RUTHERFORD COUNTY, NORTH CAROLINA

WILLS

AND MISCELLANEOUS RECORDS

1783-1868

by
James E. Wooley
and
Vivian Wooley

Please Direct All Correspondence and Book Orders to:
Southern Historical Press, Inc.
PO Box 1267
375 West Broad Street
Greenville, SC 29602-1267
or
southernhistoricalpress@gmail.com

ISBN #0-89308-413-1

INTRODUCTION

Rutherford County, North Carolina, was formed in 1779 from Tryon. It is in the southwest section of the state and is bounded by the state of South Carolina and Polk, Henderson, McDowell, Burke and Cleveland counties, North Carolina.

In 1787 part of Burke County was annexed to Rutherford and in 1791 Buncombe was formed from Burke and Rutherford. In 1794 part of Rutherford was annexed to Buncombe and part of Burke was annexed to Rutherford in 1807.

Cleveland County was formed in 1841 from Rutherford and Lincoln, and in 1812 part of Rutherford was annexed to Cleveland. McDowell County was formed in 1842 from Rutherford and Burke; and part of Rutherford was annexed to McDowell in 1844, and part of Rutherford was annexed to Henderson in 1844.

NORTH CAROLINA
AT THE BEGINNING OF
1780
Showing Approximate County Divisions
within Present State Boundaries.
Map by
L. Polk Denmark

NORTH CAROLINA
AT THE BEGINNING OF
1900
Showing Approximate County Divisions
within Present State Boundaries.
Map by
L. Polk Denmark

BOOK A

(First two pages badly torn.) Oct. Term. An agreement between WAIGHT-
SILL AVERY and JAMES MILLER. Lands mentioned on French Broad River, Cane
Cr., Hoopers Cr., Davidson River. Other names mentioned, ANDREW BLANC-
HARD, Esq., THOMAS WADTINGTON, AGNIS MILLER, ANNA MILLS, WILLIAM MILLS,
DAVID MILLER, WIDOW MILLS, BENJAMIN DAVIDSON. Dated Oct. --- ?

Page 1. 14 Apr. 1782. Proved July Term 1782. Will of WILLIAM WILLIS.
        The land I now live on to ELIZABETH HILL, during her natural
life, then to my g'son ARTHUR BUCKHANEN, son of dtr. ELIZABETH BUCKHANEN
wife of JAMES BUCKHANEN. I give my g'son URIAH, son of JACOB WILLIS,
decd. the tract of land whereon his mother ELIZABETH WILLIS now lives. I
give to my g'son HEN--? WILLIS, son of WILLIAM WILLIS, land lying on
Cabin and Hinton Creeks and the river. The moveable estate to be divided
among my three chn. and their heirs. I appoint my son WILLIAM WILLIS
sole executor. Wit: DAVIS DUFF, BENJ. X BRACKETT, JAMES WHITESIDE.
                        Signed: WILLIAM W. WILLIS.

Page 2. 20 Oct. 1779. Proved Apr. Term 1782. I, JOHN LEWIS, give to my
        wife SUSANA household furniture, 100 acres of land, one negro
woman named Hester. I give to dtr. MILDRED ROWLAND one negro girl named
Nanne, one beast & saddle, furniture & 10 acres of land. I give to my
dtr. FRANCES ROADS LEWIS one negro girl named Lidia, one beast & saddle,
furniture, to be made equal to my dtr's share in land or money. I give
to my son JULIUS C. LEWIS furniture. I give to my son DAVID J. LEWIS
furniture. Estate to be divided among all my sons, some have recd. considerable. I will give to my two youngest sons furniture, those that had
nothing given to be made equal with them that have. All land, stock,
tools, household items, negroes to be put in lott according to number of
sons, each to draw tickets for the same. I appoint my son TALIAFFERO
LEWIS, ALEXANDER MACKEY and JONATHAN HAMPTON, Esq. as executors. Wit:
THOMAS ROWLAND, JOHN MILLER, ALEXANDER MCFADIN.
                        Signed: JOHN LEWIS.

Page 1. 1 Nov. 1785. Proved Apr. Term. I, MARTIN ARMSTRONG, do give
        unto JANE & ELIZABETH ARMSTRONG my dtrs. all household stuff,
and stock that is branded ID on buttocks. Wit: WILLIAM JOHNSON.
                        Signed: MARTIN ARMSTRONG.

Page 2. (No date). Proved Apr. Term 1786. I, THOMAS EARLY, of Ruther-
        ford Co. Have made over, authorized and appointed JOHN HUGHES
of the same county my true and lawful attorney, to ask, demand, sue and
recover from ROBERT EVES in Washington Co. State of Franklin a tract of
land containing 200 acres of my rightful property, now in EVES possession, To recover the same as the law may direct. No witnesses.
                        Signed: THOS. EARLY.

Page 3. 24 Apr. 1786. Proved Apr. Term 1786. I, JOHN GASPERSON, in
        consideration of Ł 20 do sell unto HUGH GREENWOOD, two horses,
1 cow and calf, 1 sow and 3 shoats, 1 seal skin trunk, 2 beds and blankets. Wit: SCOOP EGERTON.   Signed: JOHN X GASPERSON.

Page 3. 4 Feb. 1786. Proved Apr. Term 1786. I, RUTH SINGLETON, have
        sold in open market unto JOHN LATTIMORE for the sum of Ł 100
sterling, one waggon, 4 horses, "known by the name SINGLETON old waggon
horses.". Wit: JOHN WHITESIDE, JAMES WHITESIDE.
                        Signed: RUTH SINGLETON.

Page 4. 25 Nov. 1785. Proved, date not given. I, JESSE RAKESTRAW, do
        sell a pair of hogs now on the range on Hunting Creek, formerly
RAKESTRAW property, 3 head of 2 yr. old hogs, 11 head 6 months old hogs,
unto THOMAS EARLY. Wit: MARY X BIGGERSTAFF, NANCY X DAVIS.
                        Signed: JESSE RAKESTRAW.

Page 5. 7 Apr. 1786. Proved Apr. Term 1786. I, ELISHA BROCK, Senr. of
        96 Dist., S.C. have ordained, appointed my friend, JOHN MCKINNY,
of Rutherford Co., N.C. my true and lawful attorney, to ask, sue, demand,
receive for any money or monies due me. Wit: HENRY MCKINNY, JOHN MCKINNY,

1

Junr.   Signed: ELIAS EB BROCK.

Page 6. 18 Aug. 1786. Proved in open court. I, DAVID HUDDLESTONS, do
        give unto my beloved wife HANNAH, two thirds of all the improve-
ments, with the manor house and support during her widowhood or marriage.
At death to fall to my dtr. MARY HUDDLESTONS, Also My negro woman named
Cate. At HANNAH'S marriage or death, Cate to fall to DAVID HUDDLESTONS
son of WILLIAM. One third of my moveable estate after my debts and fune-
ral charges are paid I give to my son WILLIAM, also negro called Young
Bet, also my wearing apparel. I give to my son DAVIS my negro boy called
Jo. I give to my son JOHN, my negro called Yirimus. I give to my dtr.
JANE SMART Old Jack and Old Bet, my little boy called Jule. I give to my
son JAMES my little negro called Winny, also 100 acres of land of my old
survey, joining Col. JOHN WALKER'S land. I give to my dtr. MARY HUDDLE-
STONS 300 acres of land in the middle of the old survey, also negro call-
ed Jim, 3 cows & calves, 3 head of sheep. I give to my g'son DAVID
HUDDLESTONS 100 acres of land off the old survey. To dtr. MARY my bed &
furniture, pewter, dishes, ring and clothing of her mothers. I appoint
my son WILLIAM HUDDLESTONS, WILLIAM PENNALLAND my executors. Wit: ALEX
MCGAUGHEY, JAMES KIRKPATRICK, WILLIAM ROBERTSON.
                                    Signed: DAVID X HUDDLESTONS.

Page 8. No date given. Proved in Apr. Court. ------. I, WILLIAM HAW-
        KINS, leave to my g'dtr. FANNY HAWKINS my bed. I leave my rifle
and smith tools and a bed to my son PHILIP HAWKINS. I desire that my
personal estate be left to my beloved wife PATTY HAWKINS during her life
time, then to be sold and divided amongst my chn. WILLIAM, MARTHA MAID-
ANEL, JUDAH MAIDANEL, & FANNY DAVID, PHILIP HAWKINS and SUSANAH COOPER.
Wit: THOMAS GOOD, JOHN HAWKINS, JOHN STILES.
                                    Signed: WM. HAWKINS.

Page 9. 18 Dec. 1786. Proved in open Court. I, PETER DILLS, Junr. give
        to my beloved sister MOLLY LILES 5 shillings, I give to my be-
loved BARTLET DILLS 4 shillings, I give to my beloved brother THOMAS
DILLS all my lands, Also I give to my sister ELIZABETH DILLS all my goods
and chattles, etc. I desire that NATHAN BRISCOW & WILLIAM ROBBINS as
executors. Wit: WILLIAM JOHNSON, PHILIP HENSON, JACOB DAVIS.
                                    Signed: PETER DILLS.

Page 10. 2 Oct. 1786. Proved in open court. I, WILLIAM BAKER, for the
        sum of Ł 20 paid by SAMUEL HUNTER. Hath bargained, sold and
delivered 3 horses, 7 head of cattle, household furnitur, 150 bushels of
corn. Wit: JAMES CHITWOOD, ROBERT HUNTER.
                                    Signed: WILLIAM X BAKER.

Page 11. 5 Jan. 1787. Proved in open Court. I, JOSEPH MOORE, Senr.,
        JOSEPH MOORE, Junr. have sold unto JOHN EARLE a negro boy named
Sam about 12 yrs. old. In consideration of a judgment obtained by JOHN
EARLE against JOSEPH MOORE, Junr. to satisfy execution in consign of
Judgement. Ordered by JOHN CRAWFORD Sheriff. Wit: BAYLIS EARLE, Senr.,
MATTHEW MAYBEAN.   Signed: JOSEPH X MOORE, SR., JOSEPH
                                                    X MOORE, JR.

Page 13. 10 Jan. 1787. Proved in open Court. An inventory of the pro-
        perty of MARTHA HAYS. SAMUEL HAYS denying of having any right
to the said property below. 10 cows, 6 two yrs. old heifers and steers.
6 yrs old calves, 1 horse and saddle, and household furniture. Wit:
JAMES CHITWOOD.   Signed: SAMUEL HAYS.

Page 13. 21 Dec. 1785. Proved in open Court. I, RICHARD COLEMAN, in
        consideration of Ł 100 to me paid by WILLIAM WEBB, have bargai-
ned, sold one negro named Milly, commonly called Betty. Wit: BURGUS X
LILES, PLEASANT WEBB.   Signed: RICH. COLEMAN.

Page 15. 14 May 1786. Proved July Court 1787. "This lye bill proved in
        open court and ordered to be recorded as follows." "This is to
certify that I ABRAM CLINTON and JOHN SIMMONS do acknowledge that we saw
no harm between PLEASANT WEBB concerning a cow & that it is a lye that we
said of him." As witness our hand this 4 May 1786. Wit: RICHARD COLEMAN,
BURJES X LILTES.   Signed: ABRAM CLINTON & JOHN X SIMMONS.

2

Page 15.   17 April 1787. Proved in open court. Power of Attorney, I
          have appointed my trusty friend GEORGE MOORE, Esq. my special
attorney for me and in my name. To bargain, sell, rent, or lease two
tracts of land, containing 225 acres, lying in the fork of Little and
Main Broad Rivers. Wit: JOHN HAWKINS & SAMUEL MOORE.
                              Signed: ROBT. ELLIOTT.

Page 16.   5 April 1787. Proved in open court. 96 Dist., S.C. I, FIELD
          PRUITT, have made and appointed WILLIAM TWITTY my true and law-
ful attorney in my name and use. To ask, demand, sue for recovery from
JOHN KING Ł 7 Virginia money due me. Wit: MAJOR CARSONS, WILLIAM STEELE.
                              Signed: FIELD X PRUITT.

Page 17.   6 Dec. 1785. Proved Oct. Term 1787. JAMES LOGAN, Esq. Put
          the following to probate to record as follows. The deposition
of WILLIAM SIMS Dep. surveyor. States that he made two surveys in 1765-
1766 for one JOSEPH MONFORD, some where on the North fork of Pacolet
River, for 600 acres, down said fork, for 500 acres running upward said.
He was brought to WM. ALSTON on the first and second day of Dec. 1785,
found marks that did not appear like the platt he marked for MONFORDS.
ANTHONY HUTCHINGS employed WM. DICKSON a surveyor to survey on the North
side of Pacolet, with out a grant from the Court of Claims. He found
two oaks marked WD and AH. SIMS said he never saw the markes, when he
made the survey for JOSEPH MUNFORD. Signed, WILLIAM NEVILL, J.P.
                              Signed: WM. SIMS.

Pages 20-23. Deposition of WILLIAM NEVILL, J.P. JOHN EARLE, J.P.,
          EZEKIEL POTTS and ROBERT CARRUTH on the above land dispute.

Page 24.   20 Sept. 1787. Proved April Term 1788. I, JOHN SMATHERS, for
          love and affection, that I have for my dtr. JUDAH SMATHERS. I
do give and grant my cattle, horses, household furniture, hogs, sheep as
her property absolutely. Wit: CHARLED TAYLOR, CELIA TAYLOR.
                              Signed: JOHN X SMATHERS.

Page 25.   20 Feb. 1788. I, JOHN WHITESIDE, of Green County, State of
          Georgia. Have appointed my trusty friend THOMAS STILL of
Rutherford Co. N.C. my lawful attorney, for me and in my name. To ask,
demand, sue and recover a certain tract of land on Green River in Rutherford County. Now in dispute between WHITESIDE and JOSEPH MCDONALD. To
recover said land by detress or otherways as the law may direct. Wit:
I. BAYLIS EARLE.   Signed: JOHN X WHITESIDES.

Page 26.   21 July 1787. Proved April Term 1788. I, BENJAMIN RUE, in
          consideration of Ł6 to me paid, do make over one bay mare about
9 or 10 yrs. old unto JACOB VANSANT, if said sum of money is paid before
the 6th of Oct. next. Then the writing to be void, or in full force.
Wit: WILLIAM MCMURRY.   Signed: BENJAMIN X RUE.

Page 27.   20 Nov. 1787. I, HUGH GREENWOOD, Planter, In consideration of
          Ł 155 & s5. To me in hand paid by JOHN MCKINNY. Have bargain-
ed, sold and delivered one negro man named Jack, tall, slim, yellow fellow, about 25 yrs. old. One negro boy about 4 yrs. old, named Dick. One
bed and furniture, 2 cows and calves, 31 head of hogs, one iron pot, one
mare colt. Wit: DANIEL CAMP, LUDIA MCKINNY.
                              Signed: HUGH GREENWOOD.

Page 28.   27 Nov. 1782. Proved July term 1788. I, RICHARD SINGLETON,
          have bargained, sold and conveyed unto JAMES MURRY a tract of
land containing 100 acres, lying on waters of Dunking Creek. For the
consideration of Ł20 do obligate myself and my heirs in the penalty of
Ł40 to make a good and sufficient title, right and conveyance to said
land. The above obligation is such that if RICHARD SINGLETON doth make
a good right and title to said land unto JAMES MURRY, then the obligation
to be void. Wit: DANIEL SINGLETON, JOSEPH GRAYSON.
                              Signed: RICHARD SINGLETON.

Page 29.   12 July 1788. I, GEORGE PARIS, Senr. For divers good causes
          have made, authorized and appointed my friend ROBERT PARIS of
Green Co. N.C. My true and lawful attorney. To use, sell or dispose of

3

as he thinks proper for me, a tract of land containing 36 acres, lying
in Botetourt Co. Va. On the North fork of Roanoke River, upon the North
side of a tract of land formerly belonging to GEORGE PARIS, which he sold
to WILLIAM HENDERSON. To take all lawful ways for me, to make title or
convey the land as the law may direct. Wit: THUMAN X JONES, ABSOLOM X
POTTER.   Signed: GEORGE PARIS.

Page 30. July Session 1788. The last will and Testament of WILL HAYS,
          decd. Proved in open Court, by oath of JOHNATHAN HAMPTON and
JOHN WHITESIDES & filed. (Will not copied in record book.)

Page 30. 28 March 1787. Proved Oct. Term 1788. I, MOSES MOORE, in the
          province of West Florida, District of Mobile, Planter, for
divers good causes and other consideration. Have made, ordained and
appointed my friend JOSEPH LAWRENCE in the County of Rutherford, N.C. My
lawful attorney, to use my name, recover, receive all just and lawful
debts, etc. Wit: JNO. WALTON, ANTHONY HAGGETT, JOSEPH NEWBERG.
                                  Signed: MOSES X MOORE.

Page 31. 16 April 1788. Proved Oct. term 1788. I MUMFORD WILSON in
          consideration of Ł50 to me paid by SAMUEL CARPENTER, hath bar-
gained, sold, release and confirmed unto CARPENTER a negro named Dick, 2
yrs. old. I will warrant and forever defend. Wit: SHADRACK HOGAN.
                                  Signed: MUMFORD WILSON.

Page 32. 8 Oct. 1788. I JACOB FORSYTHE for good causes and other con-
          sideration have constituted and appointed my trusty friend
JEREMIAH YEARLY, Gentleman, my true and lawful attorney. To ask, demand,
recover and receive from DAVID VANS of the State of Georgia, County of
-----?. The sum of Ł50 Virginia money. (Not witnesses).
                                  Signed: JACOB FORSYTHE.

Page 34. 31 Dec. 1788. Proved, Jan. Term 1789. I, EDWARD HAGON, in
          consideration of natural love and affection which I bear unto
my wife CHRISTIAN HAGON. Have given and granted one negro called Clov--?
during the life of Said EDWARD HAGON, then to be the property of RICHARD
HAGON son of HAGON. Wit: WILLIAM GRANT, JEREMIAH SMITH, CHARLES GRANT,
DAVID MACKY.   Signed: EDWARD X HAGON.

Page 35. 7 Jan. 1789. Proved, Jan.Term 1789. I, WILLIAM PORTER, in
          consideration of Ł40 Current money. Have paid by THOMAS ROW-
LAND, ALEXANDER MACKY, and JOHNATHAN HAMPTON. Executors of the estate of
JESSE WALKER, decd. Have given, granted, mortgage and made over unto
said executors my dwelling plantation containing 275 acres, lying on
South fork of Camp Creek. Being same plantation where Col. ROBERT PORTER
lived. Together with all my rights, claim to said land. Shall pay 12
months after this date, unto said executors the full sum of Ł40 with lawful interest. Wit: DAVID DUHY. Signed: WILLIAM PORTER.

Page 37. 29 June 1789. Proved, July term 1789. I, WILLIAM CALDWELL, of
          Lincoln County, N.C. Hath bargained and sold unto ANDREW MILL-
ER, one negro girl about 11 yrs. old, named Nancy. In consideration of
Ł30. I will forever warrant and defend aganst any claims. Wit: STEPHEN
WILLIS, J.P. & L. BUTLER.   Signed: WILLIAM CATDWELL.

Page 38. 22 March ----? Proved, July term 1789. I, CHRISTOPHER BENSON,
          of Wilkes County, N.C. Do make constitute and appoint my trusty
friend THOMAS MORRISS of Rutherford Co. N.C. my true and lawful attorney.
For me and in my name, my use, to receive the pay or sue for value of a
certain horse that CHRISTOPHER BENSON had of mine. BENSON traded the
same horse to HENRY TROUT. TROUT traded the horse to THOMAS MORRISS.
MORRISS traded him to WILLIAM GRANT. The horse then was bought by JOHN
CALAHAN & JOSEPH THOMAS for which they recovered damages. Wit: G. WHEAT-
LEY, HENRY X TROUT, DINA X WHEATLEY.
                                  Signed: CHRISTOPHER BENSON.

Page 39. 15 April 1789. Proved date not given. I, JAMES ALEXANDER, of
          Burke County, N.C. For and in consideration of the sum of Ł70
to me in hand paid by JOHN EARLE, Esq., Hath bargain, sell and deliver 5
head of horse creatures, 13 head of horned cattle, one wagon, My house-

4

hold goods. Said ALEXANDER shall cause to be paid unto JOHN EARLE, Esq. on or before 16 July next, with lawful interest. Wit: JOHN BUTLER.
Signed: JAMES ALEXANDER.

Page 40. 30 Sept. 1789. Proved date not given. I, SAMUEL and AMEY HETHERLY have made, ordained, constituted and appointed our trusty friend JAMES CAMP our true and lawful attorney. To ask, sue, demand recover and receive from -----? KECHON of Lincoln County, N.C. for the estate of JAMES WILLIAMS, decd. Wit: RICHARD COLEMAN, THOMAS X CAMP.
Signed: SAMUEL X & NEOMY X HEATHERLY.

Page 42. 17 Nov. 1789. Proved Jan. Term 1790. A mortgage of land from JONATHAN HARDIN to Mr. EDGAR WELL, of the city of Charleston, proved in open court on the oath of MICHAEL HAGON, entered on the minutes and ordered to be recorded as follows----. I, JONATHAN HARDIN, planter in consideration of Ł82 s2, in hand paid by Mr. EDGAR WELLS, the receipt is hereby acknowledge. Have granted, bargained and sold unto EDGAR WELLS a tract of land lying in the County of Rutherford, containing 600 acres, on both sides of two branches of Hickory Creek, waters of Little River. The land wheron JONATHAN HARDIN now lives, with improvement, where son JOSEPH HARDIN lives. The obligation of the above is. That JONATHAN HARDIN shall pay or cause to be paid unto said EDGAR WELLS, the sum of Ł41 in 12 months from the date hereof, also Ł41 in 24 months from the date hereof. In the total of Ł82 with lawful interest. Wit: MICHAEL HAGON, ELIJAH HARDIN. Signed: JONATHAN X HARDIN.

Page 44. 17 Nov. 1789. Proved, Jan. term 1790. I, WILLIAM SMITH, in consideration of Ł33 s19 to me in hand paid, before sealing and delivery, by Mr. EDGER WELLS of the city of Charleston, have granted, bargained and delivered, all that tract of land containing 200 acres, lying on Big Hickory Creek, waters of Little Broad River. Whereon SMITH now lives, with improvements. The condition of the above obligation is such that if the said WILLIAM SMITH shall pay unto said WELLS the sum of Ł33 s19 with lawful interest from the date hereof of 14 months. The said mortgage shall be void. Wit: MICHAEL HOGAN, MICAJAH SMITH.
Signed: WILLIAM SMITH.

Page 46. 1 June 1789. Proved, Jan. term 1790. I, JOSEPH LAWRENCE, planter, in consideration of good causes, and divers reasons. Have by virtue of a power of attorney invested in me from and by MOSE MOORE of West Florida and Mobile District. Recourse to the records in the office of our Court. Book #1 page 30 will make the same sufficiently appear. Have made ordained, constituted and appointed my trusty friends DRURY LOGAN and JOSHUA ROBERTS or either of them my true and lawful attorney, to sue, ask, demand, receive and recover all lawful debts, likewise to do the same for and in behalf of MOSES MOORE, also to appoint one or more attorneys. Wit: EZEKIAL ENLOE, MICAJAH X MORRIS.
Signed: JOSEPH LAWRENCE, Agent and
attorney for MOSES MOORE.

Page 49. 13 Aug. 1787. Proved, Oct. Term 1790. For diver good causes and love that I bear unto my g'dtr. SARAH GRAHAM, dtr. to my son WILLIAM GRAHAM and SUSANNA his wife of the Common Wealth of Virginia, County of Franklin, I do give to said SARAH GRAHAM one negro girl named Mall about 9 yrs. old. If said SARAH die without issue, negro Mall to fall to the male heirs of my two sons, ARCHIBALD & ARTHUR. Should my son WILLIAM survive his dtr. SARAH. Wit: ARTHUR GRAHAM, JACK DILLINGHAM.
Signed: ARCHIBALD GRAHAM, Senr.

Page 50. 13 Aug. 1787. Proved, Oct. Term 1790. For diver good causes and love I bear unto my son WILLIAM GRAHAM, I, ARCHIBALD GRAHAM, Senr., of the Common Wealth of Virginia, County of Franklin. Do divise unto SARAH GRAHAM dtr. of my son WILLIAM & SUSANNA GRAHAM his wife, one negro boy named Charles about the age of 11 yrs. old at this time. Said Negro boy Charles I do freely give to SARAH my g'dtr. If SARAH die without issue negro Charles to fall jointly unto the male heirs of my sons ARCHIBALD & ARTHUR GRAHAM after the death of my son WILLIAM, provided he should survive his dtr. SARAH or her issue. Wit: ARCH. GRAHAM, Jr., SAMUEL X RUPH, ARTHUR GRAHAM. Signed: ARCHIBALD GRAHAM.

Page 51. 16 Nov. 1787. Proved date not given. Received of JAMES HOL-
LAND ₤500 receipt and payment is hereby acknowledge. I have
------ Delivered to him the following negroes, viz. Dinah, a woman about
26 yrs. old, and Hannah, a girl 9 yrs. old, Lewis, Joe and Adlia chn. of
said Dinah. Which negroes I will warrant & forever defend to the said
JAMES HOLLAND and his heirs from all lawful claims forever. Wit: RICHARD
LEWIS.   Signed: WM. GILBERT.

Page 51. "Received the 25 March 1783 of Capt. ALEXANDER MCFADIN, all
debts, dues, legacies and demands whatsoever that I have had or
claimed of or to the estate of JOHN or STEPHEN MCFADIN, decd. I say received by me." Wit: HENRY LEWIS. Signed: WILLIAM MCFADIN.

Page 52. 10 Aug. 1787. Proved, Oct. term 1790. I, JOHN MCCLURE, have
bargained, sold and delivered unto WILLIAM PORTER a certain
negro called Hagar, for the sum of ₤100 to me in hand paid by said WILLIAM
PORTER, and do warrant that the said negro is of sound mind and memory.
I will defend the rights of the said negro girl of any claim. Wit: MAT-
HEW BILBOW, JOHN WATKINS.   Signed: JOHN MCCLURE, Junr.

Page 52. "I do here by certify that I saw JOHN MCCLURE, Junr. execute
the within bill of sale to WILLIAM PORTER for the purpose contained. I have had it almost every since in my memory." Dated 12 Aug.
1790, JOHN PORTER.

Page 53. 5 Oct. 1790. Proved, Oct. term 1790. Between ARCHIBALD GRAHAM,
Senr. of Lincoln Co. N.C. and WILLIAM GRAHAM of Rutherford Co.
N.C. In trust and for the sole benfit of SARAH GRAHAM, dtr. of WILLIAM
GRAHAM & SUSANNA his wife. In consideration of natural love and affection that he bear to the said SARAH GRAHAM his g'dtr. For her better
maintenance, hath given, granted, and confirmed unto said WILLIAM GRAHAM
in trust one tract of land lying on the South side of First Broad River,
containing 300 acres. Originally granted to ROBERT ARMSTRONG, dated 30
Oct. 1765. Another tract on the West side of Little Broad River, containing 400 acres. Originally granted to JOHN BEATY the 30 Oct. ----.?
Said SARAH GRAHAM to have all rights, titles, interest, and claims. Wit:
ARTHUR GRAHAM, ARCH. DILLINGHAM. Signed: ARCHIBALD GRAHAM, Senr.

Page 54. 15 Jan. 1791. Proved, Jan. term 1791. In consideration of
₤160 paid to CHARLES MCDANIEL, have sold and delivered unto
JAMES MCINTIRE of Burke Co., N.C. two negroes known by the name of Shade
and Hannah. I, CHARLES MCDANIEL, do bind myself and my heirs to warrant
and defend unto the above named JAMES MCINTIRE and his heirs forever.
Wit: JAMES MILLER, RICHARD LEWIS. Signed: CHARLES MCDANIEL.

Page 54. 22 Dec. 1790. Proved Jan. term 1791. I, DANIEL MCCLARIN, of
Spartanburg County, S.C. Doth nominate and appoint DAVIS
WHILEHEL of Rutherford Co., N.C. my true and lawful attorney for me and
in my name, to sue, recover and receive from THOMAS STILL all the arrear-
ages for rents due to me from said STILL. I do hereby give and grant
unto my said attorney full and absolute power and authority to take all
lawful ways and means for recovery. Wit: WILLIAM BARNES.
                              Signed: DANIEL MCCLARIN.

Page 55. 11 April 1791. Proved, April term 1791. I, JOHN DEVENPORT,
for deivers good causes and consideration have hereinto appointed my trusty and well beloved SAMUEL KING, Senr., my true and lawful attorney for me and in my name, to act, and do everything, and all things
touching and concerning a tract of land granted to me under the -----.
Lying and being in Bedford County, Virginia, Lying on both sides of
Blackwater River. Said tract of land KING lived on. I do hereby em-
power my attorney to him SAMUEL KING a good and lawful deed of conveyance, for the said land. Wit: JONAS BEDFORD, ADAM WATSON.
                              Signed: JOHN DEVENPORT.

Page 56. 27 Dec. 1788. Proved, July term 1791. Articles of agreement
made between WILLIAM WEBB, Senr., and RICHARD COLEMAN. The
said RICHARD COLEMAN is to take a son of WILLIAM WEBB, named JONATHAN
WEBB and to use him well & to learn him to read, write and cypher as far
the rules of three & JONATHAN WEBB to be free at 20 yrs. of age. RICHARD

6

COLEMAN to pay JONATHAN WEBB Ł40 in gold, silver or the value thereof.
In case of death of RICHARD COLEMAN or his wife MARY COLEMAN, JONATHAN
WEBB is to have the Ł40 and his learning, from the COLEMAN estate and
return home to his father. Wit: BURGES X LILES, WILLIAM WEBB, Jr.
Signed: WILLIAM WEBB & RICHARD COLEMAN.

Page 56. 9 Aug. 1790. Proved, July term 1791. I, DANIEL SWANY, in consideration of Ł43 s18 p10 paid by JAMES MILLER, Col., Have
bargain, sold and delivered my houses and two ----- ?. With all and
every part of my small tools now in my shop, all cattle, my black mare,
also furniture, household goods. I will forever warrant and defend.
Wit: EDWARD HANNONS, RICHARD LEWIS. Signed: DANIEL X SWANY.

Page 57. N.B. I, JAMES MILLER, promise and agree to make over to DANIEL
SWANY and JANE SWANY at the payment of Ł43 s18 p10 to the said
JAMES MILLER any time in one year and eleven months, to give unto DANIEL
& JANE all the above mentioned articles, except the beds and household
furniture. Wit: EDWARD HANNONS, RICHARD LEWIS.
Signed: JAMES MILLER, Col.

Page 57. 8 Aug. 1790. I, JAMES MILLER, for diver good causes, do give
to JANE SWANY and her two dtrs. ISEBIL and JEAN forever, three
beds with furniture, two ovens, 1 pot & small skillet, 1 pewter tea pot,
one basin, two card and spinning wheel, one looking glass. I do for myself and heirs acknowledge fully satisfied and contented with the above
mentioned articles. Wit: EDWARD HANNONS, RICHARD LEWIS.
Signed: JAMES MILLER, Col.

Page 57. I, MAY RUSSELL, for and in consideration of Ł100 in hand paid
by JAMES MILLER, Col., have sold and delivered a negro boy
named Jack. I will forever warrant and defend said negro boy nine yrs.
old. Except one FELBY the former wife of GEORGE RUSSELL, decd. Dated
27 March 1784. Wit: JOHN WHITESIDES. Signed: MARY X RUSSELL.

Page 58. 5 Oct. 1788. I, HUBBARD PEOPLES, of the County of Guilford,
N.C., in consideration of Ł160. Have bargain, sold unto JAMES
MILLER, Col., a negro named Isham about the age of 30 yrs. old. I will
forever warrant and defend said negro. Wit: RICHARD LEWIS, WILLIAM NEVILL.
Signed: HUBBARD PEOPLES.

Page 58. 17 March 1787. I, FELIX WALKER, in consideration of 11,500
weight of tobacco. Have sold unto JAMES MILLER, Col., one
negro man named Rodger. Will forever defend the said negro Rodger to
the said JAMES MILLER. Wit: STEPHEN WILLES.
Signed: FELIX WALKER.

Page 59. 8 Feb. 1798. I, THOMAS MORRISON, of the County of Iredell, N.C.
In consideration of Ł100 paid by JAMES MILLER, Col., I, THOMAS
MORRISON, have bargain, sold, and delivered unto JAMES MILLER, one negro
named Joe about 20 yrs. old. Said negro, I do warrant and defend unto
JAMES MILLER. Wit: JAMES MORRISON, Senr., WILLIAM MORRISON, Junr.
Signed: THOMAS MORRISON.

Page 59. 14 Oct. 1791. Proved, Oct. term 1791. I, ARTHUR OSBORN, For
diver good causes, have made and appointed MUNFORD WILSON my
lawful attorney, in my name to ask, demand and receive from all or any
persons that are indebted to me in the State of Virginia, County of Alb-
bemarle or else---- or hold any property real or personal in trust or
otherways, and more especially those in whose hands is held the late
property of ARTHUR OSBORN, decd. as executor or administrator that part
divised to me the said ARTHUR OSBORN by ARTHUR OSBORN decd. Will recorded in Clerk's office in said county. In my name to sue, recover or
pursue for recovery of property. To give receipt and release as he
thinks necessary. Wit: DANIEL SERVIL ?, JONATHAN HAMPTON.
Signed: ARTHUR OSBORN.

Page 61. 26 May 1780. Proved, July 1782. Ordered by the Court that the
depositions of JOHN NEIL, WILLIAM SMART, Senr., DAVID HUDDLE-
STON, Junr., be recorded to wit.."I met at SAMUEL ANDREWS begining corner
and JOHN NEIL appeared at the corner and declared on oath that two white

oaks on the side of a hill in the forks of Cain creek, is the North side
of Donses fork to be the corner made by him for the begining corner of
said land, which he NEIL surveyed. Sworn before me, TIMOTHY RIGGS, J.P.
Likewise, WILLIAM SMART, Senr., declared that by order and agreement...
(torn) MARLIN the above said Mr. NEIL was to ....(torn) from two certain
white oaks on the South side of Donses fork Northward. Sworn before me,
TIMY. RIGGS, J.P. and likewise, DAVID HUDDLESTON, Junr., being one of
the chain carriers of said land declared agreeable to the above Mr. SMARTS
declaration. Sworn before me.. TIMOTHY RIGGS, J.P.

Page 62. 1 March 1781. Proved, Oct. term 1782. On oath of JOHN WALKER.
          I, AARON MOORE, being sick and weak in body, but of sound mind
and perfect memory. I will that my just debts be paid. I give to my
beloved wife ....(torn) one third part of my real and personal estate,
during her life, and at her decease to be equally divided among my chn.
viz: MOSES, ELISHA, SARAH, MARY, MARGARET, RACHAEL, JOHN and ANN MOORE.
I give to my sons, all my lands except above mentioned. One horse each.
The remaining part of my moveable estate to be sold according to law, the
money to be equally divided among my dtrs. I give to my dtr. ELIZABETH
HARMON Ł5 to be paid out of my moveable estate. I appoint RACHAEL MOORE
and JOAB LAWRENCE my executors. Wit: JOHN WALKER, PETER WALKER, ELIZA-
BETH WALKER.   Signed: AARON X MOORE.

Page 64. 4 Oct. 1782. Proved, Oct. term 1782. On oath of JAMES WHITE-
          SIDES, Esq., THOS. WHITESIDES have bargained, sold in open
market unto BENJAMIN SHAW of the County of Washington, N.C. one negro
woman named Jain about 20 or 25 yrs. old. In consideration of Ł100 by
virtue of a bond due to the said BEN SHAW from JOHN LATTIMORE, bearing
date 25 March 1782, I do hereby warrant and forever defend said negro
from any person whatsoever laying lawful claim. Wit: THOS. STICTON,
ADAM WHITESIDE, JAMES WHITESIDE. Signed: THOMAS WHITESIDES.

Page 64. 16 Sept. 1782. Proved, Oct. term. On oath of TIMOTHY RIGGS,
          Esq. I, JAMES DOUGLASS, of Camden Dist. S.C. have bargain,
sold on open market, in consideration of Ł80 one negro man named Harry,
late in the possession of JAMES MILLER of Rutherford Co., N.C., Unto
JAMES WITHROW of said county, with all profits that may arise from his
service since he absented my service. I do warrant & defend said negro
from all claims. Wit: TIMOTHY RIGGS, THOS. WHITESIDES.
                         Signed: JAMES DOUGLASS.

Page 65. 15 April 1780. Proved, date not given. I, EDWARD HOPSON, of
          Burke Co. N.C. In consideration of Ł1000 to me in hand paid by
WILLIAM WEBB of Rutherford Co., N.C. Do bargain, sold, setover & deliver-
ed one negro woman named Nan, unto WILLIAM WEBB and his heirs forever.
I do warrant and forever defend from all persons, or claims. Wit: JAMES
WITHROW, AARON BIGGERSTAFF.   Signed: EDWARD HOPSON.

Pafe 66. 5 Dec. 1776. Proved, Jan. ter 1783. On oath of ALEXANDER
          MCGAUCHY. An agreement between the heirs of JOHN BATTLES, decd.
We the heirs of JOHN BATTLES decd. of Tryon County, N.C. "divided untest-
ed" That is to say the widow, SARAH BATTLES, JOHN BATTLES, NANCY ADJUT-
ANH alias BATTLES, WM. BATTLES, ANGELICKEY BATTLES, firmly agreed with
the adjusters, WILLIAM ROBERTSON, BENJAMIN ADAMS, ALEXANDER MCGAUCHY in
the manner as follows. 1st All lawful debts be paid from whole estate.
2nd. The widow SARAH to have her third part of the moveable estate, and
negroes of JOHN BATTLE est. as her part of dowery, also third part of the
upper survey, of both clear & wood land and manor house. At her death,
her part of dowery to be divided among the legatees. I, JOHN BATTLES
agree to make my brother WILLIAM equal with myself in the estate of land
that belonged to my father, JOHN BATTLES, dec. and to him a sufficient
right for land as soon as law permit. If anyone brake the agreement,
they shall forfeit all rights and titles unto the others. Wit: WILLIAM
ROBERTSON, BENJAMIN ADAMS, ALEXANDER MCGAUGHY.
                    Signed: SARAH BATTLES, JOHN BATTLES,
                            NANNY ADJUTANH, WILLIAM BAT-
                            TLES, ANGELIKEY BATTLES.

Page 69. 5 Jan. 1783. Proved, Jan. term 1783. I, JOHN PAIN, being sick
          and weak in body, but of good sense and perfect memory. I give

8

the land I now live on to my BETTY to live on till my son BENJAMIN come
of age, then to be sold and money divided between my wife, son BENJAMIN
and dtr. MARY. All my stock and household furniture in the same manner.
I appoint my wife sole executor. Wit: JOHN SUTTON, JAMES ASHLOCK.
Signed: JOHN X PAIN.

Page 70. 14 April 1783. Proved, April term 1783. On oath of JAMES
COOK. I, JEREMIAH RUSSELL, in consideration of £400 in hand
paid by GEORGE WINTERS, have sold, bargain & confirmed all my negroes
named as follows. Dianah, Esther, Frank and Silvey unto GEORGE WINTERS
and his heirs forever. I will warrant & defend against any and all claims.
Wit: JAMES COOK, EPHRAIM HAIGHS. Signed: JEREMIAH RUSSELL.

Page 71. 13 Sept. 1783. Proved, Oct. term 1783. We, JAMES HOLLAND,
JAMES WITHEROW, JOHN FLACK, WILLIAM PORTER, THOMAS WELCH,
ROBERT PORTER, RICHARD SINGLETON and FELIX WALKER. Arbitrators, indif-
ferently choosen and elected by SAMUEL ANDREW and JAMES WITHEROW to
settle a land dispute between said ANDREWS & WITHEROW. The land lying on
Cain creek between their plantations, where they now live. We do find
for the said ANDREWS all the land contained and expressed on a patent,
granted to JOHN MARLEN. ANDREWS to pay WITHEROW for all improvement on
land according to patent. Signed: JAMES HOLLAND, JOHN FLACK,
WILLIAM PORTER, THOMAS WELCH, ROBERT PORTER, JAMES WITHEROW, RICHARD
SINGLETON & FELIX WALKER.

Page 72. 29 April 1783. Proved, Jan. term 1783. On oath of PETER RENFRO.
I, WILLIAM NEIL, of 96 Dist. S.C., For and in consideration of
a certain bay gelding to me sold and delivered by HENRY WOLF, the receipt
is hereby acknowledge. I, by these present doth sell and deliver unto
HENRY WOLF one negro named Nancy, formerly the property of Col. GRAYSON,
of the State of Georgia. Condemned as forfeited property, and given to
JABES EVANS for service done in the State. EVANS sold and made over said
negro to me. I, WILLIAM NEIL, will forever warrant and defend said
negro against and person or claim. I WILLIAM NEIL shall pay and deliver
unto HENRY WOLF a Negro fellow under 25 yrs. old, and above 15 yrs. sound
and healthy, of an indefesible right and title on or before 1 Aug. next.
Wit: BAYLAS EARLE, PETER RENFROE Signed: WILLIAM NEIL.

Page 73. 11 Feb. 1784. Proved April term 1784. I, JESSE WALKER, being
sick and weak, but of perfect mind and memory. Do give to my
well beloved chn. viz: SARAH WALKER, JANE WALKER, ANN WALKER, RHODA
WALKER, WILLIAM WALKER and ELIZABETH WALKER. All my estate both real and
personal to be equally divided among them. I appoint THOMAS ROWLAND,
JONATHEN HAMPTON executors. Wit: BENJAMIN HYDER, RICHARD LEWIS.
Signed: JESSE WALKER.

Page 74. 17 April 1784. Proved, April term 1784. On oath of FELIX
WALKER. I, JOSEPH WILLIAMS, in consideration of £60 have bargain, sold and made over unto ABRAM MUSICK, the receipt is hereby acknowledge, 2 horses, six head cattle, 9 head hogs, furniture & other articles.
Wit: FELIX WALKER. Signed: JOSEPH WILLIAMS.

Page 75. 17 Sept. 1782. Proved, Oct. term 1784. On oath of SAMUEL
EARLE. I, THOMAS FARRAR, of 96 Dist. S.C. In consideration of
£200 Virginia Money. I have bargain, sold the receipt is acknowledged
from FELIX WALKER. About that tract of land lying on Sinking Creek, of
Watauga River, in Washington Co. N.C. Known by the name of Flaerys Camp
or land. Containing 500 acres. Wit: SAMUEL EARL.
Signed: THOMAS FARRAR.

Page 76. 10 Jan. 1785. Proved, Jan. term 1785. Received of JAMES HOL-
LAND £150 on behalf of monies arriving from the estate of
WILLIAM HALL (HALE). Received by me this 10 Jan. 1785. Wit: WM. JOHNSON.
Signed: ELIZABETH X HALL.

Page 77. 13 April 1785. Proved April term 1785. We the under named,
being mutually chosen and appointed to award and determined and
make a final end of all matters of debate, between THOMAS MORRIS of
Rutherford Co. N.C. and MICHAEL MCELWRATH, SAMUEL NESBIT and JOHN MC-
ELWRATH guardians of MICHAEL MCELWRATHALL of 96 Dist. S.C. Met according

to appointment and giving due audience to all evidence on both sides. We do say that said MCELWRATH shall pay MORRIS ₺250 specie indent, also pay the cost of suit that MORRIS brought against ANTHONY DICKEY, MORRIS shall pay cost of suit brought against MCELWRATH.
                              Signed: JAMES WHITESIDE, ---- CARSON, WM. PORTER, JOHN CARSON, PATRICK WATSON, BENJ. HYDER, ROBERT PORTER, JAMES WATKINS.

Page 78. 12 April 1785. Proved, April term 1785. (Same suit as above).
        MICHAEL MCELWRATH to make to THOMAS MORRIS a good and compleat title in fee simple to a tract of land, lying in the fork of Cedar & Cove Creeks. Being the same that appears to have been purchased from MCELWRATH by MORRIS. MORRIS to pay sum due MCELWRATH, by bond with a horse to the value of ₺10 MCELWRATH to pay to JOHN HARDIN for expenses in locating land.   Signed: JONATHAN HAMPTON, JAMES WITHE-ROW, JOHN CARSON, GEORGE LEDBETTER, BENJ. HYDER, WM. PORTER, PATRICK WATSON, JAMES WHITESIDES.

Page 79. 14 April 1785. Proved, April term 1785. (Same suit) We the
        Arbitrators, meet to determine matters between ANTHONY DICKEY and MICHAEL MCELWRATH. Hath rewarded and say that each discharge suits and claims for all accounts or damages.
                              Signed: JONATHAN HAMPTON, WILLIAM PORTER, JOHN CARSON, PATRICK WATSON, ROBERT PORTER, THOS. KOWLAND, JAMES WITHEROW.

Page 80. 26 March 1784. Proved, April term 1785. I, JOHN MCFADIN, of
        Davidson County, N.C. have constituted and ordain my brother ALEXANDER MCFADIN of Rutherford Co., N.C. my true and lawful attorney, in my name to make a true and lawful title in fee simple to MOSES FERGU-SON to a tract of land on Crab Creek in Rutherford County. Wit: WM. PAR-NELL, MOSES FERGUSON, JOHN GEHILLIPE.
                              Signed: JOHN X MCFADIN.

BOOK B

Page 3. 2 Aug. 1791. Personally came ELIAS MORGAN before me, DAVID
        DICKY, J.P. Saith that "WILLIAM MORGAN son to this deponant, was born in lawfull wedlock and that he is the first born after his first son JOHN MORGAN." Sworn before me this day. D. DICKEY, J.P.
                              Signed: ELIAS MORGAN.

Page 3. 27 Dec. 1788. An agreement between WILLIAM WEBB, Senr. & RICHARD
        COLEMAN to go equal shares in building a mill. RICHARD COLEMAN to have half of what the mill gets in his life time. If COLEMAN dies his heirs to have same for the term of 4 yrs. then the property to return to WEBB and his heirs forever. Wit: BURSIS X LILES, WM. WEBB, Jurat.
                              Signed: RICHD. COLEMAN & WILLIAM WEBB.

Page 3. 2 Sept. 1783. I, JOSEPH UNDERWOOD, in consideration of ₺60 in
        hand paid by JAMES MILLER. Have bargained, sold unto said MILLER a negro named Abram about 35 yrs. old, 1 negro wench named Lott and her child. I will warrant and forever defend all lawfull claims. Wit: FRANCIS BROWN, WM. BROWN. Signed: JOSEPH UNDERWOOD. Proved on oath of FRANCIS BROWN this 17 Nov. 1783. Before STEPHEN WILLIS.

Page 4. Personally came before me, TABETHA JENKINS, and on oath saith
        that some time in the summer of 1779 to the best of her know-ledge WILLIAM CAPSHAW made a deed of conveyance to BENJAMIN JENKINS for part of his upper survey, which included the land whereon they lived. Some time in the year of 1780 their house burned and she believe that the deed was burned. She believe that the deed was never recorded or register-ed, dated 29 Nov. 1791. Signed, JOHN EARLE, J.P.
                              Signed: TABITHA X JENKINS.

Page 5. 10 Oct. 1792. I, JOHN MCMULLIN, in consideration of ₺60 have
        bargained sold, and delivered unto ANDREW HAMPTON, 3 mares & colts, household furniture. Wit: LITTLETON SIMS.
                              Signed: JNO. MCMULLIN.

Page 6. 1 Nov. 179_? Proved, Jan. term 1793. I, HUGH GREENWOOD, in
consideration of ₤165 to me in hand paid by JAMES MILLER. Have
bargained, sold and delivered unto said MILLER one negro boy named Dick
about 8 yrs. old, one woman named Hager, about 23 yrs. old. 1 horse, 10
head cattle, a quantity of hogs. I will hereby warrant and forever defend any and all claims. Wit: RICHARD LEWIS, STEPHEN WILLIS.
Signed: HUGH GREENWOOD.

Page 7. 17 Jan. 1793. Proved, Jan. term 1793. I, CHARLES MCDONALD, in
consideration of natural love and affection to son JAMES MC-
DONALD, have given granted and confirmed one horse, 1 set smith tools, to
dtr. CATHARINE one filly, 15 head cattle, 9 head sheep. The rest of my
estate to be divided between the above mentioned chn. Wit: RICHARD LEWIS.
Signed: CHAS. MCDANIEL(?)

Page 8. 5 Oct. 1792. Proved, Jan. term 1793. I, WILLIAM GRANT, in consideration of ₤98 s15 p10 sterling money of S.C., paid by
ALEXANDER MCBETH and JOHN HONCRIEFFE under the firm of McBeth & Comp.
mertchants, of Union Co. S.C. Hath bargained, sold, and delivered unto
ALEX. MCBERTH a certain tract or lot of land containing 3/4 of an acre
with a two story framed house and other buildings thereon, known as #1
in the plat of the town of Rutherford. The condition of said mortgage
is such that WILLIAM GRANT shall pay to ALEX. MCBETH & Co. the sum of
₤98 s15 p10 on or before 1 March 1794, then the present mortgage to be of
no effect. Wit: I. MILLER, THOMAS GRANT.
Signed: WILLIAM GRANT.

Page 10. 18 Feb. 1793. Proved 6 April 1793. I, MUNFORD WILSON, have
bargained sold and delivered unto JOSEPH CARPENTER one negro
girl named Hannah, about 9 or 10 yrs. old. In consideration of ₤70 lawfull money, in hand paid by JOSEPH CARPENTER. I will forever warrant
and defend said negro against all claims. Wit: SAMUEL YOUNGE, JOHN TAL-
BERT.   Signed: MUNFORD WILSON.

Page 10. 29 April 1787. Proved, 6 April 1793. I, JAMES WALKER, in
consideration of ₤133 lawfull money, in hand paid by WILLIAM
MILLS, Have bargained, sold, and delivered a negro named Jean, about 16
yrs. old, and will forever warrant and defend said negro unto WILLIAM
MILLS against all claims. Wit: DAVID MUSICK, ROBERT BROOKS.
Signed: JAMES WALKER.

Page 11. 28 May 1792. Proved, April term 1793. I, FREDERICK HAMRIGHT,
have this day in plain and open market, bargained, sold and
delivered unto JOSEPH CARPENTER a negro boy named Bob, about 9 yrs. old.
In hand paid by said CARPENTER ₤57 s10. I do warrant and defend all
claims on said negro. Wit: RICHARD SINGLETON, SAMUEL CARPENTER.
Signed: FREDERICK HAMRIGHT.

Page 12. 4 July 1793. Proved, July term 1793. We ZACHARIAH GOFORTH,
GEORGE GOFORTH, EZEKIEL GOFORTH, and CORNELIUS CLEMENTS husband
of SUSANNAH GOFORTH all heirs and lawfull representives of MILES GOFORTH
decd. for certain good causes and consideration have made, ordained, and
appointed our true, trusty and beloved brother and friend JOHN GOFORTH
our true and lawfull attorney, to ask, demand, recover and use our name
for all or part of the estate of ZACHARIAH GOFORTH, decd. of Kent County,
State of Deleware. We release our said attorney from all errors that he
may commit in prosecuteing the business aforesaid. Wit: FELIX WALKER.
Signed: ZACH. X GOFORTH, GEORGE GO-
FORTH, EZEKIEL GOFORTH, CORNELIUS CLEMENTS.

Page 13. 2 June 1793. Proved, July term 1793. I, ALLEN TWITTY, this
day have sold, and delivered unto ALEXANDER MCFADIN the following property. four horses, ten head cattle, 18 head hogs, farm tools,
household furniture etc. In consideration of ₤350 current money of N.C.
to me paid in hand. I will forever warrant and defend all claims. Wit:
JOHN MILLER, SUSANNAH MILLER.   Signed: ALLEN TWITTY.

Page 15. 11 May 1793. Proved, July term 1793. I, JOSEPH GILL, in consideration of love, good will and affection I bare to my dtr.
JANE SULLINS, do give and grant to her during her natural life one negro

11

child named Betty, at her dec. to go to her dtr. ELIZABETH SULLINS, in
case Betty has issue, the first living child to be given to JANE'S eldest
dtr. SARAH. Wit: ELIAS ALEXANDER, JOHN GOOD. Signed: JOSEPH GILL.

Page 16. 6 June 1793. Proved, July term 1793. I, ALLEN TWITTY, for
divers good causes and consideration have ordained, constituted,
and appointed my trusty friend ALEXANDER MCFADIN my true and lawfull
attorney, for me and in my name, to ask, demand, recover and receive from
all and every person or persons indebted to me. Wit: JOHN MILLER,
SUSANAH MILLER.   Signed: ALLEN TWITTY.

Page 17. 4 Sept. 1792. Proved, July term 1793. I, JOHN WHITESIDES, for
divers good causes and consideration, have ordained, constituted and appointed my trusty friend WILLIAM WHITESIDES my true and lawfull
attorney, to use my name, to ask, demand receive and recover from every
person or persons that is indebted to me. Wit: THOS. WHITESIDES, ABRAM
BARNET. WILLIAM MONROE.   Signed: JNO. WHITESIDES.

Page 18. 17 July 1793. Proved, Oct. term 1793. I, ROBERT YOUNG, in
consideration of £150 in hand paid by JAMES MILLER, in plain
and open market, have bargained, sold, and delivered two negroes viz: Tom
28 yrs. old, blind in one eye, the other named Harry 20 yrs. old. I will
forever warrant and defend from any lawfull claim. Wit: RICHARD LEWIS,
JAS. NORRIS.   Signed: ROBERT YOUNG.

Page 18. 17 Oct. 1793. Proved, Oct term 1793. MARY FLACK admnr. of the
estate of JOHN FLACK, decd. and guardian for her own children &
WILLIAM FLACK guardian for the four eldest chn. of JOHN FLACK, decd. Have
agreed that the land on which the four children are now living shall remain in the quit possession of said children until the youngest comes of
full age. The land shall be under the direction of the children, the
widow dowery excepted. The land lying on Mountain Creek shall be and remain for the youngest children and without hinderance from WILLIAM FLACK
or any other person. Wit: WILLIAM PORTER, JOHN BATES.
                    Signed: WM. FLACK & MARY X FLACK.

Page 19. At the Oct. term of Court 1793 on Monday, came JOSEPH GREGORY
and on oath saith. That in the year 1773 he came to the Broad
River and that JOHN CERTAIN or (CARLIN) was then living on the East side
of Little Broad River, on a tract whereon CHARLES RAWLINS now lives &
that JOHN CERTAIN then claimed 300 acres. Said CERTAIN showed him a
marked red oak tree at the mouth of a creek where CERTAIN cabins was
built, the creek was then called Cabbins Creek. Mr. CERTAIN had receipt
from Mr. JOHN KIRCONNELL, for entry, surveying, & patent fee. Some time
later Mr. KIRCONNELL was in the area and he heard Mr. CERTAIN ask him for
his patent, was told that it was lost or misplaced in his house. Some
time later KIRCONNELL did send the patent to CERTAIN. After Mr. CERTAIN
death, he was made administrator of the estate, and did divide the land
between himself (as he had married Mr CERTAIN'S dtr.) & his wife's sister
ARASTATIA CERTAIN. He has possessed the land until Mr. NELSON came in
and lived on the place one fall & winter then left. That he had paid all
taxes and legal demand on his part of the property. ARASTATIA CERTAIN
had lived on her land also. One WILLIAM BARRON lived on part of the property during the late war. JNO. KIRKCONNELL states that he surveyed the
said land for Mr. CERTAIN in the year 1774. Land entered, 10 June 1771.
                    Signed: JOSEPH GREGORY.

Page 20. 5 Oct. 1793. Proved, Oct. term. I, WILLIAM QUEEN, of Randolph
Co. N.C. Impower, appoint my son and trusty friend WILLIAM
LEWIS QUEEN of Rutherford Co., N.C. a true agent for me, to bargain, sell,
buy or convey, it shall be as done by myself. Wit: SAML. CARPENTER, JAMES
CHITWOOD.   Signed: WM. X QUEEN.

Page 21. 13 Oct. 1791. Proved, Oct. term 1793. Received from WILLIAM
WEBB, executor of the LW&T of RICHARD COLEMAN decd. By us
RICHARD BRADLEY and RICHARD COLEMAN, legatees of said will. recd. in full
the amount bequeathed to our children and received by us. And we do
agree to pay our chn. said sum due them from the estate. Wit: JONATHAN
HAMPTON, FELIX WALKER.   Signed: RICHARD COLEMAN & RICHARD
                                        BRADLEY.

Page 21. 13 Oct. 1791. Proved, Oct. term 1793. I, RICHARD BRADLEY, have received from WILLIAM WEBB, executor of the estate of RICHARD COLEMAN, decd. the sum of Ł100 by note of hand being the full part of said COLEMAN estate bequeathed to SARAH CLATON. Wit: JONATHAN HAMPTON, FELIX WALKER. Signed: RICHARD BRADLEY.

Page 22. 13 Aug. 1793. Proved, Oct. term 1793. Know that I, THOMAS ROBINSON, for and in consideration of Ł25 to me paid by WILLIAM ROBINSON at or before the delivery, have bargained, sold and delivered 1 mare & colt, 1 cow, 1 bed and furniture forever. Wit: THOMAS PRICE, THOMAS HAWKINS. Signed: THOMAS ROBINSON.

Page 22. 13 Aug. 1793. Proved, Oct. term 1793. I, THOMAS ROBINSON, in consideration of Ł25 in hand paid by MARY ROBINSON, before the delivery. I have bargained, sold, and delivered 1 horse, 1 cow & calf, 4 head sheep, 1 feather bed & furniture, 1 dozen pewter plates, 4 dishes, 1 bason, 3 potts, 1 oven. Wit: THOMAS PRICE, THOMAS HAWKINS. Signed: THOMAS ROBINSON.

Page 23. 13 Aug. 1793. Proved, Oct. term 1793. I, THOMAS ROBINSON, Senr., in consideration of Ł25 in hand paid by THOMAS ROBINSON Junr., before delivery, I have bargained, sold and delivered 1 mare, 1 cow & calf, 1 feather bed & furniture. Wit: THOMAS PRICE, THOMAS HAWKINS. Signed: THOMAS ROBINSON.

Page 24. 9 Jan. 1794. Proved, Jan. term 1794. I, CHARLES MCDONALD, for natural love and affection which I bare unto my dtr. CATHERINE MCDONALD, have given, granted, and confirmed 2 feather beds & furniture, my pewter and other household furniture, 25 head of hogs. I will forever warrant and defend said property. Wit: WALTER CARSON. Signed: CHARLES MCDONALD.

Page 24. 9 Aug. 1792. Proved, Jan. term 1794. I, JAMES NETTLE, in consideration of Ł100. Have bargained, sold on open market unto WILLIAM NETTLE a young negro boy named Natt, about 14 yrs. old. I will warrant and defend unto said WILLIAM NETTLE against all claims whatsoever. Wit: THOMAS HESLEP, MARY X HESLEP. Signed: JAMES X NETTLE.

Page 25. 25 March 1794. Proved, April term 1794. We PHILIP NULL, HENRY NICHOLAS & THOMAS NORTON of Rutherford Co. N.C. are firmly bound unto JAMES DAVIS of Fairfield County and JAMES RUTHERFORD of Columbia, S.C. merchants, in the sum of Ł550 s6 p10 sterling or current money of S.C. We bind ourself and our heirs & executors, etc. The conditions is such of this obligation is that we or our heirs will truly pay or cause to be paid in gold or silver or proper medium at the usal discount or exchange in the following manner. Ł50 to be paid on 1 June next, Ł100 in 6 months from the date hereof, Ł50 in 9 months, and the balance remaining in 12 months from date here of, with interest at the rate of 7% from 1 May 1794. Wit: ANDW. BODDAN, JOHN LONG. Signed: PHILIP NULL, HENRY NICHOLAS, TOWNSON HORTON.

Page 26. 8 Dec. 1792. Proved, April term. Whereas before, THOMAS WHITESIDE, Esq., JAMES WITHEROW obtained judgement against MUNFORD WILSON in the sum of Ł15 s12 p6 and cost. THOMAS WHITESIDES, J.P. granted execution on the judgement which came to the hand of WILLIAM MURRY, constable, dated 15 Sept 1792. MURRY did take negro girl about 3 yrs. and advertised for 10 days according to law. Sale held 8 Dec. 1792 in consideration of Ł12 s10 being the highest bidder unto JAMES WITHEROW. Girl name Clarsey. Wit: WILLIAM WILSON, PHILIP CROWDER. Signed: WILLIAM MURRY.

Page 27. 27 Feb. 1794. Proved, July term 1794. (Marriage contract) Between GEORGE LEDBETTER of Rutherford Co., N.C. and METTA HEYER of Gramby, Lexington Co., S.C. and AMOS JUSTICE of Buncombe Co., N.C. and NICHOLAS HANE of Gramby, S.C. Whereas a marriage is intended to be shortly had and solemnized between said GEORGE and METTA, with JUSTICE and HANE as trustee GEORGE LEDBETTER is to have no part of METTA possessions, which is listed as household items. Signed, GEORGE LEDBETTER & METTA HEYER. Wit: ALEX. BOLLG. STARK, ELIJAH GREEN.

13

Signed: AMOS JUSTICE, NICHOLAS HANE.

Page 31. 18 July 1794. Proved, July term 1794. I, JOHN MCKINNEY have
        constituted, made and appointed my trusty and loving son JOHN
MCKINNEY, Junr., my lawfull attorney, for me and in my name, to my use,
to ask, sue, demand and receive all debts, rents, accounts, particularly
all my lands in the State of Pennsylvania, which fell to me or which may
fall to me hereafter by heirship or otherwise. Wit: JONAS BEDFORD, Junr.,
DAVIE LILES.   Signed: JOHN MCKINNEY.

Page 31. No date given. Proved, Oct. term 1794. I, JOHN GOODE, in con-
        sideration of love and good will I do have for my cousin PETER
GILL, I have given and granted one negro boy named Jack. I give and
grant my cousin SALLY GILL one negro woman named Jude. I give to my
cousin JOSEPH GILL, Junr., the following negroes Jo, Judy & Bob, the first
living child that Judy brings to be given to WILLIAM GILL. I give and
grant unto my cousin JENNY GILL negro girl named Nanie. I also give to
HENRY GILL one negro named George. I give to cousin JOHN L. GILL one
negro named Tom. I also give to PETER: Sally, Jimmy, Henry, William,
and JOHN LUMPKINS GILL one negro named Sam to be equally divided amongst
them as they come of age or marry. Wit: WM. HAWKINS, Junr., WM. HAWKINS,
Senr.   Signed: JOHN GOODE.

Page 33. 8 ---- 1792. Proved, Oct. term 1794. I, JOHN BRIDGES, of York
        Co., S.C. do bargain, sell and deliver unto WILLIAM CAMP &
JAMES DUNCAN of Rutherford Co., N.C. one negro man named George, also one
studd horse, one good feather bed, one trunk, one pot and dutch oven.
Without any meaning of fraud or pretents to any heir at law or creditor,
but under full consideration of WILLIAM CAMP and SM. DUNCAN being my
security in two suits at law between me and MICHAEL HOGAN, and they taking upon themselves to act as my attorney, to act, ask, demand, sue for,
and receive bills, debts and book accounts due unto me, to give receipts
and receive. Wit: JOS. CAMP. ABRAHAM CAMP.
                                      Signed: JNO. BRIDGES.

Page 35. No date given. Recorded, Oct. term 1794. "Be it remembered
        that JAMES MORRIS, eldest legitimate son and heir of JOHN
MORRIS, decd., being desireous to establish his legitimacy and also his
being the heir of the said JOHN decd. Called on TIMOTHY RIGGS, Esq., one
of the Justices of said county who voluntarily came into Court and being
and solemnly sworn in due solemn form of law deposeth and said that he
celebrated the rites of marriage between JOHN MORRIS and MARTH POWEL in
the Spring of the year 1773 and joined them together as man and wife in
due form of Law." Signed: R. LEWIS, C.C.
                                      Signed: TIMO. RIGGS, J.P.

Page 35. "Be it further remembered that THOMAS MORRIS being of age came
        voluntarily into Court at the request of the above JAMES MORRIS
and being duly sworn saith that he knew the said JAMES was the first
child born in wedlock of JOHN, decd. That JAMES was born about the lat-
ter end of June 1775 and that he hath known JAMES from his childhood till
this time and knowing that he is now in Court hath made this requisition
is the same first legitimate son and heir of JOHN MORRIS, decd." Signed:
R. D. LEWIS, C.C.   Signed: THOMAS MORRIS.

Page 37. 4 Sept. 1794. Proved, Jan. term 1795. I, JEREMIAH THOMPSON,
        in consideration of love, good will and affection I do bear
toward my loving dtr. BETSEY THOMPSON, have given, granted unto said
BETSEY one negro named Laosey and one negro boy named Charles, 2 cows &
calves, 1 feather bed, 10 head hogs, one horse and saddle. Wit: WILLIAM
HAWKINS, BARNET FOLDY.   Signed: JEREMIAH THOMPSON.

Page 38. 4 Sept. 1794. Proved, Jan. term 1795. I, JEREMIAH THOMPSON,
        in consideration of love, good will and affection which I have
toward my son WILLIAM THOMPSON, have given, granted unto said son one
negro fellow named Jack and negro boy named Joseph, one bed, 2 cows & ·
calves, 6 pewter plates, 1 gray studd horse, 10 head hogs. Wit: WILLIAM
HAWKINS, BARNETT FOLDY.   Signed: JEREMIAH THOMPSON.

Page 39. 4 Sept. 1794. Proved, Jan. term 1795. I, JEREMIAH THOMPSON, in consideration of love, good will and affection which I have to my dtr. CEALIA THOMPSON, one negro girl named Hannah, 2 cows & calves, 1 feather bed, 6 pewter plates, 10 head hogs. Wit: WILLIAM HAWKINS, BARNET FOLDY.   Signed: JEREMIAH THOMPSON.

Page 40. 4 Sept. 1794. Proved, Jan. term 1795. I, JEREMIAH THOMPSON, in consideration of love, good will and affection which I have to my son JOHN THOMPSON, one negro boy named David and another named Tom, one feather bed, 2 cows & calves, 6 pewter plates, one mare, 10 head hogs. Wit: WILLIAM HAWKINS, BARNET FOLBY.   Signed: JEREMIAH THOMPSON.

Page 41. 5 March 1795. Proved, April term 1795. I, ADLAI OSBORN, agent and attorney for the trustees of the University of N.C. in the district of Morgan, on behalf of the trustees quitclaim to and release unto JOHN LATIMORE and his heirs all rights, titles and claims to a certain tract of land lying in Rutherford Co., N.C. on Hintons Creek, containing 200 acres. Granted to WILLIAM & MARGARET WILLES. Said MARGARET conveyed to JOHN LATIMORE, in consideration of Ł10 paid in hand to said ADLAI OSBORN, Esq. Wit: M. STOKES, JESSE RICHARDSON.
                          Signed: ADLAI OSBORN.

Page 41. 12 Oct. 1794. Proved, April term 1795. I, ANTHONY METCALF, do appoint Col. JAMES MILLER my lawfull attorney for me and in my name, to sue, receive from person or persons, all trust, fees, claims coming from my father-in-law EDWARD HOGAN, which may be in the hands of Executor EDWARD HOGAN. I do appoint said JAMES MILLER to execute to JAMES WHITESIDE or his heirs a title for 50 acres of land lying on waters of Bufelow.... ? the land of JAMES GRAY, which I entered in the entery office of Rutherford County. Wit: ALEX. MCFADDEN, WARNER METCALF.
                          Signed: ANTHONY METCALF.

Page 42. 19 Feb. 1795. Proved, April term 1795. I, JOHN MCNITT ALEX-ANDER of Mecklenburg Co., N.C. Have leased and rented unto CHARLES STICE of Rutherford Co., N.C. the whole of the waters and the land under the First Little Broad River from where the line crosses the said river on High Sholes down the river to the mouth of Shoal Creek, including all the fish pots, or traps, and fishing on or in the said river, that was transfered by deed to said JOHN MCNITT ALEXANDER dated 20 Aug. 1773 and granted to RICHARD BERRY the 26 Sept. 1766. Has been leased or rented unto CHARLES STICE for the term of 6 yrs. In the sum of 1 shilling. Wit: WILLIAM BRIDGES, WM. ALEXANDER. Signed: J. M. ALEXANDER.

Page 44. 19 Jan. 1795. Proved, July term 1795. I, WILLIAM GRAHAM, have sold and delivered unto GEORGE SELLEY of Burke Co., N.C. one negro named Terry about the age of 17 yrs. old. In consideration of Ł100 of hard money in hand paid by GEORGE SELLY. I will forever warrant and defend against any and all claims. Wit: DANIEL X MILES, SAMUEL CARTER.
                          Signed: W. GRAHAM.

Page 44. 26 May 1795. Proved, July term 1795. I do hereby certify that I will not dispossess or take out of the hands of and possession of SUSANNA GRAHAM'S dowery in lifetime one negro girl named Lazal?. Also one third part of a certain tract of land containing 400 acres, being the tract that WILLIAM & SUSANNAH GRAHAM now lives on. Wit: JOSEPH GREEN.   Signed: ABRAM TROINE.

Page 45. 15 July 1795. Proved, July term 1795. I, THOMAS GOODE, in consideration of diver good causes, have constituted, appointed my trusty friend JAMES HOLLAND my lawfull attorney to use my name, to sue, recover, receive all such monies as shall be due me in the State of Virginia for two yrs. service in the regiment of that state under the command of Capt. LA.....? HOPKINS and discharged at the Vally Forge by JOHN STOKES.   Signed: THOS. GOODE.

Page 46. 4 June 1795. Proved, July term 1795. I, WILLIAM BARNETT, in consideration of Ł100 lawfull money to me paid by my friend ANDREW MCKINNEY, doth bargained, sold and delivered 2 tracts of land lying on Robinson Branch, containing 230 acres, 2 horses, 1 cow, 1 rifle, and household items. I will forever warrant and defend said property. Wit: THOMAS MULLIN.   Signed: WILLIAM BARNETT.

Page 47.   10 Sept. 1787. Proved, July term 1795. Received of the hand
          of JAMES HOLLAND L250 the receipt is acknowledged. Have sold
and delivered 2 negroes to wit: Tom a blacksmith well known & Winterford
a plantation negro, about 45 yrs. old. I will warrant and forever defend
to said JAMES HOLLAND from all lawful claims. Wit: JAMES HOLLAND, Senr.,
JAMES DUDLEY.   Signed: WM. GILBERT.

Page 48.   27 Aug., 1795. Proved, Oct. term 1795. I, FELIX WALKER, in
          consideration of 400 Spanish Milled dollars, have bargained,
sold and delivered unto GEORGE SULEY of Burke Co., N.C. a negro woman
named Poll about 23 yrs. old and her 2 chn. Candise a girl of 4 yrs. old
and Levia a boy of 14 Mo. old. Said WALKER will warrant and forever
defend negroes from all claims. Nevertheless, WALKER has told GEORGE
SULEY in express terms that negro Poll has a swelling in her legs. If
SULEY is to run her through a hazzard WALKER is not liable for any consequence. Wit: SAMUEL CARPENTER, JAMES SMITH.
                                      Signed: F. WALKER.

Page 49.   20 March 1790. Proved, Oct. term 1795. I, JOHN MCGUIRE, of
          South Carolina, planter, for diver good causes and considera-
tion, have constituted, appointed, my trusty son JOHN MCGUIRE, Junr., of
Spartanburg Co., S.C. My true and lawfull attorney for me and in my name,
concerning the 400 acres of land granted to me by the State of N.C. the
18 Sept. 1772, lying on Little Mountain Creek. Having sold said land to
ELIAS MORGAN, and he has never received a title for same. My said attorney to collect amount due and make a deed in fee simple for said land.
Wit: ELIJAH MCGUIRE, W. MCGUIRE, EVERET MCGUIRE.
                                      Signed: JOHN MCGUIRE.

Page 51.   29 Oct. 1793. Proved, Jan. term 1796. I, JAMES HOLLAND, in
          consideration of 5 shillings lawfull money to me in hand paid
by ALEXANDER MCANDLESS GILBERT, have bargained, sold and delivered the
following negroes, to wit: Hannah a woman about 16 yrs. old, Tom her
child about 4 month old, and Lewis a boy about 12 yrs. old next christ-
mas. I will warrant and defend forever from all lawfull claims. Wit:
JAMES ENGLISH.   Signed: JAMES HOLLAND.

Page 51.   31 Oct. 1795. Proved, April term 1796. Received from THOMAS
          HUNTER the sum of L40, I have bargained, sold and delivered
unto JAMES HUNTER 1 negro boy child, the identity being set forth in a
bill of sale from GEO. LEDBETTER to HUNTER and MILLER, called Dave. I do
warrant and defend for ever from all claims. Wit: RICHARD LEWIS.
                                      Signed: JAMES MILLER.

Page 52.   3 Dec. 1795. Proved, Jan. term 1796. I, JAMES REAVIS, in con-
          sideration of L30 lawfull money in hand paid by JAMES DOYLE,
have bargained, sold, and delivered one negro girl named Milla about 3
yrs. old. I will forever warrant and defend said negro from all claims.
Wit: DAVISE DOYLE, JOHN DOYLE.   Signed: JAMES REAVIS.

Page 52.   17 July 1793. Proved, Jan. term 1796. I, JAMES MILLER, for
          the sum of L125 in hand paid by RICHARD LEWIS, have bargained,
sold and delivered a negro man called Harry computed to be 18 or 19 yrs.
old. Wit: JAMES ERWIN.   Signed: JAMES MILLER.

Page 53.   -- June 1792. Proved, Jan. term 1796. I, JOHN MCCLAIN, Senr.,
          for the sum of L50 lawfull money to him in hand paid by RICHARD
LEWIS, hath bargained, sold and delivered unto RICHARD LEWIS a negro boy
called Abraham, about 7 yrs. old. I will warrant and defend said negro
from all claims forever. Wit: WILLIAM TATE.
                                      Signed: JOHN MCCLAIN.

Page 54.   15 July 179 ? Proved, Jan. term 1796. I, THOMAS GOOD, for the
          sum of $120.00 in hand paid by SAMUEL MOORE the receipt is here-
by acknowledged, have bargained, sold and delivered one negro boy named
Jack about 6 or 7 yrs. of age. Said boy to be free and sound from dis-
orders. I will forever warrant and defend negro from all lawfull claims.
Wit: WALLACE ALEXANDER.   Signed: THOMAS GOOD.

Page 54.   13 Jan. 1795. Proved, Jan. term 1796. I, JASON ISBELL, hath bargained, sold and delivered to GEORGE SEALY of Burke Co., N.C. a negro boy named Robert, about 14 or 15 yrs. old. In consideration of $230. I will forever warrant and defend all lawfull claims. Wit: JOSEPH HARRETL, ---TTIE X ISBELL.   Signed: JASON ISBELL.

Page 55. 3 Sept. 1794. Proved, Jan. term 1796. I, JOHN WITHEROW, hath bargained, sold and conveyed unto RACHEL PORTER a negro wench named Fann, about 12 yrs. old. For the sum of L60 to me in hand paid, before the sealing and delivery of said negro. I will forever warrant and defend all lawfull claims. Wit: JAMES THOMPSON, DORCUS HUEY.
                                Signed: JOHN X WITHEROW.

Page 56. 19 Sept. 1794. Proved, Jan. term 1796. I, JOHN MCCLAIN, in consideration of 150 Spanish Milled Dollars, hath bargained, and sold unto FELIX WALKER a negro girl called Pegg, 13 yrs. old, and being dumb and deaf. I will forever warrant and defend said negro from all lawfull claims. Never the less that the said JOHN MCLAIN shall at or before the first day of July next, shall pay unto FELIX WALKER the sum of L36 current money which at this time said JOHN MCCLAIN is justly indebted to WALKER in that amount. Then this mortgage and bill of sale shall be null & void, or remain in full force. Wit: NATHAN PORTER, ALEXANDER TRAVER.   Signed: JOHN MCCLAIN.

Page 56. 19 Sept. 1795. Proved, Jan. term 1796. I, EZEKIEL ENLOE, for diver good causes and considerations do appoint my trusty friend ABRAHAM ENLOE my attorney, to act in my place in a suit in law brought by myself and ANDREW MILLER against ----- TERRELL or ADAM COOPER in Buncombe Co., N.C. For the recovery of damage or possession of a tract of land containing 200 acres. Wit: RANSOM EGETON, ANTHONY ENLOE.
                                Signed: EZEKIEL ENLOE.

Page 57. 19 Sept. 1795. Jan. term 1796. I have made and constituted my trusty friend ABRAHAM ENLOE my sole attorney for me in the suit of ANDW. MILLER and myself against ----- TERRELL & ADAM COOPER for certain damages upon our premises. In consideration of L50 in hand paid by ABRAHAM ENLOE, we have sold all our rights and titles of judgement to the said suit for recover of 200 acres of land lying in Buncombe Co., N.C. on Cane Creek. Wit: RANSOM EGETON, ANTHONY ENLOE.
                                Signed: EZEKIEL ENLOE.

Page 58. 24 Aug. 1793. Proved, Jan. term 1796. JOHN HILTERBRAND, admnr. of the estate of CHRISTOPHER CANESTER, decd. have appointed and impowered my true friend JAMES CHITWOOD or his heirs to make a title to a tract of land containing 50 acres lying on Words Creek, entered by said CONESTER, being the place where DANIEL WORKMAN now lives. Wit: SAMUEL CARPENTER, SAMUEL SWANN, BENJ. BEAVER. Signed: JOHN HILTERBRAND.

Page 59. 15 April 1796. Proved, April term 1796. I, WILLIAM HAWKINS, of Rutherford Co., N.C. For good causes and consideration have made ordained, authorized and appointed WILLIAM HOPSON of Hallifax, (Co.) Va. my true and lawfull attorney, to use my name, to sell, dispose of any land belonging to me in said estate. Wit: RICHARD LEWIS.
                                Signed: WILLIAM HAWKINS.

Page 60. 23 May 1793. Proved, April term 1796. I, ABRAM ENLOE, in consideration of L80 to me paid by GRAVEL EAVES, have bargained, sold, and delivered a negro girl named Meblda. I will warrant and forever defend from all lawfull claims. Wit: SARAH X ENLOE, ELIZABETH X EDGINGTON.   Signed: ABRAM ENLOE.

Page 60. 2 April 1796. Proved, April term 1796. I, BENJ. COOK, in consideration of love and good will and affection which I bear for my son ABRAHAM COOK, having given, granted all my household furniture, horses, cattle, absolutely with out any manner of conditions. Wit: ROBERT X TRAP, WILLIAM ROLLANS.   Signed: BENJAMIN COOK.

Page 61. 21 Jan. 1796. Proved, April term 1796. I, MOLLEY BRIGGS, have sold and delivered unto JOHN MILLER a negro girl named Secy, in consideration of the sum of $257 to me in hand by said MILLER. Negro about the age of 18 yrs. old. I will warrant and forever defend all law-

17

full claims. Wit: ANDREW MILLER.   Signed: MOLLY BRIGGS.

Page 62. 24 Dec. 1795. Proved, April term 1796. I, ARTHUR JOHNSON,
        have sold unto WINFORD TONSON, two cows, two heffers and two
yearlings. I have recd. value for in full. Wit: JAMES LOVE, THOS.
HUNTER.   Signed: ARTHUR JOHNSON.

Page 62. 26 June 1795. Proved, April term 1796. I, JOSEPH GILL, in
        consideration of $100 to me paid by THOMAS GOODE, have bargain-
ed, sold and delivered a negro boy named Jack, about 6 or 7 yrs. old,
sound and sensible. I will forever warrant and defend all lawfull claims
on said negro. Wit: JAMES MORRIS, JACOB WOMACK.
                                 Signed: JOSEPH X GILL.

Page 63. 15 April 1796. Proved, April term 1796. This day came ISAAC
        HUTSON, made oath before me in due form, that he lost a bond on
JOHN HUGHES for the sum of £50 and that JOHN WILLIAMS, Jr. was the wit-
ness to said bond, the bond was lost the 13th of the present instant.
(Month) Wit: DANIEL CAMP, J.P.   Signed: ISAAC HUTSON.

Page 63. 21 Oct. 1795. Proved, July term 1796. I, THOMAS BOYD, for
        diver consideration have made, ordained and appointed JAMES
POLLY my lawfull attorney, to use my name, to make a good and lawfull
deed for 100 acres unto PHILIP MOORE. Land lying on First Little Broad
River, on both sides of Flush branch, joining land of JOHN ANDERSON.
Wit: JOHN ANDERSON, JOSEPH X ROPER.   Signed: THOMAS BOYD.

Page 64. 13 July 1796. Proved, July term 1796. Personally appeared
        MARCURIL REOU in open Court and made oath that he lost or mis-
placed a note of £120 on MATHEW MCHAN, dated 26 Oct. 1794, due 26 Oct.
1795, there is a balance on note of £37 s19 with interest. Note witness
by MARTHY MCHAN. Wit: RICHARD LEWIS, C.C.
                                 Signed: MARCURIL REOU.

Page 64. 24 May 1796. Proved, July term 1796. I, JAMES PORTER, in
        consideration of the sum of £100 to me in hand paid by PETER
PULEN, have bargained, sold and delivered a negro girl named Bynah about
the age of 15 yrs. old. I do warrant and forever defend all lawfull
claims. Wit: DANIEL CARSON, SAMUEL CARPENTER.
                                 Signed: JAMES PORTER.

Page 66. 29 Aug. 1795. Proved, Oct. term 1796. This indenture made
        between DANIEL CAMP, sheriff of Rutherford Co., N.C. and LEWIS
BEARD of Rowan Co., N.C. Whereas a writ of Fieri facias issued from
Hillsboro, N.C. Superior Court in the name of the Governor against
WILLIAM NEVILL and others, in the sum of £50, levied on a negro named
Santee, about 36 yrs. old. Said negro was sold at public out cry on the
27 Aug. 1795 and LEWIS BEARD became the last and highst bidder in the sum
of £25. Said sheriff hath bargained, sold and delivered said negro unto
BEARD, and will forever defend from all lawfull claims. Wit: ELIAS ALEX-
ANDER, J.P., STEPHEN WILLIS, J.P.   Signed: DANIEL CAMP, Sheriff.

Page 68. (No date given) Proved, July term 1796. I, NATHAN BRISCO, for
        diver good causes and consideration have made, ordained and
appointed ELIJAH ROBBINS of Chester Co., S.C. my true and lawfull attorney for me and in my name, to defend, sue, ask, recover from every person
whatsoever in the State of Maryland, any and all real estate coming to me
by decent, heirship, or otherwise, any money due me from JAMES S. BRISCO
or any others. (No date) Wit: WILLIAM X. EIBBINS, J. BEDFORD.
                                 Signed: NATHAN BRISCO.

Page 69. 11 Oct. 1796. Proved, Oct. term 1796. I, WILLIAM COXEY, for
        certain good causes and consideration, have made ordained &
Appointed my beloved friend ABRAM ENLOE my true and lawfull attorney for
me and in my name to ask, demand, sue for, recover the value of a tract
of land from PETER JONES of South Carolina of 100 acres which was sold
and conveyed by deed from PETER JONES to WILLIAM COXEY and has been since
recovered from me by operator of law hereby giving and granting to my
attorney full power. Wit: JAMES HOLLAND. Signed: WILLIAM COXE.

Page 70. 13 Oct. 1796. Proved, Oct. term 1796. I, JOHN MCCLURE, for
certain good causes and consideration, have ordained, constituted and appointed my true and trusty friend JOHN MCCLURE, Junr., my true
and lawfull attorney for me and in my name. To ask, demand, sue, recover
from the estate of ARTHUR MCCLURE, decd. To take whatever means he
thinks proper in law or equity. Wit: F. WALKER.
Signed: JOHN MCCLURE.

Page 71. 4 March 1795. Proved, Oct. term 1796. I, MARY COOPER, widow,
in Consideration of love, good will and affection, I have and
bear to my beloved BENJAMIN SHEPHERD and JOHN SHEPHERD, have given and
granted unto said BENJAMIN & JOHN SHEPHERD a tract of land containing 50
acres, lying on waters of Bullons Creek known by the name of the Weber
place. I have given and granted unto said BENJAMIN & JOHN the said land
without any manner of conditions, and disbaring any person from laying
claim to said land, after the death of WILLIAM COOPER. Wit: HENRY SEARS,
JOHN MILLS, RICHARD YEALAIN.   Signed: MARY X COOPER.

Page 71. 22 Dec. 1795. Proved, Oct. term 1796. I, BENJAMIN DUMAS,
living upon the Pedee, have constituted, made and appointed my
trusty friend WILLIAM FREZIER of Rutherford Co. N.C. my true and lawfull
attorney in my name, to act, recover in my name a tract of land in
Whitesides Settlement, lying on the South side of Little Broad River,
being the land whereon Mr. STEPHEN HOGUE now lives on. What ever is
needfull to be done about the premises. Wit: SILAS DUMAS.
Signed: BENJAMIN DUMAS.

Page 72. 12 Jan. 1797. Proved, Jan. term 1797. I, EDWARD GOOD, for the
sum of £60 to me in hand paid by LEMUEL MOORE have bargained,
sold, and delivered one negro boy named Jerry about 4 yrs. old being of
sound mind and body. I will forever warrant and defend said negro from
all claims. Wit: WALLACE ALEXANDER   Signed: EDWARD GOOD.

Page 73. 10 Jan. 1797. Proved, Jan. term 1797. I, MARTHA MORGAN alias
JENNINGS, in consideration of diver good causes, have constituted and appointed my trusty friend GEORGE SUTTLES my lawfull attorney to
act and do for me in all respects. To act and do in a suit I obtained in
Henry County (no state given), wherein THOMAS ROBINSON was plaintiff and
MICHAEL ROWLAND defendant in the sum of £220 and cost of judgement granted by said court. Wherein Col. MARTIN did concur, also JOHN KNOX, Clk.
of said Court, is required to give satisfaction from the records as my
attorney may require. Wit: MICHAEL HOGAN, NATHANIEL HAMMRICK.
Signed: MARTHA X JENNING Alias JENNING.

Page 74. 12 April 1797. Proved, April term 1797. I, JONAS BEDFORD,
Senr., for diver good causes and consideration, have made,
ordain and authorized JONAS BEDFORD, Junr., my loving son, my true and
lawfull attorney, in my name and proper use, benfit, to act demand, sue,
recover and receive of and from any true consule, or other commissioners
whatsoever who may be appointed for that purpose by the Government of
Great Britain, all such sums of money as now or hereafter shall become
due, owing or payable unto me as claiment on the British Government and
take all lawfull ways and means for the recovery thereof. Wit: JOHN MC-
KINNEY, DANIEL SWANN.   Signed: JONAS BEDFORD.

Page 75. 13 April 1797. Proved, April term 1797. I, MARTHA MORGAN,
widow of JOHN MORGAN, decd. For diver good causes and other
consideration, have made, ordained, constituted and appointed JAMES BED-
FORD, Junr., my true and lawfull attorney for me, and in my name, to ask,
demand, sue, recover and receive from the Sheriff of Henry County, Virginia. Such sums as has been, shall be recovered in a suit in Henry Co.,
Va. From THOMAS ROBINSON or MICHAEL ROWLAND, also such sums of money,
debts, judgments, which are now due or owing to me in the State of
Virginia. Wit: JOHN MCKINNEY, DANIEL SWANN.
Signed: MARTHA MORGAN.

Page 76. 15 April 1797. Proved, April term 1797. Whereas, AMBROSE
MILLS, decd. died intestate in the year 17-- leaving a widow
ANNA MILLS, and seven chn. to wit: WILLIAM MILLS, THOMAS MILLS, JOHN
MILLS, AMBROSE MILLS, MILLY MILLS, POLLY TWITTY, PAMILEA MILLS, ANNA

19

MILLS the youngest. Col. JAMES MILLER, in the year 1782 administered on the estate. The said ANNA MILLS (the widow) intermarriaged with JOHN CARRICK in Feb. 1790. Such proceeding have been had and such management with the estate as appeared in the copy annexed, and certified. RICHARD LEWIS, Esq. & WILLIAM MILLS has been appointed guardian of AMBROSE, MILLY, and ANNA MILLS, one petition is to require bond and security for the estate and action of debts, in part of the second sale of a negro, a waggon, a note on MCCAFFENTY, horses, cattle. Bond to be on Admnr. JAMES MILLER, JOHN CARRICK & ANNA his wife. This indenture witnesses that WILLIAM MILLS & JOHN CARRICK have agreed to settle their suit in law, and other disputes about the estate of the decd. The widow to have her dower in the old home place, WILLIAM MILLS to pay court cost, attorney fees. JOHN CARRICK shall not claim any more of the personal estate of the decd. than he had or left at the old home place when he went to Cumberland. Wit: WAIGHTSILL AVERY, JOHN MCKINNEY, JOHN GOODBREAD.

Signed: WILLIAM MILLS & JOHN X CARRICK.

Page 80. 15 April 1797. Proved, April term 1797. Whereas some disputes between me FRANCIS BEATY and JONATHAN HARDIN, which is my desire to settle now, the present. I will agree and consent to release forever a quit claim deed to JOHNATHAN HARDIN and his heirs for ever the 12 acres of land, including his mill and improvement thereinto, which has been in his possession for 20 yrs., which land is within his grant also within the lines of my grant. Said 12 acres to be laid off in a long square up the hill. Wit: DANIEL CAMP, JAMES CAMP.

Signed: FRANCIS BEATY.

Page 82. 18 May 1796. Proved, April term 1797. This indenture made between SAMUEL SWANN and WILLIAM HORTON, in consideration of £25 in hand paid by said HORTON, the receipt is hereby acknowledged Have granted, bargained, and sold the messuage and tenements and all the land lying on Second Broad River, known by the name of ROBERT SWAN. Adj. lands of SAMUEL SWANN and his son ROBERT SWANN. Containing 100 acres. (lease & release). Wit: WM. WEBB, Junr., DANIEL SWANN.

Signed: SAMUEL SWANN.

Page 85. 10 July 1797. Proved, July term 1797. We, JOHN DALTON, JOHN MCCANN, heirs by marriage of the dtrs. of WILLIAMS SIMS, decd. For divers good causes, have constituted and appointed JOHN DANING of Rockingham Co. N.C. our true and lawful attorney, for us, and in our name, to ask, demand, receive from representative of the estate of WM. SIMS, decd. in the State of Virginia, Albemarle County, to claim our part of said estate. Wit: JNO. SUTTON, DAVID LEWIS.

Signed: JOHN MCCANN & JOHN DALTON.

Page 86. 3 April 1797. Proved, July term 1797. Commissioners appointed by the County Court to divide the land of JOHN FLACK, decd. among and between the legatees. We give unto ANDREW & GEORGE FLACK eldest sons of decd. all that tract of land on Catheys Creek, whereon said decd. last lived. Containing 380 acres, valued at £585. We give to JOHN & WILLIAM FLACK, Jr. sons of decd. a tract of land of 200 acres lying on Ricely Fork of Mountain Creek. Valued at £150. For the widow dowery, she to have £71 & s5 from the first allotment and £31 & s17 from the second allotment. Signed: F. WALKER, J. HAMPTON, SAMUEL CHERRY, ROBERT CHERRY, ROBT. GILKEY.

Page 88. 5 June 1797. Proved, July term 1797. I, SARAH HAMILTON, in Consideration of £100 good and lawfull money, in hand paid, have bargained, sold, and delivered unto BARKLY WILLIAM FINLY, one negro girl named Camby, one lot of land in Morristown, in Buncombe Co., N.C. also 100 acres in Rutherford Co. N.C. two miles from town, joining land of ADAM WATSON. I will warrant and forever defend from all claims. Wit: SAMUEL D. FINLY.   Signed: SARAH HAMILTON.

Page 89. 28 Aug. 1797. Proved, Oct. term 1797. I, JAMES COCKERHAM, in consideration of the sum of $60 to me in hand paid by JOHN GREENWOOD have bargained, sold and delivered unto JOHN GREENWOOD a sorrel filly, about 14 hands high, 2 yrs. old. I will warrant and forever defend said filly from all claims. Wit: CHARLES RICHARDSON.

Signed: JAMES COCKERHAM.

Page 89. 13 Oct. 1797. Proved, Oct. term 1797. I, WILLIAM GARNER, Senr. in consideration of the natural love and affection which I have and bear to my son WILLIAM GARNER, and for other good causes have given, granted and confirmed unto said WILLIAM GARNER, Junr. First I give him the plantation whereon I now live containing 172 acres, also 100 acres joining the same on the South East side, also 50 acres on both sides Magnesses Creek, Including the mill. Also one mare and 2 young horses, all cattle beast, hogs, sheep and my household furniture. Wit: ABRAHAM CROSS, DANIEL JOHNSTON.   Signed: WILLIAM X GARNER.

Page 91. 26 Jan. 1797. Proved, Jan. term 1798. This indenture made be-tween JOSHUA ELLIS and WILLIAM F. WHITESIDES, saddler, the said ELLIS resides in Iredell Co., N.C. and WHITESIDES resides in Rutherford Co., N.C. Whereas JOSHUA ELLIS have placed his son JAMES ELLIS apprin-tice in order to learn the saddler and saddle bag trade, and every branch belonging to said trade carefully. To be taught by Mr. WHITESIDES for the term of two and a half years from above date. Said JAMES is to dwell and live with said WHITESIDES. The said apprintice being cripple. Mr. WHITESIDES is to supply meat, drink, lodging and apparrel. When his term is up, he is to be supplied with a crediable suite of clothes. Wit: ABEL LEWIS, DRURY ALLEN.   Signed: JOSHUA ELLIS, WM. F. WHITESIDES.

Page 92. 11 Nov. 1795. Proved, Jan. term 1798. CALEB LINDSEY, do nominate, constitute, and appoint my friend JAMES LINDSEY of the State of S.C. to be my lawfull attorney, to make a good lawfull title to a tract of land that I formily lived on. Lying on Green River at the mouth of Polls Creek, containing 80 acres, as will appear from a deed of GEORGE GREEN to JAMES & CALEB LINDSEY. My attorney to make a lawfull title to CHALTON LINDSEY & CHARLES ROSS. Wit: THOMAS JUSTICE, JOHN MC-COUREY.   Signed: CALEB LINDSEY.

Page 93. 12 Feb. 1798. Proved, April term 1798. I, JAMES CONNER, for love, good will, and natural affection that I have for my son HUGH CONNER, and other consideration doth give, grant and convey unto my son the following species of my personal property, to wit. A negro woman named Tye, about the age of 26 yrs. with her two children, Dinah a girl of 5 yrs. and Isaac 2 weeks old. 2 mares, 5 cows, 4 heffers. Wit: F. WALKER, ABRAM ENLOE.   Signed: JAMES CONNER.

Page 94. 12 Feb. 1798. Proved, April term 1798. I, JAMES CONNER, for love, good will, natural affection that I have for my dtr. ELIZABETH (alias) BETSY CONNER, for other good causes and consideration. Doth give and grant unto my dtr. a negro girl named, Patt, age 7 yrs. old. I do hereby invest the right of property, exclusive of all other persons, in the ELIZABETH CONNER. Wit: F. WALKER, ABRAM ENLOE.
Signed: JAMES CONNER.

Page 95. -- April 1798. Proved, April term 1798. This is to certify that I have bargained, sold for value received to WILLIAM JONES & WILLIAM FRASURE, a studd horse, and one gray horse, that I had of OBEDIAH TURPIN, 2 feather beds & Furniture, with other household items. Wit: THOMAS STOCKTON.   Signed: WM. TURPIN.

Page 96. 21 Oct. 1795. Proved, April term 1798. I, THOMAS BOID, for diver consideration, do make, ordain, constitute and appoint EBENEZER NEWTON my lawfull attorney to make a good and lawfull deed to JOHN MCCARVAN of Lincoln Co., N.C. for a tract of land containing 150 acres, on the waters of First Broad River. Lying on both sides of Long branch of Knob Creek. Joining land of WILLIAM RILLEN. Wit: JAMES POLLY, JOSEPH ROPER.   Signed: THOMAS BOYD.

Page 97. 9 Oct. 1797. Proved, July term 1798. I, DAVID DUMAS, Junr. of the county of Montgomery, N.C. doth bargain, sell and deliver unto STEPHEN HOGUE of Rutherford Co. N.C. 2 negroes named, Sook, and a boy named Cane. I will warrant and forever defend from all lawfull claims. Wit: JNO. METTON, WILLIAM FRASER.
Signed: DAVID DUMAS, Junr.

Page 97. 5 July 1798. Proved, July term. "I do hereby forwarn all persons in dealing with NANCY FLIN or intertaining of her, as

she has abandoned her bed and left me, I have taken this method to inform
the public against trading with her on my account or showing of any
favours in any respect." Signed: JOHN FLIN.

Page 98. 16 July 1798. Proved, Oct. term 1798. I, EDWARD GOODE, being
          sound in judgement, memory, and understanding, but weak in body.
First my debts be paid. I give to my wife MARY GOODE during widowhood
all my real and personal estate, viz: All lands, stock, and household
furniture of every kind, except 5 shillings I give to each of my chn.
when they come of age. Dtr. SARAH WATSON 5 shilling, son JOHN GOODE 5
shillings, THOMAS GOODE 5 shillings, Dtr. PATSEY GOODE 5 shillings, dtr.
ELIESTON ? 5 shillings, I give to son RICHARD 5 shillings, dtr. NANCY 5
shillings, Son BENJAMIN 5 shillings, Dtr. AGNESS 5 shillings, son LUSBY
5 shillings, dtr. PRESCILLA 5 shillings. In case my wife marry, she to
have one third part of estate, the other to be divided among the chn.
equally. I appoint OBEDIAH WATSON, Rev. DENNIS CARROL, Capt. WILLIAM
GREEN executors. Wit: SAMUEL YOUNG, WILLIAM MURIAW, JOSEPH JAY.
                              Signed: EDWARD GOODE.

Page 99. 29 Dec. 1794. Proved, Oct. term 1798. JOHN HARRIS, LW&T being
          weak in body but perfect in mind and memory. First I give to
my wife all the estate both real and personal for her benfit and bring-
ing up the children during her life or widowhood at the expiration of
either my land to be divided among my sons, PETER, JOHN and REUBIN. My
personal estate to be divided among my 4 dtrs. SALLY, BETSY, AMNY, and
JUDAH and my beloved wife FRANCIS also. Wit: JOS. CAMP, JOHN WILSON.
                              Signed: JOHN X HARRIS.

Page 99. 24 Nov. 1792. Proved, Oct. term 1798. I, JOHN BRIDGES, of
          York Co. S.C. for divers good causes, have made, ordain,
authorized and appointed WM. CAMP & JAMES DUNCAN of Rutherford Co. N.C.
my true and lawfull attorney for me and in my name, and to my use, to
ask, demand, sue, and receive all debts, dues, bonds, bills, and book
accounts from my debtors that stand indebted to me in North & South
Carolina. Wit: JO. CAMP, ABISHAI CAMP. Signed: JOHN X BRIDGES.

Page 100. 11 Dec. 1798. Proved, Jan. term 1799. I, LEVY JACKSON, in
          consideration of $85 to me in hand paid by DAVID FORBUS, being
fully satisfied have bargained, sold and delivered 1 bay mare, 1 colt, 16
head cattle. Wit: A. GLASS, JAMES SELLERS.
                              Signed: LEVI X JACKSON.

Page 101. 1 Jan. 1799. Proved, April term 1799. I, JOHN BARBER, being
          very sick and in weak condition, but of perfect mind & memory.
First all lawfull debts paid. Next I will unto my beloved wife SARAH
BARBER the third of my estate both real and personal, with the two oldest
negroes York & Phillis. I will unto my sons JOHN & ROBERT the remaining
part of my land, JOHN to have negro Little Sam & ROBERT to have negro
James. Dtrs. MARGARET, ANNA and MARY BARBER I will an equal part of the
remaining personal estate. I will to friend THOMAS NITT 5 shillings, I
will to my son-in-law ROBERT & ISEBEAL PATTERSON 5 shillings. I will to
JAMES & SARAH WATSON 5 shillings. I will to WILLIAM & KATHARINE MARTIN
5 shillings, I will to ROBERT & JANE ADAMS 5 shillings. I appoint SARAH
BARBER & JOHN BARBER executors. Wit: ISAAC WHITE, DAVID MOFFITT, HUGH
W. REYNOLDS. Signed: JOHN BARBER.

Page 103. 25 May 1798. Proved, July term 1799. I, THOMAS WALKER, being
          in a low state of health but of perfect mind & memory. First,
I give to my dtr. MRSILLA WALKER a negro girl named Rachel and one named
Hetty, also to dtr. SARAH WALKER one negro named Winny and her child
Nellie, I give the two dtrs. MRSILLA & SARAH my household furniture, my
money and money due, to be equally divided between them by my executors.
I give to my son JAMES WALKER all my lands, farm tools, negroes Lucy &
Frederick. I appoint JONATHAN HAMPTON and NOAH HAMPTON executors. Wit:
MARY X HAMPTON, JAMES HAMPTON, BETSEY HAMPTON.
                              Signed: THOMAS WALKER.

Page 105. 1 Oct. 1794. Proved, Jan. term 1800. I, JESSE CLARK, do or-
          dain, appoint TIMOTHY RIGGS, Esq. my lawfull attorney. to make
a good title to ALEXANDER COOPER for 100 acres of land on Grog Creek,

where I lately lived, according to a grant when it is obtained, by sign-
ing my name to a good warrantee deed for the same to ALEXANDER COOPER.
I do ratify and confirm all my said attorney shall do. Wit: WILLIAM
EAVES, ISRAEL RIGGS.   Signed: JESSE X CLARK.

Page 105. 9 Nov. 1799. Proved, Jan. term 1800. I, JESSE KUIKENDALL,
           have bargained, sold, conveyed and delivered unto JOSEPH CAR-
PENTER, one negro man named Hary, about 26 yrs. of age. In hand paid by
said CARPENTER $400. I do warrant and forever defend all lawfull claims.
Wit: SAMUEL CARPENTER, MARGARET CARPENTER.
                         Signed: JESSE JUIKENDALL

Page 106. 23 Aug. 1795. Proved, Jan. term 1800. I, THOMAS STREET, of
           perfect mind and memory, but very sick and weak in body. I
give to my youngest dtrs., NANCY, FRANKIE, LUSIANY and LUCY each one cow
& calf & household furniture to make them equal with my eldest dtr. ELIZ-
ABETH, as they come of age. I give to my youngest son NIMROD one horse,
and is to be raised out of the estate, until he comes of age. The
balance I give to LUCY my beloved wife, as long as she lives, my land &
tenements, at her death, the estate to be equally divided as aforsaid
among my chn. without exception, to wit: ANTHONY, ELIZABETH, SIMON, JOHN,
NANCY, FRANKIE, NIMROD, LEWVINA, and LUCY. If wife die before chn. come
of age, est. to be keep together. Wit: ROBERT TAYLOR, JOSEPH GRAYSON,
WM. X FOBES.   Signed: THOMAS STREET.

Page 108. 13 April 1800. Proved, April term 1800. I, JOSEPH MILLER,
           for & in consideration of natural love and affection I have to
my dtr. NANCY KING, have given, granted, 1 mare, cow & calf, bed and
furniture. Wit: CHAS. LEWIS.   Signed: JOSEPH MILLER.

Page 109. 8 May 1799. Proved, April term 1800. I, WILLIAM E. STOTT, in
           consideration of $25 in hand paid by THOS. HUNTER & Love Co.
I do hereby deliver unto said Hunter & Love Co. 1 bed & furniture, bed
matt, cups, potts, juggs, dutch oven, 5 tea spoons, 1 tea kittle, mugs,
canister, pails, medicine, vials, papers & other items now in their possession. I will warrant and forever defend. Wit: I. MILLER, JAMES SCOTT,
LEWIS HUNTER.   Signed: WM. E. STOTT.

Page 110. 27 March 1800. Proved, July term 1800. Articals of an agree-
           ment & bargain made between SUSANNAH JOHNS & MICAJAH PUCKET to
live together, during his natural life, to care for his person & property,
and to behave as a good wife does to her husband till seperated by death.
Said MICAJAH hath bargained with SUSANNAH to give one negro woman named
Cloey & her mulatter child Rachel, 1 mare, 1 horse to work, 1 woman saddle, one third part of household furniture, cattle & hoggs. In case
SUSANNAH dies first, the child named Rachel to be given to SUSANNAH JOHNS,
dtr. SARAH JOHNS & her heirs forever, the other property to remain in
MICAJAH hands. SUSANNAH to live on the land lying on the South side of
Whiteoak Creek, during her natural life, then to return to MICAJAH'S
heirs. Wit: SAMUEL YOUNG, ADAM THOMPSON.
                   Signed: MICAJAH PUCKET & SUSANNAH JOHNS.

Page 111. 23 May 1800. Proved, July term 1800. I, DANIEL WATKINS,
           being very sick and weak of body but of perfect mind and
memory. I give to my beloved wife ELIZABETH all my cattle, horses and
household furniture of all kinds. I make and ordain my ----- executrix
of my last will & testament. I leave my land unto my sons ERVIN & DANIEL
to be equally divided between them when they come of age. The whole to
stay in possession of my wife, to raise my children. (not signed).
Appeared in open Court PATRICK SULLIVAN & MARY WATKINS and on oath,
stated they were present and heard DANIEL WATKINS, decd. make the above
will or disposition and he wished Mr. SULLIVAN to witness which was done,
and he died within two hours, unable or was prevented from signing by his
death. Signed PARRICK SULLIVAN, R. T. LEWIS, Clk.
                         Signed: MARY X WATKINS.

Page 113. 6 June 1794. Proved, Oct. term 1800. I, MARY RUSSELL, in
           consideration of £50 to me in hand paid by THOMAS WHITESIDES,
have bargained, sold and delivered a negro named Jeff near seven yrs.
old. I do warrant and forever defend all lawfull claims. Wit. D. DICKEY.

23

Signed: MARY RUSSELL.

Page 113. We the Commissioners appointed by an act of the assembly seat-
        ed at Raleigh on the 18 Nov. 1799 to lay out a town on Main
Broad River between the mouth of first Little Broad River and the mouth
of Green River, have conveaned at Rutherford on the 18 Oct. 1800. When
& whose a majority of the said Commissioners agreed that the aforesaid
town should be established some small distance above Poors ford on Main
Broad River on the land of JOHN MCKINNY and the Commissioners have also
agreed that JAMES MILLER, Junr. & JONAS BEDFORD, Junr. shall take and
give all the obligation required in purchasing the land whereon the above
mentioned town shall be established hereby. Radifying, confirming &
holding for good all that they may lawfull do in the execution of the
same. In testimony whereof we have hereunto set our hands & affix our
seal the above date.   Signed: JOHN LEWIS, J. BEDFORD, WM.
GREEN, CHARLES WILKINS, GEO. MORE for G. BLANTON, JAMES MILLER, Junr.,
JNO MILLER, in place of T. ROBISON. Recd. Oct. term 1800.

Page 114. 23 Sept. 1800. Proved, Jan. term 1801. I, ANDERSON WELLIAM-
        SON, in consideration of £140 hard money to me in hand paid by
DAVID NOWLIN, Junr., have bargained, sold and delivered one negro woman
named Alice about 18 yrs. old. Will warrant and forever defend all lawful claims. Wit: DAVID NOWLAND, JAMES NOWLAND, JOHN X MATHIS.
                        Signed: ANDERSON WILLIAMSON.

Page 115. 20 July 1799. Proved, Jan. term 1801. I, DAVID NOWLIN, Senr.
        in consideration of £80 lawfull money to me paid in hand by
DAVID NOWLIN, Junr., I do hereby acknowledge the receipt. Have bargained,
sold and delivered one negro man named Charles, about 22 yrs. old. I
will warrant and forever defend all lawfull claims. (no witnesses)
                        Signed: DAVID NOWLAND.

Page 115. 3 Oct. 1800. Proved, Jan. term 1801. REBECCA SELLERS, hath
        agreed voluntarily to put their son JOHN SELLER & ELIAS SELL-
ERS to learn to write & read in manner directing the full term of six
years next. Said master is to leave him a horse and saddle worth twenty
pounds, one suit of clothing, Sons to serve master day and night and will
not waste masters goods at cards, dice, or any other unlawfull gaming
during said term. Signed: JOHN STREET.
                        Signed: REBECCA X SELLERS & JOHN
                                SELLERS.

Page 116.? -- Jan. 1801. Proved, Jan. term 1801. I, WILLIAM BOMAN,
        Senr., in consideration of the love and affection which I
have for my dtr. ELIZABETH BOWMAN, I give and grant the following goods
and items one feather bed & furniture, one cow & heffer, one woman saddle
& bridle, one chest, six peuter plates, one bason, to have and hold said
forever. I will warrant and forever defend. Wit: DAVID DALTON, STEPHENS
PHILLIPS.   Signed: WILLIAM BOWMAN.

Page 117. 11 Apr. 1801. Proved, April term 1801. We the undersigned
        chosen by JAMES SMITH & WILLIAM HENDERSON as arbitrators to
settle a controversy between them. Certain slanderous words spoken by
the wife of HENDERSON against said SMITH, and after hearing the witnesses
on both sides, concluded that said BETSEY HENDERSON, has spoken rediculous
and slanderous words against the character of said SMITH, without just
grounds. We therefore award said BETSEY shall before as many witnesses
as SMITH can convene at the house of Maj. JOHN LEWIS on Monday next pub-
lickly acknowledge that the slanderlous and base words that she spoke of
said SMITH are false and groundless. If BETSEY refuses to make this
acknowledgement, she is to pay 50 Spanish dollars.
                        Signed: JOHN LEWIS, JOHNIAS WALCROOP,
JOHN HOLLIN, DANIEL GARNER, ALEXANDER CARRUTH.

Page 117. We sho have hereunto set our name do certify that being pre-
        sent at the house of Maj. JOHN LEWIS. We heard BETSEY HENDER-
SON acknowledge in the presents of a number of witness the required award.
                        Signed: ALEXANDER CARRUTH, JOHN HOLLAND,
                                DANIEL GARNER.

24

Page 118. 20 Dec. 1800. Proved, April term 1801. I, WILLIAM BOWMAN, in
consideration of $400 in hand paid by WILLIAM ELLIOTT, have
bargained, sold and confirmed a negro named Hanah about 19 yrs. old. Will
warrant and forever defend all lawfull claims. Wit: WILLIAM SPIVEY,
JONAS SPIVEY.   Signed: WILLIAM BOWMAN.

Page 118. 1 Nov. 1800. Proved, April term 1801. I, SAMUEL YOUNGE, for
and in consideration of the natural love and affection which
I have for my son FRANCIS YOUNGE. have given, granted and confirmed, two
negroes, viz: one negro woman named Sennu and her dtr. Ann a child, ten
head cows, bed and clothing. I will warrant and forevr defend. Wit:
JOSEPH JAY, MARTHA X HOOTEL.   Signed: SAMUEL YOUNGE.

Page 119. 20 Oct. 1800. Proved, April term 1801. I, SAMUEL YOUNGE, in
consideration of natural love and affection, that I have for
my son JOHN YOUNGE, have given granted him two negroes boys viz: Bob &
Clem, ten head cattle, one bed and furniture. I will warrant and forever
defend, said property. Wit: JOSEPH JAY, MARTHA X HOOTEL.
                                    Signed: SAMUEL YOUNGE.

Page 120. 19 Jan. 1801. Proved, April term 1801. I, GEORGE PETTY, being
weak in body, but of perfect mind and memory. I, give to my
beloved wife SARAH ANN PETTY, my land and all my goods and chattles of
every kind during her life, at her death to be equally divided amongest
all my children that are single to wit: MARY, JAMES, LETTICE, FANIA. I
give to my dtr. ELIZABETH 10 shillings, I give to dtr. CLERSY 10 shillings,
I will to my son ORASHA 10 shillings, I will to son JOSEPH one cow and
10 shillings. I appoint my wife and son JOSEPH as Executors and Executrix. Wit: CHARLES RICHARDSON, JAMES YOUNGE.
                                    Signed: GEORGE PETTY.

Page 121. 30 March 1801. Proved, July term 1801. I, GLOUD LONG, being
very sick and weak of body, but of perfect mind and memory.
First I give to my loving wife JANE LONG my land I now live on and my
negro fellow Abe during her life or widowhood, then to be the property
of our son GLOUD LONG. Also all stock, beds & furniture and kitchen
furniture during her life time. I give to my son PATRICK LONG $15 out
of the bond that I have against MIKE TANNER also a good feather bed &
furniture. I give unto my son JAMES LONG $20. I give to my dtrs. JESEBEL
& PEGGY $10 a peace out of TANNER bond. I give to my son GLOUD LONG $8
out of said bond. I give to my two youngest dtrs. JANE & POLLY $8 a
peace from said bond. Also $5 from said bond to son JOHN LONG for the
use of grave yard. The balance of said bond to pay my just debts. The
ballance if any left with the money I may have to buy my wife a negro
girl. I appoint JOHN LONG, PATRICK LONG, JAMES LONG my executors. Wit:
JAMES BABER, GLOUD LONG.   Signed: GLOUD X LONG.

Page 122. 17 March 1798. Proved, July term 1801. I, DAVID THOMPSON,
being sick likely for a change to another world, in my proper
senses, I allow my just debts be paid. My little estate I leave to my
wife ELEANOR THOMPSON while she lives and at her death and if the child
ELEANOR MURRAY continue with my wife, she is to have what the old woman
has. Not to be disinherited on the account of marriege. I allow JOHN
TABOUR, Senr., to be executor, and WILLIAM THOMPSON my son to be another.
Wit: JOHN TABOUR, JOHN GARRET, Jurat.   Signed: DAVID THOMPSON.

Page 123. No date. I, WILLIAM QUEEN, Senr., hath bargained and sold
unto STEPHEN HOUGE a certain mare, now in his possession, likewise six plates, three dishes, three basons. I will warrant and defend
from all persons whatsoever. Wit: DAVID FORBUS, WILLIAM HOUGEN.
                                    Signed: WILLIAM X QUEEN.

Page 124. 31 Jan. 1801. Proved, Oct. term 1801. I, PETER WATKINS,
being very sick & weak in body but of perfect mind & memory.
I give unto my beloved wife HANNAH WATKINS all goods and chattles as
long as she lives, then to be sold on 12 month credit. The money to be
equally divided among my chn. to wit: DAVID WATKINS, WILLIAM WATKINS,
EVAN WATKINS, ESTHER CAPSHAW, NANCY MCKINNEY, ELLENDER PHILLIPS, I give
unto my grand son EVAN WATKINS £10 from the sale to be put to education
said EVAN WATKINS. I appoint my sons WILLIAM WATKINS, & EVAN WATKINS AS

25

executors. Wit: JACOB X DAVIS, PHILIP DAVIS, J. B. LASWELL.
                        Signed: PETER X WATKINS.

Page 126. 10 Sept. 1801. Proved, Jan. term 1802. I, MARY MCDONALD,
            being sick & weak in body, but of perfect mind and memory.
First all my just debts be paid if estate is sufficent. My will is the
dtr. of JAMES MCDONALD called SUSANNA & the dtr. CATHERINE MOSS wife of
JAMES MOSS, called ELIZABETH MOSS shall hold and enjoy my estate, both
real and personal. I appoint RICHARD LEWIS as my executor. Attest:
THOS. GRANT.   Signed: MARY X MCDONALD.
The expenses for attending me in my sickness & family charges to be paid
first. Attest: THOM. GRANT.   Signed: MARY X MCDONALD.

Page 127. 24 Nov. 1801. Proved, Jan. term 1802. I, MARY COLEMAN, in
            consideration of natural love and affection that I bear for my
grandson ELIAS WEBB, son of my dtr. USLEY CAROLINE WEBB, have given &
granted unto said ELIAS WEBB my negro mulatto wench named Bash and her
four children viz: Reuben, Patience, Selinie & Jordan. To have and hold
said negroes forever. I will warrant & forever defend all lawfull claims.
Wit: SAMUEL YOUNGE, ROBERT HANEY, (Jurat).
                        Signed: MARY X COLEMAN.

Page 128. 17 Sept. 180?. Proved, Jan. term 1802. I, JAMES RUTHERFORD,
            of Columbis, S.C. merchant. Have for diver good causes. Have
ordain, authorized and appointed FELIX WALKER of Rutherford Co., N.C. my
true and lawfull attorney, for me and in my name, use and benfit, to ask,
sue, demand, recover, demand all money and demands whatsoever. From
PHILIP NUELL, HENRY MILLES, and TOUNSON HORTON late of Rutherford Co.,
N.C. to possess, attachment or arrest to recover money due me from named
persons. Wit: A.M. GILBERT, (Jurat)   Signed: JAMES RUTHERFORD.

Page 129. 14 April 1797. Proved, Jan. term 1802. I, ROBERT MCMINNS,
            Senr., being very sick and weak in body, but of perfect mind
and memory. I will and do order first my just debts be paid with burial
charges. I give unto my wife JANE all my estate both real and personal,
to keep and use as myself for the common support of the family, during
her natural life or widowhood. After her death to be equally divided
among all my children. I appoint my wife JANE and ALEXANDER DAVIDSON,
Senr., executors. Wit: JOHN REAGAN, JAMES KURKENDALL.
                        Signed: ROBERT MCMINNS,

Page 130. 3 Feb. 1802. Proved, Jan. term 1802. I, ARTHUR CLARK,
            nominated, constituted and appointed Maj. ROSS ALEXANDER to
use my name by all legal ways and means whatsoever to sue for, recover
debts due and demands to me in this county. Wit: ELIAS ALEXANDER, NEVILL
HOPSON.   Signed: ARTHUR CLARK.

Page 132. 22 Aug. 1800. Proved, April term 1802. I JESSE KURKENDALL of
            Lincoln County have bargained sold and delivered unto SAMUEL
YOUNGE of Rutherford County, a negro named Lewis, about six yrs. old. In
hand paid 150 silver dollars, by said SAMUEL YOUNGE. Will warrant and
defend said property. Wit: JOSEPH CARPENTER, SAMUEL CARPENTER.
                        Signed: JESSE KURKENDALL.

Page 132. 14 April 1802. Proved, April term 1802. I, JANE M. CLAINS,
            in consideration of love, good will and affection that I have
and bear unto my dtr. REBECCA BYERS, living near myself, have given,
granted unto said REBECCA and her heirs one negro woman named Pegg forever. Wit: B. FINLY, HUGH KILPATRICK.   Signed: JEAN CLAIR.

Page 133. 14 April 1802. Proved, April term 1802. I, JEAN M. CLAIN, in
            consideration of love, good will and affection that I have and
bear towards my dtr. MARGARET MURRY. Living near myself, have given,
granted one negro boy named Peter forever. Wit: B. FINLY, HUGH KILPAT-
RICK.   Signed: JEAN CLAIR.

Page 134. 1 May 1801. Proved, Jan. term 1802. I JAMES KETER being in
            perfect health, strength, mind and body. I give to my son
JAMES KETER 50 acres where he now lives. I give to my son JOHN KETER
50 acres more. JOSHUA KETER 50 acres more. BENJAMIN KETER 50 acres

more. Son JAMES to have house and land where he now lives, after my death, and one gray horse, JOSHUA to have one bay mare, BENJAMIN to have what is left. Wife LUCY to have all stock during her life time or widowhood. Dtrs. BETSEY & NANCY to have a cow & calf a piece. when they marry. Household furniture to be divided between sons JOSHUA & BENJAMIN, POLLY the wife of THOMAS SMITH shall have 5 shillings. I wish HENRY & JOHN KETER to be executors, and HENRY KETER to have $10 from the estate. Wit: WILLIAM S. SLATE, JAMES KETER, JOSHUA KETER.
Signed: JAMES X KETER.

Page 135. 12 April 1802. April term 1802. Whereas there has been a report prevailing in the county, that Mr. ABRAM IRVINE of this county did attempt to rob the widow RAGAN, and that the said widow RAGAN did propigate said report her self. Therefore the said IRVINE brought suit against her for damages & which said CATHARINE RAGAN, widow, does this day 12 April 1802 by these present do acknowledge that she was mistaken that the said Mr. IRVINE is absolutely clear of the fact and report are false against him, therefore we have settled the matter this by paying all cost of said suit. The said suit is therefore dismissed. Wit: WILLIAM GRAHAM, RICHARD HOGAN. Signed: CATY REAGAN.

Page 136. 6 ---- 1802. Proved, July term 1802. I, LEVI JACKSON, in consideration of $85, to me in hand paid by JOHN JACKSON, have bargained, sold and set over and delivered 25 acres of land joining the improvement, one bay mare & two coults, one 3 yrs. old the other sucks, 12 head horned cattle, two work oxen, two head sheep, one large kettle, one pott & oven, feather bed & furniture, two bee hives. I will warrant and forever defend from all persons. Wit: JAMES JACKSON, JOHN SILLERS.
Signed: LEVI X JACKSON.

Page 137. 12 March 1802. Proved, July term 1802. I, WILLIAM GREENWOOD, have bargained and sold to HENRY COCHRAM my right title and interest to a tract of land containing 250 acres, on waters of Broad River & Maple Creek for which we HUGH GREENWOOD, WILLIAM GREENWOOD and HUGH BIRD GREENWOOD have a bond on JAMES MILLER to make a title for the above mentioned land. I, WILLIAM GREENWOOD, do hereby sign away my right title & interest to the said bond on the said JAMES MILLER to the said HENRY COCHRAM. Wit: JAMES COCHRAM, THOMAS MAUNOR, JOSEPH SHARP.
Signed: WILLIAM GREENWOOD.

Page 138. 21 July 1802. Proved, Oct. term 1802. I, ARTHUR CLARK, by bond or obligation by these present in the sum of $4,780 with a condition there under written, for the payment of $2,390, unto JAMES MAIR & ROBERT MEANS at the period herein stated. To better secure the sum of $2,390 unto said JAMES MAIR & ROBERT MEANS, I have sold and delivered five negroes to wit, one negro man named Philip about 30 yrs. old, Nelly his wife about 22 yrs. old also a girl about 4 yrs. old, also a girl about one year old, also a girl named Milley about 6 yrs. old. Said CLARK shall pay the sum of $2,390 (no date given) or the said JAMES MAIR & ROBERT MEANS shall possesse all lands tenements goods and chattles of the said CLARK. Wit: WILLIAM SMITH, WILLIAM GEVING.
Signed: ARTHUR CLARK.

Page 140. 21 July 1802. Proved, Oct. term 1802. ROBERT CLARKE of Rutherford Co. N.C. of the one part and JAMES MAIR & ROBERT MEANS both of Charleston, S.C. of the second part. In better secureing the bond of $2,390. Have bargained sold unto JAMES MAIR & ROBERT MEANS all the several tracts of land lying & being in Rutherford County, N.C. Tract # 1 for 150 acres. tract #2 150 acres. tract #3 200 acres. tract #4 200. tract #5 200 acres. tract #6 100 acres. tract #7 100 acres. tract #8 150 acres. For a total of 1250 acres more or less. ROBERT CLARKE to pay the full sum of bond or JAMES MAIR & ROBERT MEANS to take possession of the land. Wit: WM. SMITH, WILLIAM GEVING.
Signed: ARTHUR CLARKE.

Page 144. 22 Jan. 1796. Proved, Oct. term 1802. I, GEORGE BLANTON, being weak & frail in body but sound mind and memory. Executors are BUNEL BLANTON & WILLIAM BLANTON. First all debts to be paid. I leave to my beloved wife SUSANAH BLANTON, all and every part of my estate, both real and personal during her life or widowhood. After her

27

death to be divided among my children, viz. BURRELL BLANTON, ANN BRIDGES, CATHARINE BRIDGES, WILLIAM BLANTON, BETSEY BRIDGES, FRANCES BLANTON, JOHN BLANTON, MARY BLANTON, PEGGY BLANTON, and RICHARD BLANTON. Wit: JOHN BLANTON, JEREMIAH RANNEGES.   Signed: GEORGE BLANTON.

Page 146. 6 Sept. 1802. Proved, Jan. term 1803. I, JOHN SCOTT, in consideration of good will and affection which I have for my wife LETTICE SCOTT, if my death is before hers, I give and grant unto my wife LETTICE SCOTT and her heirs all my goods & chattles, lands and tenements belonging to me, after my just debts are paid. Wit: JAMES SCOTT, LETTICE SCOTT.   Signed: JOHN SCOTT.

Page 147. 9 March 1802. Proved, Jan. term 1803. I, JOHN DANEIL, being very sick and weak in body but of perfect mind and memory. I give and bequeath to my sons WILLIAM and HARDY DANIEL, to be equally divided between them, all my lands, messuage, and tenements after the decease of my wife ABIGAL DANEIL and moveable property as stock and house-hold furniture, to be equally divided among my children after the death of my wife. Wit: ROBERT WELLS, WILLIAM WILSON.
                         Signed: JOHN X DANEIL.
NB. I constitute and ordain my wife ABEGIL DANEIL & WM. DANEIL executors.

Page 148. 2 March 1802. Proved, Jan. term 1803. I, JOHN WATSON, being in a low state of health, but of perfect mind and memory. Just debts to be paid. I give to my wife ANN my negro man Dick, Cate and China, also stock and household furniture, and such debts that may be due to me. I give to my dtr. JENING WATSON my negro boy Ceason, I give to dtr. DELPHEY WATSON, negro boy George, To my son SAWNEY WATSON I give my negro girl Sall, and all land on the South side of Green River, after the death of my wife. To my son OBEDIAH WATSON, I give one shilling. I give to my son JOHN WATSON £17. I give to my son MATHEW WATSON, the lower end of my land on the North side of Green River, up to the line run by Eq. DUKEY, containing 60 acres. I give to my sons JOSEPH & WILLIAM WATSON, all the land on the North side of Green River above the line run by said DUKEY. I give to my son DAVID WATSON one shilling. I desire that my son DAVID WATSON shall have a reasonable support during his life, and from the property I have given my wife. Executors, ZACHARIAH WOOD, GEO. WHERSEY and JOSEPH WATSON. Wit: RUSSELL TWITTY, JONATHAN MURICK.
                         Signed: JOHN WATSON.

Page 149. 20 Sept. 1802. Proved, Jan. term 1803. I, SAMUEL REED, being weak of body but sound memory. I give to my wife SARAH the tract of land whereon I now live, with the house and improvements. One half of the furniture in the house and farming tools of every kind. One Black filly, and one half of the land that I now own. I give to my son JOHN REED my bay mare that he now has, he paying his three sons as follows, the youngest son JAMES to have the coult, and sons WILLIAM & JOHN each to have one third of the value of the mare. I give to my dtr. RACHEL REED 100 acres of land that I bought from MILES GOFORTH with im-provements. One Black mare named Fly & her colt. One half of the live stock, and half of the furniture in my house. I give unto my SARAH the remainder of the time of my negro boy John Define, Wife to pay one half, and dtr. the other half of his freedom. Wife & dtr. to share all debts due unto him, and share all debts he may have. I appoint my son JOHN REED & RACHEL REED as executor and executrix. Wit: WM. FLACK, PEYTON GOFORTH.   Signed: SAMUEL REED.

Page 151. No date. Proved, April term 1803. I, WILLIAM EARLE, being very sick in body, but of perfect mind and memory. I give to my son NATHANIEL EARLE the house wherein I now live, with 100 acres of land, the other 200 acres to be equally divided between sons PLEASANT & ELYAH EARLE. I give to my dtrs. ? LEDBETTER, SUSEY EARLE, MARGARET EARLE a negro woman named Cate, my two youngest dtrs. to have a feather bed each. I give to my sons BENNET EARLE, WILLIAM EARLE, JOSHUA EARLE 10 shillings each. My just debts to be paid from the debts due me. I give to my wife my house and ballance of my moveable estate during her life, then to go to my three dtr. named. I appoint my son NATHANIEL EARLE my sole executor. Wit: ROBERT HARDEN, R. MASTERS, ROBERT JNO. ROBERTS.   Signed: WILLIAM X EARLE.

Page 152. 3 Dec. 1802. Proved, April term 1803. I, JOHN HUGHS, being in a low condition of health, but perfect mind and memory. I give to MARTHA my beloved wife, my land and negroe property during her natural life, but she is not to sell any part thereof. The debts oweing me to be collected, from them to pay my just debts or demands. The ballance if any with my stock, tools and furniture to be at the disposal of my wife MARTHA, and at her decease the whole I give unto my dtr. ELIZABETH MCCAIN and if CHARLES MCCAIN the present husband survives her, he to have the use during his life time, But not to sell or convey any part thereof. At his decease to be divided equally among the children of my dtr. ELIZABETH lawfull heirs of her body. Except a negro boy named Joe I have already give to CHARLES, which is to remain as confirmed property. I leave it to my wife to give MOURNING WILLIAMS any sum under $50. Wit: ELIAS ALEXANDER, FRANCES ALEXANDER.   Signed: JOHN HUGHS.
NB. I, JOHN HUGHS, on the 3 Dec. 1802 have appointed ELIAS ALEXANDER & FRANCES ALEXANDER executors. Wit: SAMUEL YOUNGE, JAMES MURRAY.
                            Signed: JOHN HUGHS.

Page 153. 19 Sept. 1802. Proved, April term 1803. I, JAMES LOVE, Merch. Being perfect and sound of mind but present laboring under bodely afflictions. I will my executor to pay my debts. I give unto JAMES the son of CLEMENTINA GRANT the sum of $50. I give to my wife ANN & my dtr. NANCY SIMMS, my son JOHN and brother DAVID, all the residue of my estate and property to be equally divided among them, if my wife should have another child, it is to share equal. I appoint my friend THOMAS HUNTER, Merch. of Pendleton, S.C. my beloved wife, and friend WILLIAM TOMS, Merch, my executors. Wit: LEWIS HUGHS, JNO. MCGUAFHY.
                            Signed: JAMES LOVE.

Page 154. 11 April 1803. Proved, April term 1803. "I, NATHANIEL EARLE, son of ELIZABETH EARLE do lease to ELIZABETH EARLE the house where she now lives and what part of the land she wants to tend for her own use and half of the peach orchard and SUCY EARL and MARGRET EARLE daughters of ELIZABETH EARLE do give or lease to ELIZABETH EARLE a negro wench by the name of Cate to waite on her, her lifetime or widowhood and PLEASENT EARLE give to his mother all the land she wants to tend or use for her own use during her widowhood or lifetime." Wit: JNO. ROBERTS, MARTIN ROBERTS.   Signed: NATHANIEL X EARLE, PLEASENT X EARLE, SUSCY X EARLE, MARGRET EARLE.

Page 155. 29 May 1793. Proved, July term 1803. I, SAMUEL MCMURRY, being weak of body but of sound mind and memory. First I allow my lawfull debts to be paid from my moveable estate. I give to my wife MARGARET MCMURRY a third of my moveable estate, she to have her living from the plantation as long as she is a widow. I give to my son ANDREW MCMURRY the land lying over the creek. I give to my dtr. JEAN MCMURRY one horse and saddle & two cows and one bed and furniture. I give to JAMES MCMURRY the plantation I live on that lyes on the same side of the creek that I live on. And all the tools for working the same and one cow. I give to MARGRET MCMURRY one horse, saddle, two cows and one bed & furniture. I give to SAMUEL MCMURRY, 5 shillings, I give to son THOMAS MCMURRY 5 shillings, I give to dtr. SARAH BOULDERIDGE 5 shillings, I give to my dtr. ELIZABETH CALLAHAN 5 shillings, I give to my son JOHN MCMURRY 5 shillings. I allow my wife MARGRET MCMURRY all the furniture in the house. The remainder if any to be divided among my chn, viz: ANDREW, ELENOR, JANE, MARY, AGNESS and MARGRET MCMURRY. I appoint my wife MARGRET & son ANDREW MCMURRY as executors. NB I allow my waggon to be equally divided between my sons ANDREW & JAMES MCMURRY. Wit: ALEXANDER MCGAUGHY, CORNILUS MELTON, Jurat.   Signed: SAMUEL X MCMURRY.

Page 157. 23 Dec. 1802. Proved, July term 1803. I, have occasion to alter my will concerning my chn. ANDREW has got his land and sold it, AGNESS & ELENOR has married. I therefor allow ELENOR GROVES, 5 shillings, ANDREW MCMURRY, 5 shillings, AGNESS GROVES, 5 shillings. Wit: ALEXANDER MCGAUGHY.   Signed: SAMUEL MCMURRY.

Page 157. 11 March 1801. Proved, July term 1803. I, JAMES REAVIS, being in a low state of health but of perfect mind and memory. First my just debts to be paid by sale of my waggon & horses as can be spared. The land I bought from JAMES and BIRD SLUGHTER should be given

29

up to them again if they will consent to it. The estate to remain in the
hands of wife MARTHA until my eldest son WILSON come of age, then the
estate to be valued, and my wife to have equal part with my chn. viz:
POLLY, MORGAN, WASHINGTON, BETSEY, LUCYNDA. Chn. to have their part
when come of age or marry. I appoint JOHN HEADEN, JOHN BRADLEY & my wife
MARTHA as executors. Wit: JAMES DOYLE, JAMES BRADLEY, WILLIS BRADLEY.
Signed: JAMES REAVIS.

Page 158. 19 April 1803. Proved, July term 1803. I, WILLIAM ROBINSON,
farmer, being weak of body but of sound memory and mind. First
I allow my just debts and fueneral charges to be paid from my moveable
estate. I give to my beloved wife ELIZABETH the dwelling house and land
on which we now live, with all household furniture, farming tools, one
negro man named Jack, three head horses, six cows & calves, also my stock
of hogs & sheep. My wife may despose of any of the above mentioned property at any time she thinks proper. At her death her property to be
equally divided among my legatees. I also give to my son JONATHAN ROBIN-
SON 100 acres of land lying between me and GOUD LONGE, also 180 acres
where I now live at the death of my wife, The other property divided
among my chn. viz: THOMAS ROBINSON, REBECCA, WILLIAM, ELIZABETH, BENJAMIN
& JONATHAN. I appoint my wife ELIZABETH and JONATHAN HAMPTON and ROBERT
SMITH my executors. Signed JOSEPH GREEN, JAMES MOOREHEAD, JOHN MCCONNELL.
Signed: WILLIAM ROBERTSON.

Page 160. 12 July 1803. Proved, July term 1803. We, JOHN WEBB & DAVID
NOWLAND, being men of credit appeared in open court on the 4
July 1803 and made oath that ANDERSON WILLIAMSON, late of this county
died on the 4 June last past, and the above wittness in the last sickness
of the decease, about night said before his death, they were called upon
by the decendants to bear witness of the following. He declared that this
was his last will. "I leave my property to my wife and my three boys to
be equally divided between them" Mr. DAVID NEWLAND further said "that
the property is to stay in the hands of my wife until the children are
raised, then the property to be divided among the boys and his wife."
Signed: JOHN WEBB, DAVID NOWLAND.
This 12 July 1803.

Page 161. 1 Nov. 1802. Proved, July term 1803. We SARAH WALKER & RHODY
WALKER of the County of Woodford & state of -----?. do nominate and appoint our friend WM. WALKER our true and lawfull attorney. To
settle all our business and interest in the property of JESSE WALKER,
decd. in the State of N.C. to receive and receipt the money or otherwise.
(There is a Woodard County, Ky.) Signed: SARAH X WALKER, RHODY WALKER.

Page 162. 5 Oct. 1803. Proved, Jan. term 1804. I, DAVID MILLER, being
very sick & weak in body but of perfect mind and memory. I
give to my son JOHN MILLER the following lands, messuage, and tenements,
lying in Rutherford & Buncombe Counties. (There are 48 tracts, with 7,106
acres.) I give to my second son ANDREW MILLER the following land,
messuage and tenements, lying in Buncombe & Rutherford Counties. (there
are 41 tracts, with 7,177 acres.) I give to my son in law ALLEN TWITTY,
husband of my dtr. MARTHA, the following lands, messuage and tenements,
in Rutherford & Buncombe Counties. (there are 58 tracts, with 6,495 acres)
I give to my grand son DAVID BRIGGS a tract of land containing 150 acres,
lying in the fork of the branch of Floyd Creek. I give to my son JOHN
MILLER my Roan horse, my riding saddle, 3 head of young cattle, one bed
& furniture, one large oven, one half of pewter plates. Also the following money, to wit: JAMES KUYKENDALL bond & open account of 450 Ł 18
shillings, 4 pence. FRANCES ALEXANDER bond of 50 Ł. Also my great coat,
one waistcoat, & one pair of briches. I give to my son ANDREW MILLER, my
young soral horse with Phils saddle, one cow & calf, one black heffer
which I gave to his dtr. POLLY MILLER, my waggon & gear, with farming
tools, my Walnut table, a large pewter bason, other items listed. The
money as follows. Bonds & accounts to wit. ROBT. ORSBORN bond, DAVID
RAMSOUR, bond, JOHN DAVIDSON bond, ABRAHAM KUYKENDALL bond, JOHN DOLTON
bond, JOSEPH SPRNCER bond, THOMAS MCENTRIE note. I give to my son in law
JESSE BRIGGS, husband of my dtr. ESTHER each and every tract of land with
my signature thereto. One cow & calf, one bed & furniture that stands
next to the front door, one looking glass, my corner cubbard, my table
and dresser furniture. I give to my son in law ALLEN TWITTY my negro

woman Sall, one cow & calf, bed & furniture. I appoint JOHATHAN HAMPTOM, GEORGE WATSON, JOHN MILLER, ANDREW MILLER and ALLEN TWITTY my executors. Wit: WM. TWITTY, ALEX. M. LADIN, CHARLES EDWARDS.
Signed: DAVID MILLER.

Page 178. 4 Nov. 1803. Proved, Jan. term 1804. I, BENJAMIN HAWKINS, in consideration of $350. $210 in hand paid by & $140 to be paid on or before Christmas and before the signing and sealing by SARAH THOMP-SON, of Spartanburg County, S.C. Have bargained, sold a negro woman called Jane about 22 yrs. old. Wit: WILLIAM MILLICAN.
Signed: BENJAMIN HAWKINS.

Page 179. 1 April 1804. Proved, July term 1804. I, JOHN MCKINNEY, Senr., being sick in body but of sound mind and memory. I give to my wife JEAN, one good feather bed and furniture, and is to live in my dwelling house as long as she lives. I give to my son JOHN MCKINNEY 200 acres where he now lives, and the remainder of the tract that I sold to ANDERSON & $100 in money. I give to my son JAMES MCKINNEY 308 acres of land that I bought from SHARP, also 100 acres that I took up joining it. Also $50 in money. I give to my son HENRY MCKINNEY the land where he now lives, begining where GEORGE CAMPBELL and I made some marks, thence to the back line, down said line to the river, And $200 in money, to be paid within three years. I give to my son WILLIAM MCKINNEY the land where he now lives, also $50 in money. I give to my son GEORGE MCKINNEY the plantation where I now live. I also give to my son in law THOMAS GORE $100 in money. I give to my son in law JONAS BEDFORD $25 in money. I also give to my son in law JOHN ROBERTS a negro wench named Pat, also $50 in money. I give to my dtr. SALLY CAMP $100 worth of property at my decease. I give to my dtr. DEDAMI 300 acres of land where SALLY CAMP now lives also a negro girl named Hanah and a boy named Tom, and $100 in money. I give to my grand son WILLIAM MCKINNEY son of HENRY MCKINNEY a tract of land joining WILLIAM ROBBIN (discribed). I give to my grand dtr. LYDA CAMP dtr. of SALLY CAMP (discribed) contaning 150 acres. I appoint JAMES MCKINNEY, HENRY MCKINNEY, and GEORGE MCKINNEY my executors. Wit: BENJ. HICKS, JAMES HUMPHERY, THOMAS X SEMMONS.
Signed: JOHN MCKINNEY.

Page 182. 2 Nov. 1805. Proved, Oct. term 1805. I, ANDREW MITCHELL, being weak in body but of perfect mind and memory. I give to my grand son JOHN MITCHELL, son of WILLIAM MITCHELL all my land in Ruther-ford County on the waters of Little Cub Creek. Containing 35 acres. The right now lies with my son WILLIAM, he is required to make a true and lawfull deed of conveyance to said JOHN MITCHELL or pay him full value thereof. I give to my grand dtr. MARTHA MITCHELL, dtr. of WILLIAM MIT-CHELL my bed and furniture, one duch oven & lid. four plates, one pewter bason. I give to my grand dtr. POLLY MITCHELL dtr. of WILLIAM MITCHELL one cow & two iron potts, 1 pewter Bason and a mantle. I give to my grand son WILLIAM MITCHELL, son of WILLIAM, my bay horse now in possess-ion of my son WILLIAM, one axe, two hoes, & a set of plow irons. I give to my dtr. JANE MITCHELL dtr. of WILLIAM MITCHELL, one pewter dish, four pewter plates, one coffee pott & five pewter spoons. I give to my Grand dtr. NANCY, dtr. of WILLIAM, one smothing iron, one iron pott rack & spinning wheel. I give to my son WILLIAM MITCHELL my clothes, one large Bible and other books, saddle & bridle. (other items). I give to my dtr. FRANCES AYOCK four pewter spoons, one small pewter bason, (other items). I give to my son ANDREW MITCHELL the sum of $5. to be due any time after this will is in force. I give to my grand dtr. POLLY, dtr. of PEGGY MITCHELL, decd., one heifer to be deposited with my son WILLIAM, until, she comes of age then WILLIAM to give said POLLY a cow and calf. I appoint my son WILLIAM MITCHELL as executor. Wit: CLAYBOURN CANDRY, WILLIAM L. PRICE.
Signed: ANDREW X MITCHELL.

Page 184. 20 July 1805. Proved, Oct. term 1805. I, ANDREW HAMPTON, being in low state of health, but of perfect mind and memory. First I will my just debts be paid of whatever nature they may be and with receipt. I give to my youngest son WASHINGTON the land which I now live on, being part of several tracts, also a negro boy named Jack, one fourth part of the growing crop. I leave to the care and use of dtr. ELIZABETH PRICE, my negro woman Dinah, I also leave to the care & use of my dtr. NANCY BRADLY my old negro man named Will. The remainder of my

31

property both real and personal, including negroes, Tom, Eae, Ben, Patt, Sall & Miria to be valued by three freeholders, a just distribution made among my chn. except son WASHINGTON. Chn. are: JONATHAN, SUSANAH, ANDREW, JOHN, ELIZABETH, NANCY, BENJAMIN, ALICE, RACHEL, MARY, ADAM, MICHEL, & CATHERINE, decd. whose part is to be paid to her heirs. I appoint my son JONATHAN HAMPTON executor. Wit: CHARLEY LEWIS, THOMAS ROWLAND.
Signed: ANDREW HAMPTON.

Page 186. 9 June 1803. Proved, 6 July 1805. I, SAMUEL ANDREWS, being weak in body but of perfect mind and memory. I allow all my just debts to be paid. I allow my beloved wife SARAH a comfortable maintenance off the tract of land I now live on, also all household Furniture in the house or kitchen and one black mare named Drea, saddle & bridle. One third of cattle, sheep & hogs. One third of the cash debts, and the remainder of the price of the young horse I sold. I give to my son JOHN $25. I give to my dtr. CHRISTAIN the young man that they have recd. and $25 to be paid in trade. I leave to my son JAMES all my land lying up Cane Creek above MARLINS line. I leave to my son HUGH $150 to be paid by my son BANJAMIN in two years after my death also a saddle & bridle and a bought suit of clothe at his own choosing to be paid from my moveable property. I leave my son BENJAMIN all the old tract of land I now live on, and a horse named Sealer & I allow the horse that my son BENJAMIN sold, that was loaned his for my son JAMES to get half the price. I allow after my sons JAMES & BENJAMIN pay up what was before mentioned. I allow any over plus of my property to be equally divided among them. I appoint my wife SARAH ANDREWS & my son BENJAMIN ANDREWS executors. Wit: PATRICK WATSON, POLLY ROBERSON.
Signed: SAMUEL ANDREWS.

Page 187. 4 March 1805. Proved, 6 July 1805. I, RICHARD RIGHT, being very sick and weak in body but of perfect mind and memory. I give to JUDITH WRIGHT all my personal estate during her natural life, and after her decease, I give to my dtr. NANCY LEE one feather bed & furniture, and my property to be equally divided amongest the rest of my chn: JOHN WRIGHT, MARY RAN---? (blured), ELIZABETH LEE, NANCY LEE, SARAH MCCOMBY, FEBY HAMBRICK. I appoint OWEN LEE & GEORGE HAMBRICK as executors. Wit: JULLET WRIGHT, BENJAMIN DAILY.   Signed: RICHARD WRIGHT.

Page 188. 24 Sept. 1805. Proved, Jan. term 1806. I, JOHN TABOR, being sick and weak in body but of perfect mind and memory. I give to my wife ELIZABETH all my lands and other estate for her while she re-mains a widow during her life and or afterwards to be equally divided amongst all my chn. Or if my wife marry again she to have a child part. I allow my youngst son ELY one young horse, the value of $50, before he come of age exclusive of his equal part. I appoint my wife ELIZABETH, my son SOLOMON TABOR and THOMAS TABOR my executors. Wit: WILLIAM CAPSHAW, (jurat) DAVID CAPSHAW, WILLIAM WASH CAPSHAW.
Signed: JOHN TABOR.

Page 189. 23 Jan. 1806. Proved, April term 1806. I, WILLIAM WEBB, being of perfect & sound mind, but in low state of health and body. I give to my dtr. NANCY EARL a negro named Moses. I give to my dtr. SARAH SCOGGINS a negro named Aaron. I give to my wife URSELA CAROLINA, during life or widowhood one negro boy named Frank. At her decease or marriage said negro to be given to dtr. POLLY. I give to my wife URSELA CAROLINA, during her life or widowhood a negro girl named Ann, at her decease or marriage said negro to be given to dtr. SUCKY. The remainder of my estate both real & personal I leave to my wife, during her life or widowhood, after death or marriage just debts to be paid and then the property to be divided among my sons, ISAAC, JONATHAN, ELIAS and dtrs. SALLY, POLLY, NANCY and SUCKY all to have an equal share. I appoint my wife URSELA CAROLINA my executrix. Wit: JESSE MORROW, WM. TOMS, GEORGE MORROW. (Jurat).   Signed: WILLIAM WEBB.

Page 190. 14 April 1806. Proved, July term 1806. JESSE TATE, Being of sound and perfect mind and memory. I give to my wife MARY TATE 500 acres, 2 cows & calves and personal estate, during her life or widowhood. After my just debts are paid and at her death. I give to my sons SAMUEL TATE, REBIN TATE, JAMES TATE, 500 acres of land to be equally divided amongst them. I give unto my son RANDAL TATE 100 acres of land

32

where he now lives, joining, WM. BLANTON, and WILLIAM HUMPHRIES land. I
give to my dtr. KIPSEY TATE one feather bed & furniture, one horse, one
cow & calf. I give no more to my two dtrs. PATSEY TATE & NANCY ARRNOL
than the law allows. My personal estate to be equally divided between
my dtrs. FANNY WELLES, SARAH HESTER, SUSANNAH MCRAN, MARY MCRAN and
KIPSEY TATE. I appoint SAMUEL TATE, executor. Wit: CHARLES WILKINS,
RANDEL TATE, (Jurat) WM. BLANTON.   Signed: JESSE X TATE.

Page 191. ----- 1806. Proved, July term 1806. I, ROBERT CAMPBELL, being
             of sound mind and memory. I allow my just debts to be paid
from my personal property. I give to my son WILLIAM 50 acres lying highest up the creek to run across. I give to my son ROBERT 50 acres of land
lying lowest down on the creek too in the manner above. I give to my son
JOHN 50 acres of land joining his brother WILLIAM to be run as above. I
give to my son THOMAS 50 acres joining his brother ROBERT & JOHN to be
run as above. Each is to hold their land until the youngst come of age.
I bequeath unto my four sons and three dtr. my personal property, viz:
WILLIAM, ROBERT, JOHN, THOMAS, ELIZABETH, MARY, and CATHY. To my eldest
dtr. MARGARET I bequeath 20 shillings. Wit: JAMES GUFFY, CONNELIUS
CLEMENT.   Signed: ROBERT CAMPBELL.

Page 192. 2 June 1806. Proved, July term 1806. I FREDRICK MARCH, yeo-
             man, being of sound mind & memory, but weak of body. I give
to MARGARET my beloved wife one bed and furniture, her choice of the
horses, her choice the cattle, four of the cows, & her saddle & bridle.
When the crop are gethered she to have grain & pork, all flax & cotton.
The use of the land till the chn. come of age. Then to be sold and
divided between herself and her two chn. I give to dtr. one bed & furniture. I give to my son JOHN MARCH one bed & furniture and $10. I appoint
JOSEPH CARPENTER & JACOB CARPENTER executors. Wit: JOHN ORR, Jr., HENRY
HOYLE. (Jurat).   Signed: FREDRICK X MARCH.

Page 193. 22 March 1807. Proved, July term 1807. I, WILLIAM DAVIS,
             being in a low state of health but in perfect mind & memory.
First, I will that my just debts be paid. I give to my wife CATY one
half of my tract of land dividing it with a line North & South, during
her widowhood and then to my son TOLIVER DAVIS and all the rest of my
estate to my wife during widowhood. The other half of the land I give to
THOMAS PATRICK that now lives with me, I also give him a horse, to be
worth about $70 when he becomes 20 yrs. old, also a bridle & saddle and
cow & calf. I appoint my wife CATY & HENRY DAVIS as executors. Wit:
JOSEPH GOODE, (Jurat) THOMAS ALLHAN.   Signed: WILLIAM X DAVIS.

Page 193. No date given. Proved, 6 Jan. 1806. I, JOHN SIMMONS, being
             very low in body but of perfect mind and memory. I give to my
well beloved wife my man saddle & bridle, household goods, one cow. I
give 8 shillings to my son JOHN, also 8 shillings to my son JOSEPH. Also
I give to my dtr. RUTH one cow. Also my land equally to my two younger
sons, viz. JOEL & JONATHAN and one heifer each. I appoint JAMES KIDD &
my wife JANE SIMMONS executors. Wit: MARTAIN SISK, JAMES KIDD. (jurat).
                Signed: JOHN X SIMMONS.

Page 194. 7 Dec. 1806. Proved, July term 1807. I, WILLIAM WILSON, being
             in perfect health, mind and memory. First I give to my oldest
son SPENCER WILSON the sum of 5 shillings. I give to my beloved wife
DIANNA WILSON 120 acres of land with the dwelling house forever. I give
to my son MOSES WILSON $20. I give to my dtr. PHEBY WILSON 5 shillings.
I give to my son JAMES WILSON 5 shillings. I give to my son ROBERT
WILSON 50 acres, that I bought from WILLIAM GREEN & a new saddle. The
balance to be equally divided among my chn. named: MOLLIE, WILSON, JOHN
WILSON, SALLY WILSON, NANCY WILSON, MOSES WILSON, WILLIAM WILSON, THOMAS
WILSON, JAMES WILSON, ROBERT WILSON. I appoint my son THOMAS WILSON
executor. Wit: JESSE GIBBS, LOTT WOOD, JAS. SHEARER.
                Signed: WILLIAM X WILSON.

Page 195. 20 May 1807. Proved, July term 1807. I, CLAUDIUS LONG, of
             Washington County, State of Tennessee. Being sick and in a
low condition of body but of sound mind & memory. First, I allow all my
just debts and funeral charges to be paid from my personal estate. I
give to my beloved sister ELIZABETH LONG wife to JOHN LONG $150. I give

33

to my eldest brother PATRICK LONG $140. I give to my brother JAMES LONG
$140. I give my sister MARGARET TEMPLING wife to JACOB TEMPLING $150.
I give to my sister JENNY LONG $150. I give to my sister MARY LONG $150.
I give to my brother in law JOHN LONG my saddle & bridle, and other articals that may be at his house at my death. I appoint JOHN LONG my
brother in law & my brother PATRICK LONG executors. Wit: WILLIAM PORTER,
---- PRICE, G. ERWIN.   Signed: CLAUD LONG.

Page 196. 27 April 1807. Proved, July term 1807. I, JOHN MILLER, of
           Rutherford Co. N.C. Now lying in the house of ANDREW ERWIN,
Esq. in the town of Asheville in the County of Buncombe. Being of perfect mind and memory. I give to my beloved wife SUSAMAH MILLER the
plantation she lives on with two other plantation with the grist mill &
distillery, & two negroes named Bradick & Dave and negro woman named Bet.
All household furniture at her death to be equally divided between my
two sons DAVID & WILLIAM. I give to my son DAVID a man negro named Dick,
with a set of blacksmith tools, one negro man named James, one negro girl
named Nancy, with 140 acres of land, another tract of 350 acres between
myself & WILLIAM MILLS, in the County of Buncombe., and $125 for a horse,
bridle and saddle. I give to my son WILLIAM MILLER, two negroes named
Stephen & Jack and a negro girl named Serena, Also 200 acres of land,
known as the Patterson place on French Broad River, another tract on
Little River in Buncombe County, A note of $350. Also $125 for a horse,
saddle and bridle. I give to my dtr. SUCKY a negro woman named Sally &
her three children. A negro woman named Annie. One horse worth $100.
Also $100 in money, a good saddle & bridle, two feather beds & her house-
hold furniture. I give to my dtr. BETSY one negro girl named Liza, two
negro boys the chn. of (from here over a half of a page is too blurred
to be read) He wish the children stay with their mother until they come
of age. The negroes left to sons DAVID & WILLIAM to be hired out for
their use. ROBERT MCAFEE is not to have any share of the notes or bonds.
I appoint my friends JOHN LEWIS, JONATHAN HAMPTON, DAVID DICKY, ROBERT
MCAFEE and my wife SUSANNAH executrix & executors. Wit: A. FERGUSON,
ANDREW ERWIN, DANIEL MATHEWS.   Signed: JOHN MILLER.

Page 199. 1 March 1806. Proved, Oct. term 1807. I, ROBERT TAYLOR, Being
           far advanced in life, but of perfect mind and memory. I give
to my son JOSHUA TAYLOR two negro men named Sam & Mark, with all my stock
of horses, Cattle, Hogs, sheep. Also my working tools & my bed and
furniture. Also one half of the growing crop. The other half of the
crop, I give to my grand son ROBERT TAYLOR. I give to my grand son
JEREMIAH TAYLOR one negro man named Jack. I give to my grand son JESSE
TAYLOR one negro man named Tom. I give to SUSANNAH NELSON a bed and
furniture, and one woman's saddle, also $60 in money being one fifth of
what ROBERT TAYLOR owes me. The balance of money due me which is $240,
to be divided equally among HARTWELL HONEYCUT, husband to my dtr. MARY
HONEYCUT. GEORGE NELSON husband to my grand dtr. POLLY NELSON. JOHN
DEVENPORT husband of my grand dtr. REBECCA DEVENPORT. CYNTHIA TAYLOR my
dtr. to be paid to her on her marriage or of age. I appoint JONATHAN
HAMPTON, ROBERT TAYLOR. Wit: JAMES BRADLEY, JOHN X BALLARD.
                                  Signed: ROBERT TAYLOR.
NB. The within named ROBERT TAYLOR on his death bed expressed his desire
that his grand dtr. POLLY NELSON to have the bed, being the same on which
he now lies with furniture, Also that PETERS horse which he now claims
to remain for his use. Wit: WILLIAM CHRISTOPHER, MOSES DUKYE.

Page 202. 20 Oct. 1806. Proved, Oct. term 1807. This indenture made
           20 Oct. 1806. Between PHILIP GOODBREAD & DRURY MATHEWS. In
consideration of $10 in hand paid, the receipt is hereby acknowledged.
The said DRURY MATHEWS for and during the term of 50 yrs. from this date,
hath promised, agreed to and with PHILIP GOODBREAD to serve him as an
indented servant. To obey as a servant in all things. The said PHILIP
GOODBREAD shall supply clothing & lodging of a servant, he shall pay his
taxes and all things necessary to be done as a master. Wit: JAMES
HARRISS, EDWARD BRADLEY, ZADOC HARRIS.   Signed: DRURY X MATHEWS &
                                                  PHILIP GOODBREAD.

Page 203. 19 Dec. 1807. Proved, Oct. term 1807. This indenture witnes-
           ses that CATY JOHNSON a free woman of color. Have this day
of her own free will and accord put her two children, a boy named RICHARD

34

WALTON & a girl named JEMIMA WALTON under the guardianship of PETER FISH-
ER where CATY doth agree that the chn. shall continue during minority,
they being born on the third Aug. 1805. Said PETER is bound to make
reasonable provision for the chn. as to food & clothing, and refrain from
all unmerciful useage. Wit: WM. BRYSON, JACOB FISHER.
Signed: CATY X JOHNSON & PETER FISHER.

Page 203. 16 Feb. 1806. Proved, Oct. term 1807. I, MICHAEL TANNER,
being very sick but of perfect mind & memory. I give to my
children the sum of ₤10 to be paid by my son DANIEL whom I appoint my
sole executor. Namely: EVA PAINTER ₤10, MECHAEL TANNER ₤10, BARBRA HUD-
LONG ₤10, MAGDALON SHUNK ₤10, MARGARET HARMON ₤10, MARY HEAD ₤10, JOHN
GARNER ₤10, I give to my dtr. CATHARINE ₤10 one cow & year old heifer,
also one steer of the same age. I give to my dtr. ESTHER ₤10 and cattle
to be equal with CATHARINE. The balance of my est. both real & personal
I give to my son DANIEL. I give to my dtrs. ESTHER & CATHARINE to have
a colt each. I give to MAGDALON SHUNK the Gray Mare that I have. ESTHER
& CATHARINE to have the household furniture. Wit: JONATHAN HAMPTON,
HENRY X DAVIS, JAMES X TRUELOVE. Signed: MICHAEL X TANNER.

Page 205. 10 May 1805. Proved, Oct. term 1807. I, LEONARD PAINTER, at
this time being of sound & perfect memory. I give to my son
GEORGE PAINTER the tract of land lying in the fork of Second Broad River
and Cain Creek, the land we now live on bought from THOMAS WALKER. Also
all moveable property., except the pewter and cubbard furniture, beds
and furniture to be equally divided between my two dtr. CHRISTEAN DECK
the wife of HENRY DECK & BETSEY DECK the wife of JACOB DECK. It is my
will that one year from my decease my son GEORGE shall pay unto JACOB
DECK the sum of $50. I appoint my trusty friend JACOB DECK & JOHN CARSON,
executors. Wit: F. WALKER, AM. ENLOE, BUCKNER X EAVES.
Signed: LEONARD PAINTER.

Page 207. 5 Sept. 1803. Proved, Oct. term 1807. I, NATHAN BRISCOE,
calling to mind the certainty of death but uncertainty of the
time. First I give to my wife ELIZABETH all my land during her life
time or widowhood, Also all stock of cattle, hogs, sheep also household
& kitchen furniture, I also lend to my wife during her widowhood my negro
man Philip and enough money to buy a negro girl between the ages of 10 &
25 yrs. The money to buy said to me from my brother JAMES SOUTHERN
BRISCOE, decd., estate. At my wife death or remarriage the above property to go to my two chn. PHILLIPS & SARAH BRISCOE. I give to three
dtrs. MARY CRAWFORD, ELIZABETH MORROS, NANCY ROBBINS. NANCY to recd.
first ₤12 and the balance to be equally divided among the last three
named dtrs. I appoint my beloved wife ELIZABETH, PHILP ROBBINS, and my
son PHILIP BRISCOE, executors. Wit: DANIEL MADDIN, WM. X ROBBINS, PHILIP
X HENSON. Signed: NATHAN BRISCOE.

Page 208. 3 Feb. 1808. I, FRANCES KITS, being in a low state of health
but of sound mind and memory. I appoint CHARLES RICHARDSON
& my wife NANCY KITS as executor & executrix. I give to my wife NANCY
one half of all my goods & chattles, debts due me after my just debts
are paid. The other half I give to my only son FRANCES together with
the land I now live on, and 100 acres tract lying on the Middle Fork of
Walnut Creek, bought from JAMES MILLER, Junr. Wit: SHADRICK WIER, (Jurat)
CHARLES RICHARDSON, Jr. Signed: FRANCES X KITS.

Page 209. 28 April 1808. I, PRECELLA HAMRICK, being sick in body but of
sound mind & memory. First I give to my son WILLIAM HAMRICK
$15, also I give to my dtr. JENNY $5, I also give to my dtr. REBECCA $5.
Then an equal division of my part of the whole est. of JAMES HAMRICK,
my decd. husband, among all my chn. MOLLY HARDIN, SUSANNAH HARROLD, SALLY
BRIDGES, GEORGE HAMRICK, ANN HAMRICK, ELIZA HAMRICK, JENNY HAMRICK,
WILLIAM HAMRICK, REBECCA HAMRICK, and JESSE BRIDGES my grand son. I
appoint SAMUAL HAROLD & GEORGE HAMRICK my executors. Wit: BERRY HICKS,
WILLIS JOHNSON. Signed: PRICELLA X HAMRICK.

Page 210. 2 July 1808. I, ANDREW COULTER, being of sound mind & memory.
First I will my just debts be paid. I give my house and lot
in the town of Rutherford to my dtr. MATILDA KENNAD born of the body of
NANCY KENNAD to hold the said house in fee simple forever. To my brother

JOHN COULTER, the Parish of Invec, in the County of Donegal, in the Kingdom of Ireland, I give my negro slaves called, Jim, Joshua, Sandy. I
give to my sister MARGARET COULTER of the Parish, County & Kingdom aforesaid, a negro woman named Becky, known by the name Hunters Becky & her
two chn. Hannah & ----. I give to CATHARINE COULTER of the same place,
my woman named Betty and her child Mary. My negro boy named Charles?, I
give to my sister HANNAH COULTER. I give to my brother JOHN negro boys
Patrick & Jack. Also the residue of my estate. I appoint JONATHAN
HAMPTON & Merchant, JOHN MOORE executors. Wit: JOSEPH HAMILTON, ARTHUR
MULLIN, S. DONOHO.   Signed: ANDW. COLTER.

Page 211. 20 Sept. 1807. I, SAMUEL STOCKTON, being now old and infirmed
           but of perfect mind and memory. I give to my wife PRUDENCE
STOCKTON the plantation on which I now live on. Two cows & household
furniture during her life time. I give to my eldest son DAVIS STOCKTON
all my lands and tenements at the death of his mother. I give to my only
dtr. ANN LATTIMORE $20. The remainder of my moveable property to be
divided as follows, namely: one third to my son DAVIS, one third to my
dtr. ANN LATTIMORE. The other third to be equally divided between my
two grand sons SAMUEL, THOMAS JEFFERSON STOCKTON. I appoint my friends
DAVIS STOCKTON, DANIEL LATTIMORE, PRUDENCE STOCKTON my executors. Wit:
---- ROSS, (jurat), JAMES WHITINDES, ANNA STOCKTON.
                    Signed: SAMUEL STOCKTON.

Page 213. 11 June 1808. I, RACHEL LOGAN, being sick and declining in
           bodily strength but of sound mind. First I will that my just
debts and funeral expenses be paid from my personal est. I give to my
only dtr. SALLY SELENA all my lands and personal estate. The property
to be put on lease yearly and the money put on interest, until said SALLY
SELENA comes of age. So that it may be known when she come of age. I
certify that she was born the 24 Nov. 1807. My daughter I leave to the
care of my dear mother MARY LOGAN, to raise and direct her education.
Should my child die before comming of age, the estate shall be divided in
six equal parts, and one part to my dear mother MARY LOGAN, one part to
my sister MARGARET LOGAN, one part to my sister MARY CARRUTH, one part
to my brother GEORGE LOGAN, One to my sister KATHARINE ANNE LOGAN, and
one share to be divided among my sister SARAH CARRUTH, decd. four dtrs.
viz: LINDAMAE CARRUTH, FARILLA K. CARRUTH, POLLY H. CARRUTH, and PEGGY
P. CARRUTH. I appoint My brother GEORGE MITCHELL LOGAN as executor.
Wit: ALEXANDER CARRUTH, JAMES X FISHER.   Signed: RACHEL LOGAN.

Page 215. 6 July 1805. I, ELIZABETH WALKER, widow of Col. JOHN WALKER,
           decd. Being of sound & perfect mind & memory, but feable state
of body & health. I give to my son JACOB WALKER a negro woman named
Sarah which I purchased from my sister ALICE ALEXANDER in her life time.
With all my live stock, household furniture & the residue of my legacy
left to me by my brother WILLIAM WILSON, decd. of York Dist., S.C. This
being my whole estate. JACOB WALKER to collect all money due me at my
death, and act as my executor. Wit: F. WALKER, JAS. SCOTT.
                    Signed: ELIZABETH X WALKER.

Page 216. 6 April 1808. Oct. Term 1808. I, ROBERT ANDERSON, being in
           a sick & weak condition of body but of sound mind & memory.
First I will that my just debts & funeral charges be paid. To my dtr.
AGNESS I give two cows & calves. To my dtr. MARGARET I give my brown
mare called Keed & also two cows & calves. To my dtr. RACHEL I give my
horse called (blured) also two cows & calves. To my dtr. MARY I give
two cows & her dtr. one cow, to my grand son ROBERT, I give my bed and
furniture. All the rest of my household furniture to be equally divided
among my three dtrs. that is at home with me. To my dtr. JENNY I give
5 shillings also her son ROBERT I give $10. to get it in schooling. My
negro Man, I give to work for my three dtrs. while they remain together,
then to be AGNES'S while she lives and at her decease to be my son
SAMUELS. To my son SAMUEL I give my plantation, wagon young cattle. I
appoint my son SAMUEL as executor. Wit: EPHRAIM X DAVIS.
                    Signed: ROBERT X ANDERSON.

Page 217. 1 Oct. 1808. Proved, Oct. term 1808. I, JOHN WILSON, being
           very sick & weak but in perfect mind and memory. I give to
my wife ANNA WILSON all and every part of my estate now in possession,

36

during her life or widowhood. I also give to ANNY WILSON, my wife, one negro girl named Candell during her life, then to be equally divided among POLLY, JOEL, & JASON. I appoint my wife & JOHN & JOEL as executors. I desire that my wife give to the chn. as they marry or come of age what she can spare, keeping a record of the same so all will be made equal. Except the negro girl above mentioned. Chn: JAMES WILSON, NICEY, HANNAH, JOHN, PEGGA, ANNY, JOEL, POLLY, & JASON. JAMES has had $60 & NICEY had $100. Wit: DAVID BURGE, JOEL SMITH.   Signed: JOHN WILSON.

Page 218. 17 Aug. 1808. Proved, Oct. term 1808. I, JOHN MCCLURE, being in very low state of health but of perfect mind and memory. I will to my eldest dtr. MARTHA KILPATRIC the sum of $20. Also IZABELLA GRAY the sum of $20. Also my eldest son RICHARD MCCLURE I leave him the land he now lives on, agreeable to a deed I made to him also $30. To my son JOHN MCCLURE all the rest of the land I hold on South side of Broad River, also $20. To my dtr. JANE SWENY the sum of $30. To my son ARTHUR MCCLURE all the land I hold on the north side of Broad River and Mountain Creek also Horses, cattle, Sheep & hogs with the plantation tools and waggon and gun. JOHN MCCLURE the sum of £5 also to his ---- the sum of $4. To the rest of the chn. one dollar each. To MARTHA KILPATRIC chn. one dollar each. IZABELLA GRAY'S one dollar each. JOHN F. MCCLURE five £. JINNY MCCLURE $4. To ---- LITTLE the sum of $20, to MARGARET, her dtr. $10. Respecting the small est. coming to me from the State of Pennsylvania to be divided among my three sons. I appoint my sons JOHN MCCLURE & ARTHUR MCCLURE my executors. Wit: LETTIE X LITTLE, MARY MC-CLURE.   Signed: JOHN MCCLURE.

Page 220. 22 Aug. 1808. Proved, Oct. term 1808. I, CRANSHAW CAMP, being of sound & perfect mind & memory. First I give to my brother GEORGE CAMP my negro boy Embra and all that part of my Campfork tract of land, Lying on the East side of the old Waggon Road, two rifle guns, my working tools, one half of my legacy from my father's estate. In consequence, he must pay to my sister RUTH CAMP $250 or a negro girl of that value. To my brother JOSHUA CAMP I give all that part of the Campfork tract of land lying West of the old Waggon Road, my cotton gin and half of the work of the machine and a 50 acres tract of land on Floyds Creek, which I have a title from PETER FISHER, according to a contract between ASAN CAMP and myself. Also the other half of my father's estate, which he must pay my friend & brother SAMUEL BROADWAY $50. Unto my brother AARON CAMP I give the land where he lives of 100 acres and my saddle. I appoint my brother GEORGE and JOSHUA CAMP my executors. Wit: D. GOLD, NOBLES HAMILTON.   Signed: CRANSHAW CAMP.

Page 222. 20 Nov. 1806. Proved, Jan. term 1809. I, ANDREW TAYLOR, being of sound mind & memory but of infirmed body. As to my worldly estate, let it be disposed of to pay all my legal debts, for I am indebted for the whole amount. First to my wife JEANNETT if she serves me, I give a child part of my personal est. which will be one fifth of the whole. Hereby acknowledgeing the following chn. viz: JOHN TAYLOR, JENNETT, PATSEY, ANDREW TAYLOR and JANE SPENCER to whom I give 5 shillings. I give to my grand dtr. NANCY CASKY (who has in a quite degree ameliorated my condition for years past during which time I have been sorely afflicted in body and mind and deserted by my wife and children) The whole of my real & personal property to her forever, as the only compensation I am able to make for the service she rendered me. I appoint her my sole executrix. Wit: J. H. ALLY, WILLIAM NEWTON.
                              Signed: ANDREW TAYLOR.
Acknowledged before me the 5 July 1807.   Signed: J. P. HOLLAND.

Page 223. 8 Jan. 1808. Proved, Jan. term 1809. I, DAVID MCDOW, being in a poor state of health but of sound mind & memory, after my just debts and funeral expenses are paid, I give to my dtr. AGNESS, son WILLIAM, Dtrs. JANE & ELIZABETH, son THOMAS MITCHEL, dtrs. MARY & SARAH the sum of one quather of a dollar, they having received from me their full share of my property. I give to my wife ELIZABETH for & during her life time or widowhood all and every part of my property both real & personal, at her death I give unto my dtr. MARGARET one feather bed & a cow. Unto my son JOHN, I give the tract of land on which I reside, containing 150 acres. Also a tract I entered & hold containing 100 acres, one set of smith tools., Unto my dtr. ESTER I give my negro

boy Tetey. Unto my dtr. MARTHA I give my negro girl Sylvia. Unto the
before named dtrs. ESTER & MARTHA I give my negro wench Carander. I
appoint my wife ELIZABETH and my friends MAY & WILLIAM GREEN as executors.
Wit: WILLIAM MCBRAYER, WILLIAM TOMS.   Signed: DAVID MCDOW.
My wife having property when we married, that was willed to her during
her life time. at her death said property to return to the children of
her first husband WILLIAM EARLY. Wit: WILLIAM MCBRAYER, (Jurat) WILLIAM
TON, (Jurat)   Signed: DAVID MCDOW.

Page 225. 1 Jan. 1809. Proved, April term 1809. I, GEORGE MUSICK,
          being of sound mind and memory. I will and direct my just
debts be paid. I give to my son JONATHAN MUSICK all that tract of
land bought by me from RUSSELL TWITTY on the North side of Green River on
which he now lives. I give to my grand son WILLIAM HAWKINS when he
reaches the age of 21 yrs. a horse valued at $80. I give to MICHAEL
HAWKINS 5 shillings. I give to my dtr. PHEBE RA-----. a tract of land
on the South side of Green River, containing 150 acres. All other property both real and personal I give to my wife LURETER during her natural
life. I give to my son AUSTIN MUSICK, after the decease of my wife, all
the land lying on the North side of Green river. that I bought from
MATHEW WATSON. I appoint my sons AUSTIN & JONATHAN MUSICK as executors.
Wit: JOHN MOORE, ---- DICKEY.   Signed: GEORGE X MUSICK.

Page 227. 7 Jan. 1809. Proved, April term 1809. I, BENJAMIN JONES,
          being weak of body yet of sound mind & memory. I give to my
wife NELLY JONES my mill with 61 acres of land adjoining, with one third
part of my stock & one third part of my household furniture during her
natural life or widowhood, then to become the property of my son DANIEL
JONES. I give to my son WILLIAM JONES that tract of land known by the
name of the Barnett Place also one third part of the of my stock & one
third part of the household furniture. I give to my son THOMAS JONES
100 acres of land adjoining the Mill place on which he now lives, also
one third part of the stock & household furniture. I appoin WILLIAM
JONES & ABRAHAM CROW my executors. Wit: ABRAHAM CROW, JOHN PRICE.
                        Signed: BENJAMIN X JONES.

Page 228. 14 March 1809. Proved, April term 1809. "REUBEN GETTEY being
          in a very low state of health but in his perfect sense did
make known to us that this should be his last will and testament he did
give unto his beloved wife SUSANNAH GUTTEY all his estate both personal
and real in our presents."   Signed: THOMAS X CAWOOD, SARAH X HAINES.
"This day came THOMAS CAWOOD and SARAH HAINES before me and made oath
that the above was the last will of said REUBEN GUTTEY who passed away
on the 17th instant early in the morning." Sworn to, this 21 March 1809,
SAML. MOORE.   Signed: THOMAS X CARWOOD, SARAH X
                                  HAINES.

Page 229. 1 July 1806. Proved, July term 1809. I, HOUSAN HARROLD,
          being under the decay of nature, but of sound sense and memory.
I will my just debts and expenses be paid. My will that my son STREET
HARROLD be paid $75. My son RICHARD HARROLD to receive one feather bed
& furniture and the sum of $25. My beloved wife FRANCES HARROLD to
possess the balance of my est. both real & personal during her widowhood
or natural life, and after either the property to be equally divided
among my chn. PHILDELPHIA STREET the wife of WILLIAM STREET. DICY
BRIDGES, wife of JAMES BRIDGES, SAMUEL HARROLD, ELIZABETH JOHNSTON wife
of JOHN JOHNSTON, JOHN HARROLD, EDY SMITH wife of DAVID SMITH, GILBERT
HARROLD and PHEBE RAYNOLDS wife of THOMAS RAYNOLDS. I appoint my wife
FRANCES HARROLD and JOHN HARROLD executors. Wit: JAMES GAGE, HAMILTON X
REYNOLDS, DANIEL GOLD.   Signed: HOUSAN HARROLD.

Page 230. 3 Dec. 1808. Proved, July term 1809. I, JAMES PAULY, being
          in a weak & low condition but of perfect mind & memory. First
my just debts shall be paid out of my estate. I will unto my beloved
wife AGNESS PAULY the whole of my personal estate except articles hereafter mentioned. Wife to have one third of the tract of land on which
I now live including the mansion house, during her natural life. At her
death to become the property of my nephew THOMAS NEAL. I also give to
my wife a tract of land containing 200 acres of land, joining JOHN
ANDERSON and ---- ANDREWS, which land is to be at her own disposal. I

give unto my wife negro man named Jack & a negro woman named Dina. At my wife death said negroes to be emancipated and set free, and they may live on the place with NEAL. I give to my beloved nephew a tract of land containing 150 acres, joining ISAAC WHITE & THOMAS WHITE. I give to my nephew THOMAS NEAL 100 acres lying on the West side of the river, two head of cattle, and the bed and furniture he now lies on and wearing apparel. I give to my nephew JAMES PAULY son of JOHN PAULY, 150 acres of land, joining THOMAS WHITE & ANDREW PELER. I give unto SARAH PAULY dtr. of JOHN PAULY the sum of $100, to be paid when she comes of age. I appoint AGNESS PAULY & JAMES BEATH exors. Wit: THOMAS WHITE & ISAAC WHITE (Jurat).   Signed: JAMES PAULY.

Page 232. 20 Nov. 1809. Proved, Jan. term 1810. I, PATRICK WATSON, being weak of body but of perfect mind and memory. First of all my lawfull debts to be discharged by my wife and son DANIEL from the estate. I give to my son HUGH a tract of land. (amount not given). I give to my son DANIEL a tract of land of 50 acres, likewise one mare named Juel. I give unto my dtr. ELIZABETH 3 shillings. I give to my dtr. ANN 10 head cattle that she claims, bed & furniture, With saddle, bridle & wheel. I give to my dtr. SARAH one cow & calf, bed & furniture, one saddle, bridle & wheel. I give to my wife ANN the remainder of my land, during her life time, one mare called Jolly, household furniture not given already, balance of stock, sheep, hogs & farming tools. At my wife decease the lands to be divided between my sons. I likewise allow my sons to pay PATRICK W. CARSON the sum of $5 each to be paid in three years. What is in the hands of JOUSH LEWIS, I give to my dtrs. SARAH & ANN when received. I appoint my wife ANN & HUGH WATSON my executors. Wit: GEORGE WATSON, DANL. WATSON, (Jurat).   Signed: PATRICK WATSON.

Page 234. 13 Feb. 1810. Proved, Apr. 1810. I, MARY COLLINS, feeling infirmed, but in sound mind & memory. I give to my dtr. MARY WILLIAMS two cows & calves, my wearing cloths, and saddle. I give unto my son JACOB COLLINS two cows. I give to my son ABRAM COLLINS 50 acres of land on Jumping branch joining WILLIAM MOODE, what hogs I have, one mulatto girl named Charity, two cows & calves, household items named. I give unto SEBARD 10 shillings. I give unto ISAAC COLLINS my son 5 shillings. I give unto MARY WILLIAMS my grand dtr. daughter of WILLIAM WILLIAMS one cow. I give unto my sons ISAAC, ABRAM & SEBAND all the money that I have in my possession at death. ABRAM to have the balance of my chattles. I appoint ABRAM COLLINS. Wit: LEWIS HUNTER, (Jurat). Signed: MARY X COLLINS.

Page 236. 16 Jan. 1810. Proved, April term 1810. I, WILLIAM MODE, being weak in body but of sound memory. I give unto my wife the tract of land that I now live on, containing 120 acres, and at her death to my son SAMUEL MODE, also to my wife one cow and yearling of her choosing, all household furniture, all stock of hogs & sheep. I give to my son SAMUEL MODE one mare and four head of young cattle, one sow & pigs. I give to my son ISAAC MODE tract of land that he now lives on containing 80 acres. I give to my dtr. MARY, her bed & furniture, loom & implements also two cows named Pet & Rose. I give to my dtr. FANNY HIENS one cow named Dayse, also my axes and plantation tools for the use of the plantation. I appoint ISAAC & SAMUEL MODE as executors. Wit: JOHN GORDAN, (Jurat), WILLIAM WHITE.   Signed: WILLIAM X MODE.

Page 237. 19 Jan. 1806. Proved, April term 1810. I, ISAAC LOLLAR, being of sound and perfect mind & memory. I give to my beloved wife MARTHA all the stock as they stand with all household furniture, except the waggon during her life time. I will that my son ACHIBALD live with my wife on the plantation and divide the profits. I will unto my son ACHIBALD the waggon & gears with one stud colt, one rifle gun. I appoint my son ARCHIBALD & my wife MARTHA Executors. Wit: ROBERT MCAFEE, (Jurat) POLLY MCAFEE.   Signed: ISAAC LOLLAR.

Page 238. 12 June 1809. Proved, April term 1810. I, THOMAS MOORE, In a low state of health but of perfect mind & memory. My burial expenses and just debts to be paid. My estate depends on the issue before the County Court & Equity in S.C. I am therefore obligated first to devise my negroes. I will then make out a list of obligations in my hand for money, when collected are to be despose of in the manner

herein after mentioned. A total of $5770.00. To my brother MICHAEL
MOORE of Fairfield Dist. S.C. The following negroes. Stephen a black
man for $500; Levi a yellow man for $500; Tom an old black man for $300;
Silvia & child for $450. To my brother JOHN MOORE of Rutherford Co. N.C.
The following negroes. Charley an elderly man for $375; Leah a black
woman for $400; Betty a dark mulatter for $375 & one horse & bay horse
for $200; Frank a negro boy for $375; Mary a small girl for $300. To
the chn. of WILLIAM MOORE, decd. of Rutherford Co., N.C. The following:
Milly a buding woman for $400; Perry & Esther for $300; Nancy for $375;
Sam a little boy for $270; Daniel for $450; Bill for $200. The amount
of money due me from: MALACHI HOWELL, of Richland $250, JOHN HOOKER of
N.C. $93, R. MILLIGANY $122, Doctor SAMUEL GREEN $115, ELISHA HAGWOOD
$150, ELISHA HAGWOOD, on note $340, JOHN & ELISHA HAGOOD $270, PHILLIP
SLIGH $302, ROBERT CAMPBELL, N.C. $290, JOHN BROWN of Fairfield $240,
ROWLAND WILLIAMS Fairfield $75, WILLIAM MILLS $20, MICHAEL MOORE, cash
lent $100, SAML & THOMAS NELSON $78, HENRY RUFF of Newberry $300. ROBERT
RABB, total of $3,400. Tract of land on Little River $450. a tract of
land on Cannons Creek. a note on Morrow $130. The and last mentioned
negroes to be sold at private sale. My executors to keep $400 for their
truble in handleing my busness. The remainder to be divided among
MICHAEL MOORE, Senr. JOHN MOORE, and the children of WILLIAM MOORE, decd.
To MICHAEL MOORE I give my holster & pestol also a debt against THOMAS
DAVY. Also a note on EDWARD CORNWALL for $350. To JOHN MOORE I leave
my watch & mahogany sideboard, that stands in the house of MICHAEL MOORE
in Columbia. I appoint my brother JOHN MOORE sole executor. Wit: DAVID
BYERS, (Jurat), LACK. WOOD, (Jurat). Signed: THOS. MOORE.

Page 242. 20 July 1809. Proved, July term 1810. I, THOMAS EARLY, being
sick in body but of perfect mind & memory. To my dear wife
ELIZABETH EARLY I leave 150 acres of land, being the same on which I now
live, likewise all household furniture, tools, stock, etc. At her death
or marriage to be equally divided between herself and ten children which
she now has living, but no division to be made until the youngest comes
of age. I appoint my friend RICHARD GARRISON & WM. F. WHITESIDE executors. Wit: NEOMY X EDWARDS, L. A. ROSS. Signed: THOMAS EARLY.

Page 243. 1 Feb. 1810. Proved, July term 1810. I, ISAAH BLACKWELL,
being weak in body but perfect mind & memory. I give to my
wife MOLLY BLACKWELL one third of my land, which I allow to be divided
into equal shares by my son JOHN BLACKWELL & STEVEN TOMKINS, Junr., &
my wife, likewise, one bed & furniture, what corn & meat we now have,
flax wheel, one oven, one cow & calf. and other household items. I give
to my grand dtr., name not known, dtr. of WILLIAM BLACKWELL a third of
the land. I give to my dtr. MARY one part of my land, one horse, and
what cattle & hogs I have, one feather bed. I give to my dtr. SARAH, my
horse & saddle, two iron pots, one bason. The rest of my chn. I have
divided my property with, and have no more for them. I appoint my son
JOHN BLACKWELL, STEVEN TOMPKINS, Junr., & my brother JOEL BLACKWELL
executors. Wit: GEORGE X SUTTLE, MERION X DORAM, ---- SUTTLE.
Signed: ISAAH BLACKWELL.

Page 244. 24 Oct. 1809. Proved, July term 1810. The following agreement was admitted to go to record as follows. viz: We LEMUEL
SCOGGIN, BURGAS LARKIN, JESSE SCOGGIN & RICHARD SCOGGIN as legatee of
FRANCES SCOGGIN decd. do hereby certify that we have this day laid off &
survey into lots the land of the deceased, and have all agreed on the
lots that we are to have to wit. LEMUEL SCOGGIN have the lot #3. BURGAS
SCOGGIN take for himself and for ELIZABETH SCOGGIN lots #4 & #5. LARKIN
DYCUS take for himself & SALLY WORTHBURN lots #6 & #7. JEREMIAH SCOGGIN
as guardian of JESSE & RICHARD SCOGGIN takes lots #1 & #2. Test. ISRAEL
RIGGS. Signed: JEREMIAH SCOGIN, LEM. SCOGIN,
BURGES SCOGIN, LARKIN DYCUS, RUBEN WASHBURN, JASSE SCOGIN, RICHARD SCOGIN.

Page 246. 25 July 1810. Proved, Oct. term 1810. I, CATHERINE ANNE
LOGAN, being in a declining state of health but of sound mind
& health. First I will my just debts & funeral expenses to be paid from
the money on hand. I give to my mother MARY LOGAN $100 from the estate
excluding what she owes me, also the use of my negro girl named Alpha
during her life time. I give to my sister MARY CARRUTH said negro Alpha
after the death of my mother. Should my sister MARY not live the negro

40

Alpha to go to her two dtrs. POLLY MICHEL CARRUTH & ELIZA KING CARUTH.
I give to my sister MARY CARUTH $50, out of which is to be discounted
what JAMES CARRUTH owes me. I give to my sister MARGARET $50 to be put
on interest for her use as she may need. The remainder of the estate to
be divided into two parts. One part I give to my brother GEORGE M. LOGAN
and the other part to be divided among the four dtrs. of my sister SARAH
CARRUTH. I also give to my brother GEORGE the chest named in my sister
RACHEL'S will, should it fall to my estate. I appoint my brother GEORGE
M. LOGAN my executor. Wit: ALEX. CARRUTH, JOHN BABER. (Jurat).
Signed: CATHERINE X LOGAN.

Page 247. 20 Sept. 1810. Proved, Oct. term 1810. I, PATRICK MCFARLAND,
being of perfect mind & memory. First I will that my just
debts be paid. I desire that the plantation be keep together for the use
of my wife & children. Wife PEGGA to sell a few cattle to raise some
money for the children education, and use. I wish one son to take the
blacksmith trade and use my smith tools. Should my wife remarry, she is
to have a child's part, after the youngest becomes of age. I appoint my
friend WILLIAM MCFARLAND & JAMES MCFARLAND executors. Wit: ROBERT H.
TAYLOR, & ELIZABETH X DONING. Signed: PATRICK MCFARLAND.

Page 249. 29 May 1810. Proved, Jan. term 1811. I, GEORGE FLEMING,
being in a sound mind and perfect memory. After my just debts
are paid I give unto my son JOHN FLEMING, my eldest son, one tract of
land containing 150 acres, being the upper part of my land on Cathey
Creek, also one cow, one bay horse, an equal part of the sheep. I give
to my son, GEORGE FLEMING, all the plantation where I now live, being the
lower part of said land, also one bay mare five yrs. old, one cow, an
equal part of the sheep. I give to my son, WILLIAM FLEMING, one tract of
land of equal value to his brothers, said tract to be purchased by said
JOHN & GEORGE FLEMING in a reasonable time, also one bay mare, one cow,
an equal part of the sheep. I give to my dtr. ELIZABETH FLEMING one bay
mare, one bed & furniture, one cow, an equal part of the sheep, one big
& little wheel. I give to my dtr. JENNET FLEMING, one gray mare, one
bed & furniture, one cow, an equal part of the sheep, also one big & one
little wheel. I give unto my dtr. REBECCA FLEMING one bay coult at this
time, one bed & furniture, one cow, and equal part of the sheep, one big
& one little wheel. I give to my grand dtr. NANCY FLEMING one cow 2
yrs. old. The household furniture divided as listed. I appoint JOHN
FLEMING & CHARLEY LEWIS my sole executors. Wit: ROBINSON TRUMAN, WILLIAM
E. STARR. Signed: GEORGE FLEMING.

Page 252. -- March 1811. Proved, April term 1811. I, WILLIAM EDWARDS,
being in low health but sound mind & memory. First I allow
my lawfull debts to be paid, and the remainder of my estate both real and
personal I give to my wife OMA EDWARDS during her natural life and at her
death to be equally divided between my sons JOHN & ISAAC EDWARDS and my
two step sons JOHN ADAMS & RICHARD EDWARD ALLEN. I make and appoint my
two stepsons JOHN & RICHARD ALLEN my lawful executors. Wit: WILLIAM X
FORTUNE, CORNELIUS MELTON, (Jurat). Signed: WILLIAM EDWARDS.

Page 253. 4 Feb. 1811. Proved, April term 1811. I, JOHN DRISKILL, being
low in health and weak in body but sound in mind and memory.
First allowing my just debts & funeral charges to be paid. To my beloved
wife MARY the plantation where I now live during her natural life or
widowhood, a bay mare, a 2 yr. old heifer, her bed and furniture & farming tools. To my dtr. JINNY I give a cow named the big heifer and her
bed & furniture. To my dtr. ISBEL I give a white spoted 3 yrs. old
heifer, a bed & furniture, a saddle, or $15. To my dtr. BETSEY, I give
a brown 3 yr. old heifer and a saddle, or $15. The 2 yr. old sorrel mare
is for the family use and the women to ride. The old cow, and hogs I
lease for the use of the family, If any choose to live on the plantation,
they may do so and help with the work, business and share the profit.
To my son WILLIAM I allow a bed & furniture besides what he has received.
To my son SAMUEL the black 4 yr. old mare, when he goes to himself, a
bed & furniture. To my son JONATHAN I leave the coult the mare is with,
also a bed and furniture. I appoint my son JOHN DRISKILL, and friend
DAVID GRAY as executors. Wit: DAVID TWITTY, SHADRICK WREN, (Jurat) D.
DICKEY (Jurat). Signed: JOHN DRISKILL.

41

Page 256.   16 Oct. 1810.   Proved, July term 1811.   I, ROBERT PORTER,
          First I allow my just debts and funeral charges be paid from
my personal estate. I allow my beloved wife, ELIZABETH PORTER, to be
supported out of my estate, if this be insuffient the balance to be paid
from my son ROBERT'S part, my executor to see this taken care of. I give
to my eldest son DAVID PORTER one 2 yrs. old steer or heffer, and the
value of $5 in other property. I give to my son ALEXANDER PORTER one
$10 cow or the amount in other property. I give to my son THOMAS PORTER
$5 worth of cattle or other property. I give to my dtr. POLLY FLACK $10
worth of cattle or other property. I give to my son ROBERT PORTER that
part of the land on which I now live to be divided between him and his
brother WILLIAM by the line agreed on between them heretofore. I also
give him the large Bible, the big chair, and third part of the household
furniture. I give to my son WILLIAM the other part of the land on which
he lives to the line agreed on before. I give to my dtr. BARBARY, one
third part of my household furniture. I give to my dtr. one third part
of the household furniture and all the other property not mentioned. I
appoint GEORGE FLACK, Esq. & my son WILLIAM PORTER my executors. Wit:
WM. PORTER, (jurat) WM. WALLACE, RUTH X WALLACE.
                    Signed: ROBERT PORTER.
A codicil made the 18 Dec. 1810. I allow my two horses, a gray mare and
a bay mare unto my dtrs. BARBARY & ELIZABETH, I also allow them my loom
& tackling when the family divides, until then the use of the family.
Wit: WM. PORTER, (jurat) JOHN FLEMING.   Signed: ROBERT PORTER.

Page 259.   15 Oct. 1808.   Proved, Oct. term 1811.   I, JOSEPH ALEXANDER,
          of Burk Co. N.C. have ordained and appointed ---- DONOHO of
Rutherford, N.C. my true and lawfull attorney to collect and appopriate
the following money to the use of WILLIAM STEPHENS of Charleston, S.C.
to wit: A balance of a judgement on WM. FISHER of Ł30 15-0 another note
of Ł21-10-0. It is understood that the money to be collected and applied
to the debt that I am in with WILLIAM STEPHENS. The above was proved before THOS. LOCKE, Judge.   Signed: JOSEPH ALEXANDER.

Page 260.   9 June 1811.   Proved Oct. term 1811.   I, DAVID HARDIN, weak in
          body but of sound memory. I give unto my two sons JOHN &
JOSEPH HARDIN two tracts of land where my mill now stands, containing 200
acres, the Mill Creek being the line between them, the East side to my
son JOHN. I give to my son DAVID HARDIN the tract of land where I now
live, containing 200 acres. I give to my wife HANNER HARDIN my negroes
named Harry, Moll, Jake, Sall, Kell, Luie and their increase, during her
natural life, then to be equal divided among my chn. viz: JANE HARDIN,
JNO. HARDIN, REBECCA HARDIN, SUSANNA HARDIN, JOSEPH HARDIN, DAVID HARDIN,
HANNER HARDIN, SALLY HARDIN. I give to my wife HANNER HARDIN, all my
horses, stock, household furniture during her life time, at her death
personal property to be sold and divided betweed my above named chn.
(part of page torn.) Wit: M. ROBERTS, JACOB X MECRUM.
                    Signed: DAVID HARDIN.

Page 261.   30 Dec. ----.   Proved, Jan. term 1812.   I, RICHARD HICKS, being
          sick in body but sound mind and memory. First I give to my
wife MARY during her natural life or widowhood my household furniture.
I also give to my dtr. DICY MARTIN Ł10 to be paid by my executors. I
also give to my dtr. EDITH DURHAM Ł10 to be paid by my executors. I also
give to my grand son BERRYMAN HICKS all my stock of cattle, hogs, horses
and working tools. Said BERRYMAN HICKS is to give unto my grand son
WILLIAM HICKS, when he comes of age, one horse worth $30. I appoint
BERRYMAN HICKS executor. Wit: ROBT. HARDIN (Jurat) SALLY X HARRISS.
                    Signed: RICHARD HICKS.

Page 262.   7 March 1811.   Proved, Jan. term 1812.   I, WILLIAM WESSON,
          being in sound and perfect mind & memory. I give unto my
beloved wife REBECKEY WESSON my personal estate, during her life or
widowhood after paying all my just debts. After her death or widowhood
to be equally divided amongst my living chn. I make & ordain REBECAH
WESSON executrix & JAMES JOLLY executors. Wit: CHARLES S. WILKINS (Jurat),
ARON X BRIDGES, NANCY X ARNOL.   Signed: WILLIAM WESSON.

Page 263.   19 Aug. 1811.   Proved, Jan. term 1812.   I, WILLIAM MCMURRY,
          being under the decays of nature but of sound sense & memory.

42

After my just debts are paid. I will and desire that my wife MARGARETT
MCMURRY be possed of all my real & personal estate during her life time.
I give unto my son SAMUEL MCMURRY an equal part with all my chn. after
the death of my wife. I give unto my son JAMES MCMURRY the tract of land
over the river. I give unto my son JOHN MCMURRY half of the land lying
on the West side of Broad River. (Part of the bottom of the page torn
off). I give unto ----- MCMURRY the upper half of the tract of land
mentioned. I give to every one I shall name an equal share of the personal estate after the death of my wife. Viz: SAMUEL, MARY, MARGARETT,
JAMES, JOHN, CATHERN, WILLIAM, SARAH & PATSEY. I appoint my wife executrix & JOHN Executor. Wit: ROBT. PATTERSON, (jurat) D. BURGE.
Signed: WILLIAM X MCMURRY.

Page 265. 27 April 1812. Proved July term 1812. I, DAVID PORTER,
            being of sound mind and memory. After my just debts and
funeral charges are paid. I give to my wife JANE PORTER all my real and
personal estate. Except my brother JAMES PORTER my wearing clothes and
his son DAVID my gun. To RUTH WALLAS, my waggon & gears. To my sisters
VILET ENLOW & ANN CANADAY cash of 5 shillings a piece. I make JANE
PORTER executrix & ... Wit: JOHN TUIKES, JAMES X HOWELL, JOHN X HOWELL.
Signed: DAVID PORTER.

Page 266. 29 April 1811. Proved, July term 1812. I EBENEZER NEWTON,
            being in a weak & low condition. I will unto my wife ELIZA-
BETH NEWTON all the whole of my personal estate should she survive me
and I leave to her how she leave to the children the said property while
she lives or to keep for her own support, also 100 acres of land. I
desire my executor to sale of part of my estate to defray funeral charges
and pay the legatees, and the remaining to my wife. I give to my chn.
BENJAMIN NEWTON, WILLIAM NEWTON, JOHN NEWTON, MARTHA BUCKHANSION, EBENE-
ZER NEWTON, THOMAS NEWTON and GEORGE NEWTON I will the sum of one dollar
to each, which I consider as sufficient to discharge me from any further
duty or obligation to them. Wit: ISAAC WHITE, MARTHA X NEWTON.
Signed: EBENEZER X NEWTON.

Page 267. 1 Nov. 1811. Proved, Oct. term 1812. I, JOHN MURRUNE, being
            weak in body but of sound memory. I give unto my wife FRANKEY
MURRUNE the plantation whereon I now live, containing 200 acres during
her life time and then to be divided among three sons, JOHN MURRUNE,
PETER MURRUNE, & SAMUEL MURRUNE. I give my moveable property as follows.
My household furniture, stock, and horses to be equally divided among my
chn. CHARLETT MURRUNE, ELIZABETH MURRUNE, SARAH MURRUNE, SUSANNA MURRUNE,
JANE MURRUEN, I give unto my dtr. SUSANNA one bed and furniture and one
cow as part of her share. I leave to my wife to divide the said property among the named chn. I appoint my wife executrix and GAVIN MURRUNE
as executor. Wit: W. ROBERTS, (jurat) JOHN SQUIRE.
Signed: JOHN X MURRUNE.

Page 268. 26 Sept. 1812. Proved, Oct. term 1812. This indenture made
            between LURANEY CHAVIS and ALEXANDER M. GILBERT both of Ruther-
ford Co. N.C. The said LURANEY CHAVIS in pursuance to an act of the
General Assembly in such cases doth place and bind unto ALEXANDER M. GIL-
BERT an orphan of the age of one & half years, named SALLY AMANDA to live
after the manner of an apprentice and servant, until the age of 18 yrs.
She shall obey her master, and at no time absent herself without his consent. ALEXANDER M. GILBERT doth promise and agree to teach the said
SALLY to read and write & understand the first five rules in arithmetic,
or cause it to be done, he shall supply her with supply of diet, lodging,
wearing apparel, and all things in sickness & health. JAS. HAMELTON,
J.P. (jurat).   Signed: LURANEY X CHAVIS & A. GILBERT.

Page 269. 22 April 1812. Proved, Jan. 1813. I, PETER PULER, being of
            sound & perfect mind and memory. I give unto my wife ELIZABETH
the brown mare named Fly, her saddle & bridle and half of all household
furniture, two cows & calves. I allow her support from the plantation,
and the negro woman named Benar. If my wife should leave the place or
marry, the named property to be divided among my three youngest sons,
viz: DAVID, JOHN & JOSEPH PULER. I give to my dtr. NANCY the wife of
DAVID HOYLE the sum of $1 and no more. I give unto my son BARNETT PULER
the tract of land I bought from JOHN HENRY in Lincoln Co. and the note

of hand I have on ROLING WILLIAMSON living in S.C. I give to my son
DAVID, the McCay tract of land lying on Nab Creek, and a negro boy named
Isaac and girl named Lyd, the horse I gave him. I give to my son JOHN
the house & tract of land I bought from RUSSELL, and the 40 acres I entered ajoining the same, one negro girl named Peg and a negro boy named Bill,
the mare & my new saddle. I give to my son JOSEPH, the upper end of the
tract of land where I now live. and two negro girls named Eam & Jen. A
colt and the money coming from my father's estate. I desire DAVID to
have six months schooling, JOHN to have one year schooling, and JOSEPH
to have 2 yrs. schooling. I appoint my friend CHRISTY AKER & HENRY
BEANICK of Lincoln Co. executors. Wit: JOSEPH CARPENTER, PETER CARPENTER,
JOHN CARPENTER.   Signed: PETER PULER.

Page 271. 18 Sept. 1812. Proved, Jan. term 1813. I, JOHN ELMS, being
          weak in body but sound in mind & memory. First of all I de-
sire my just debts to be paid by my beloved wife NANCY ELMS and the remainder of my estate both real and personal to continue in the hands of
my wife in order to raise our children and to educate all the small ones
as well as the mostly grown. If my wife NANCY should marry again, she
is then to have a child's part. I appoint my wife NANCY Executrix and
RICHARD LEDBETTER JR. executor. Wit: ABRAHAM CROW, RICHARD BRADLEY.
                         Signed: JOHN ELMS.

Page 272. 25 Dec. 1812. Proved, April term 1813. I, DANIEL JOHNSON,
          being at present in a low state of health yet of perfect mind
& memory. First I give to my beloved wife MARY JOHNSON all my estate
both real and personal during her natural life or widowhood, then the
youngest chn. PATSEY, DANIEL, and MARION shall have equal shares of said
est. To my dtr. AMY JONES 5 shillings, To my son JOHN JOHNSON 5 shillings, To my dtr. BETSEY 5 shillings, To my dtr. LEANNER, 5 shillings, To
my dtr. LOIS five shillings, To my dtr. UREAH 5 shillings, To my son
WILLIAM JOHNSON 5 shillings, To my son JOEL JOHNSON 5 shillings, To my
Dtr. PHEBE 5 shillings. I DANIEL JOHNSON appoint DAVID JOHNSON & JOHN
(torn), and my wife MARY JOHNSON. executors & executrix. Wit: WILLIAM
WHITE, (jurat) CARTER JOHNSON, (jurat) THOMAS JOHNSON.
                         Signed: DANIEL JOHNSON.

Pages 274 to 277 are missing.

Page 278. 15 Jan. 1810. Proved, April term 1813. I, ROBERT GILKEY,
          being of sound mind & memory. I allow all my just debts to be
paid from my personal est. I give unto my beloved wife JEANEY GILKEY the
possession of the plantation with all cattle, horses and tools to carry
on the farm. She is authorized by this will to give and divide the personal estate between JOHN, ANNEY and REBECCA as she may think proper,
after the several sums are paid to the other children as by this is
ordered. She is authorized to sell and convey one of the small entries
of land to SAMUEL D. FINLEY for the money I owe him, if he will take it.
I give to dtr. LETTY $2. I give unto my dtr. SALLY $2. I give my dtr.
JENNY $2. I give to my son JOHN, the main tract of land at his mother's
death, also I allow JOHN (negro) Tom at the death of his mother. I appoint my wife JEANEY GILKEY & son JOHN GILKEY executors, I appoint Maj.
WILLIAM BRADLEY FINLEY guardian to said executors. Wit: WM. PORTER,
CHARLES LEWIS, JAMES CHERRY.   Signed: ROBERT GILKEY.

Page 279. 11 May 1812. Proved, April term 1813. I, JOHN WATSON, Being
          weak in body but of sound mind and memory. First all my debts
be paid. I give to my beloved wife JUN one bed & furniture, one filly
and her saddle, I give to my son WILLIAM if he returns alone, my executor
to purchase him a saddle, if he remain at home and work, he will then
share equal. I give to my dtr. ELIZABETH C. a horse and saddle, one bed
& furniture. I give to my son HUGHY, one horse & saddle when he comes
of the age of 21 yrs. I give to my sons GEORGE & JAMES and my dtrs.
ISABELLA & MARY all equal shares with the others. I appoint my wife JUN
and son WILLIAM and my brother GEORGE WATSON executors. Wit: WILLIAM
FLACK, (jurat) HUGHEY WATSON (jurat).   Signed: JOHN X WATSON.

Page 283. No date given. Proved, July term 1813. "JOHN MELTON late of
          Rutherford Co. made his last will testament as follows." He
gives to his son CYRUS MELTON $400 & a rifle gun. 500 pounds of pork to

his wife SARAH MELTON, one bed & furniture, one (torn), one flax wheel, one check reel, and a woman (torn) during her life time or widowhood, at death to her youngst dtr. BETSEY, also the plantation during life time or widowhood. He willed to his wife SARAH all real and personal property till her youngst child come of age, then to be equal divided between his wife and children share and share alike. He appointed ABRAHAM ENLOW & JOHN FORTUNE executors.   NOT SIGNED.

Page 284. 10 July 1813. Proved, July term 1813. "WILLIAM GRAHAM
          proved a deed of gift from JAMES MCFEE to ROBERT MCFEE the
same recorded."

Page 284. 20 April 1813. Proved, July term 1813. I, JOHN SORRELS, being
          weak of body but of sound mind & memory. I allow my lawfull
debts and funeral charges to be paid. I give to my beloved wife CHRIS-
TEAN SORRELS all my lands & moveable estate. She can despose of as she
pleases among her chn. JOHN, WALTER, NANCY, REBECCA, CHRE(torn), SUSANN,
CATHERINE & MARGARET. I appoint my son WALTER SORRELS and CHARLEY HILL
my executors. Wit: (blurred) GILKEY, (blurred) BATES.
                    Signed: JOHN SORRELS.

Page 1.   21 Feb. 1813.   Proved, July term 1813.   I, JOSEPH MILLIGAN, at
          present of Rutherford Co., N.C.   For diver causes, appointed and
constituted my friend JAMES S. TERRELL of said county my true and lawfull
attorney for me and in my name.   To apply, call for, and receive from
this State my land warrant as heir to JAMES MILLIGAN, deceased, Lieutenant who died in the service of his country.   Agreeable to a resolution
past in my honor during the setting of last General Assembly.   Receive
such warrant, to give receipt, discharge me in my name.   Wit: MOSES LOGAN,
WILLIAM HILL.   Signed: JOSEPH MILLEGAN.

Page 2.   7 July 1812.   Proved, July term 1813.   REBECCA EARLE, of Ruther-
          ford Co., N.C. for diver good causes done to me by POLLY ANDER-
SON of Wilson Co., Tenn.   Have give unto said POLLY a negro girl, Nance,
9 yrs. old, during her life time and at her death, said Nance and her
increase to be equally divided between the heirs of said POLLY ANDERSON'S
body.   I will forever warrant and defend all lawfull claims.   Wit: GEORGE
MILLER, WILLIAM PRINCE, EDWIN HARMON. Signed: REBECCA EARLE.

Page 2.   18 Apr. 1802.   Proved, July term 1813.   Paid and delivered to
          WM. JONES of Rutherford a negro boy Dave for the consideration
& sum of sixty dollars the interest of two ??? for six months.   Wit:
ABRAM IRVINE, ?? DILLINGHAM.   Signed: GEORGE DOGGET.

Page 3.   4 Oct. 1813.   Proved, Oct. term 1813.   I, JOSEPH MILLIGAN, at
          present of the County of Rutherford, N.C. for diver good causes,
have appointed & constituted my friend, JONATHAN HAMPTON, of said County,
my true and lawfull attorney, for me and in my name to apply, to ask,
call for, and receive from the State my land warrant as heir to JAMES
MILLIGAN, decd., Lieutenant who died in the service of his Country.
Agreeable to a resolution past in my honor at the setting of the last
General Assembly.   To receive such warrant, to give receipt, discharge me
forever. Wit: MICHAEL MOORE, N. HAMPTON, Jurat.
                                       Signed: JOSEPH MILLIGAN.

Page 3.   23 May 1813.   Proved, Oct. term 1813.   I, WILLIAM GETTYS, Being
          of sound mind and memory.   I give to my beloved wife, Agness,
her living on the plantation, one mare colt, all my stock of cows, hogs,
& sheep.   Her side saddle & farming tools.   At her death I give my land
to my sons JAMES & WILLIAM GETTYS my sons now living with me, to each I
give one cow & calf.   To my dtr., ANN, being with me I give one horse,
and a saddle, one cow & calf, a bed & furniture.   I give to my son,
SAMUEL, a long bore gun, a four year old cow.   I give to my son, JOHN
GETTYS, a cow at the expiration of two years after my decease.   My dtr.,
ISABELL MCFARLAND, and MARY PRICE one side saddle each.   I appoint my
friend SAMUEL GETTYS & JAMES MCFARLAND as executors.   Wit: WM. MCFARLAND,
JAS. CARSON.   Signed: WM. GETTYS.

Page 4.   28 Dec. 1812.   Proved, Oct. term 1813.   I, JAMES LONG, now in
          my natural senses.   I will unto my friend, GEORGE HAY, all the
money that may be coming to me as a soldier of the United States, and
two notes now in the hands of ARTHUR MCCLURE.   One on JOHN DRESKABLE for
$24 and the other on GEORGE HAY for $12.   I also give to my dtr., SALLY
HAY, my land that is coming to me as a soldier of the U.S.   I appoint my
friend, GEORGE HAY as executor.   Wit: GEORGE WALTON, JAMES MILLER. (Copy
inf. 28 April 1815) sic.   Signed: JAMES X LONG.

Page 4.   6 Jan. 1814.   Proved, Jan. term 1814.   I, JOSEPH MILLIGAN, of
          the County of Rutherford, N.C.   Have diver good causes have
constituted & appointed ASAPH HILL of West Tennessee at present in the
county & state aforsaid, my lawfull attorney to apply for and draw a
military land warrant from the state aforsaid as heir to JAMES MILLIGAN,
decd., agreeable to a resolution passed in my favour by the legislator
of 1812.   Wit: JAMES HILL, REUBIN HILL.   Signed: JOSEPH MILLIGAN.

Page 4.   8 June 1811.   Proved, Jan. term 1814.   I, BENJAMIN HAWKINS, of
          the State of Kentucky and County of Christian, doth make ordain
and constitute JAMES L. TERRELL of the county and state aforsaid my lawfull attorney, to ask, demand and receive all moneys or property that

may be due or conveyed to me. ELIAS ALEXANDER, (jurat), Mr. ALEXANDER,
(Jurat).   Signed: BENJ. HAWKINS.

Page 5. 17 Oct. 1813. Proved, Jan. term 1814. I, CHARLES BOSTICK,
          being under the decay of nature, but of sound mind & memory. My
will & desire that my just debts are paid the tract of land whereon I
reside containing 100 acres, I give to my son, RICHARD BOSTICK, also my
negro named, Saul, forever. I give my negro woman, Judah, to my dtr.,
SUSANNA PARROTT, with her increase forever. My negro boy named Hugh I
lend to my son, CHARLEY BOSTICK, during his natural life, at his decease,
to be sold and money divided equally among his chn. by his first (wife),
Also I give my negro girl Hannah with her increase to be equally divided
among the chn. of MARGARET BOSTICK that she had by REUBEN BOSTICK, decd.
to them & their heirs forever. My negro boy named Fuller, I give to my
dtr., LUCY REYNOLDS, to her and her heirs forever. Also I desire that
my estate of horses, cattle, hogs, and household furniture, farm tools,
etc. to be sold and the money equally divided among JAMES HARRELL, POLLY
HARRELL, & BETSEY HARRELL chn. of JOHN HARRELL, Esq. and RECY WALKER wife
of JOHN WALKER, Junr. My desire is that my beloved wife, RUTH BOSTICK,
to possess the whole of my estate both real and personal during her
natural life, at her decease to be divided as above mentioned. I appoint
RICHARD BOSTICK, executor. Wit: D. GOLD, JOEL SMITH, (Jurat).
                                   Signed: CHARLES BOSTICK.

Page 6. 23 May 1811. Proved, Jan. term 1814. I, ELIAS WEBB, being in
          perfect health and sound mind & memory. First I allow my just
debts and funeral charges be paid from the whole estate. I give to my
well beloved brothers & sisters, viz: ISAAC WEBB, JONATHAN WEBB, NANCY
EARLE, SALLY SCOGGEN, POLLY SCOGGEN to each $50. I give to my youngest
sister, SUSANNA WEBB $300. I give unto COLEMAN BUCHANAN, son of NANCY
BUCHANAN, decd., & the said COLEMAN whereas born and raised with me the
remainder of my estate what I now possess & also that which will fall to
me of my father's estate according to his last will & testament. I
appoint WILLIAM GREEN, JOHN WALL, ROBERT HANEY my executors. Wit: JOHN
MCGAUHEY, RICHARD GOODE.   Signed: ELIAS WEBB.
CODICIL: I, ELIAS WEBB by this codicil give unto my son COLEMAN BUCHANAN
          WEBB my negro boy named Ruben to be kept for his use by my
executors. Dated 23 May 1811. Wit: JOHN MCGAUGHY, RICHARD GOODE.
                                   Signed: ELIAS WEBB.

Page 7. 29 Nov. 1813. Proved, Jan. term 1814. I, RICHARD GARRISON,
          being weak in body but of good and sound mind and memory. First
I will all my debts & dues that I owe be paid. I give to my well beloved
HANNAH, my goods & chattles except hereafter named. To possess the
plantation where I now live, also the other plantation known by the
Hundred Acres I bought from JOHN JOHNSON for JOHN HARDEN to live on as
his own. I give to my son, GARRETT, $30 over and above the other chn. I
give unto my son, JOSEPH, the plantation where I now live with all the
land I own, and my shot gun. I give to my son, JOHN, mountain plantation
of 56 acres. I give unto my son, JACOB, after the decease of my wife,
HANNAH, 100 acres of land, that I bought from JOHN JOHNSON, also a tract
of land joining COOROD WESSON on Robinson Creek, that I bought from THO-
MAS EARLY, Senr. decd. After the death of my wife, the property not already given to be sold and the money equally divided among the chn. to
wit: GARRETT, WILLIAM, GEORGE, ROBERT, BARBARY, JOHN, JOSEPH, & JACOB. I
appoint GARRETT and WILLIAM GARRISON my executors. Wit: ANDREW TAYLOR,
SOLOMON ROSS, (Jurat).   Signed: RICHARD X GARRISON.
CODICIL: I also give unto my beloved wife, HANNAH, my chest of drawers
          or desk that was willed to her by her step father as her right
and property, to dispose of in life or at death. Wit: ANDREW TAYLOR,
SOLOMON ROSS.   Signed: RICHARD X GARRISON.

Page 10. 13 Sept. 181?. Proved, April term 1814. I, HARDY JONES, being
          of perfect mind and memory. Being enlisted in the United
States Army, considering the danger, I think necessary to leave a
statement of my wordly affairs. In case of death JOHN GORDON son of
SAMUEL GORDON, Esq. shall be entitled to all or any of my estate both
real or personal. Such lands and wages as I am to receive by my enlist-
ment. To be executed by SAMUEL GORDON & BENJAMIN SLATON. Wit: ZAC.
WOOD, JOEL WOOD.   Signed: HARDY JONES.

Page 10. 2 Feb. 1814. Proved, April term 1814. I, DRURY ALLEN, being
of disposing mind and memory. First I desire my just debts be
paid. I give unto my beloved wife, SUSANNY ALLEN, the whole of my estate
during her life and at her death to be divided between my children. Except my land I give unto my son, DAVID ALLEN, only that son DAVID pay my
son, JAMES ALLEN, the sum of $100. I appoint my sons DAVID ALLEN &
CHARLES ALLEN my executors. Wit: JAMES BABER, WILLIAM HOUSE.
Signed: DRURY ALLEN.

Page 11. 9 March 1811. Proved, April term 1814. I, JOHN ANDERSON, being
of perfect mind and memory. I give unto my dtr., MARGARET MOR-
GAN, 5 shillings & no more. I give to my son, ROBERT ANDERSON, all my
wearing apparel & saddle & bridle, big Bible, & $50. I give unto my dtr.,
AGNESS ANDERSON, her wheel and loom tacklings, and all the tract of land
that I now live on, & her bed & bedding. I give unto my dtr., ESTHER
WILSON, 2 cows, 2 sheep & one buckskin saddle. I give to JOSEPH WILSON
son of AGNESS ANDERSON 195 acres of land on the South side of First Broad
River. I give unto my dtr., SARAH ANDERSON, all the rest of my estate
both real and moveable property, except 5 shillings to AGNESS BOYD. I
appoint PHILIP MOORE, and my dtr. AGNESS ANDERSON my executors. Wit;
JOSEPH STEPHENSON, ROBERT CROWDER, SIMPSON LOUNON.
Signed: JOHN ANDERSON.

Page 12. 1 March 1814. Proved, April term 1814. I, JOHN SMITH, being
of sound & perfect mind. I will my just debts be paid. First
I wish a public sale and dispose of all my property, that is the land I
now occupy, and my stock of hogs, cattle, and personal property, which is
to be returned for the use of my wife during her life time. At her death
the remaining to be divided among all my chn. except what is mentioned
hereafter. I give to my grandson NEWTON SMITH son of ROBERT $50 which is
to be taken from his father's part. I appoint my friend JAMES SMITH,
executor. Wit: WILLIAM SMITH, JAMES MCFARLAND, (jurat).
Signed: JOHN X SMITH.

Page 12. 1 July 1809. Proved, April term 1814. JOHN BABERAM held and
firmly bound unto TURNER HENRY in the sum of $150 for value
received. To be void on condition that the said JOHN BABER shall make a
title unto said HENRY for 100 acres of land, lying on the main road from
Rutherford to ROBERT WEBBS, in the fork of the said road and the island
ford & High sholes. Wit: A. WESSON. Signed: JOHN BABER.

Page 13. 31 Jan. 1814. Proved, April term 1814. For the sum of $100
to me in hand paid by JAMES MOORE. I have sold & delivered
unto said MOORE a negro girl named Sal about 19 yrs. old. I will warrant
and forever defend all lawfull claims. Wit: THOMAS BRADLEY.
Signed: RICHARD BRADLEY.

Page 13. 6 April 1814. Proved, April term 1814. I, DELELA WATERS, of
Rutherford County, widow, for and in consideration of the love,
good will and affection which I bear towards my dtr., SALLY WATERS, have
given & granted unto said SALLY WATERS and her heirs forever one negro
girl named Mary from henceforth as her own property without any manner of
condition. Wit: SAMUEL LOURY, ELISH SIMMONS.
Signed: DELEA X WATERS.

Page 14. .. June 1814. Proved, July term 1814. I, ANDREW CROOKS, being
of sound mind & memory. First I will my just debts be paid.
I wish the debt due me from WILLIAM JUSTICE be given to the use of the
family. I wish my legitimate son, JOHN EMANUEL CROOKS, to have $100
cash. I wish all my property both real and personal be sold on 2 years
credit. I also wish my dtr., M.A.C. CROOKS, to be educated from the
money of the sale. I wish JAMES BABER & my wife SARAH CROOKS executors.
Wit: WM. ENTIRE, JOHN LOGAN, jurat. Signed: ANDREW X CROOKS.

Page 15. 28 Dec. 1807. Proved, July term 1814. JOHN GOODBREAD, being
very sick & weak in body, but perfect mind & memory. First I
give to my beloved wife, MARY GOODBREAD, one negro named Buster, one man
named Lewis, one woman named Nan, one girl named Silee. At the death of
my wife I give negroes Buster & Lewis to CATHY WORTON MORRIS & SARAH
GOODBREAD, negro Silee to son, PHILIP, and negro Nan to son, JOHN GOOD-

48

BREAD. I also give to my dtr., CATHY WORTON MORRIS, one negro woman
named Peg & one child named Charles, and a tract of land of 50 acres
lying in Burke County. I give to my dtr. SARAH GOODBREAD one negro named
Annie & her child Hanner. I give to my son PHILIP GOODBREAD one negro
man named Sigh and woman named Agnes & her child Mary. I give to my son
JOHN GOODBREAD one negro man named Solomon & one woman Hagrow. I give
to my son BENJAMIN GOODBREAD son of THOMAS GOODBREAD, decd. one negro
woman named Beck & her child Timothy, said property to stay in hands of
PHILIP GOODBREAD until said BENJAMIN HYDER GOODBREAD becomes of age. I
give unto my son PHILIP & JOHN GOODBREAD my lands and wagons, tools, etc.
to be divided between them. I appoint my son PHILIP GOODBREAD as executor. Wit: ZADOR HARRIS, JAMES HARRIS. Signed: JOHN GOODBREAD.

Page 17. 11 Nov. 1811. Proved, July term 1814. I, GEORGE DOGGETT,
        being of sound mind & memory. I give to my dtr. ELIZABETH
ELLIOTT the negroes she now has in her possession, that is to say, Comon,
Minervia, & Hannah. I give to my son CHARLES Y. DOGGETT the following
negroes he has in his possession, Adam & Philis. The remaining of my
estate to remain in the hands of my wife ANN to be disposed of as following. The personal estate to be divided into lotts and as a child become
of age they to receive their share. Wife ANN to pick any three negroes
from the whole as her own, and keep possession of the land. After her
death to be equally divided among my sons viz: CHARLES, YOUNG, WILLIAM,
GEORGE, RICHARD LEWIS, COLEMAN, & JAMES. I appoint ANN DOGGETT, WILLIAM
DOGGETT, GEORGE DOGGETT and ABRAM IRVIN, executors. I desire my just
debts be paid from money in hand and ELISHA SIMMONS in partnership. Wit:
ABRAM IRVINNE, ELISHA SIMMONS, WILLIAM DOGGETT, CHARLES Y. DOGGETT.
                        Signed: GEORGE DOGGETT.

Page 17. 24 May 1813. Proved, July term 1814. I, ALLEN HENDERSON,
        being weak in body but of sound mind & memory. First I desire
that all my just debts & funeral charges be paid. I give to my son
GABRILE HENDERSON all my right & title to my lands, likewise my household
furniture, horses, cattle, & hogs. I appoint him my sole executor. Wit:
PHILIP HENSON, JAMES ROBERTS. Signed: ALLEN X HENDERSON.

Page 18. 19 Nov. 1813. Proved, July term 1814. I, MARY RUSSELL, in
        consideration of love good will & natural affection which I
bear to my son JOHN WHITESIDES. I give unto said WHITESIDES three
negroes viz: Peggy about 24 yrs. old, Lucy about 4 yrs. old, & Susan
about 2 yrs. old. Wit: JAS. DOYLE, L. DICKEY, JOHN WHAREY.
                        Signed: MARY X RUSSELL.

Page 19. 19 Nov. 1813. Proved, July term 1814. I, MARY RUSSELL, in
        consideration of love, good will and affection which I have &
bear unto my dtr. MARY KELLY. I give unto MARY KELLY 2 negroes namely,
Let, a woman about 22 yrs. old, and a boy about 3 months old named Jack.
Wit: JAMES DOYLE, D. DICKEY, JOHN WHAREY.
                        Signed: MARY X RUSSELL.

Page 19. 25 Feb. 1807. Proved, Oct. term 1814. "Certified that I,
        ABNER WOMACK have received of ABRAHAM ENLOE two deeds of land,
one for a piece where JANE HAMMER lived, the other THOMAS DAVES lived
which are not recorded. I do, hereby bind myself to make them good in
law and soon." Signed, JOHN EDGERTON.
                        Signed: ABNER WOMACK.
The above instrument given to JOHN LOGAN agent for ABRAHAM ENLOE.

Page 20. 5 Nov. 1813. Proved, Jan. term 1815. I, HAMILTON REYNOLDS,
        being of sound mind & memory. I give unto my son JESSE the
tract of land I now live on, containing 250 acres, except 12 acres at the
end joining the land of JAMES IRVINE. Also a negro girl named Patsy &
one feather bed & furniture over & above the rest of my chn. I give to
my son JOHN $40. I give to my son THOMAS one feather bed & furniture.
I give to my beloved wife SARAH the balance of all my personal & real
estate. After the death of my wife the estate to be equally divided
among all my chn. viz: ELIJAH, GEORGE, ELIZABETH, JOHN, UNICE, THOMAS &
JESSE REYNOLDS. I appoint my friends JESSE REYNOLDS & JESSE EVANES as
executors. Wit: LEMUEL MOORE, SAMUEL BIEDRY.
                        Signed: HAMILTON X REYNOLDS.

Page 21. 22 March 1815. Proved, April term 1815. I, CHARLY MULLINS,
being of sound mind & memory. First I wish my just debts to
be paid. I will for all my property to be equally divided between my
wife PEGGY and my two dtrs. VINA MULLINS & BECKEY MULLINS. Some parts of
his property to be sold to the best use of the family, the money to be
divided equally between the above mentioned wife & dtrs. I appoint my
friend JAMES BABER & DAVID W. BRAYER executors. Wit: WM. BABER, jurat,
SALLEY X JOHNS.   Signed: CHARLEY MULLINS.

Page 22. 4 May 1813. Proved, April term 1815. I, JESSE HORN, being
weak in body, but of sound mind & memory. First I leave to my
beloved wife MARY HORN my negro girl Lucy during her natural life and at
her decease to be divided between my dtr. REBEKAH M. KNIGHT & my son
HAMBLIN HORN, and my dtr. NANCY MCKINNY, and my son HENRY HORN, and my
dtr. ELIZABETH HOW---. I wish my real & personal property to be left to
my wife during her natural life or widowhood. At her death the messuage
land to become the property of my sons JOHN & JAMES HORN who are now two
yrs. old. The other property in this county to be equally divided among
all my chn. I appoint my wife & my oldest son HAMBLIN HORN as executors.
Wit: JAMES MCKINNEY, WILLIAM MCKINNEY, jurat.
                              Signed: JESSE X HORN.

Page 23. 14 March 1811. Proved, April term 1815. "We do here certify
that we hereby agree & acknowledge, us, JOHN GUTRY, NELSON
GUTRY, THOMAS LOW & BARTHOLERY THOMPSON do give up all the rites titles
of the land and all the personal & moveable property that RUBIN GUTRY
possessed when he died to SUSANNAH GUTRY widow." Sgn. WILLIAM HOLLAND,
Jurat. Signed: JOHN GUTRY, THOMAS LOW, B. THOMPSON, NELSON GUTRY.

Page 24. 8 March 1814. Proved, April term 1815. I, GEORGE ROBERTSON,
being in a low state of health but perfect mind & memory. I
give unto SARAH my beloved wife my estate, my negroes and all my household furniture, with my land & working tools so long as she remains a
widow, if she marry then to have her equal part with my chn. At her
decease, if she never marry, the estate to be equally divided among my
chn. viz. I give unto GEORGE & THOMAS ROBERTON my land to be equally
divided between them. I give unto MARTHA ROBERTSON 5 shillings. Unto my
granddaughter ELIZABETH HARRIS if she stays with her granny till she is
grown one bed, furniture & one cow also my son-in-law ISAAC HARRIS 5
shillings. My negroes and all moveable property to be equally divided
between SUSANNAH LAWIN, ISRAEL ROBERTSON, GEORGE ROBERTSON, POLLY HILL,
THOMAS ROBERTSON, & LILLY CARVER. The said ISRAEL ROBERTSON, & ROBERT
HILL my executors. Wit: CHARLES HILL, WILLIAM COOK, EPHRAIM COOK.
                              Signed: GEORGE X ROBERTSON.

Page 26. 20 May 1809. Proved, July term 1815. I, WALTON LEDBETTER, in
consideration of $1200 in hand paid by PHILIP GOODBREAD. Have
bargained, sold unto PHILIP GOODBREAD my negro man (blurred) & my negro
woman named Anes also her child Hannah. Wit: JAMES MORGAN, JOHN BRADLEY.
                              Signed: WALTON LEDBETTER.

Page 26. 21 Sept. 1814. Proved, July term 1815. I, RACHAEL LEVEZY,
being in sound mind & memory. First I wish all my just debts
be paid. I give to my son WILLIAM BURNETT the sum of 5 shillings. I give
unto my dtr. HANNAH WEBB & POLLY WEATHERS 5 shillings. I give to my son
JAMES BRYSON my Jack horse & 2 cows at my death. I give unto my son
ELIJAH LEVEZY 66 acres of land to be taken off my old survey of 100 acres
on the lower end including JAMES BRYSON field & spring. I allow my son
ELIJAH LEVEZY stock (named) farm tools & household items (named). I
give my son JOHN 60 acres of land, including my dwelling house, & spring,
Cattle (named) household items (named). I give unto my dtr. PEGGY
LEVEZY, stock (named) household items (named) & wearing apparel. I allow
my dtr. HANNAH WEBB (nothing is listed). To my dtr. PEGGA household
items (named) stock (named). I allow five dollars & three quarters to
son ELIJAH. Three dollars to son JOHN. JAMES WEATHERMAN seven dollars.
Three dollars & 75 cents to widow DICUS. I appoint JAMES WITHEROW &
MARGARET ETHERINGTON as executors. Wit: THOS. GALBERTH,(Jurat), J.
WEATHROD.   Signed: RACHAEL X LEVEZY.

Page 30. 1 May 1813. Proved, July term 1815. I, MARY LOGAN, being weak

in body but of perfect mind & memory. First I desire my just debts &
funeral charges be paid. I give to my dtr. PEGGA LOGAN $150 to be paid
unto my executors & money put on interest, which is to be for her support
during her life time, at her decease said money to be divided between my
dtr. MARY CORRUTH & my son GEORGE LOGAN. I give to my dtr. MARY CORRUTH
my negro woman named Lucy & two chn. Anderson & Nelly, a young sorrel
mare now in the hands of JAMES CORRUTH, my saddle, my large iron pot, My
own bed & furniture, & half of my wearing apparel & other items. I give
to my son WM. LOGAN my young black mare. I give to my son JAMES LOGAN
My young bay horse, four yrs. old. I give to my son GEORGE M. LOGAN all
my land being two tracts, 100 acres each, and other items named. I give
to my son ROBERT LOGAN $20. To my grand dtr. LINDA ELMIRA CORRUTH I give
one year old filly, now in the possession of JAMES CORRUTH. I give to
my granddtrs. SILERS LYNDAMIRA CORRUTH, MERRILLA CORRUTH, POLLY R.
CORRUTH & PEGGA P. CORRUTH each $20 to be paid by GEORGE M. LOGAN. Unto
MIRRILLA CORRUTH the colt that my mare is now in foal, and unto POLLY R.
CORRUTH the next child born unto my negro Lucy. I give unto grand dtr.
SALLY SILENA LOGAN when she comes of age the sum of $10. I appoint JOHN
MOORE, JOHN LEWIS Executor. Wit: JOHN COLDWELL, NICHOLAS GOSNELL, jurat.
                               Signed: MARY LOGAN.

Page 33. 9 Oct. 1815. Proved, Oct. term 1815. EDWARD REPPY, of Ruther-
          ford Co., N.C. For divers good causes me there unto moving
have constituted, appointed JOHN GLEN of the State of Georgia, County of
Jackson my true & lawfull attorney for me & in my name to ask, demand &
receive from LUCION WHITE of the same State & County, admnr. of JAMES
ELMORE, decd. all such sums of money due or coming to me as one of the
heirs and legal representive of said decease. Wit: VOLENTINE MARTIN,
jurat, EDWARD REPPY, jurat.   Signed: EDWARD X REPPY.

Page 34. 10 Oct. 1815. Proved, Oct. term 1815. I, WILLIAM MCCURRY, in
          consideration of natural love & affection that I bear unto
ELIZABETH HENDERSON, dtr. of BENJAMIN & PHIBA HENDERSON. Have given unto
ELIZABETH one bed stead with a good ----- & furniture thereon, one pot
with iron lid & three pewter plates, one cow and the increase. Wit: JOHN
H. CROW, jurat.   Signed: WILLIAM X MCCURRY.

Page 35. 9 Oct. 1815. Proved, Oct. term 1815. This indenture made by
          BRITTAIN LYLES who hath released his son JOHN LYLES from his
service & control of him with free priviledges to bargain, sell & possess
& inherit in his own name. To plea and implea in every manner & shape as
if he the said JOHN LYLES was twenty one years of age. Wit: SOLOMON A.
ROSS, WILLIAM GARRISON.   Signed: X LYLES.

Page 36. 8 ---- 1815. Proved, Jan. term 1815. I, ROBERT SMITH, finding
          that my business calls me to the Western Country and having
placed full confidence in my wife ELIZABETH SMITH and sons WM. R. SMITH,
JAMES M. SMITH, NATHANIEL A. SMITH, and ROBERT H. SMITH. That they will
secure the property with full power and authority to take and forever
such business at will in their opinion the production of increasing the
same. My wife is to give me my horse, bridle & saddle and wearing
clothes, with half of the money that we have on hand. To make over to
the sons the dwelling house whereon we now live at her decease. Test:
R. H. TAYLOR.   Signed: ROBERT SMITH.

Page 37. 3 Nov. 1815. Proved, Jan. term 1816. We, THOMAS TABOR, JOSIAH
          CAPSHAN, and ELIZABETH CAPSHAN of the States of Tennessee &
Kentucky do constitute & appoint ELI TABOR of Rutherford Co., N. C. our
true & lawfull attorney, for us and in our name. To bargain & sell to
JOHN MOORE of Rutherford Co., N.C. all our rights & titles and interest
in a tract of land lying on both sides of South fork of White Oak Creek,
where JOHN TABOR resided at the time of his death, and since where his
widow ELIZABETH lived. Lately sold to JOHN MOORE. ANSEEL GREEN, Jurat.
                  Signed: THOS. TABOR, JOSIAH CAPSHAW,
                          ELIZABETH X CAPSHAW.

Page 38. 15 July 1814. Proved, Jan. term 1816. "Dear Sir, This is to
          inform you that after maturely consideration your request with
respect to making you a title to your land. I do not consider myself
bound as I have once made a deed to the same land to do it again, but

this much I·am willing to do which I consider to be sufficient to make all matters safe & easy. This shall certify to all persons who it may concern that I do hereby certify that I did bargain and sell to ---- SMITH lying on the Broad River on a creek known as the name of Maple Swamp, a certain piece of land, the quarterly I do not remember and I do hereby relinquish all my right & titles to the said land to the said JAMES SMITH or his assigns forever and I do hereby warrant & defend said title against all claims brought hereafter by me or my heirs whatsoever." Wit: B. TEETER, HUGH MCREYNOLDS.   Signed: HENRY REYNOLDS.

Page 38. -- Jan. 1816. Proved, Jan. term 1816. I, JOHN LANKFORD, for diver good causes do give unto my trusty friend ROBERT THOMPSON 100 acres of land including the house whereon I now live, lying on the East fork of Skywicky. After the decease of myself and my wife ELIZABETH. Also my household furniture and stock and all I possess. Wit: JOS. CLOUD, jurat., ANDREW THOMPSON.   Signed: JOHN LANKFORD.

Page 39. 21 Nov. 1814. Proved, Jan. term 1816. I, MARY THOMPSON, of Anderson County, Tenn. for diver good causes and other consideration have made, ordained, and appointed PEHUDA THOMPSON of the State & County aforesaid our true & lawfull attorney for us and in our name. To demand, sue, ask, recover, & receive from JOHN MOORE of Rutherford Co., N.C. all money that may be coming to me or may be due me from the estate of JOHN TABOR, Senr. decd. and do authorize said THOMPSON to sign any deed in my name, and all other business to be done.
                        Signed: MARY X THOMPSON.

Page 39. 21 Nov. 1814. Proved, Jan. term 1816. State of Tenn., County of Anderson. I, HUGH BARTON, Clerk of the Court of Pleas & quarters sessions for said county do certify that ARTHUR CROZIN Esq. who signed the within certificate was at that time and still is a J.P. for the said County.   Signed: HUGH BARTON, Clk. C. C.

Page 39. 22 Nov. 1814. Proved, Jan. term 1814. This person personally appeared before me ARTHUR CROZIN, one of the J.P. for the said county, MARY THOMPSON which signed the said power of Attorney and acknowledge the same for the purposes contained.
                        Signed: ARTHUR CROZIEN, J.P.

Page 40. 25 Dec. 1815. Proved, Jan. term 1815. I, WILLIAM ROBINS, being sick in body but of sound mind & memory. I give to SARAH my beloved wife all my lands and personal estate. Also my negro woman Silve & Cloe Thompson. If my wife remarry she is to have a child's part. I give to my two sons JOHN ROBINS & THOMAS all my land at my widow's death, to be divided between them. I give to HENRY MCKINNY 20 shillings, I give to PHILIP ROBINS and JAMES ROBINS, TARLTON SMITH, and JAMES SPLAWN & JOSEPH STEADMAN & JOHN COLE also my grandaughter SAREY MCKINNY one equal part of my other property at my widow's death. I appoint JAMES ROBINS and JOHN COLE Executor. Wit: GEO. MCKINNY, CHS. SUMMOND, DEIDOMUS HUMPROREY.   Signed: WILLIAM X ROBINS.

Page 41. 8 Jan. 1816. Proved, April term 1816. This day came JACOB HOUSE before me, JOHN HOYLE, one of the Justice for said County and acknowledged himself in debt to the County Court of said County the sum of £200 to be levied of his goods, chattels, lands and tenements.
                        Signed: JOHN HOYLE.
The condition of the above obligation is such that if the above bound JACOB HOUSE. (error: This is recorded on the minutes.)

Page 41. 17 Oct. 1799. Proved, April term 1816. I, JAMES MILLER, am held and firmly bound unto WILLIAM JONES in the just and full sum of £100 good & lawfull money payable in twelve months from date. The condition of above obligation is such that said JAMES MILLER shall & will in twelve months from date make or cause to be made to WM. JONES or assigns 25 feet in front of the lott #2 adjoining JOHN GOODBREAD and on the South side 50 feet back then the above obligation to be void. Wit: JOHN MCFEE, JAS. MILLER.   Signed: JAMES MILLER.

Page 41. 26 April 1815. Proved, April term 1816. I, ARTHUR CLARKE, in consideration of $170.80 to me in hand paid by ZACH. SULLIN,

52

have bargained, sold & delivered one negro girl named Phoebe about the age of eight. I, ARTHUR CLARKE, for myself and my executors etc. do forever warrant and defend all lawfull claims. Provided that ARTHUR CLARKE shall and will truely pay unto said ZACH. SULLIN his executor or assignes the sum of $170.80 on the 17 Oct. next with lawful interest for the redemption of the bargained property then their bill of sale to be good. I, SAMUEL ROSS, do set my hand & seal this day as security for said ARTHUR CLARKE. Test: ------ RHESON, jurat.

Signed: ARTHUR CLARK, SAML. ROSS.

Page 43. 8 March 1816. Proved, July term 1816. I, MARY MADDEN, It is my will that all my just debts be paid. I then will all my estate to TARLTON SMITH both real & personal. One tract on which I now live amount not known, one tract on Green River of 50 acres, 2 others tracts on Green River granted to DANIEL MADDEN both containing 150 acres. Likewise all money, stock, & household furniture. I appoint WILLIAM M. MCKENNY, Senr., HUMPHREY PARISH my executors. Wit: GEO. MCKENNY, jurat., WM. MCKENNY, jurat.   Signed: MARY X MADDEN.

Page 44. 1 Feb. 1816. Proved, July term 1816. I, GEORGE SUTTLE, being very sick & weak of body but of perfect mind & memory. First I will my just debts be paid. I give to my beloved wife ------? Dassa negro woman, Frank & Matilda & her 2 chn. Alma & Ned to be hers during her natural life. I will that my Personal property to remain in the possession of my wife to support the family. My negroes viz: Henry, Violet, Ben, Lewis, Jack, Jerry, Jenny, Harry, Hannah, Lucky, Celia, Davie, and Lucy to be valued by four men appointed by the July Court in 1819 said men to meet 1 Aug. 1819 and value said negroes and divided into lotts agreeable to my chn. Viz: WILLIAM BYAR SUTTLE, SARAH, ELIZABETH, JOSEPH, BENJAMIN, NANCY, GEORGE, SUSANNAH, and JOHN SUTTLE. At the death of my wife the whole of my property to be sold and divided equally among all my chn. I appoint my son WILLIAM B. SUTTLE, my friend WM. B. MCKENNY, GEORGE MCKENNY executors. Wit: JONATHAN HAMPTON, A. MILLER.

Signed: GEORGE X SUTTLE.

Page 46. 23 Jan. 1815. Proved, July term 1816. I, JOHN COLLINS, being very sick in body but of perfect mind & memory. I give to my son SAMUEL COLLINS 3 two year steers. I give to my son JOHN COLLINS ten head of hogs. I give to my son JAMES COLLINS one horse, saddle that he took away with him. I give to my son JOSEPH COLLINS one mare & colt, bridle & saddle and my rifle gun, three head hogs. I give to my son WILLIAM COLLINS the plantation whereon I now live, but my dtr. RUTH COLLINS is to have the use of the part of the property as long as she shall live single. I give to my dtr. RUTH COLLINS & my granddaughter EDY HOOKS 6 cows & calves. My household furniture to be equally divided between them. With enough feed to take them through the winter. I appoint my son JOHN COLLINS & WILLIAM COLLINS my executor. Wit: J. ROB-ERTS, J. FONDERON.   Signed: JOHN COLLINS.

Page 48. -- April 1811. Proved, Oct. term 1816. Articals of agreement between GEORGE M. LOGAN & ROBERT LOGAN, on the division of the land of their late father JAMES LOGAN, decd. ROBERT to have all the land on the North side of North Pacolet from Spreggs old place up to the mouth of Little Creek, then up the creek to the old fence, then on the South side to or near the old school house then a due West course to the back line. GEORGE to have the mill and land, race, with other items. GEORGE to pay ROBERT $50 on or before 15 Feb. next. Another $100 in six months afterwards. Wit: ALEX. CORRUTH, LINDON M. CORRUTH.

Signed: GEO. M. LOGAN, R. LOGAN.

Page 49. 16 Sept. 1816. Proved, Oct. term 1816. I, AGNESS PAULY, in consideration of natural love & affection which I have and bear unto my beloved Nephew THOMAS NIELL and better maintenance and perfor-ments have give & granted all my goods & chattels, three horses, three milk cows, & five head young cattle, 13 head hogs, all household furniture except one large pot and the desk, the books, these are JAMES BEATY'S if he will pay THOMAS NIELL $30. Wit: JAS. WILSON, BASTLEY CROWDER.

Signed: AGNES X PAULEY.

Page 50. 10 April 1806. Proved, Oct. term 1816. I, NINIAN COCHRAM, of

Greenville Co., S.C. For diver good causes & consideration. Have appointed my brother ROBERT COCHRAM of Rutherford Co., N.C. my true and lawful attorney, for me & my use to ask, demand & sue and receive from HENRY SLINKARD or any other person whatsoever, any money due me or owing or payable to me on account of my father's estate. Wit: IGNATIUS BRUCE, GEORGE W. LEDBETTER.   Signed: NINIAN COCHRAM.

Page 52. 1 Sept. 1803. Proved, Oct. term 1816. I, JOHN COCHRAM of
          Greenville Co., S.C. For diver good causes and other consider-
ation have appointed my beloved brother ROBT. COCHRAM of Rutherford Co.,
N.C. my true & lawfull attorney, for me and in my name, and for my use,
to ask, demand, sue, recover and receive from HENRY SLINGARD or any other
person any money or whatever may be due, owing, or payable to me on
account of my father's estate which they may be possessed with in the
County of Lincoln. Wit: JONATHAN HAMPTON.   Signed: JOHN X COCHRAM.

Page 55. 3 Jan. 1816. Recorded, Jan. Court 1817. I, SUSANNAH SUTTLE,
          being in a low state of health, but of sound mind & memory.
First, My will is that my brother BUSHROD SUTTLE be my executor. All
just debts to be paid. "I give to my child CELUS LURAY SUTTLE and my
brother BUSHROD SUTTLE all my part of the estate which I consider myself
entitled to being the ninth part of the estate in a negro or negroes,
which was formerly willed by BUSHROD DOGGETT, formerly of Virginia, to
MOLLY SUTTLE his dtr. perhaps this will alluded to of BUSHROD DOGGETT
was or may be in the words of MOLLY BLACKWELL be this as it may, my claim
is founded on the claim of my mother whether or not I am entitled to it
before my mother's death I trust will be immaterial." I give to my
brother BUSHROD SUTTLE my bed & furniture, as to my clothes, I leave to
my mother to dispose as she pleases. I wish my brother BUSHROD to keep
my son CELUS, until he arrives at full age. To educate him as much as
situation will admit. In case BUSHROD'S death, I desire my son CELUS to
be bound out as a merchant till he comes of age. Wit: JAS. TERRELL,
BENJAMIN SUTTLE, Jurat.   Signed: SUSANNAH X SUTTLE.

Page 57. 14 April 1817. Recorded, April Court 1817. I, JAMES SUMMER-
          HILL, do give unto my son WARREN SUMMERHILL all my property
that I possess to wit: Lands & tenements stock, such as horses, cows,
hogs, sheep and poultry, household & kitchen furniture, farming tools,
etc. Will warrant and forever defend any lawful claims. Wit: HENRY
MONROE, AARON WEATHERLIE, WILLIAM GREEN.
                              Signed: JAMES X SUMMERHILL.

Page 58. 6 March 1817. Recorded, April Court 1817. I, JAMES BRADEN,
          have bargained & sold to GEORGE LOGAN for the sum of $250 four
horses, three milk cows & one heifer, 25 head of hogs, four head of
sheep, one side saddle, two feather beds & furniture. Other household
items. (named) I will defend all lawfull claims. Wit: ELI CORRUTH,
JOHN D. WILLIAMS.   Signed: JAMES BRADEN.

Page 59. 7 March 1817. Recorded, April Court 1817. I, CHARLES S. WIL-
          KINS, being sick in body, but of sound mind & memory. First I
desire all my just debts be paid form the money or debts due me. I give
to my beloved wife ELIZABETH WILKINS my negroes, David, Joseph, Riley &
girl Edy, also negro Jesse & Amy, all household & kitchen furniture.
The use of the plantation tools, lands during her natural life. Also
all live stock during her natural life. I give to POLLY WILKINS negro
girl Maria, I give to SUSANNA W. WILKINS (now RANDLE) negro girl Paritena,
I give to ELIZABETH P. WILKINS, negro girl Malinda, I give to MARIAH
WILKINS, negro girl Sally, I give to HARRIET, negro girl Lucinda to be
delivered at marriage or full age, with such bedding & other household
furniture as their mother may give them. I give to my sons viz: DRURY
WILKINS, SMITH WILKINS, THOMAS WILKINS, ZACHARIAH WILKINS, RUBIN WILKINS,
HEZEKIAH WILKINS, JOSEPH WILKINS, PETER WILKINS, ANDERSON S. WILKINS to
share equal, and be educated, from the property I have left my wife.
The executors to have the sons learn a trade before the age of 21 yrs. I
give to my grandson HEROD WILKINS $100 worth of stock when he comes of
age. I decree that my first set of children, that is the chn. of my
first wife (to wit) RICHARD WILKINS, CHARLES WILKINS, SARAH BLANTON,
FRANCES BLANTON have received all the property that I allow them to
receive from me. I appoint my son DRURY WILKINS, SMITH WILKINS & my wife

ELIZABETH as executors. Wit: HUGH QUINN, CHARLES BLANTON, jurat.
Signed: CHARLES S. WILKINS.

Page 63. 4 April 1814. Recorded, April Court 1817. I, ROBERT CORRUTH,
being in such weakness of body and advanced age in life but of
sound mind & memory. I give to my beloved wife MARGARET all my personal
estate of every kind, except such as theretofore dispose of, and to live
on my lands during her natural life. I give to my dtr. MARY CORRUTH a
tract of land on the South side of North Pacolet, containing 60 acres,
known as the Dinslyard tract lately occupied by JAMES NEIL, also one
black horse called jack & one white cow called lilly. I give to my
grandson LEROY my still & vessels, also my smith tools. I give to my son
ALEXANDER CORRUTH after his mother's decease the plantation on which I
now live, containing 220 acres, with all houses. I appoint my wife
MARGARET & my son ALEXANDER CORRUTH as executors. Wit: ROBERT BRADON,
ROBERT M. BRADON, RUSSELL TWITTY.   Signed: ROBERT CORRUTH.

Page 65. -- March 1817. Recorded, April Court 1817. I, GEORGE MOORE,
being weak in body but sound mind & memory. I lend to my beloved wife ELIZABETH two negroes named Joshia & Kisiah, one feather bed
& furniture, to have the use of the land that I now live on during her
natural life, except that part that my son JOSEPH sold to JOSEPH HAMILTON.
At the death of wife land to be sold by executors & the money divided
among my four children, viz: REBECCA, JAMES, LEMUEL, JOSEPH. My will is
that my two old negroes Bob & ____? should be at liberty to work for
themselves. The ballance of my negroes, Dave, Anny, Jesse, Bird, Eli,
Margaret, Betty, Burton, & Jerry and the rest of my estate to be equally
divided among my four named children. I appoint my two sons LEMUEL &
JOSEPH MOORE as executors. Wit: RICHARD BOSTICK, THOMAS MORELAND.
Signed: GEORGE MOORE.

Page 67. 25 May 1815. Recorded, April Court 1817. I, SAMUEL SWANN,
being of sound mind & memory, but sore afflicted with sickness.
First I wish my just debts & funeral expenses be paid. I give to my
dtr. CATHERINE all my household furniture. I give to my dtr. CATHERINE
bay mare now in possession of my dtr. MARY, and 8 head of hogs. I give
to my dtr. CATHERINE a tract of land lying on second Broad River adj.
CLINTON WEBB & WILLIAM BAXTER containing 25 acres. Being granted to me
by the State. I appoint my dtr. CATHERINE as executrix. Wit: WILLIAM
TOMS, ROBERT SWANN.   Signed: SAMUEL SWANN.

Page 68. 30 Jan. 1817. Recorded, April Court 1817. ELIZABETH GOODING,
LWT, I give to my dtr. SALLY all the property I possess, only
exception, One feather bed & furniture I give to my granddtr. FANNY
GOODING. I do give to SALLY my part of the land that we bought of RICHARD
MCDANIEL, and my wearing apparel I want them divided equally with BETSEY
VANHANDE & FATELHY FISH (executor not named). Wit: DANIEL LYLES, Jurat.
Signed: ELIZABETH X GOODING.

Page 69. 30 March 1814. Recorded, July Court 1817. I, JOHN SUTTON,
Senr. being of sound mind & memory but in a low state of health.
First I desire my just debts to be paid from the money on hand, if that
is not enough, the ballance to be paid from what I will to my dtr.
ELIZABETH & sons ROBERT and WILLIAM SUTTON. I will to my daughter (not
named) 50 acres of land where I now live to be taken off in one body as
she may choose, all my household furniture, my young mare, two cows,
other items named. Having paid for and given to my son JOHN MOORE their
fair distuibutive share of my est. I will him $5. I give to my dtr.
SARAH SUTTON my old sorrel mare now in the possession of my son JAMES,
also $10. I will to JAMES KING $80. I will to COLBY SUTTON $80. I will
to JOSIAH ASJCOCK $40. I Will the ballance of my estate to JAMES ROBERT
& WILLIAM SUTTON to be equally divided between them. I give to my
grandson WILLIAM SUTTON one speckled heifer three years old. I will to
NANCY YOUNG one 2 yrs. old heifer. (executors not named). Wit: ZACHARIAH
SUTTINS, jurat., GIDION THOMPSON. Signed: JOHN X SUTTON.

Page 71. 4 July 1817. Recorded, July Court 1817. I, JOHN JONES, Junr.
in consideration of $1500 in hand paid by JOHN JONES, Senr. at
or before signing & sealing the receipt is hereby acknowledge by JOHN
JONES, Junr. have bargained, sold unto JOHN JONES, Senr. all household

furniture, implements and other personal property, negroes Viz: one
negro woman named Lucy age about 68 yrs. another named Minsa 21 yrs of
age, another named Alice about 9 yrs. old another named Prince about 6
yrs. old and Joseph one year old, four horses, 6 head hogs, I will
warrant and forever defend all lawfull claims on said property. Wit:
SAMUEL MOORE, Jurat., EDMOND JONES.   Signed: JOHN JONES.

Page 72.   28 May 1816. Recorded, July Court 1817. I, SAMUEL REAVIS, of
            St. Louis County teratory of Missoury (sic) have nominated,
constituted, and appointed DAVID REAVIS of State of N.C. County of
Rutherford, my true and lawfull attorney for me and in my name, to ask,
sue for, demand and receive the money or legacys that is coming to me by
my wife REBECCA REAVIS, daughter of GEORGE STEELMAN, decd. To receive
and give receipt for any money due unto me. Wit: JOSEPH REAVIS, Jurat.
                              Signed: SAMUEL A. REAVIS.

Page 74.   4 Oct. 1814. Recorded, Oct. Court 1817. I, THOMAS STARKS,
            Senr. of perfect mind & memory. "I give to ELIZABETH STARKS
on a settlement made between her & myself, all the real & personal property that I the said STARKS got by her. Which was nine negroes, 612
acres of land lying on Taylor's Creek, which she agreed to take in full
satisfaction of my property as our parting settlement. More than that I
give to NELLY MARR for the respect and love and good service to me that
I have for her one negro named Constant, Josh, Tom, & Amos at my death
for her to take in possession and to do as she thinks proper with. Likewise a horse worth $120, all my household furniture, 4 cows & calves, 10
head of hogs. This to be her property to do as she pleases as long as
she lives. If she has any children by me, the said STARKS she may divide
it as she thinks proper, and then if she has none at her death the property goes to my children such of them that is alive, to be divided among
them share & share alike. The rest of my property, my debts, is to be
paid out of. The rest to be equally divided amongest my three children,
DANIEL, WILLIAM & LOUISA share & share alike, "to be divided by TURNER
STARKS." Wit: J.L. PICKETT, CHARLES PICKETT, ROBERT COCKRAM.
                              Signed: THOMAS STARKS.

Page 75.   14 April 1804. Recorded, Oct. Court 1817. I, JAMES RUTHERFORD
            of the town of Granby, State of S.C. for reasons & consideration
well known & for purposes herein after expressed. Have made and appointed my friend FELIX WALKER of Rutherford County, N.C. my true & lawfull
attorney for me and in my name, to ask, demand, sue for, & recover a
debt due from PHILIP NULL, HENRY NICHOLAS, TOWNSEND HORTON to me by judgement obtained in Rutherford County Court, against PHILIP NULL, & HENRY
NICHOLAS. Giving my said attorney full power to collect the same and for
that purpose he may sell or dispose of said judgement to any person or
persons for my use. Said mortgage given to me by deed for land on Cain
Creek in Rutherford County. Wit: A. M. GILBERT, NOBLE HAMILTON.
                              Signed: JAMES RUTHERFORD.

Page 77.   22 Nov. 1816. Recorded, Oct. Court 1817. RUSSELL TWITTY have
            this day bargained, sold & delivered a negro girl named Judy
about 16 yrs. old to ALEXANDER MCFADDIN & SUSANNA MILLER, for the sum of
$500 to her in hand paid by the above mentioned. I do warrant and for-
ever defend all lawfull claims aginst said negro. Wit: WM. GRAHAM, JOHN
MCFADDIN, Jurat.   Signed: RUSSELL TWITTY.

Page 77.   2 Nov. 1814. Recorded, Oct. Court 1817. I have bargained &
            sold unto JAMES G. BEATY one negro boy named Squire for the
sum of £100 to me in hand for which negro I will warrant & defend all
lawfull claims whatsoever. Wit: WILLIAM DEDMAN, Jurat.
                              Signed: SOLOMON BUSOW.

Page 78.   2 April 1817. Recorded, Oct. Court 1817. I, OWEN LEE, being
            of sound mind & memory. All my just debts to be paid out of
the money on hand. My wife, ELIZABETH, to keep possession of the mantion
house & lands belonging thereto, all stock of every kind, so long as she
remains a widow, if she should marry, she is to have one third part of
the real & personal property. My wife to give to the children as they
come of age or marry what property she thinks suitable. At her death all
property to be sold and equally division made giving account for them

that has received. I appoint my sons JOHN & IVERY LEE as executors.
Wit: ABRAHAM IRWIN, Jurat., SAML. FONDROW, Jurat.
Signed: OWEN LEE.

Page 79. 25 April 1808. Recorded, Oct. Court 1817. I, PRICE HAMBRICK,
under the decay of nature, but of sound mind & memory. First
after my just debts & expenses are paid my son JOHN HAMBRICK to have one
sorrel horse, saddle & bridle, one cow & calf. I give to my son, JAMES
HAMBRICK, to have one horse beast about the value of son JOHN'S., also
one cow & calf. I give to my son, MOSES HAMBRICK, one horse beast,
saddle & bridle, one cow & calf of equal value with my other sons. I
give to my son, SAMUEL HAMBRICK, one horse beast, saddle & bridle, one
cow & calf, to be equal with the others. I give to my son, RICHARD HAM-
BRICK, one horse, saddle & bridle, one cow & calf, equal with the others.
To be raised and delivered as they come of age. I give to my dtr. SARAH
HAMBRICK & MARY HAMBRICK one horse, saddle & bridle, one cow & calf each,
and all my household furniture after the decease of my wife, after they
come of age or marry. I desire my beloved wife, NANCY HAMBRICK, be
possessed with the ballance of my estate both real & personal during her
widowhood or natural life. My land to be divided among my five sons
after the death of my wife. The daughters to have no land. I appoint my
wife NANCY HAMBRICK & friend JAMES BRIDGES executors. Wit: THOMAS REY-
NOLDS, SAMUEL BRIDGES, jurat.   Signed: PRICE X HAMBRICK.

Page 81. 20 Sept. 1816. Recorded, Oct. Court 1817. I, STERLING JONES,
being of sound mind & memory. First I give to my beloved,
FANNY JONES, all my real & personal estate during her natural life or
widowhood and for her to give to my chn. as they come of age. I give to
my dtr. ELIZABETH 50 acres of land lying on the South side of the branch
I now live on, and running to THOMAS MORELAND corner. I give to my son
JAMES JONES 100 acres of land lying on the North side of the branch. he
also to have the ballance of my land at his mother death. I give to my
son NANTHANIEL one negro boy named Pampy. Sons JAMES & NATHANIEL to take
the negro girl with increase if any at her appraised value and ELIZABETH
to have her part. I appoint my friend EDMOND JONES & JOHN JONES, Junr.
executors. Wit: STEPHEN JONES, BURNIE MCKINNEY, jurat.
Signed: STERLING X JONES.

Page 82. 16 Oct. 1816. Recorded, Oct. Court 1817. I, JOHN SCOTT, being
of sound mind & memory but having arrived at an advanced age.
I will that my just debts be paid. I give to my wife, LETITIA SCOTT, all
my real & personal property, except herein after named property, also
negroes, to wit. Lett, Smart, Sall, Vinay & her two chn. Elvira & Daniel.
The above named property to remain with my wife during her natural life,
the above mentioned negroes to be given to my chn. & grand chn. To my
son, JAMES SCOTT, my negro Tom; Conditionally as follows, he is to pay to
my granddaughters MELINDA CLEGHORN & ABIGEL LUCINDA CLEGHORN dtrs. of JOHN
CLEGHORN of the State of Georgia the sum of $100 each, when they reach
lawfull age. I give to my son DUNLAP SCOTT, the following negroes, Ann,
Narcissa & Jonathan. To my son MOSES, I give Mira, Lewis, Guy. To my
dtr. LETITIA I give, Jennie, Minerva, Marvel & Abraham. To my dtr. MARY
I give Charlotte, Sylva, & Morning. To my dtr. ELIZABETH, I give Hester,
Mary, & Harriett. After the death of my wife, my lands to be divided
among my sons, DUNLAP, MOSES. To my son PATRICK SCOTT & REBECCA YOUNG
wife of GRIFFIN YOUNG, to my dtr. SARAH FINLEY wife of ROBERT FINLEY
have received their share of my property before, also JOHN CLEGHORN the
husband of my decease dtr. ABIGAL CLEGHORN shall receive no more. I
appoint my wife LETITIA SCOTT, & son DUNLAP SCOTT & MOSES SCOTT my executors. Wit: JOHN MOORE, jurat., ZACHARIAH JOHNS, jurat.
Signed: JOHN SCOTT.

Page 84. 13 June 1817. Recorded, Jan. Court 1818. I, JOHN LEDBETTER,
being sick but of perfect mind & memory. First want my just
debts paid & collected. I give to my wife ELIZABETH the ballance of my
estate during her widowhood. She shall give to her children an equal
share of my estate as she see proper, and to give to each of her children
good schooling, but if my wife change her widowhood I give her one third
part of my estate. I appoint my wife with WILLIAM WHITESIDES & MOSES
WHITESIDES my executors. Wit: A. DICKEY, GEORGE RUSSELL, jurat., ROBERT
WETMOTH.   Signed: JOHN LEDBETTER.

Page 86. 28 June 1816. Recorded, Jan. Court 1818. I, WILLIAM BOWMAN,
          am held & firmly bound unto JOHN LOGAN in sum of $1,000. The
condition of the above obligation is such that the above WILLIAM BOWMAN
shall make or cause to be made unto said JOHN LOGAN a good and sufficient
title in fee simple for one tract of land, lying on the South Fork of
Mountain Creek, to include all the land on the North side of said creek,
including the Western corner about 40 acres. Reserving the benfit & use
of the springs below the dam. Wit: CHARLES LEWIS, jurat.
                                  Signed: WILLIAM BOWMAN.

Page 87. 1 Nov. 1817. Recorded, Jan. Court 1818. I, ABRAHAM CROW, in
          consideration of the sum of $500 in hand paid PHEBE SIMMONS,
hath bargained, sold unto said PHEBE SIMMONS a nigro woman named Chet &
girl named Moll to her own proper use. Will quit all claims on said
negroes & deliver them to PHEBE SIMMONS. Wit: JOHN BAYLE, jurat.
                                  Signed: ABRAHAM CROW.

Page 87. 4 Nov. 1807. Recorded, Jan. Court 1818. I, CHRISTOPHIL LEEMAN,
          of Burke Co., N.C. being weak in body but of sound & disposing
mind & memory. First I desire all my just debts & funeral charges be
paid. I give to my wife all my lands, cattle, household goods and all
other property so long as she lives and at her own disposal at her death.
I appoint DANIEL WORKMAN & JOSEPH CARPENTER my executors. Wit: JAMES
KIDD, SAMUEL X BROWN, Jurat.   Signed: CHRISTOPHEL X LEEMAN.

Page 89. 12 Nov. 1817. Recorded, April Court 1818. I, JOHN LEDBETTER,
          in consideration of $250 to me in hand paid by THOMAS HICKS,
have bargained, sold & delivered unto said THOMAS HICKS one negro girl
named Sinia, five yrs. old. I warrant & forever defend all lawfull
claims. Wit: JAS. HICKS, jurat., GEORGE WITMATH.
                                  Signed: JOHN LEDBETTER & ELIZABETH
                                          LEDBETTER.

Page 89. 29 Oct. 1817. Recorded, April Court 1818. This day came be-
          fore me, WILLIAM TOMS, J.P. THOMAS GOOD and made oath in due
form of law that he bought a note from JOHN C. BURNETT, given by ROBERT
JOHNSTON to the said BURNETT for the sum of $200, which became due on the
25 Dec. next. That on or about the end of July last he took his pocket-
book with the said note therein. Wit: WILLIAM TOMS, J.P.
                                  Signed: THOMAS GOOD.

Page 90. 15 Feb. 1818. Recorded, April 1818. On this day recd. of
          ROBERT JOHNSTON the just and full sum of $200 which sum of $200
discharged a note JOHNSTON gave to JOHN C. BURNETT, A note I purchased of
BURNETT, this are therefore to certify that I have received full value
for this time and will stand between JOHNSTON and all damages inconse-
quence of the same. Wit: NANCY X CABINESS, J. C. BURNETT.
                                  Signed: THOMAS GOOD.
The above was acknowledged in open Court.

Page 90. 19 March 1818. Recorded, April Court 1818. Recd. of, THOMAS
          WHITESIDES, $400 in full payment for one negro girl named Mary,
which negro I warrant to be sound, healthy, sensible. Will warrant and
forever defend all lawfull claims. Wit: SALLY WHITESIDES.
                                  Signed: JOHN WHITESIDES.

Page 91. 14 Jan. 1818. Recorded, April Court 1818. I, WILLIAM COVING-
          TON, being very sick and weak in body but of perfect mind &
memory. I give to my son ELIAS COVINGTON the land where I now live, but
my wife to have use of said land during widowhood. Should my wife marry,
the land is to be rented until my son is of age. I give to my wife all
household furniture, farming tools, two cows & calves, one horse, bridle
& saddle, two sows & pigs. The property not divised to be sold and my
just debts paid and the balance to be for the use of my son ELIAS COVING-
TON. I leave my father JOSIAH COVINGTON & JOSEPH HARDEN. (executors)
Wit: JOHN FONDEREN, jurat. W. ROBERTS. Signed: WILLIAM COVINGTON.

Page 92. 26 Dec. 1817. Recorded, April Court 1818. I, ADAM MOONEY,
          being weak & infirm of body but of perfect mind & memory.
First I request all my just debts be paid. I give to my beloved wife,

SUSANNAH MOONEY, 100 acres of land including my grist mill & mantion house & all other buildings to be laid off the upper end to include the land purchased from TILPHA ? HOGEN & JAMES QUEEN, also my negro boy named Mingo. At death or marriage negro Mingo to go to my son PETER MOONEY. All other property given to my wife at her death to be sold and the money divided among all my chn. to wit. I give to my two dtrs. CATY & FANNY MOONEY a tract of land containing 200 acres lying on Brushey Fork, purchased from EDGERTON. I give to my four dtrs. CATY, FANNY, RACHEL, and OLIF, each a cow & calf & each a bed & furniture & other items named. I give to my son PETER MOONEY all that tract of land lying on First Broad River containing 100 acres, purchased from EARWOOD. I desire that PETER MOONEY be schooled. Plantation to be rented until youngest dtr. OLIF come of age. Then sold and money equally divided viz. Wife SUSANNAH, HENRY MOONEY, CATY MOONEY, ELIZABETH PATTON, SARAH MELTON, FANNY MOONEY, RACHEL MOONEY, PETER MOONEY, OLIF MOONEY. I appoint my friends ROBERT PATTEN, JOHN MORRISON executors. Wit: CHRISTYNE MOONEY, jurat. LEWIS STOCKTON. Signed: ADAM MOONEY.

Page 94. 26 Jan. 1814. Recorded, April Court 1818. I, JAMES SMITH, being weak of body but of sound mind & memory. I will my just debts to be paid. I give to my beloved wife, NANCY, her choice of three cows & calves, 15 head hogs, other items named, at her decease to be divided between my two dtrs. CATHERINE & MIRIA. I give to my wife one third part of my real estate. I give my two sons TELIAFERRO & JAMES SMITH the whole of my real estate at the decease of my wife. They to pay their sisters CATHERINE & MIRIA $150 each within 3 years after they come of age. My executors to school my chn. as the estate will allow. I appoint ALEXANDER CORRUTH, EDWIN HANNON executors. Wit: JOHN LEWIS, jurat., MATHEW GARRETT. Signed: JAMES SMITH.

Page 97. 6 March 1818. Recorded, July Court 1818. I, JOSIAH COVINGTON, being very sick but having good memory. I give all my land to my son DAVID COVINGTON, until my son JOSIAH COVINGTON become of age and all my negroes to my son DAVID until the same time. I leave $60 to finish a house in the hands of my wife MARY COVINGTON. I leave to my three dtrs. NATELY COVINGTON, SALLY COVINGTON, MARINA COVINGTON $100 each. I give to my son JOSIAH COVINGTON $100. After my just debts are paid I give the balance of my money to my wife MARY. I leave the balance of my moveable property to my son DAVID until my children come of age then to be divided equally. I leave to CHARLES LOVE, my neighbor, 2 acres of land running up my spring branch to his new saw mill. I appoint my son DAVID, CHARLES LOVE & MARTIN ROBERTS, executors. Wit: J. FONDEREN, WILLIAM COVINGTON, jurat. not in his mind. sic. Signed: JOSHIA X COVINGTON.

Page 98. 27 May 1818. Recorded, July Court 1818. I, JAMES MCINTIRE, Senr. being sick & weak of body but of perfect mind & memory. I give to my wife LUCRETIA MCINTIRE one third of my personal estate and full possession of my plantation during her life. I give to my son JAMES MCINTIRE land I contracted to him. Said JAMES MCINTIRE shall pay $100 to be equally divided among MARY MORELAND, SARAH MATHEWS, REBECCA, DRUCILLA, RHODA, ANNA MCINTIRE. I give to my youngest sons to be equally divided among them. JOSIAH shall pay $60 to the above named female legatees, before he shall be entitle to the above land. I give to my dtrs. all the balance of my personal estate after the decease of my wife. I Appoint WILLIAM COVINGTON, jurat., WILLIAM MCINTIRE, jurat., JOHN LUSK. Signed: JAMES MCINTIRE.

Page 100. 16 Sept. 1816. Recorded, July Court 1818. I, AGNESS PAULEY, spinster, being of sound mind & judgment. I give to my brother JAMES BEATY 220 acres devised to me by my husband, JAMES PAULY, decd. I give him also 2 books "Bostons Fourfold State" and "The Marrow of Modern Divinity". I divise that JAMES BEATY pay SARAH PAULY $100 divised to her by JAMES PAULY, decd. I give to my sister DEBORAH HOPE all my body clothes also my large Bible. I appoint my friends WILLIAM LOVE & THOMAS NEILL my executor. Wit: JAMES WILSON, jurat., BRETLEY CROWDER, jurat. Signed: AGNESS X PAULEY.

Page 101. 16 March 1818. Recorded, July Court 1818. I, ELIAS ALEXANDER, Senr. being sound in mind & memory. I give to my wife AGNESS her dower of the land whereon I now reside, her bed & furniture & other

necessary articals on the premises for her comfort during her natural
life, also I give her the negro girl Harriet during her life and at death
shall devolve his heirs. My son FRANCES has received his full proportion,
that he heir no part of the property. To the heirs now or to be born of
my dtr. ANN the wife of STEPHEN CAMP all that tract of land whereon she
now resides, said ANN to have full use & profits from the land during
her life time. My daughter JANE shall inherit no part of my property.
My dtr. MARGARET wife of DAVID REINHARDT, I give the first child of my
negro Hannah shall have at the age of 2 yrs. I give to my dtr. PATSEY
the wife of JACOB FISHER the negro girl Delsey during her life time, and
at her death to her heirs. To my son, MAJOR ROSS ALEXANDER, a tract of
land adjoining whereon I now live. (described). I give unto MAJOR ROSS
the following slaves, George, Milly, & Terry, two mares, my sorrell
filley, six cows & calves, one third part of the other stock. To my son,
WILLIAM ALEXANDER, I give the two negroes John & Sally also the Comet
filley. To my son, JAMES TAYLOR ALEXANDER, I give negroes Fox & Venus
and the black mare Kate. Having already given to dtr. MARGARET the first
born of Hannah, I will the next born of Hannah, Fanny & Rachel shall be
given as follows, first born, at the age of two yrs. To my son ELIAS,
the next to my son WILLIAM, the next to my son JAMES, the next to my
granddaughter MELINDA MCBEE, the next to my granddaughter, EMMALINE E.
REINHARD, the next to my grandson, WILLIAM D. FISHER. I appoint VARDRY
MCBEE, DAVID REINHARDT & ELIAS ALEXANDER, Junr. my executors. Wit: ZADOC
HARRIS, EDWARD GOODE.   Signed: ELIAS ALEXANDER.

Page 109. 11 March 1818. Recorded, July Court 1818. I, JOHN W. BLAN-
          KENSHIP, in consideration of the sum of $300 to me in hand
paid by WILLIAM MELTON for & in behalf of his son JOHN MELTON have
bargained, sold & delivered one negro boy named Allen. Will warrant and
forever defend said negro against all law claims. Wit: R. M. TAYLOR,
jurat.   Signed: JOHN W. BLANKENSHIP.

Page 110. 13 July 181?. Recorded, July Court 1818. I, JOHN JONES,
          Senr. In consideration of $1000 to me in hand paid by STEPHEN
JONES, have bargained, sold & delivered unto STEPHEN JONES three negroes
(two boys & girl) named Hannah, Prince & Joseph. Hannah is about 12
yrs. old, Prince is about 8 yrs. old & Joseph about 2 yrs. old last May.
Do warrant said negroes to be free of disorder. I will warrant and forever defend all lawfull claims. Wit: LEMUEL MOORE, jurat.
                                    Signed: JOHN JONES.

Page 111. 8 March 1818. Recorded, July Court 1818. I, BENJAMIN DREW,
          of the State of Georgia, Jones County. Have bargained, sold
& delivered unto ROBERT WEBB one negro man called Will, for the consideration of $400 to me in hand paid. I will warrant and forever defend all
claims. Wit: AFRED WEBB, jurat.   Signed: BENJAMIN DREW.

Page 112. 19 Feb. 1817. Recorded, Oct. Court 1818. I, WILLIAM MCDOWELL,
          being in perfect health and mind & memory. I give unto my
dtr. ----? FORBUSH $5 if demanded, I give unto my dtr. MARGARET HUGGINS
$5 if demanded, I give unto JOHN & ROBERT HUGGINS all my wearing apparel,
I give unto my dtr. CATHERINE ROBERTSON 5 shillings, I give unto GEORGE
ROBERTSON, son of said CATHERINE, $50 in cash. I give to my dtr.,
ELIZABETH MCDOWELL, a tract containing 100 acres, that I now live on,
with the household & kitchen furniture, all farming tools, with all cattle,
hogs, sheep & geese, also one negro fellow named Simon on condition
she pay $150 hereafter mentioned. I give to my dtr. HANNAH JORDON $50
in cash, also to my granddaughter CATHERINE LAMBERT $50 one year after my
decease, Also one fether bed & furniture. I appoint my dtr. ELIZABETH
MCDOWELL & FREDERICK J. ALLEY my executors. Wit: F.J. ALLEY, JOHN CAIN,
jurat.   Signed: WILLIAM MCDOWELL.

Page 113. 21 Oct. 1816. Recorded, Oct. Court 1818. JAMIMA JORDON, do
          hereby impower DANIEL FORNEY of the County of Lincoln my
lawfull attorney for me & in my name, to ask, demand, receive or claim
of the paymaster of this State or the United States any or all the sum
or sums due to the STEPHEN JORDON by contract of survice, also to make
application to the secretary of the War Department or any person appointed to discharge the demands against the United States for land and other
boundties & monthly wages as are lawfully due to the said JORDON. No

witnesses.   Signed: JAMIMA JORDON.

Page 115. 24 June 1819?. Recorded, Jan. Court 1819. I, JOSEPH SMART,
          Sr. being in perfect mind & memory. I give unto my wife,
ELIZABETH SMART, 100 acres of land where I formerly live during her life
time or widowhood. Reserving 20 acres of said tract to my son, JOSEPH
SMART, which is the old improvement part of the tract, Also I give to my
wife 5 head cattle, all household furniture. I give unto son, THOMAS
SMART, 184 acres of land where I now live. I give to my dtr. 5 shillings.
I give to my son REULAINS SMART 5 shillings. I give to my son JOHN SMART
5 shillings. I give to my dtr. DICEA BURNS one cow & calf. I give to
my grandchild, after my wife's death, RACHEL BROOKS one cow & calf. I
give to my three sons all my tools, viz. JOSEPH, WM., & THOMAS SMART.
The land I left to my wife, at her death to become the property of my son
THOMAS SMART. I appoint my son THOMAS & wife ELIZABETH SMART as my
executors. Wit: JAMES BABER, jurat., W. GREEN, Ser.
                          Signed: JOSEPH X SMART.

Page 117. 19 July 1818. Recorded, April Court 1819. I, JOHN GUFFEY,
          Senr. being weak in body but of sound mind & memory. First I
allow all my just & lawfull debts be paid. I give to my son JAMES GUFFEY
my half of the waggon. I give to my sons WILLIAM & JOHN GUFFEY all my
tract of land that I now live on, being on the East Fork of Camp Creek,
each having an equal division. I give to my son THOMAS GUFFEY the tract
of land on Second Broad River where WILLIAM BERRY lived. I give to my
dtr., JANE WALKER, the value of one second rate cow. I give to my dtr.,
AGNESS, her bed & furniture, one cow & calf the pick of the stock, one
half of the crop at my decease, all wool, flax & cotton that I possess.
I give to my dtr., ELIZABETH MARSH, the value of a second rate cow. I
give to my dtr., SARAH KENNEY, the value of one second rate cow. I give
to my grandson JOHN GUFFEY son of AGNESS GUFFEY the sorrel horse and a
part of the crop at the discretion of his mother. The balance of my
property to be sold and divided among my four sons. I appoint my sons
WILLIAM & JOHN GUFFEY my executors. Wit: JOHN CARSON, JENNY CARSON.
                          Signed: JOHN X GUFFEY.

Page 120. 20 Feb. 1819. Recorded, April Court 1819. I, THOMAS READER,
          being in perfect mind & memory. First I desire that all my
just debts, dues & demands be paid. I lend unto my loving wife, LUCY
READER, my land & tenements during her natural life, then to be equally
divided between my two sons WILLIAM & JAMES READER. I give my rifle gun
& shot pouch to my son WILLIAM forever. I appoint my wife LUCY READER
my executrix. Wit: WM. ROOKER, MAMRID MULLINS, JOHN NESBICE.
                          Signed: THOMAS READER.

Page 121. 10 Dec. 1818. Recorded, April Court 1819. I, JANE PORTER,
          being of sound mind & memory. First after paying my just
debts & funeral expenses. I give unto my brother, WILLIAM BIERS, one
note of hand for $30 on WM. MCENTIRE. I give to my brother, SAMUEL BIERS,
one note of hand on JNO. HOWEL for $18, also another note on HOWEL for
$8.75, also one note on JNO. HOWEL for 21 silver dollars & 68 cents, also
one note on JNO HOWEL for $15.68, one note on JESSE SPRULIN & JNO. HOWEL
for 12 silver dollars. The place whereon I now live and the old place to
be sold to pay any debts, money left & one horse & gear & farming tools,
kitchen furniture. I give unto my sister, ANNA DIVER, & her dtr. JANE
PORTER BALLANGER my chest of cloths & all the note on WM. MCENTIRE for
$23.60. I give unto my three sisters in law VILET ENLOW, ANN KANADA &
RUTHY WALLIS 100 acres of land joining JAMES ADAMS & THOMAS CONNER where
I now live to be divided between them. I appoint JOHN TUCKER, WM. MC-
ENTIRE & ROBERT CHARRY my executors. Wit: MOSES ROSS, JOHN TUCKER, JOHN
WILSON, JOHN X ROSS, JOHN X HOWEL. Signed: JANE PORTER.

Page 123. 25 May 1819. Recorded, July Court 1819. I, LOUIS HOGUE, who
          am weak in body but sound in mind & memory. First I give my
brother JESSE HOGUE full power at my death to act as my administrator
to collect in my accounts & pay my debts. I give to my beloved mother my
negro Orange to have & hold her lifetime, and at her death to my beloved
JESSE HOGUE with my whole possessions forever. Wit: SAMUEL MCCULLOUGH,
WM. SUEWELL, ELIJAH MELTON.   Signed: LOUIS HOGUE.

Page 124. 15 July 1815. Recorded, July Court 1819. I, ROBERT HAMILTON,
being old & infirm of body but of sound mind & memory. First
I allow all my just debts & funeral expenses to be paid out of my personal
estate. I give unto my beloved ELONOR all my real & personal estate,
except such parts as is hereafter disposed of. The household & kitchen
furniture to her and at her disposal. The land, live stock, farming
tools & negroes for her use during her widowhood for the support of herself and sons JOHN & JAMES. At the termination of her widowhood the
profits of the land to be used during the natural life of both or either
of my sons. If both live the land to be equally divided between them.
I allow JOHN & JAMES each a cow & calf after their mothers rights ceases.
Negroes Tom, Charles & Amecy and the live stock, and all other property,
after the decease of my wife to be equally divided among my sons, ANDREW,
JESSE, WILLIAM, & my dtr. NANCY. If a division canot be agreed on, my
executors to sell the property and divide the money after the death of
JAMES. I appoint SAMUEL YOUNG & ALEX. CARROUTH executors. Wit: CHARLEY
BAILEY, JOHN X NEEL. Signed: ROBERT X HAMILTON.

Page 127. 9 Sept. 1816. Recorded, July Court 1819. I, SAMUEL POSTON,
being weak in body but sound in mind & memory. First I give
unto my beloved wife, RACHEL POSTON, all my estate (except my land). She
to use the land just as before, and after her death said land to be divided between my two sons, when they come of age. First I give the tract
that I purchased of ROBT. SMITH & half of the 150 acres to my son JOHN
and the remaining land to my son WILLIAM POSTON where I now live. I
appoint my wife Executrix. Wit: GEO. CABANISH, ROBERT ELLIOTT, HENRY
SANDON. Signed: SAMUEL POSTON.
Rutherford County, N.C. This day came HENRY LONDON, AARON MCENTIRE, &
ELENDER MCENTIRE & made oath on the 23 instant they heard SAMUEL POSTON,
decd. say that he wanted a small part of his last will, that is to say,
that bears date 9 Sept. 1816 altered in words that will not authorize no
body to turn his daughters off the plantation where he now lives, while
they live single, they also say they think he was in his right mind when
they heard him say the words above written. Signed: AARON MCENTIRE,
ELENDER X MCENTIRE. Sworn to & subscribed this 27 May 1819. Test: JOHN
HAMILL, J.P.

Page 129. 28 Oct. 1816. Recorded, Oct. Court 1819. I, RICHARD SCRUGGS,
being of sound mind & memory. I give to my beloved wife,
PRUDENCE, the full use of all my land & personal property during her
natural life. I give all my lands between all my sons to wit: RICHARD,
JOHN, ELLIS, ROBERT & JESSE SCRUGGS at the death or marriage of their
mother. All my personal property to be divided among my chn. to wit:
RICHARD, JOHN, ELLIS, ROBERT, JESSE, ELIZABETH, MARTHA, PRUDANCE, RIZA-
MOND, & SARAH at the death or marriage of their mother. I appoint my
sons RICHARD & JOHN SCRUGGS my executors. Wit: JOHN HANEY, jurat., JOHN
CALAHAN. Signed: RICHARD X SCRUGGS.

Page 130. 14 Feb. 1819. Recorded, Jan. Court 1820. I, JOEL TERRELL,
being of sound mind. First I wish my just debts be paid. I
will that my negroes be hired out for the support of my wife & children.
As my children arrive at mature age or marriage they shall have their
equal portion of the negroes. My executors may sell my land or cultivate
for the support of my wife, MARTHA, and children, viz: EVELINA A. TERRELL,
JAMES O. TERRELL, JOHN H. TERRELL, JOEL LYNCH TERRELL, FRANCIS MARION
TERRELL. I desire that my wife, MARTHA, shall have an equal part with
my children, at her death her part to be divided among my chn. I appoint
my friend JAMES L. TERRELL & my wife MARTHA executors. Wit: JOHN BRADLEY,
WILLIAM GRAHAM. Signed: JOEL TERRELL.

Page 132. 12 Dec. 1819. Recorded, Jan. Court 1820. I, JOHN WALKER,
being in a low state in body but of good mind & memory. After
all my just debts are discharge, I leave unto my son, ROBERT WALKER, $13.
I leave to my dtr., MARGARET WALKER, one note on JOSEPH DAWSON of $100
also my mare, two cows, beds with all other furniture. The ballance of
the property to be sold, and equal divided between ROBERT, WILLIAM &
SALLY WALKER. I appoint my friend ARTHUR MCCLURE, MARGERY WALKER my
executors. Wit: JOHN MCCLURE, NANCY MCCLURE.
Signed: JOHN X WALKER.

Page 133. 12 April 1818. Recorded, Jan. Court 1820. I, ELIZABETH
          BRISCO, being sound in mind & memory. I give to ELIZABETH
HENSON and SARAH HENSON wife & dtr. of PHILIP HENSON. I give all my
clothes, except one petticoat, also one chest & lock to ELIZABETH HENSON,
the dtr. of said PHILIP & SARAH. I give one bed, two cows, cotton wheel,
one tin pan, one half dozen of white plates, one smoothing iron, one
baking pan, half dozen knives & forks, also one cow & calf, one pewter
bason. I give to MARY GILES one petticoat, also to my son, BARTLETT
DILLS, one steer, and to my son, PHILIP BRISCO, one looking glass & dish,
and to my son, THOMAS DILL, my hat. I appoint PHILIP HENSON & JOHN COAL
executors. Wit: JOSEPH COAL, jurat., SUCKY X COAL.
                              Signed: ELIZABETH X BRISCO.

Page 135. 5 Sept. 1819. Recorded, Jan. Court 1820. I, JAMES THOMPSON,
          being at present weak & in a low state of health but of sound
& perfect memory. I allow all my just debts to be paid. I give to my
loving wife, NANCY, my dwelling house & furniture as long as she lives,
and to be divided between my son JAMES THOMPSON and ELIZABETH CARSON at
my wife's decease. I also give my wife one cow. My dtr., ISABELLA
SELLERS, and son, WILLIAM THOMPSON, have received their part of my estate
before this will was made. I leave to my dtr., ELIZABETH CARSON, one
colt & weaving loom. I leave to my son, JAMES THOMPSON, all my (land)
one gray mare & her colt, with the working tools. I allow my son, JAMES
THOMPSON, to maintain his mother decently as long as she lives on the
plantation. That JOHN STERLING is to live with his aunt and work on the
place with my son to maintain her till he comes of age. JOHN THOMPSON
is to pay STERLING his proportion when he comes of age. I allow my dtr.,
ELIZABETH CARSON, to live with her mother as long as she lives if she
continues single. I appoint JOHN CARSON & WILLIAM GROVES my executors.
Wit: BENJAMIN ANDREWS, jurat., WILLIAM WATSON.
                              Signed: JAMES X THOMPSON.

Page 137. 16 Aug. 1819. Recorded, Jan. Court 1820. I, ELIZABETH MOORE,
          being low in health but sound in mind & memory. First I will
to my granddaughter, JANE HAWKINS, one cow & calf. I give granddaughter,
ELIZABETH HAWKINS, one cow & calf. I give to my grandson, HENRY HAWKINS,
my mare, these grandchildren being the chn. of my son JOSEPH HAWKINS.
After my debts are paid the residue of my estate I will to JAMES L.
TERRELL. I appoint JAMES TERRELL my executor. Wit: WILLIAM ALEXANDER,
JOEL L. HACKET.   Signed: ELIZABETH X MOORE.

Page 139. 9 Jan. 1820. Recorded, April Court 1820. I, ROBERT CROWDER,
          being weak in body but of sound and perfect mind. I give to
my beloved wife the benfit of the plantation where I now live during her
life time, a negro girl named Mary, for the same term of time. Also a
negro woman named Hannah during her widowhood also her bed & furniture,
an equal share with one of the legatees for part of the household furniture. One horse, saddle, cow & calf, I give to my son ALLEN one negro
boy named Dick, & Hannah at my wife's marriage. I give to my son WILLIAM
$10. I give to my son, JOHN, the land he now lives on containing 150
acres. I give to my son, BARTLEY, one negro boy named Cesor and a negro
woman named Mary, at his mother's death, also the plantation where I now
live & the mill at my wife death. I give to my dtr., POLLY CURTIS'S,
children $100 to be divided among them. I give to my dtr., BECKY LEDFORD,
$1. I give to my dtr., FANNY NEWTON, $1. I give to my dtr., DELILA
WILSON, $1. Three tracts of land mentioned to be sold and the money
divided among the legatees named, ALLAN, JOHN, BARTLEY, BECKY, FANNY &
DELIAH. I appoint my son ALLEN & ROBERT WELLS my executor. Wit: THOMAS
P. WELLS, MARY ANN X CLARK.   Signed: ROBERT CROWDER.

Page 142. 17 Jan. 1820. Recorded, July Court 1820. I, JOHN WALKER,
          under the decay of nature but sound mind & memory. I give my
son, JAMES WALKER, the tracts of land where he now lives, joining lands
of DAVID BEAM, and my lands patent dated 23 Nov. 1805. I will is that my
beloved wife, URCILLA WALKER, the whole of my estate both real & personal.
The whole of my estate and the money equally divided among my chn. to
wit: THOMAS, JOHN JR., WILLIAM, ELIJAH, JAMES, JESSE, JOEL, URCILLA
DICUS, & SUSANNH WALKER, the rest of my children not to share any part
of the above estate. I appoint my sons THOMAS & ELIJAH WALKER my
executors. Wit: DANIEL GOLD, jurat., WILLIAM HORTON, JOHN FREDK. COOL.

Signed: JOHN WALKER.

Page 143. 14 April 1820. Recorded, July Court 1820. I, NATHANIEL SMITH,
        being of sound & perfect mind & memory. First I desire that
my wife, JINNEY SMITH, have all my estate, both real & personal during
her natural life or widowhood. To ELIZABETH WOODARD I give $175 and one
mare & saddle, bridle, bed & furniture, one cow & calf & the sow & pigs
she has received. To my dtr., MARGARET CONNER MCMURREY, I give one mare,
one bed & furniture, one sow, cow & calf & $60 paid. To my son, JOHN
SMITH, 100 acres of land, one bed & furniture, one cow & calf. This
property he is to receive when my will is in force. I give unto JINNEY
LUKEWAER? one horse, one cow & calf, bed & furniture, six plates, dish
& bason she has received $65. I give to ELIZABETH SMITH my granddaughter
DAVID SMITH'S daughter is to have an equal part with the rest of my chn.
I appoint JINNEY SMITH & JOHN MCMURREY my executors. Wit: DAVID BURGE,
JAMES X BRIDGES.   Signed: NATHANIEL SMITH.

Page 145. 22 March 1820. Recorded, July Court 1820. I, GLOUD LONG, in
        a low state of health but with a perfect mind & memory. I
give to my beloved wife, SARRAH LONG, the home plantation and every
thing on it, joining the lands of ELISHA BLANKENSHIP and ROBERT CAUHORNS?
& JOHN LONGS lines during her widowhood. I give unto my wife $375 what
she does not make use of to be divided among my chn. At my wife's death
the land to be divided between ANDY MORRISON & GLOUD MILLER LONG. I give
to ANDY MORRISON LONG all the land on the East side of the creek. I give
unto GLOUD M. LONG one negro boy named Ransom. I give unto my wife
household furniture, all my negroes during her life time, at her death
the negroes to be sold, money to be equally divided. Except the boy
Ransom. To my wife all stock, except my son JAMES, dtr. POLLY, son ANDY
& son GLOUD to have a horse, bridle, saddle, cow & calf, bed & furniture
when they come of age. To my son WILLIAM 150 acres of land where he now
lives. I give to my son JAMES the other part of said tract, containing
150 acres. I give to my son HUGH LONG 100 acres of land, joining JOHN
BELL. I give to JOH LONG lying on Sellers Branch, joining ELIJAH BLANKEN-
SHIP & ELISH SHEMWELL lines. I appoint JOHN LONG, Senr. & HUGH LONG my
executors. Wit: ELISHA SHEMWELL, JOHN LONG.
                                Signed: GLOUD LONG.

Page 148. 5 Nov. 1819. Recorded, Oct. Court 1820. I, ISAAC ARLIDGE,
        being of sound mind, To my wife SALLY I give the whole of my
real & personal estate during her natural life. At my decease my will is
that LEVI ARLIDGE son of JONATHAN ARLIDGE shall be sole heir of all my
lands & a negro boy named Harry. At the death of my wife the remainder
of my property be divided among the four chn. of JONATHAN ARLIDGE to wit:
LEVI, ISAAC, GREENBERRY, MATHISON & the next child of said JONATHAN now
born, but not named. With respect to a negro named Pender, I will she
remain to the use of my wife during her life time. (No executor names).
Wit: ROBERT HENRY, JOSEPH HALBERT, JOHN STEEL.
                                Signed: ISAAC ARLIDGE.

Page 150. 14 Dec. 1820. Recorded, Jan. Court 1821. I, ALEXANDER POOL,
        being in a low state of health but perfect mind & good memory.
I give to my wife, ANNA POOL, all my land & improvements, during her life
or widowhood, also all stock & cattle except what is hereafter mentioned.
Should my wife marry she to have her bed & furniture, her big trunk, one
fourth part of the kitchen furniture, MILES has received his share one
mare. POLLY has two beds, furniture, saddle & chest. JOHN his one mare
& colt. DICY her one bed, furniture, saddle & chest. CARRY one bed,
furniture and I desire for THOMAS to have $10. FANNY have her bed &
furniture and PATSY and SUSY to have as much out of the estate as FANNY.
I give my lands & possessions to my son JAMES at the death of his mother,
also one third part of the stock. The remaining part of my property to
be sold and money equally divided among my chn. I appoint my wife ANNA
& son MILES my executors. Wit: LEWIS GARNER, WILLIAM GARNER.
                                Signed: ALEXANDER POOL.

Page 151. 15 May 1818. Recorded, April Court 1821. I, CORNELIUS MELTON,
        being in low health but sound in mind & memory. Unto my son,
ABNER MELTON, I give a part of my land, with the 45 acres that I purchased from JOHN EARLY, likewise one horse saddle, bridle, one cow & calf,

sow & pigs, bed & furniture which he has received. I give unto my son,
MARVILL MELTON, I give 110 acres of land that I purchased of JOHN EARLY,
one horse saddle, sow & pigs. Unto my son, HIRAM MELTON, a part of the
tract of land that I live on, marked in the presence of WILLIAM FORTUNE,
Senr. and joining land of BENJAMIN FREEMAN, likewise one horse saddle,
bridle, one cow & calf, one sow & pigs. To my son, SINDREY MELTON, I
give all that tract of land I purchased of JOHN EARLY not otherwise disposed of, except 20 acres, which is to be laid off for my son, GREEN,
also one horse saddle, bridle, one cow & calf, one sow & pigs. To my son,
SHADRACK GREEN MELTON, I give all my land not otherwise disposed of at
his mother's death, also one horse saddle, bridle, one cow & calf, one
sow & pigs, when he come of age. I also give to my wife the ballance of
my estate, to be divided amongst my dtrs. If she thinks necessary to
give TELITHA CUMA a greater share as she is not able to make a support,
also I desire that my four sons pay HIRAM $10 after they come of age. I
appoint ROBERT K. WILSON, JOHN FORTUNE, PLEASENT FORTUNE my executors.
Wit: EPHRAIM HEART, BENJAMIN X FREEMAN, Senr. jurat.
                         Signed: CORLELIUS MELTON.
CODICIL: Dated 14 March 1819. The land formerly willed to my son,
MARVILL MELTON, shall extend to Magahy spring on the original line. The
land which I willed to my son, ABNER, extend no further down the branch
than his still house. Wit: JAMES BELL, JESSE X SMELLY, jurat.
                         Signed: CORNELIUS MELTON.

Page 156. 26 July 1817. Recorded, April Court 1821. I, JOEL BLACKWELL,
          being sound in my mind & memory. I give unto my wife, SARAH,
all the property received by her on our marriage, that is my river
plantation, and my negro woman named Win and all her increase, except
Win's dtr. Easter which I have given unto BUSHROD DOGGETT, which he is to
have no further demands on my wife's estate. Win's son, Dick, I have
given at the death of my wife unto ANN SUTTLE, widow, for her part of my
wife's estate. I also give unto my wife two mares, 3 cows & calves, one
feather bed & furniture, household items (named) 12 months provision to
her & to her heirs by WM. BYERS. I have given some of my chn. as follows,
sons JAMES, CHARLES, & PETER, dtr. SALLY & REBECCA MARTIN $200 in pro-
perty. It is also my will my other chn. have $200 in property extra
allowed them in the division of my estate. I give unto my son, DANIEL,
250 acres whereon I now live as his $200 extra. I give to my granddaugh-
ter HARRIET BLACKWELL a young mare named Pall. The ballance of my estate
to be equally divided among all my chn. The Chn. of my son JOEL shall
have $100 extra of the estate when they come of age. I appoint my sons',
DANIEL & GEORGE BYERS, my executors. Wit: GEORGE CAMP, DAVID POPE.
                         Signed: JOEL X BLACKWELL.

Page 159. 15 Sept. 1819. Recorded, July Court 1821. I, JOHN JONES,
          being under the decay of nature but of sound mind & memory.
I give to my four eldest dtrs. SARAH BUCHANAN, MARTHA GREEN, ELIZABETH
BUCHANAN, & NANCY GREEN one feather bed each with the furniture belonging
to each bed. I give to my wife, ANN JONES, 2 heifers which she brought
with her. I desire the ballance of my estate be sold and the money to be
divided as follows. First I allow my just debts be paid. Then $50 to
my wife, ANN JONES, 20 shillings to my son, STEPHEN JONES, The balance of
the money to be divided between SARAH BUCHANAN, MARTHA GREEN, ELIZABETH
BUCHANAN & NANCY GREEN, FRANCES BRIDGES, MILDRED MCKINNY, and STERLING
JONES, decd. (his children to have a share with the others) of what
should have been their father's part, LEWIS JONES, ELIJAH JONES, JOHN
JONES, Junr., EDWARD JONES, ROBERT JONES & ATHA JONES. I appoint my sons
EDWARD & ROBERT JONES as executors. Wit: JOHN HORD, AUDLEY HAMILTON,
RICHARD BOSTICK.   Signed: JOHN JONES.

Page 160. 10 Jan. 1821. Recorded, July Court 1821. I, ELIZABETH POUNCE,
          being infirmed by age and knowing my certain doom, yet of
perfect mind & memory. I will my just debts & funeral charges be paid.
To my son in law WILLIAM STATON & his wife NANCY I give my four slaves
Abram, Dick, Ceiler, & Bill during their natural life, after the death
of WILLIAM & NANCY I give to my granddaughter, SALLY TART, the above
named Dick & Ceiler and to JONATHAN TART, my grandson, I give the above
named Abram & Bill. I appoint JAMES MORRIS & EDMUND WALDROP my executors.
Wit: JOHN LANCASTER, WILLIAM X WOOTEN.
                         Signed: ELIZABETH X POUNCE.

Page 162.   17 May 1821.   Recorded, July Court 1821.   I, JOHN HALBERT,
            being of sound & perfect mind & memory.   I give unto my wife,
SARAH HALBERT, all my estate real & personal after my just debts are paid
during her life or widowhood.   At my wife's decease I give to my son,
JEROME BONAPARTE HALBERT, & JOHN MAKEAN HALBERT each one half of my real
estate, unto my dtrs. POLLY PAMELA HALBERT & BLANCHY CAROLINE HALBERT I
give each one half of my personal estate.   I hereby certify that my sons
JOSEPH, BENJAMIN, & MARVILLE HALBERT & my dtr. ALVAMARIAH HALBERT have
heretofore received of me equal shares with the first four heirs.   I
appoint my friend JOSEPH HALBERT executor.   Wit: EDWARD M. QUIN, jurat.,
JOHN HICKS, jurat., TOLLIVER CROW, Jurat.
                            Signed: JOHN HALBERT.

Page 163.   27 April 1821.   Recorded, Sept. Court 1821.   I, DANIEL HARRIS,
            being weak in body but sound in mind.   I lend unto my wife,
SARAH, all my estate during her natural life or widowhood.   At her decease or marriage, I wish my estate to be divided as follows.   I give
unto my son, ROBERT HARRIS, 5 shillings, I give unto my son, JAMES, 5
shillings, I give to my son, MATHEW, 5 shillings, I give to my dtr.,
MARGARET DELLINER, 5 shillings, I give to my dtr., MARY DOBBINS, 5 shillings, I give to my dtr., SARAH STASEY, 5 shillings, I give to my dtr.,
ROSEY MORRISON, 5 shillings, I give to my son, LEAVEN, 5 shillings, the
ballance of my estate to be equally divided between my other three chn.
Viz: JOHN, CHARLES & DELETHA.   I appoint my friend LEMUEL MOORE & my wife
SARAH executors.   Wit: LEMUEL MOORE, Jurat., STEPHEN JONES, Jurat.
                            Signed: DANIEL HARRIS.

Page 164.   4 Sept. 1821.   Recorded, Oct. Court 1821.   I, WILLIAM ALEX-
            ANDER, being of sound mind & memory.   I give unto my brother,
ELIAS ALEXANDER, my negro girl Carolina, I give unto my brother, ELIAS,
all my part of the land now owned by my brother, JAMES T. ALEXANDER &
myself, land lying on both sides of Floyd's creek.   I will unto my
brother, JAMES, my negro, John, Sally Ann, all my part of the land that
JAMES & myself bought of JAMES MURPHY, Esq. of Burke County, N.C. land
lying on both sides of North Fork, now known by the name of Bedford's
place.   The balance of my estate both real & personal to be equal divided
between my brothers ELIAS & JAMES ALEXANDER.   I appoint ELIAS & JAMES
ALEXANDER my executors.   Wit: ZADOCK HARRIS, jurat., THOMAS CAMP.
                            Signed: WILLIAM ALEXANDER.

Page 166.   13 Aug. 1821.   Recorded, Oct. Court 1821.   I, SAMUEL F. CUTLER,
            merchant, I will that all my debts be paid.   I give all my
clothes & wearing apparel to SETH BANSTER of Brookfield, Mass.   I will my
watch & it --------? to my honored father Gen. JOHN CUTLER of Brookfield,
Mass.   I will all the property I own in Rutherford Co., N.C. to SARAH
HAMILTON, eldest dtr. of Doctor JOSEPH HAMILTON, except so much as may be
sufficient to purchase a pair of grave stones over my grave, which is to
be enclosed.   I appoint JOSEPH BOWEN my executor.   Wit: JAMES GRAHAM,
AMOS P. GANER, jurat.   Signed: SAMUEL F. CUTLER.

Page 167.   28 April 1821.   Recorded, Oct. Court 1821.   I, WILLIAM MORRIS,
            being very sick in body but of perfect mind & memory.   I will
all my just debts & funeral charges be paid.   I give SOPHA MORRIS, my
beloved wife, all my whole estate, with every part & parcel thereof except my land together with profits & rents arising therefrom with $200.
I give unto my brother JOHN MORRIS'S son JAMES MORRIS my land to be his
forever, he paying the said $200 after two years.   I appoint WILLIAM
KIMSEY & BENJAMIN POSEY my executors.   Wit: THOMAS RODES, WILLIAM KIMSEY,
jurat.   Signed: WILLIAM MORRIS.

Page 169.   31 July 1821.   Recorded, March Court 1822.   I, MARY COLLINS,
            being in a low state of health.   After paying my just debts.
I give to my dtr., MARY SMART, 5 shillings, to my son, JOHN COLLINS, 5
shillings, to my dtr., MARGARET REDEY, 5 shillings, to my dtr., JANE DEAN,
5 shillings, to my dtr., SALLY COLLINS, I leave the balance of my estate
both real and personal.   I appoint JOSEPH GREEN, Senr. & SALLY COLLINS my
executors.   Wit: JOSEPH X SMART, jurat., ELIZABETH X SMART.
                            Signed: MARY X COLLINS.

Page 170.   11 April 1820.   Recorded, April Court 1822, I, CLATER SMITH,

66

of sound & perfect mind & memory. I desire my just debts to be paid. I give to my loving wife, MARY SMITH, all my estate both real & personal during her natural life. I give to my dtr., ELIZABETH BRIDGES, all the stock & furniture that she has received. To my son, WILLIAM S. SMITH, all the land, stock, household furniture that I gave him with 20 shillings. MINOR W. SMITH all the lands, stock, and household furniture that I gave him before, 20 shillings. I give to my dtr., SARAH HARRELL, all the stock & household furniture that I have given her. I give unto my son, JOHN SMITH, all household furniture that I have given him before. I give to my son, CHARLES C. SMITH, all household furniture that I have given him before. I give to my son, CLAYTER C. SMITH, all the household furniture that I have given to him before. I desire my executors to divide the balance of my estate among the following 8 children. ELIZABETH BRIDGES, SARAH HARRELL, JOHN, CHARLES, CLATER, NANCY, BRAXTON, BENJAMIN SMITH. I appoint my wife, MARY SMITH, & BRAXTON & BENJAMIN SMITH my executors. Wit: THRO. BIRCHETT, jurat., M. DAVIS.
                    Signed: CLATER SMITH.

Page 1.   5 June 1814.   Recorded, Oct. Court 1822.   I, MARY ORR, being
          very sick & weak but of perfect mind & memory.   I give unto
MARY QUEEN one bed & furniture, all my clothing, all household Furniture
and the balance of my property (to wit) 5 head cattle, 6 hogs, one foot
wheel & one saddle I give in the manner & form.   It shall continue in
the hands of my executor for MAXWELL QUEEN, JEAN QUEEN, OLIVINE QUEEN,
MARY QUEEN, & MARGARET QUEEN until the youngest comes of age, then divided equal if property will admit, if not, it shall be sold and the money
equally divided among them.   I appoint WILLIAM L. QUEEN as my executor.
Wit: JAMES MCNEELY, jurat., WM. DOWNS, ELIZABETH DOWNS.
                              Signed: MARY X ORR.

Page 3.   3 July 1822.   Recorded, Oct. Court 1822.   I, JOHN WILSON, Senr.
          Being in a perfect mind & memory.   I give unto my beloved wife,
MARGARET WILSON, the plantation whereon I now live, with all land adjoining the same, two horses named Royal & Dill, all farming tools, all
household & kitchen furniture, all my stock of cattle, except one cow &
calf, all hogs & sheep, all my negroes that is Kate, Liss & Will to remain in her possession during her life time or widowhood.   I give to my
dtr., ELIZABETH, my negro girl Liss at my wife's death.   Also one colt,
one cow & calf and to live on the place as long as she remains single.
I give to my dtr., MARY, the wife of WILLIAM ALLEN $100.   I give to son,
JAMES WILSON, the tract of land on Ward's Creek, called Bracket's old
place in case he returns.   The balance of my property both real & personal at the decease of my wife to be equally divided among my son, JOHN
WILSON, SAMUEL WILSON, JAMES WILSON, THOMAS WILSON & my dtr., ELIZABETH
WILSON, each to share alike.   In case JAMES does not return his share to
be divided among the other four.   I appoint JOHN WILSON, SAMUEL WILSON,
& THOMAS WILSON my executor.   Wit: SAMUEL WILSON, DANIEL KING, ZLENEN
TUCKER.   Signed: JOHN X WILSON.

Page 5.   12 Nov. 1822.   Recorded, Dec. Court 1822.   Being in my perfect
          mind & memory.   I will to DRUCILLA MCENTIRE all that I received
from her parents with her.   I will to my beloved child, JOSEPH MCENTIRE,
all that I received from my father, other property two horses, two cows
& calves and hogs.   Wife to have one year provision, the balance to be
sold and money put on interest for my son.   I appoint my father WILLIAM
MCENTIRE executor.   Wit: JOHN LANSING, JAMES LANSING, both jurat.
                              Signed: SAMUEL MCENTIRE.

Page 6.   8 Nov. 1822.   Recorded, Jan. Court 1823.   I, ZACHARIAH SULLINS,
          being in a low state of health but with perfect senses & sound
memory.   I leave all my lawful debts to be paid.   I give to my wife,
PHEBE, 100 acres of land, from the Bedford 50 & the adjoining 50 acres
including the house & advantages.   At her death to belong to my son,
JOHN FLACK.   I give to my son, JOHN FLETCHER, 100 acres joining his
mothers above.   I give to my son, NOAH, 100 acres next above joining JOHN
FLETCHERS.   I give to my son, JONAH, 100 acres above NOAH & 18 acres off
the Bedford tract.   I give to dtrs., NANCY & SALLY, 100 acres the remainder of the Bedford tract.   NANCY at the lower & next to JOHN MORELAND
and the upper 50 to SALLY.   I give to my son, JESSE, all the land North
of Shoal Creek, including the Mill shoal, with liberty to improve the
same.   Should be 100 acres, with the use of the spring.   I give to my
son, WILLIAM, all the rest of the Lyles tract, with the house, orchards
for his support, to be rented, with the profit of the still to him & his
mother, and at his death to be divided among his 4 brothers.   I appoint
my sons JOSIAH & JESSE my executors.   Wit: JESSE RICHARDSON, JOHN C.
ERWIN, JOHN L. RICHARDSON, jurat.   Signed: ZACHARIAH SULLINS.

Page 8.   6 June 1818.   Recorded, Jan. Court 1823.   I, JOHN CHAMPION,
          enfeeble by age but sound of mind & memory.   Wife, KIZIAH, to
have possession of property, she is not to withhold from dtr., TEMPER-
ANCE, the usual maintenance which we have given her.   After the decease
of my wife, I give to my dtr., TEMPERANCE, & son, ABNER, the tract of
land on which the family now lives to be divided between them.   I give
to my dtr., TEMPERANCE, 2 beds & usual furniture, one walnut chest & my
large Bible.   I give to my son, RICHARD CHAMPION, all my wearing apparel.

After the payment of my just debts, the residue of my property to be
divided between my dtr. TEMPERANCE & son ABNER. All rest of my chn. have
received their portion, and I will they have no more. I appoint my son
ABNER & dtr. TEMPERANCE as executors. Wit: GEORGE JONES, EPHRIAM LITTLE-
JOHN, jurat.   Signed: JOHN CHAMPION.

Page 10. 5 May 1820. Recorded, April Court 1823. I, JONAS BEDFORD,
        being in perfect health of body and perfect mind & memory. I
give to my dtr., UNICE LYLES, all debts dues or demands, also all lands
proved to be my property, provided the debts & lands are recovered. I
give to my son, RAYMOND BEDFORD, Ł5, likewise I give to my son, JONAS,
Ł5, I also give to my son, JAMES, $100, also to my son, STEPHEN BEDFORD,
Ł5. I also give to my dtr., ELIZABETH BYARS, $100. To my dtr., REBECCA
HUNT, $100. I appoint DAVID LYLES & THOMAS LYLES my executor. Wit:
ANDREW SHERRER, JOHN LYLES, jurat.   Signed: JONAS BEDFORD.

Page 12. 30 May 1823. Recorded, July Court 1823. I, RECHEL MCENTIRE,
        being sick & weak of body, yet of perfect sound mind & memory.
I give to my four dtrs. REBECCA MCENTIRE, ELIZABETH CRAIN, LYDIA CORN-
WALL, ANN PEGGA BAILEY my bed & furniture and all my wearing clothes
equally divided between them if they can agree, if not sell them. All
household furniture, cattle, & every thing else that I possess. I will
to my grandson, JAMES COLLINS. To be his property free & clear. (No
executors named). Wit: JEREMIAH GARNER, jurat., WILLIAM CRAIN.
                        Signed: RACHEL MCENTIRE.

Page 13. 13 Aug. 1823. Recorded, Oct. Court 1823. I, ARTHUR MCCLURE,
        being weak in body but of sound mind & memory. I allow all my
just debts to be paid. I will my wife all her dowry of land & other
property. At the death of my wife her part of the land to fall to the
boys, the balance to be divided among the rest of the legatees. I will
unto my two sons, ISAAC D. MCCLURE & JAMES A. MCCLURE, all my lands to
be divided between them. The balance of the property to be divided among
all the rest of the legatees, ELIZABETH, SAM S., ISAAC D., MARY E.,
JAMES A., & PAMELA N. MCCLURE to receive their part as they come of age.
I appoint my friend DAVID GRAY, W.D. KILPATRICK & MARY MCCLURE, my wife,
executors. Wit: JAMES WRAGG, jurat., JAMES GRAY, RICHARD MCCLURE.
                        Signed: ARTHUR MCCLURE.

Page 14. 6 Oct. 1823. Recorded, Oct. Court 1823. I, CHARLES RICHARD-
        SON, Being in health & of sound mind & memory. First my will
is that all my just debts be paid from my perishable property by my wife,
MARY RICHARDSON, which I give her. 130 acres of land, with two 50 acres
tract adjoining, also all stock, household furniture for her use. After
her decease the land to be sold and divided among my five sons to wit:
WILLIAM, CHARLES, HYMEN, HIRAM & JAMES RICHARDSON. I give to my three
dtrs: ISABELLA, ELIZABETH, MARY RICHARDSON each a feather bed and all
other property that my remain to be divided amonst my eight chn. I
appoint WILLIAM RICHARDSON, JACOB MICHAEL my executors. Wit: WILLIAM
HALL, Senr., jurat. WILLIAM HALL, Junr., jurat.
                        Signed: CHARLES RICHARDSON, SENR.

Page 16. 15 March 1822. Recorded, Dec. Court 1823. I, MARGARET CARRUTH,
        being of an advanced age & much inpared in body but of sound
mind & memory. I give unto my son, ALEXANDER CARRUTH, $100 to be paid
out of the money from the sale of my property. I give unto my dtr.,
MARY CARRUTH, one bed & furniture, one chest, small table, one mare, one
cow. I give unto, EPHRAIM CARRUTH, my grandson $100. Also to GEORGE
BARCLAY, ROBERT BARCLAY, MARGARET PACE my grandchildren $33 each. I
give to the chn. of ADAM CARRUTH, decd. $100 to be divided between them.
I give unto POLLY M. CARRUTH, ELIZA K. CARRUTH, KATHERINE ANN CARRUTH
dtrs. of JAMES CARRUTH, decd. $33 each. I give unto LEROY CARRUTH
grandson the colt of the mare given to MARY CARRUTH, also all plantation
tools of all kinds. The residue of my estate I allow to be put to sale
and the money from sale to be divided amongst my dtrs. ELIZABETH CARRUTH,
RUTH CUNNINGHAM, MARY CARRUTH, MELINDA SLOAN. I appoint my son, ALEX-
ANDER CARRUTH, executor. Wit: JOHN LEWIS, jurat. GEORGE WILLIAMS.
                        Signed: MARGARET X CARRUTH.

Page 18. 9 Feb. 1820. Recorded, Dec. Court 1823. I, HENRY JOHNSTON,

being weak in body but in perfect mind & memory. I give unto
my son, WILLIAM CAMP, the land he now lives on containing 140 acres,
lying on Second Broad River, also one cow & calf. I give unto my dtr.,
AMY KEETER, one bed. I give to my son, GEORGE JOHNSTON, the balance of
my land, 2 feather beds & furniture, all the balance of my stock of
cattle & my household & kitchen furniture. I appoint my son, GEORGE
JOHNSTON, & JOHN KEETER my executors. Wit: F. F. ALLEY, SUSAN ALLEY.
                        Signed: HENRY JOHNSTON.

Page 20. 10 Sept. 1823. Recorded, Jan. Court 1824. I, THOMAS HALL,
          being of sound mind & memory. I wish all my just debts to be
paid. It is my will that my brother, JOHN HALL, shall live, reside, in
the same manner, on the same premises, on the same conditions and be
provided for as long as he lives. I will that FERRABY COGAN who now
lives on my premises to remain on the same & be provided for as equal.
It is my will that my son, THOMAS COGAN, born of the body of FERRABY
COGAN. I do for the love & affection I have for him do make appoint &
order him my true & lawful heir, to have all the property that I may die
in possession of. It is my will that WILLIAM OWEN shall live where he
now lives until my son THOMAS COGAN come of age, no part of the property
to be sold. My negroes to shall remain all together on the same place
they now live. It is my will my son, THOMAS COGAN, shall have a good
English education. I appoint Gen. GEORGE WALTON & WILLIAM OWEN to be
my executors. They shall become the guardian of my son, THOMAS COGAN.
Wit: THOMAS HENSON, jurat., JOSEPH COLE, JOHN COLE, jurat.
                        Signed: THOMAS X HALL.

Page 22. 7 Aug. 1820. Recorded, May Court 1824. I, WILLIAM NEWTON,
          being of sound mind & memory. First I desire my just debts &
expenses be paid. I give unto my beloved wife, MARGARET, all her beds &
furniture, all household furniture, 2 cows during her widowhood. I give
unto my son, EBENEZER NEWTON, the sum of $1 & no more. I give unto my
2 sons, WILLIAM & JAMES NEWTON, all the land I now hold. I give to my
son, JAMES, one horse. I give unto my sons, WILLIAM & JAMES, my wagon
& gears, tools. All my clothing to be divided among my 3 sons JOHN,
WILLIAM & JAMES NEWTON. I allow all my books to be divided between my
dtr., MARTHA NEWTON, and all personal estate to be divided among my sons
JOHN, WILLIAM & JAMES. I appoint JAMES NEWTON & Capt. SAMUEL WILSON of
Lincoln Co., N.C. my executors. Wit: WILLIAM ELAM, jurat. DANIEL G.
CALLIS.   Signed: WILLIAM NEWTON.

Page 24. 20 May 1824. Recorded, Aug. Court 1824. I, LETITIA SCOTT,
          being of sound mind & memory. I give to my son, DUNLAP, a
negro child named Lewis about 4 mo. old, also one bed & furniture. To
my son, MOSES, I give negroes Daniel, Jason & Jack, also one bed & furniture. and a filly. I give to my dtr., LETITIA CARRUTH, one heifer. I
give to my dtr., POLLY, negroes, Letty, Vina & Elvira, one mare, cow &
calf & 2 beds & furniture. I give to my dtr., BETSEY, a negro boy named
Adolphus, one mare, a cow & her calf, 2 beds & furniture. My own bed &
furniture I give to my granddaughter, LETTY M'KINDRICK YOUNG, of GRIFFEN
YOUNG. To my dtr., POLLY & BETSEY, I give the balance of my household &
kitchen furniture, all stock, other personal property in the house. I
have given the above mentioned property by the last will of my late husband, JOHN SCOTT. I appoint my son MOSES & dtr. POLLY my executors.
Wit: JOHN MOORE, jurat. ZACHARIAH JOHNS, jurat.
                        Signed: LETITIA X SCOTT.

Page 25. 6 June 1824. Recorded, Aug. Court 1824. I, LARKIN LEE, being
          weak in body but of sound mind & memory. I desire all my law-
full debts to be paid. I give to my loving wife 200 acres of land, all
household furniture and personal property during her widowhood, if she
should marry I want SALLY NARCISSA LEE, dtr. of JOHN LEE, to have $10.
FELIX WALKER LEE, son of widow LEE, to have $10. I want EASTER BAXTER,
dtr. of WILLIAM BAXTER, $10. I want DARCAS MORELAND, dtr. of JOHN MORE-
LAND, to have $10. But if she should not marry I want her to keep the
whole herself. (No executors named.) Wit: JOHN STEIRN, MOSES SPLAWN,
jurat.   Signed: LARKEN LEE.

Page 26. 13 Jan. 1823. Recorded, Sept. Court 1824. I, JOHN D. NEAL,
          being of sound mind & memory. To my son, MOSES NEAL, I give

70

that part of land on which he now lives, and to his wife Should she
survive him I give unto her a tract of land containing 120 acres, joining lands of HASKEW FOSTER & DANIEL FOSTER'S line. To my grandson NEAL
WILLIAMS I give the other part of my land, containing 120 acres including my dwelling house. Joining lands of JAMES NEAL, HASKEW FOSTER &
DANIEL FOSTER. Reserving to my dtr., SARAH WILLIAMS, a supply from the
land devised to her son, during her life & her chn. that is now with her.
I desire that one acre of land to be laid out for a buring ground. I
give to my dtr., SARAH WILLIAMS, a chest, one feather bed & furniture.
The rest of my personal property to be sold by my executors and money
divided among JAMES NEAL, MOSES NEAL, SARAH WILLIAMS. I do not devise
any part of my present property to my son WILLIAM NEAL, except what I
have heretofore given to him. I appoint JOHN LEWIS executor. Wit:
JOSEPH CLOUD, jurat. BAYLIS W. LEWIS.
                                    Signed: JOHN D. X NEAL.

Page 28. 13 June 1824. Recorded, Oct. Court 1824. I, JOSEPH HAMILTON,
          being of sound & disposing mind & memory. First I give unto
my sister, LETTY MCGINNISS, wife of ROBERT MCGINNISS of Tennessee four
negroes to wit. Unity & her two children, and a girl named Suckey, now
in possession of said MCGINNESS, also $200. I give unto my sister,
FANNY MARTIN, the wife of RICHARD MARTIN a negro girl named Nancy now in
possession of said MARTIN. Also the sum of $600 to be put on interest
by my executors and the interest paid unto said FANNY annually during
her life time, and at her decease to be divided between her chn. I give
unto my beloved wife, NANCY, during her natural life my plantation on
Sandy Run where on I now live, also negroes, Nancy & her 3 sons, Ben,
George & Prince, Also Charlotte's dtr. to ABBY & Beckey's dtr. to SILVIY.
All household furniture, stock, Cotton gin, & sulkey and $1,000. At the
decease of my wife the aforsaid land & negroes to be divided between my
dtrs. MARY & SARAH. I give to my dtr. SARAH the house & lot in Rutherfordton & 100 acres of land which I purchased from ANDREW CROOKS, I give
to said dtr. the following negroes, Daniel, Robert, Rose & her 4 chn.
named Beck, Arthur, Luissa, Eliza, Jude, Moses, & wife and their chn.
named Rosannah, Little Mose, & George. Also all money due or may be
coming to me from the business of James M. Erwin & Company or the partnership now existing between us & three feather beds & furniture. I
give unto my dtr. MARY my plantation on Mountain Creek now under lease
to her, to her & her heirs. Also the following negroes named, Bubit,
Henry, Robert, Abbey, Ausin, Clarissa, and her child Adeline, William,
John, Big Silvey, Little Silvey, Levi, Harrison, also three beds & furniture. I Give unto my friend Dr. CHARLES SCHUFFELIN my thermometer.
I also leave all my wearing apparel & clothing to my brother AUDLEY
HAMILTON. I appoint my friend JOHN MCDOWELL, my brother AUDLEY & my
wife NANCY all of Rutherford County my executors. Wit: JOHN HORD, jurat.
EDMOND JONES, jurat.   Signed: JOSEPH HAMILTON.

Page 30. 17 June 1824. Recorded, Oct. Court 1824. I, WATSON COLLINGS,
          being much afflicted in body but of sound mind & understanding.
First my just debts & funeral expenses be paid. My real estate I give
to my wife, MARY COLLINGS, during her widowhood, except one feather bed
& furniture which to be the property of my dtr., SUSSANNA. At the death
of my wife, my sons HEZEKIAH & IRA to take the real estate & dtr.
SUSSANNA to have the personal property, if enough, if not the balance to
be made up by the other two legatees. I appoint my sons HEZEKIAH & IRA
COLLINGS my executors. Wit: ALEX. CORNETH, jurat. NATHAN X LANKFORD.
                                    Signed: WATSON COLLINGS.

Page 31. 14 July 1824. Recorded, Oct. Court 1824. I, LARKINS LOGAN,
          being in sound mind & memory but of weak body. I will all my
just debts be paid. I give to my wife, FANNY LOGAN, one bed & furniture.
I give to my dtr., SILLA LOGAN, bed & furniture, one loom & implements.
I will all the remaining property be sold & the amount thereof to be
divided among my chn. to wit: FREEMAN LOGAN, REASON LOGAN, SILLA LOGAN,
BRISON LOGAN, JIMMY LOGAN, SAMUEL LOGAN, & ROBERT LOGAN, to receive
their share as they come of age or marry. I will that my land be rented
yearly and every year unto my youngest child comes of age, then sold and
the money divided among children. I appoint EDWARD RIPPEY my executor.
Wit: JOSEPH LOGAN, jurat, THOS. LOGAN, jurat, WM. LOGAN.
                                    Signed: LARKIN X LOGAN, SR.

Page 32. 8 Aug. 1824. Recorded, Feb. Court 1825. I, ZACHARIAH WOOD,
being in a poor state of health but of perfect mind & memory.
My just debts (if any) to be paid. To my dtr., DOSHA FOWLER, I give
all the land above the road from the Flat Shoals on Green River, of which
she now has possession. To my son, JOEL WOOD, I give all my land above
Edmond Waldrop's which the said Waldrop signed me a deed of conveyance.
To my son, RANDOLPH WOOD, I give all land between EDMOND WALDROP and my
North line. To my dtr., SUSANAHA GUTHRIE, all the land below the land
I now live on and, and the fish trap to Wilkins's line. To, MIDDLETON
WOOD, my son I give land on North side of Green River, below the part
given to son RANDOLPH. To my sons NELSON WOOD & CARTER WOOD I give all
the balance of my estate real and personal. None of the land is to be
sold from my legatees, if any wish to sell, another willing to purchase.
"And knowing the exorbitant and perfidicous principles of my wife and
fearing she will to the injury to her children claim her lawful right as
a preventative means should she thus act I give the whole estate to the
State of Virginia." I appoint my son JOEL WOOD sole executor. Wishing
him to in every case to obtain the advise of my friends JOHN MOORE and
AMBROSE MILLS. (No witnesses). Signed: ZACHARIAH WOOD.
State of N.C., Rutherford County. Court of Probate, Feb. Term 1825.
"The above written paper purporting to be the last will & testament of
ZACHARIAH WOOD, decd. was presented in open Court for probate to which
there being no subscribing witnesses.. JOHN MOORE, mercht., JOHN MORRIS
& JAMES MORRIS being sworn deposed that they believed the body & signa-
ture of instrument to be of proper handwriting of the testator. Court
ordered it recorded & registered in full length." Witnesses: J. CRATOW,
Clk. By: THEO. F. BIRCHETT.

Page 35. 16 Feb. 1825. Recorded, April Court 1825. I, NATHAN HAMRICK,
being of sound, perfect mind & memory. I give to my wife,
DELILAH HAMRICK, the following negroes, Spencer, Hansick & Harry. Also
one fourth of the land and plantation whereon I now live. Stock, household & kitchen furniture (named) & all ready money during her natural
life. I give unto my son, NATHAN HAMRICK, the negro boy Ben. I give
unto my dtr., NANCY HAMRICK, Jin & Peter and their increase. I give to
my dtr., NARCISSA HAMRICK, negro Rhoda & her increase. I give unto my
son, DAVID HAMRICK, negroes Sarah & Tom. I give unto my son, WILLIAM
HAMRICK, negroes, Phill & Willis. I give to my son, LORENZO D. HAMRICK,
negroes Edvey & Bets and their increase. I give to my son, JEREMIAH
HAMRICK, negroes Europe & Winney and their increase. I give unto my
dtr., SARAH MAGNESS, a negro girl called Fatima and her increase, also 2
beds & furniture, and all other property I have hereinto given her. I
give unto my dtr., SELAH SUTTLE, all my tract of land on Mouse Creek, in
McMin County, Tenn. during her natural life, at her decease to be equally
divided amongst her heirs forever. I give unto NEVIL SUTTLE, HENRY
SUTTLE, & WILLIAM SUTTLE, my grandsons & sons of HENRY SUTTLE, a negro
girl named Irene & her increase, said negro is now in possession of
HENRY SUTTLE. I give unto my granddaughter, IRENE SUTTLE, a negro girl
to be bought at $200 by my executors & her increase to her forever. I
desire that my land be undivided until after my wife's death, then to be
divided amongst my four sons, NATHAN, DAVID, WILLIAM & LORENZO D. HAMRICK.
The rest of my estate not mentioned at the end of four years, balanced
& divided to make all equal. After my wife's death I give to NATHAN,
negro woman Hannah. To DAVID I give negro boy Harry, to NARCISSA negro
man Spencer. The personal property left to my wife to be divided amongst
my dtrs. I appoint my sons DAVID & WILLIAM HAMRICK my executors. Wit:
THEO. BIRCHETT, jurat, JOHN L. GLADDEN, A. C. IRWIN.
Signed: NATHAN X HAMRICK.

Page 37. 26 March 1825. Recorded, April Court 1825. I, SUSANNA MILLER,
widow of JOHN MILLER, decd. being by the will of my said husband left some property & have procured some in my own rights. It is my
will that my son-in-law, ROBERT MCAFEE, be content with what he has
received. I give unto JOHN TWITTY MILLER 90 acres of land secured by me
joining the old tract, also 2 cows & calves. I give to my son, DAVID
MILLER, 2 cows & calves, 2 horses. The remainder of my stock to be
equally divided between DAVID MILLER, JOHN TWITTY MILLER, SUSANNA LOURY,
& BETSEY CRATON. To my son DAVID, I give negroes Dave, Betley, Nancy,
& William. To POLLY MCAFEE, and her dtr. SUSANNAH MIRIA, I give to each
of them a bed & furniture. Dtrs. SUSANNA LOWRY & BETSEY CRATON each to

have a bed & furniture. I appoint my son-in-law ISAAC CRATON & THEODO-
RICK BIRCHETT my executors. N.B. I allow MILLER MCAFEE $20. Wit: T.
BRICHETT, jurat., D. DICKEY, jurat.   Signed: SUSANNA MILLER.

Page 39.   5 July 1823.   Recorded, July Court 1825.   I, WILLIAM HUMPHRIES,
        Senr., being in a very low state of health and under some
afflictions yet in sound mind & memory.   I appoint my two sons, SAMUEL
& DAVID HUMPHRIES, as my executors.   I wish my debts if any to be paid.
I will to my beloved wife, FRANCIS HUMPHRIES, to be possessed of my
dwelling house, plantation, all live stock, waggons, tools, household
& kitchen furniture during her natural life or widowhood.   I give to my
sons, ANDERSON & HENRY HUMPHRIES (at death) of my wife, all my land to
be divided between them by my executors.   I give my step daughter, NANCY
SERRATT, one feather bed & furniture, which she now claims.   I give to
my dtr., MARGARET, one feather bed & furniture which she now claims.   I
give unto LEASY SERRATT one bed & furniture which she now claims.   I
will at the death of my wife the remaining property shall be divided
between the following legatees, NANCY SERRATT, MARGARET, ANDERSON & HENRY
HUMPHRIES, LEASY SERRATT.   Wit: BENJAMIN ELLIS, BYARD X MCCRAW, JOHN
ALLISON.   Signed: WILLIAM X HUMPHRIES.

Page 40.   16 Feb. 1824.   Recorded, July Court 1825.   I, JOHN JONES,
        Senr., being in the use of my perfect senses.   I give to my
beloved wife, SARAH COLLY, one cow & calf & one 3 yrs. old heifer, one
sow & ten pigs, all household furniture & one negro man named Frank during her life time and at her death to be sold and the money divided
among all my chn.   I give to my son, CHARLES JONES, one still now in
possession of WILLIAM JONES also one cow.   To my dtr. USLEY QUEEN also
one mare.   I appoint my son, EDWARD JONES, my executor.   Wit: JOHN ROOKER.
                        Signed: JOHN X JONES.

Page 42.   9 July 1819.   Recorded, Sept. Court 1825.   I, JOHN REED, Junr.,
        being in common health but in perfect mind & memory.   First I
allow all my lawful debts to be paid.   I give unto my sons, JOHN &
ARCHIBALD REED, my plantation whereon I now live at the decease of my
negro man Ace.   I give to my dtrs., AGNESS FLESSION, MARTHA GUFFEY,
MARY GININS, ELIZABETH GUFFEY, LETTESSE COCKRAM & FANNY HOOD all my stock
of cattle not mentioned, divided equally and $8 in cash each.   I allow
FANNY HOOD my large looking glass.   I give to my dtr., JANE REED, my
horse, one bed & furniture and half of all household furniture.   I give
to my trusty servant, Ace, all my tract of land, my farming tools,
utensils, one horse, one cow & 2 heifers, my stock of hogs, one feather
bed & furniture, one large bed, rug, kitchen items, during his natural
life, at his death to be divided between my two sons JOHN & ARCHIBALD
REED.   I also allow servant, Ace, one half of my chairs & table.   I allow
my dtr., JANE, all my books.   I appoint my son-in-law, ROBERT COCHRAM &
JOHN CARSON, my executors.   Wit: JOHN CARSON, jurat, JOHN LONG, jurat.
                        Signed: JOHN X REED.

Page 44.   24 Sept. 1825.   Recorded, Oct. Court 1825.   I, JOSEPH BOWEN,
        I give to my beloved wife, MILLEY, all the land I received
from her, in fee simple.   I give to my wife the negro girl named Mary
which she had at our marriage, as her property forever.   I give to my
wife, MILLEY, & our two chn., MARY ANN & THOMAS, any increase the said
negro Mary may have, to be divided equally when the oldest child become
the age of 21 yrs.   I give to my wife all personal property & $300 and
interest from 1 May 1823.   I give my wife all my interest I possess in
the firm of Reinhardt & Bowen & Co.   I give to my brother-in-law, ROBERT
G. TWITTY, my planes, hand saw & iron square.   I appoint friend, ROBERT
G. TWITTY, my executor.   Wit: JACOB MICHAEL, jurat, OSSUER B. IRVINE.
                        Signed: JOS. BOWEN.

Page 45.   24 Dec. 1824.   Recorded, Oct. Court 1825.   I, JOSEPH EAKINS,
        Senr., being in a low state of health but sound mind & memory.
I give unto my loving wife, ISABELLA, my negro woman named Caty during
her life and at her death to my dtr., SALLY BIGGERSTAFF, also the plantation I now live on during her natural life, to be divided between my
sons JOHN, & GEORGE at her death, also all money on hand & due me for
her support with the household furniture & stock.   The tract of land
lying on Buffalo Branch containing 200 acres to be sold and $50 to be

paid to each of SAMUEL BIGGERSTAFF sons: BENJAMIN & JOSEPH. The balance
of my est. to be sold and divided amongst my lawfull heirs, SALLY BIGGER-
STAFF, ISABELLA WILKISON, THOMAS EAKINS, SAMUEL EAKINS, GEORGE EAKINS,
& JOHN EAKINS. I appoint SAMUEL BIGGERSTAFF & JAMES MCGAHEY my executors.
Wit: R. K. WILSON, jurat., JOSEPH CARPENTER.
                                   Signed: JOSEPH X EAKINS.

Page 47. 12 Sept. 1822. Recorded, Jan. Court 1826. I, GABRIEL WASHBURN,
          being of sound & perfect mind & memory. I give unto my dtr.,
MARY DAVIS $5. I give to my dtr., ELIZABETH MORRIS $5. I give THOMAS
MARTIN Junr., and the four children by my dtr. RHODA, his wife, who is
since dead $5. I give to my dtr. MARTHA HARRELL $5. I give to my son
JOSIAH WASHBURN, one saddle & bridle, 2 cows & calves, one feather bed
& furniture. I give to my wife, PRISCILLA WASHBURN, all my estate both
real & personal during her life or widowhood. She may swap or convey
any part of my estate except the lands & two negroes girls, Polly &
Rachell. At the death of my wife I give to my son ABRAHAM WASHBURN 300
acres of land above Dill's branch, joining lands of MARTIN ELLIOTT,
RICHARD COVINGTON, & CHARLES DURHAM, also the negro named Polly. After
the death of my wife I give the balance of my real estate to my son,
JONAH, also the negro girl Rachel all farming tools. After the death of
my wife, I give my personal estate to my following chn. JOHN WASHBURN,
THOMAS WASHBURN, SARAH LAWS, REUBIN WASHBURN, MARGARET LAWS, GABRIEL
WASHBURN, LURANY MCSWAIN, SUSANNAH HARRELL, ABRAHAM WASHBURN, JOSIAH
WASHBURN to be divided among them. I appoint my wife, PRISCILLA, my
sons ABRAHAM & JOSIAH WASHBURN my executors. Wit: ACHILLES DURHAM, Junr.
Jurat., FARMER MOORE, jurat., JOHN MOORE.
                                   Signed: GABRIEL WASHBURN.

Page 49. 28 Dec. 1825. Recorded, Feb. Court 1826. I, NATHAN LANKFORD,
          being sick & afflicted in body but of sound mind & memory. It
is my will that my just debts be paid from my personal estate. I give
to my wife, MERON LANKFORD, the use of all my estate both real & personal
during her natural life or widowhood except two heifers I give to my
dtr., MERON, for herself & her chn. If any should marry or leave, she
is to furnish them with a bed & furniture. Should my wife die or marry,
I give the tract on Skywicker below the mill to my son, JOHN LANKFORD.
The tract on Long Branch known as the Buice place I give to my son,
CURTIS LANKFORD. The tract that I live on I give unto, ROBERT L. LANK-
FORD, under the direction & guardianship of his brother, JOHN LANKFORD.
If my negres should increase, I allow the first to my dtr., ELIZABETH
and the second to my dtr., MERON. The residue of my estate I allow my
executor to sell and divide into shares. I allow my dtr., ELIZABETH,
one share, if she should not receive said negro, I allow her $50 more.
I allow my son, JOHN, one share. My dtr., MARY HOBBS, one share. I
allow my dtr., SARAH LOGAN, & dtr., SEBBY CARRUTH, one share each. The
chn. of my dtr., RHODDA BRADEN, one share. My dtr., MERON, one share,
if the negro should fail to increase, she to have $50 more. My dtr.,
MARTHA HOBBS, one share. My son, MINOR L. LANKFORD, one share. My son,
CURTIS C. LANKFORD, one half a share & my son, ROBERT L. LANKFORD, one
half a share under the guardianship of his brother, JOHN LANKFORD. I
appoint my wife, MERON, Executrix & my son, JOHN LANKFORD, executor.
Wit: ALEX CARRUTH, jurat., EZEKL. GRAHAM.
                                   Signed: NATHAN X LANKFORD.

Page 51. 12 Sept. 1815. Recorded, March Court 1826. I, JAMES WESSON,
          will to wife, NANCY, the land whereon I now live, all stock,
horses, cattle, & hogs and household furniture during her life time or
widowhood. At her death the furniture & stock to be divided amongst
HENRY, CLARYMON, WILLIAM, LUKE, REBECCA PEARSON, and EDWARD CLANTON and
the land to be divided equally between the boys HENRY, WILLIAM, LUKE,
& EDWARD CLANTON the home place. I leave my dtr. PATSEY $30. I leave
my dtr. NANCY $30. That tract of land on Ganay's Branch of 200 acres,
I leave to be sold, one half of the money be left in the executors hands
to buy land for the boys, the other half to be equally divided between
my two dtrs., CLARYMON & REBECCA PEARSON. I allow REBECCA, WILLIAM &
LUKE one year schooling each and EDWARD CLANTON to be paid out of the
estate. I appoint my wife NANCY WESSON & HENRY WESSON my executors.
Wit: JESSE X MARSHALL, JAMES X DOLLAR, WILLIS PUTMAN, jurat., RICHARD X
MARSHALL.   Signed: JAMES X WESSON.

Page 52. 2 Feb. 1826. Recorded, March Court 1826. I, JOHN WALKER,
being sick & very low in body, but of sound & perfect mind.
I give to my beloved JEREMIAH WALKER all my land & perishable property,
my household goods, working tools, to care & maintain me and my wife
ANNE as long as we both live. To pay all my just debts. I appoint my
son, JEREMIAH WALKER, my executor. Wit: DAVID MOONEY, jurat., JONATHAN
X MOONEY, jurat., JOHN WALKER. Signed: JOHN X WALKER.

Page 53. 17 March 1823. Recorded, April Court 1826. I, HENSON QUEEN,
of Burke Co., N.C. being weak in body but of perfect mind &
memory. I give to my wife, SARAH QUEEN, two negroes named Dick & Landon,
all my working tools & farming tools, household furniture during her life
time, at her death the negroes I will to my son, JOHN QUEEN. I will to
my dtr., SARAH QUEEN, my negro woman named Seal. I will to my dtr.,
RUTH UPTON, $50. I will to my dtr., JANE JOHNSTON, $50. I will to my
dtr., CATY HICKS, $50. I will to my dtr., SELEY CASTER, $50. I will
to my son, WILLIAM, $50. I will to my son, JOHN QUEEN, all my household
furniture & farming tools, I further appoint JOHN QUEEN my executor.
Wit: D. GLASS, jurat., F. P. GLASS, jurat.
Signed: HENSON X QUEEN.

Page 54. 5 March 1825. Recorded, June Court 1826. I, ROBERT CHERRY,
Being of sound mind & memory. I give unto my wife the planta-
tion, the farming tools, household & kitchen furniture, cattle during
her life time, also two negroes, Millia & Fanny. I give unto my son,
JAMES CHERRY, at his mother's death the plantation where I now live, of
100 acres, the whole of the personal property, three negroes named Candas,
Moses & Tinah. At his mother's death JAMES to pay unto my dtr., MARY
WALLACE, 2 cows & calves, one horse. I give unto my grandchildren,
ETTULINDA, ROBERT ADOLPHUS & WILLIAM ALVIN WALLACE, 100 acres of land
adjoining the lands of Kester & Johnson. I also give unto my above
named grandchn. one negro girl named Chloe. I appoint my son JAMES
CHERRY & my friend JOHN GILKEY my executors. Wit: J. GILKEY, jurat.,
BENJAMIN LOGAN. Signed: ROBERT CHERRY.

Page 57. 20 May 1826. Recorded, Sept. Court 1826. I, JECHONIAS WALD-
ROP, Senr., being weak in body but of sound mind & memory.
First I will all my just debts to be paid. I give unto my beloved wife,
MARGARET WALDROP, the house & plantation where I now live, Containing
300 acres, including the land where JECHONIAS WALDROP, Junr., now lives.
I give unto my wife her support by the childrens' labor & behavior and
at her death to be divided amongst the four, RICHARD, MARY, MARY ANN &
REBECCA WALDROP. I give unto my 2 sons, LUKE & JECHONIAS WALDROP, 250
acres of land, they paying a third value of said land unto my decd. son,
JOSEPH WALDROP heirs, viz: ROBERT & ZACHARIAH WALDROP. I give to my
dtr., MARGARET PETER.,? & $5 to the heirs of my son, JOHN WALDROP. Sons,
LUKE & JECHONIAS, to have 2 yrs. to pay other legatees. ALFRED HESTER,
if he stays with the old lady to have a horse & saddle worth $40. What
remains to be sold at my wife's death, and money divided between son
JOSEPH, ROBERT, & JECHONIAS and MARGARET PETER. I appoint my sons LUKE
& JECHONIAS WALDROP my executors. Wit: TERRELL WILKINS, jurat., JOHN
WILKINS. Signed: JECHONIAS WALDROP.

Page 58. 17 July 1826. Recorded, Sept. Court 1826. I, JOHN JONES,
being sick and weak in body but of perfect mind & memory. I
give to my wife, SARAH JONES, 100 acres of land, also all stock, tools,
& household furniture to dispose as she think proper. I give my dtr.,
MARY PATTON, 10 shillings at the decease of her mother. I give to my
son, THOMAS JONES, 28 acres of land of the old tract. I give to my son,
DAVID JONES, I give the 100 acres that I lent to my wife until her death.
To my dtr., JANE BALDRIDGE, I forgive the interest of a note of $100
that I hold of hers. I give to my dtr., NANNY JONES, that 15 acres where
DAVID lives, & 30 acres joining known as the Edwards survey & 27 acres
of the old survey. I give unto JOHN P. JONES 10 shillings at his mother's
death. I give to my dtr., SARAH JONES, 72½ acres of land of the old
survey, joining DAVID & NANNY below & ELIZABETH above. I give to my
dtr., ELIZABETH JONES, 72½ acres of the old survey, joining THOMAS &
SARAH. I give to my dtr., FRANCES ELENDER CURRY, $30 at the death of
her mother. I appoint THOMAS JONES & DAVID JONES my executors. Wit:
WILLIAM ADAIR, jurat. THOMAS MARLOW, jurat. Signed: JOHN JONES.

75

Page 61.   28 April 1824. Recorded, Oct. Court 1826. I, JOHN SCHROEBEL,
being in a low state of health but of sound mind. I request
any debts if any to be paid. I give to my beloved wife, SALLY SCHOEBEL,
all my real & personal estate, during her widowhood, should my wife die
my widow, then our children to divide & each receive an equal share, at
present we have but one son whose name is THOMAS. I allow not any
children born of a marriage after my death or any children I had by a
former marriage. I appoint ABSOLOM WARLICK, JERRALL CROWDER, JERRY
BLANTON my executors. Wit: AMOS WALL, JOSEPH GREEN, SAMUEL MELTON,
jurat.   Signed: JOHN SCHROEBEL.

Page 62.   15 Oct. 1826. Recorded, Jan. Court 1827. I, MARY ANN YORK,
being in an ill state of health but of sound & perfect mind.
I give to my son, JOHN YORK, one feather bed & 2 sheets. I give unto my
son, WILLIAM YORK, .75¢ for himself & his heirs forever. I give unto my
son, ABNER YORK, for himself & his heirs forever. I give unto my dtr.,
SALLY YORK, 200 acres of land on the waters of Crooked Run, which was
patented by CHRISTOPHER WALBERT, also the mare & the colt to be SALLY'S
son LEVI, also cow & 9 hogs, farming tools, household & kitchen furniture. I give to my dtr., NANCY YORK., .75¢ for herself & her heirs forever. I give to my dtr., DICEY DILE, .75¢ for herself & her heirs forever. I give my dtr., MARY ANN DILE, .75¢ for herself & her heirs forever. I allow that SALLY pay all debts & bequeaths, also I make my dtr.,
SALLY YORK, my executor. Wit: SAMUEL GIDNEY, ROBERT WELLS, jurat.
                          Signed: MARY ANN X YORK.

Page 64.   18 March 1823. Recorded, Jan. Court 1827. I, BENJAMIN HYDER,
being stricken in years but of sound mind. I will that my
just debts & funeral expenses to be paid. I give to my beloved wife,
CATHERINE, my plantation on which we live, with all negroes, stock,
tolls, & furniture during her natural life. She to have negro Jack &
to despose of as she pleases. To my son, BENJAMIN HYDER, give all lands
I possess on the waters of Mountain Creek, after the decease of myself
& wife. The lot holding in the town of Rutherfordton, & my smith tools,
son, JOHN, to have liberty to use the said tools, also waggon & gear, &
negro Luke, to my grandson, ADAM LEWIS HYDER, I give the negro Squire.
To my deaf & dumb son, JOHN HYDER, I give the negroes Sylvia, & Virgin.
As to the chn. of CATY MCMURTRY, I allow the negro Hercules to be sold &
divided amongst the said chn. I will that all the personal property we
leave at death to be laid off in five lots, one lot to MARY LOGAN, chn.
JULIUS, NANCY, & CATY, chn. (not named) one lot to NANCY BAGWELL, chn.
(not named). I appoint my wife, CATHERINE, & son BENJAMIN HYDER &
friend DAVID DICKEY my executors. And my friends JONATHAN HAMPTON, JOHN
BRADLEY, & JOSHUA TAYLOR, trustees. Wit: ELIAS MCFADDIN, D. DICKEY,
jurat.   Signed: BENJAMIN HYDER.

Page 66.   4 Dec. 1826. Recorded, Jan. Court 1827. I, JAMES MOORE, being
of sound & perfect mind and memory. All my just debts to be
paid. I wish all my estate to be divided into 2 lots, with my wife
NANCY to have choice of the lots to her own benfit, the other lot I wish
to be sold and then divided equally between the heirs of JOSEPH MOORE,
my brother, and the heirs of my two sisters ELIZABETH WILSON & MARY
BRADLEY. I appoint my friend GEORGE WALTON & JACOB MECHAEL my executors.
Wit: H. HARRIS, ISAAC LEDBETTER.   Signed: JAMES X MOORE.

Page 67.   10 Nov. 1826. Recorded, Jan. Court 1827. I, JOHN MORRISON,
being weak of body yet of perfect mind & memory. First I wish
all my just debts to be paid. I give unto FRANCES WILLIAMS & JAMES
MORRISON the land and property they have received whereon they now live.
I give unto my sons, JOHN & ROBERT MORRISON, the plantation on First
Broad River called the Hoge place to be equally divided between them,
also to JOHN 3 head cattle, and to ROBERT the horse & saddle he now
claims, 2 head cattle, to each one bed & furniture. I give the plantation I now live on to my beloved wife, during her natural life, then to
be divided amongst my 3 sons THOMAS, ANDREW & JOSEPH MORRISON. To THO-
MAS the horse & saddle he now claims, two head cattle, one bed & furniture. To ANDREW & JOSEPH each two horses & one saddle, each two head
cattle & bed Furniture. I give unto my dtr., CATY MORRISON, one horse
& saddle, two head of cattle, two beds & furniture & $200 in money. I
give to my dtr., MARY MORRISON, one horse & saddle, two head of cattle,

76

two beds & furniture, also $200 in money. I give to my dtr., BETSY
MORRISON, one horse & saddle, two head of cattle, two beds & furniture
and $200 in money. I allow my still and three negroes named Loose,
Phillis & Abe to be sold and the money to be used in settling the claims
against the estate. I give unto my wife a negro girl named Sel, the
balance of the estate not named to be her property until death then
equally divided amongst the above named children. I appoint FRANCIS &
JOHN MORRISON my executors. Wit: HUGH WATSON, SAMUEL SPRATT, jurat.
Signed: JOHN MORRISON.

Page 69. 5 Aug. 1826. Recorded, Jan. Court 1827. I, JESSE EVANS, being
          very weak & frail in body but in my perfect senses. I give to
my three dtrs. that is still with me, FRANKY, LUCINDA and my youngest
that we call the baby., when they need to go to themselves, each to have
the value of $50 In such property as will suit them. The rest of my
property both real & personal I leave to my wife UNICE during her natural
life or widowhood. After that I give what land I possess unto THOMPSON,
JEFFERSON & JESSE. What remains to be divided amongst all my chn. BETSY,
FRANKY, LEWIS, SALLY, POLLY, DAVID, ANNA, THOMPSON, LUCINDA, JEFFERSON,
JESSE, and the youngest we call the baby. I give unto my wife EUNICE
one negro girl of her choice & for her disposal. I appoint JAMES LONG
& DAVID EVANS. Wit: JAMES YOUNG (see min. docket P 120 for probate).
Signed: JESSE EVANS.

Page 71. 3 April 1827. Recorded, May Court 1827. I, WILLIAM GROVES,
          being weak in body but of perfect mind & memory. I will my
just debts to be paid. I give to beloved wife, NANCY GROVES, the land
where I now live with the house & furniture for the raising & support of
the family., with one mare, colt & one horse with the cattle & hogs
during her widowhood. I give unto my son, JESSE GROVES, the land where
he now lives, containing 145 acres and the property he has received. I
give unto my dtr., JENNY, the property she has received and a mare. I
give unto my son, WILLIAM GROVES, one mare that he now owns with a saddle
& bridle, five head of cattle & 11 head of hogs. I give to my dtr.,
ELIZABETH GROVES, one horse saddle & bridle, one bed & furniture, one
wheel, one cards & one cow & calf. I give to my son, GEORGE W. GROVES,
one horse saddle & bridle, one cow & calf, one sow & pigs. I give to my
son, JAMES A. GROVES, one horse saddle & bridle, one cow & calf, one sow
& pigs. I give to my son, ANDREW GROVES, one horse saddle & bridle,
one bed & furniture, one cow & calf, one wheel & cards. I give unto my
son, NELSON W. GROVES, one horse saddle & bridle, one cow & calf, one
sow & pigs. I allow at the death of my wife all the land to be equally
divided among my five sons WILLIAM, GEORGE, JAMES, ANDREW, NELSON GROVES.
I allow cotton machine, one waggon, one still, set of smith tools, one
horse to be sold, and the money divided amongst my five youngest sons.
I appoint my wife NANCY & son JESSE GROVES my executors. Wit: HUGH
WATSON, Junr., jurat. WILLIAM H. GROVES.
Signed: WILLIAM GROVES.

Page 73. 27 June 1827. Recorded, July Court 1827. I, AARON MCENTIRE,
          being of advanced age but of sound mind & memory. I will all
my just debts to be paid from my personal estate. I lend to my wife,
ELLENDER, the whole of my estate during her life or widowhood. At her
death or marriage my estate to be divided equally. I give unto my dtr.,
SUSANNAH MCKINNEY, $200 worth property, which JAMES MCKINNEY has received
from me and must be put in their share of my estate. Likewise I give
unto my son, WILLIAM MCENTIRE, $110 worth of property. Likewise I give
unto my son, THOMAS MCENTIRE, $185 worth of property. Likewise I give
unto my son, JOSIAH MCENTIRE, $200 worth of property. Likewise I give
unto JACOB WOLF $200 as being married to my dtr., NANCY. The children
that now live with me, when of age or marry to have $200 worth of pro-
perty. I appoint WILLIAM COVINGTON & BIRD MCENTIRE my executors. Wit:
LEWIS CAMP, jurat., JOHN MCENTIRE. (No exor. sworn nor copy made out
T.B.)   Signed: AARON X MCENTIRE.

Page 76. 26 July 1827. Recorded, Oct. Court 1827. I, STETH MAYS,
          being of a sound & perfect mind & memory. First all my just
debts to be paid. I give unto my beloved wife, SISSLY MAYS, all my real
& personal estate during her natural life or widowhood. At her death or
at marriage all my property to be divided amongst all my children,

77

BOSEMAN MAYS, DOLLY BLANTON, STETH MAYS, JOHN MAYS, STEPHEN MAYS,
SUSANNAH ROACH, SALLY MAYS, NANCY THOMPSON MAYS, JAMES FLETCHER MAYS,
PATSEY MAYS. Wife to have support during her life time. I appoint my
son STEPHEN MAYS & WRYLEY BLANTON my executors. Wit: JOHN WALL, Jurat,
JEREMIAH BLANTON, jurat, JOHN M. HALL, jurat.
                         Signed: STETH MAYS.

Page 77. 12 May 1827. Recorded, Oct. Court 1827. I, TEMPIA CHAMPION,
          being weak in body and sick. I give the interest I have in
the real estate of my father, I allow to my three nephews, JOHN BLALOCK,
ABRAHAM CHAMPION & DAVID BLALOCK on their taking care of my mother while
she lives. The personal property I have after my just debts are paid.
I allow NELLY WOOD one cow & calf, one calico dress, my wearing apparel.
To my sister BETSY HEFLIN, my saddle. I allow to TEMPIA CHAMPION, my
bed & furniture I allow to be equally divided between POLLY HEFLIN,
TEMPY CHAMPION, SARAH CHAMPION, POLLY CHAMPION. I appoint ABRAM CHAMP-
ION & JOHN BLALOCK my executors. Wit: D. DICKEY, jurat., DAN EDWARDS,
jurat.   Signed: TEMPIA X CHAMPION.

Page 78. 14 Aug. 1827. Recorded, Oct. Court 1827. I, JOSEPH GOODE,
          after my just debts are paid, I give unto my loving wife,
PATSEY, all my estate real & personal during her natural life or widowhood, except one mare colt which JONATHAN LIVERTEE is to have if he lives
with us & behaves himself until he is 21 yrs. old. Estate to be sold
on 12 months credit and money divided among my heirs at the death or
marriage of my wife. I appoint MICHAEL HUDLOW & wife PATSEY GOODE executors. Wit: R. K. WILSON, jurat, HARBERT HORTON.
                         Signed: JOSEPH GOODE.

Page 79. (No date). Recorded, Oct. Court 1827. He wishes to get back
          the land from his brother if he will consent to sell it, his
executor to sell other property to buy the land. He leaves the residue
of his property to his wife after paying his debts. At her death the
property to be divided between the children. He appointed his wife &
JAMES BLACKWELL his executors..N.B. "After making the above memorandum
I read it to G. YOUNG, he approved of it. He obsereved that more than
what property he had left, came to him by his wife and that she was best
entitled to it for her life. He appeared to be of sound mind." (for
probate of this writing see minutes docket of this term page 192). No
witness or signature. (nuncupative will of GRIFFIN YOUNG.)

Page 80. 17 Oct. 1827. Recorded, Nov. Court 1827. JACOB MOONEY, to
          my wife, SUSY MOONEY, I give negroes, Lige & girl named Loose,
the plantation where I now live & the other tract, all household furniture. The Neel's tract & the Beaty tract to my son, PETER MOONEY. To
my dtr., BETSEY, a negro boy named Sam, to my dtr., BECKEY, the negro
boy named Tom. To my dtr., SUZA, $150. To my dtr., SALLY, $150. To
my dtrs., PEGGY & MARY MOONEY $150 each. The balance of my property to
be sold and divided equally with my wife SUZA. Wife SUZA & JACOB CAR-
PENTER my executors. Wit: JNO. LUCAS, PETER SPANGLER. (last name in
German.)   Signed: JACOB MOONEY.

Page 81. 3 Feb. 1827. Recorded, Feb. Court 1828. I, BENJAMIN MAGNESS,
          being under the decay of nature but of sound mind & memory.
After my just debts are paid, my will is that my beloved wife, NANCY
MAGNESS, be possessed with the whole estate both real & personal during
her natural life or widowhood, except what is hereafter named. I give
to my son, JOSEPH MAGNESS, 150 acres of land, on Brushy Creek, one negro
named James, one horse, saddle & bridle, he to receive the property when
he comes of age twenty-one years old. I give unto my dtr., SALLY MAG-
NESS, 100 acres of land lying on Sandy Run, known as the saw mill tract,
one negro girl worth $200 to be received when she come of the age of 18
yrs., one horse, saddle & bridle, one bed & furniture. SALLY not to
receive the full possession of her land until the death of her mother.
I give unto my son, SAMUEL MAGNESS, one negro boy called Adam, one horse
worth $75, saddle & bridle. I give unto my son, ROBERT MAGNESS, one
negro boy called Albert, one saddle & bridle, I also give unto my sons,
ROBERT & SAMUEL MAGNESS, the tract of land where I now reside, containing 274 acres, to be divided between them, they are not to possess said
land until the death or marriage of my wife. At my wife's death, I will

my personal estate to be divided amongst my chn. PERRYGREEN, JACOB, JAMES, BENJAMIN, WILLIAM MANGESS, MARY WASHBURN, CATHERINE REYNOLDS, JOSEPH, SALLY, SAMUEL & ROBERT MAGNESS. My tract of land in Lincoln County, lying on both sides of Buffalo Creek to be equally divided amongst all my chn. I appoint my son JOSEPH MANGESS, ELIJAH WALKER my executor. Wit: DANIEL GOLD, HOUSEN HARRELL, jurat.
Signed: BENJAMIN MAGNESS.
CODICIL: And further more to my last will & testament, I give to my sons: JOSEPH, SAMUEL, & ROBERT MAGNESS two cows & calves each when they arrive at full age and to my dtr., SALLY MAGNESS, three cows & calves when she arrives at 18 yrs. or marry. This 3 Feb. 1827. Wit: DANIEL GOLD, HOUSEN HARRELL.   Signed: BENJ. MAGNESS.

Page 84. 15 Oct. 1827. Recorded, Feb. Court 1828. I, JOHN ALLEN, being sick & weak in body but of perfect mind & memory. I give to my beloved wife, MARY, all my stock & household furniture, MARY ALLEN to have possession of my lands during her life time, then my land to be sold & divided among sons, dtrs., MARY BRADLEY, JOHN, WILLIAM, LEMUEL, WILLIS ALLEN, NANCY MORRIS, CARTER ALLEN. Be it understood that his son JAMES ALLEN is not an heir in this will, his father willing him a tract of land of 80 acres, joining PETER KOONE. I also give to my dtr., SALLY MAYFIELD, 20 shillings, and MARY BRYSON is to become an equal heir in my estate. I appoint son WILLIAM & JAMES ALLEN my executors. Wit: JOHN WHITAKER, jurat., WADE BATES, jurat.
Signed: JOHN X ALLEN.

Page 86. 14 April 1827. Recorded, March Court 1828. I, ELIJAH PATTON, Senr. being in a low state of health, yet in my proper mind & memory. First I desire all my just debts paid. I will to HUGH PATTON, Junr., 5 shillings. I will my two grandsons, PATRICK A. WATSON & ELIJAH P. WATSON, my negro girl Miry, also two notes one on JOSEPH CARSON of $200 another on JOHN REED of $200. I will to my son ELIJAH PATTON the tract of land I now live on lying on Cane Creek. My wife, MARGARET PATTON, I will her support, use of the house, negro man named Harry & woman named Sally & household furniture (items named) I will to my dtr., CHARITY H. MORRIS, negro named Esther & negro boy named Daniel. I will to my dtr., PEGGY MORRIS, a negro man Jesse & a negro woman named Jude & my negro boy named Ellison. I will to my dtr., RACHEL MORRISON, my negro boy Isaac & boy Hial. I appoint my son, ELIJAH PATTON, my executor. Wit: WILLIAM J. LONG, jurat., THOMAS S. LONG, jurat.
Signed: ELIJAH PATTON.
(Written in margin: ELIJAH PATTON born 31 Aug. 1766. M.6-6-<u>1799</u>, written by son of grand son.)

Page 88. 4 June 1825. Recorded, March Court 1828. I, WILLIAM SMART, being weak in body but of sound mind & memory. I give unto my wife, JEAN, all the household furniture & money she now possesses. I give unto my dtr., ELIZABETH REED, $100 that I lent to JOHN REED, the said note to be given up at my death. Another note of $17, & one for $10 due by order from GEORGE MITCHELL to old WM. SMART. I give to my dtr., JEAN LONG, 100 acres of land as the last of her share, a deed made to WILLIAM LONG her husband for said land. I give to my dtr., MARGARET BLACK, a tract lying on Reed's branch, joining lands of SARAH REED, JOHN REED, Cockran line, I allow 30 acres out of said tract unto HUGH BLACK for a filly he let ISABELLA have and the balance to MARGARET, I also allow said MARGARET $5 in cash. I give to my dtr., ISABELLA GOFORTH, one tract of land lying on Reed's branch, begining at Carson's corner up branch to SARAH REED'S line then to WILLIAM ALLEN'S line & Baldridge's line. I give to my son, THOMAS, two tract of land containing 75 acres, one cow & calf, & smith tools. A judgment on JOHN P. JONES near $20 & a note on DRURY LOGAN of $5 if recovered to my wife JEAN. I give my two guns to my grand son, JOHN BALDRIDGE SMART. I appoint my two sons-in-law JOHN REED & WILLIAM LONG my executors. Wit: JAMES HUDDLESTON, jurat. THOMAS SMART, jurat, RESTON GOFORTH.
Signed: W. SMART.

Page 90. 6 June 1827. Recorded, May Court 1828. I, WILLIAM BALDRIDGE, being sound in mind but frail in body. First I allow my just debts to be paid. I give unto my beloved wife, MARY, all my household goods during her natural life, if any remain at her decease it to be

79

sold and equally divided amongst my grandchildren. Likewise the real &
personal property to be sold for wife's support, if any left to be divided amongst the g. chn. viz: WILLIAM, POLLY, JAMES & JINCEY BALDRIDGE.
I appoint JOHN GILKEY & GEORGE FLACK my executors. Wit: JOHN FLACK,
ANDREW FLACK, jurat.   Signed: WILLIAM X BALDRIDGE.

Page 91. 16 Sept. 1817. Recorded, May Court 1828. I, JOSHUA MELTON,
          being of sound mind & memory. First after my just debts are
paid I give unto my beloved wife, SARAH, the tract of land whereon I
now live & all my personal property during her natural life or widowhood.
In case of marriage, she is to have only a child's part. At her death
all the property to be divided amongst the heirs. I appoint my wife,
SARAH, executrix. Wit: WILLIAM X DAVIS, HENRY NORVILL, ALFRED MELTON,
jurat.   Signed: JOSHUA MELTON.

Page 92. 28 Jan. 1828. Recorded, May Court 1828. I, MARY BORDIN, being
          of sound mind & memory. I give to my dtr., ROSANNAH SWEEZY,
$50 to be raised from a note due me from JESSE LEDFORD in the sum of
$100 also one bed & furniture, two cows & calves two thirds of my stock
of hogs, I give to my dtr., NANCY BELL, one big oven, one third of the
balance of JESSE LEDFORD'S note, one third of my cattle, one nineth of
my hogs. I give to my dtr., SARAH HARRIS, one small oven, one wheel,
one third of balance of JESSE LEDFORD note, one third of cattle, one
ninth of my hogs. I give unto my dtr., POLLY MURRAY, my walnut chest,
one third of the balance of JESSE LEDFORD note, one third of my cattle,
one ninth of my hogs. I give unto my grandson, JAMES W. MURRAY, my
looking glass, & one small heifer. I give unto my grand son, ELIJAH M.
SWEEZY, one small heifer. I appoint my friends, SOLOMON A. ROSS & JOHN
SWEEZY, my executors. Wit: S. A. ROSS, jurat. SARAH X ROSS.
                         Signed: MARY BORDIN.

Page 94. 15 July 1828. Recorded, Aug. Court 1828. I, JACOB WILLIS,
          being advanced in years and in ill health but of sound & per-
fect mind & memory. I give unto my beloved wife, LYDIA, all my land
belonging to it, all farming tools, household & kitchen furniture, all
cattle, three head horses, all hogs during her life time in widowhood,
should she marry the land to be divided among the chn. I give to my
dtr., SARAH WILLIS, one feather bed & furniture. I give unto my son,
WM. WILLIS, one scythe cradle and one axe. I give unto my son, JAMES B.
WILLIS one scythe cradle & one axe. I give unto my son, JOHNSTON WILLIS,
75¢. I give unto my dtr., AGNESS WILLIS, one feather bed & furniture.
I give unto my dtr., ANN WILLIS, 75¢. I give unto my son, JOHN WILLIS,
75¢. I give unto my dtr., POLLY WILLIS, 75¢. I give unto my son,
JACOB CRAVEN WILLIS, 75¢. I give unto my dtr., RACHEL WILLIS, 75¢. I
give unto my son, RICHARDSON WILLIS, 75¢. I give unto my son, JOSEPH
GALLISHAW WILLIS, 75¢. I appoint my wife, LYDIA, & son, JAMES BLACK
WILLIS my executor. Wit: SAMUEL S. GIDNEY, jurat. JOSEPH THOMAS, jurat.
                         Signed: JACOB WILLIS.

Page 96. 7 June 1828. Recorded, Sept. Court 1828. I, RACHAEL GRAYSON,
          being weak in body but of perfect mind & memory. First all
debts to be paid. I give unto JANE CROW, all my body clothing except
two silk handkerchiefs, one loom, all the delph ware that's on my
dresser with one saddle, she has in her possession. I give unto RACHEL
CROW dtr. of JANE CROW one new side saddle, with my largest bake pan &
one scarlet cloak. I give unto ELIZABETH CROW one little wheel & my
best oven. I give unto LETTIS CROW one big wheel, one new 4 gallon pot,
with one check reel. I give unto ELIZABETH LETTIS CROW dtrs. of JANE
CROW one feather bed & under bed with stead & cord & furniture to be
divided between them. I give unto ISAAC, JAMES, and ABRAHAM CROW sons
of JANE CROW $5 each, money to be put on interest until they are of age.
I give unto GREEN CROW one $25.50 note to be delivered to him by my ex-
ecutors. I give unto LEWIS VANZANT all the remainder of my household
furniture & stock, with one still, farming tools & one log chain. I
allow my executors to collect one $9 note from GREEN CROW & put it on
interest for the sons of JANE CROW until they are of age. I appoint
LEWIS VANZANT and JOSEPH GRAYSON my executors. Wit: HUGH WATSON, jurat.
WM. GRAYSON, jurat.   Signed: RACHEL GRAYSON.

Page 98. 17 Sept. 1828. Recorded, Oct. Court 1828. I, WILLIAM MCCURRY,

being very weak and low in body but of perfect mind & memory.
I give unto, ELIZABETH MCCURRY, my beloved wife after my just debts are
paid. I give unto my wife all my household & kitchen furniture, my land
& plantation whereon I live & the working tools, my loom, & my negroes
except one, which is to be sold & the stock except what is hereafter
mentioned. I give unto my dtrs. now living with me a cow & calf each
to wit: REBECCA, CYNTHIA, MAHALY, MARENY, & MATHENY, also one bed &
furniture. To my son, JAMES MCCURRY one horse or the money to buy one
with when he comes of age. The tract of land lying on the waters of
Sandy Run & Brushy Creek also the negro before mentioned to be sold, and
the balance of my stock to be sold also, and the money equally divided
amongst all my chn. PEGGY MELTON, PHEBE HENDERSON, JOHN MCCURRY, WILLIAM
MCCURRY, AMOS MCCURRY, REBECCA MCCURRY, BETSY LEDFORD, NANCY WEBB, SILAS
MCCURRY, CYNTHIA, MAHALY, MARENY, & MATHENY, the last two named children
are not of age, & JAMES, except MARENY which I give $12 more than the
others. I appoint ELIZABETH MCCURRY & MICAJAH MCCURRY my executor.
Wit: JOSEPH TAYLOR, jurat.   Signed: WILLIAM X MCCURRY.

Page 100. 13 July 1815. Recorded, Jan. Court 1829. I, AGNESS MILLER,
          widow & relict of JAMES MILLER, being of sound mind & perfect
memory, but being far advanced in years. I give unto my dtr., MARY,
wife of JAMES ERWIN a negro woman named Judy, also I give all my plates
& cupboard furniture, also I give my clothing, all table & kitchen
furniture, three feather beds & furniture to her. I give unto my grandson, ARTHUR ERWIN, second son of JAMES ERWIN a negro boy named Dick. I
give unto my granddaughter, SARAH, dtr. of said JAMES ERWIN, a negro
girl named Lina. I give unto my granddaughter, MARY MATILDA ERWIN, dtr.
of JAMES ERWIN, a negro girl named Betsey. I give unto my grandson,
JAMES MILLER ERWIN, two feather beds & furniture. I give unto my grandson, RICHARD LEWIS ERWIN, son of JAMES ERWIN, all the horses & cattle.
The balance of my estate I give unto my dtr. MARY ERWIN. I appoint
JONATHAN HAMPTON, Esq. & JOHN MOORE, Esq. my executor. Wit: ROBERT
WILLIAMSON, Jurat. A.T. ERWIN, jurat.
                         Signed: AGNESS X MILLER.

Page 102. 4 Jan. 1828. Recorded, May Court 1829. I, LUKE WALDROP,
          Senr., being in good health & of sound mind & memory. I give
unto my well beloved wife, MARY, the land whereon I now live of 50 acres,
with my other property during her natural life, then to be divided
equally between my two dtrs., SARAH & MARY, & each to have a cow & calf
& a feather bed. I give my son, ASA, a cow & calf, then my property to
be divided between my dtrs. & my son, ASA. I appoint my dtr. SARAH & my
son ASA my executors. Wit: JOHN LANKFORD, LUKE WALDROP, Junr., jurat.
                         Signed: LUKE WALDROP.

Page 103. 7 Dec. 1827. Recorded, July Court 1829. I, WILLIAM WADE,
          planter, being of sound mind & memory. Just debts & funeral
expenses to be paid. I give unto my beloved wife, MARTHA WADE, all my
estate both real & personal, except the increase of my negroes, which
she is entitled unto one half. I have thought it proper that she have
the disposal of the half of my personal property. At the request of my
wife I give unto EDMOND ROOKER & MARTHA, his wife, of Rutherford Co.,
N.C. and to their heirs forever all my real estate either in N.C. or
S.C. at the death of my wife. The other half of my personal estate &
half of the negroes that may be born after my death unto the heirs of
my brother, EDWARD WASHINGTON WADE, of Barnwell Dist., S.C. I appoint
my wife, MARTHA WADE, my sole executor. Wit: JAMES JACKSON, jurat.
WILLIAM JACKSON, jurat. MOSES JACKSON.
                         Signed: WM. JACKSON.

Page 105. 29 March 1829. Recorded, July Court 1829. I, JAMES WILSON,
          Senr., being of sound mind & memory. I give unto my son,
JAMES WILSON, a tract of land including his improvements, land described.
I give unto JOHN WILSON a tract of land including his improvements. I
give unto my two dtrs. that is ELIZABETH & JEAN WILSON a tract of land,
described. They to get their timber from the land of my son, ALEXANDER'S
part, as long as they remain single, then the property to fall to son,
ALEXANDER WILSON. I give unto my son, ALEXANDER WILSON, the balance of
my land described. I give unto my dtr., MARY, wife of MILES POOL 150
acres of land including his improvements, joining lands of WILLIAM ELAM

& MILES & THOMAS POOLS land. I give unto my dtr., SARAH, wife of THOMAS
POOL the fox horse they have now in their possession & $30. I give unto
my son, ANDREW WILSON, $10. I give unto my dtr., EASTER, wife of JAMES
WILLIS $10. I give unto my two dtrs. that is ELIZABETH WILSON my fly
mare, two cows & her choice of the stock. JEAN WILSON I give the colt
of the fly mare, & two cows, and all my household & kitchen furniture to
be divided between them. All property not mentioned to be sold. ELIZA-
BETH & JEAN WILSON to have $100, the balance to be divided among my chn.
JAMES, ALEXANDER, MARY POOL, ELIZABETH, SARAH POOL, JEAN WILSON each a
part. I appoint JAMES & ALEXANDER WILSON my executors. Wit: SAML. WIL-
SON, JACOB CLYNE, jurat.   Signed: JAMES WILSON, Senr.

Page 108.   19 June 1829. Recorded, Aug. Court 1829. I, BUSHROD DOGGETT,
            being in a low state of health but of sound & memory. It is
my will that my wife, SUSSANNAH DOGGETT, have negroes, Jacob, Jenny,
Spenser, & Abram, the tract of land where I now live, containing 200
acres, all my stock, waggon, still, household furniture & farming tools.
At my wife's death the negroes & their increasase, with the land and
other effects to be divided amongst my children then living or their
issue. Reserving the first child that Jenny may have for BUSHROD DOG-
GETT the son of my son RICHARD, for him to receive at maturity. I will
to my dtr., SARAH WILMOTH, a negro girl named Selah, with a mare & cattle,
which she has received, which I estimate worth $280. I will to my dtr.,
NANCY MOSELY, the tract of land on which she now lives, consisting of
50 acres, also a negro girl named Harriet, a horse, & cattle she has
received, worth $430. I will unto my dtr., ELIZABETH, a negro girl
named Rachel with my lots & improvements in Rutherfordton with 30 acres
of land, worth $580. I give unto my dtr., MARTHA BUTLER, a negro girl
named Jude, 100 acres of land where she now lives, $20 worth of cattle,
worth $520. It is my own will & pleasure to put in the possession of
WILLIAM SUTTON who married dtr. MARY a negro girl named Dinah for the
use of my two grandchn. ELIZA LOVE SUTTON, & ELIAS R. SUTTON. I have
given unto my son, WILLIAM DOGGETT, land, negro, stock, & $560. I have
given un my son, GEORGE DOGGETT, land, negro, stock, & $520. I have
given unto my son RICHARD DOGGETT land, negro, stock, & $520. I appoint
my son WILLIAM DOGGETT & OTHNEIL BUTLER my executors. Wit: JAMES L.
TERRELL, jurat. M.R. ALEXANDER.   Signed: BUSHROD X DOGGETT.

Page 111.   1 July 1829. Recorded, Sept. Court 1829. I, JANE REED, in
            a weak state of health but of sound mind & memory. First I
allow all my lawfull debts to be paid. I give unto my beloved niece,
ELIZABETH GUFFEY, all my plantation now occupied by her & STUART, also
4 feather beds & furniture, also I allow her all my other estate that I
may die possessed of, except my notes & what is here after named. I
give unto my sisters, AGNESS FLEMMINGS, MARTHA GUFFEY, LETITHIA COCKRAM
three dollars each when my notes are collected. I give unto my sister
ELIZABETH GUFFEY one cow & calf. I give unto FREE ACE one half of a
note I have on JAMES CHERRY when collected, one cow & other items named.
I give unto my niece, ELIZABETH GUFFEY, the balance of my notes. I
appoint JOHN GUFFEY Senr. my executor. Wit: JOHN CARSON, jurat. WILLI-
AM ERWIN, jurat.   Signed: JANE X REED.

Page 112.   15 Sept. 1829. Recorded, Oct. Court 1829. I, DAVID WEBB,
            being of sound & perfect mind & memory, though much effected
in body. I give unto my beloved wife, MARY WEBB, all my land where I
now live, with all my personal estate during her natural life, or widowhood, if she should marry I allow her a child's part with my three
youngest children viz: JOHN WEBB, GEORGE WEBB & ANDREW WEBB, and one
other yet unborn. At my wife's death or marriage I give unto my oldest
children, MARY LYLES, SPICEY WEATHERS, RICHMOND WEBB, DAISEY WALKER,
NOAH WEBB, CHAMBERS WEBB, RACHEL RANDLE, MARGARET COCHRAM one dollar to
each of them. I appoint JOHN WALL executor. Wit: JOHN GOODE, Jurat.
EPHRAIM PADGETE, jurat. ELIAS PADGETE.
                            Signed: DAVID X WEBB.

Page 114.   10 May 1829. Recorded, Jan. Court 1830. I, JAMES HARRIS,
            being some what stricken in years, but of sound mind & memory.
To my beloved wife, PATIENCE, I allow all my possessions, stock & furniture during her life or widowhood. But if she marry I allow her one
third of the land & a child's part of the property. To my son, ZADOCK

HARRIS, I give the negro man Bob, with all he has had from me to the present date. To my son, JOHN WASHINGTON HARRIS, I give the negro woman Patty & her child with all other he has received to this date. To my dtr., LUCY WILLIAMS, the negro girl Zelpha with all other property received by her till date. To my dtr., SALLY ELLIOTT, I give the negro girl, Nancy, with all property she has received from me till this date, Also $80 over & above. To my granddaughter, LAVINIA ELLIOTT, the negro boy, Sam, & all the property she has received till this day. To my granddaughter, ZELPHA LEDBETTER, I allow $200. The remaining property be equally divided between my four chn. ZADOCK, JOHN W., LUCY & SALLY. I appoint my sons ZADOCK & JOHN WASHINGTON HARRIS my executors. Wit: LEWIS HARRIS, jurat. H. HARRIS, jurat. WILLIAM X HARRIS.
Signed: JAMES HARRIS.

Page 115. 29 Dec. 1829. Recorded, Feb. Court 1830. I, ELIJAH MCHANN, being weak in body but of perfect mind & memory. All my just debts to be paid after the payment of my debts, the plantation on which I now live with the present crop and stock of all kinds, farming tools, & household furniture, all money on hand notes I give to my wife, ELIZA- BETH MCHANN, during her natural life & at her death all the property to be sold and the money to be equally divided amongst all my children. I appoint my wife ELIZABETH MCHANN my executor. Wit: MOS. LOGAN, JAMES MCHANN, jurat.
Signed: ELIJAH X MCHANN.

Page 117. 6 June 1818. Recorded, April Court 1830. I, DANIEL WORTMAN, being in perfect mind & memory. I give unto my son, DANIEL WORTMAN, that tract of land lying on the head of Woods Creek as his deed calls for, containing 125 acres. I give unto my son-in-law, JOHN HOYLE, & his wife, my dtr. REBECCA HOYLE, 125 acres lying on the head of Knob Creek & Ward's Creek agreeable to his deed. I give to my son, HENRY WORTMAN, 133 acres lying on Coxes' Creek, whereon he now lives agreeable to his deed. I give to my son, MICHAEL WARTMAN, 133 acres where he now lives, to the line run by ANDREW TAYLOR. I give to my dtr., ELIZABETH WORTMAN, 133 acres on Ward's Creek also I give to my said dtr. one cow, 2 heifer, 6 pewter plates, one bason & her bed & furniture she now claims. I give unto my beloved wife, MARY MARGARET WORTMAN, the dtr. of CHRISTO- PHER KENETSER?, all stock, farming tools, household & kitchen furniture, not above given, during her natural life or widowhood. In case of marriage the property to be sold & the money to be equally divided among her & my children. I appoint R. H. TAYLOR & JAMES MCNEALY my executors. Wit: JAMES MCFARLAND, ROBERT DEVENY, jurat., AARON THOMAS, WILLIAM HULL.
Signed: DANIEL X WORTMAN.

Page 119. 4 Jan. 1825. Recorded, April Court 1830. I, JOHN MATHIS, being of sound & perfect mind. All my just debts to be paid. I give to my son, ALLEN MATHIS, all the land between the creek & LEWIS MATHIS' line. I will to my son, WILLIAM MATHIS, 150 of land joining Parker's old line & AARON MCENTIRE'S & my old line. It is my will that my beloved wife, SUSANNAH MATHIS, shall have the use of the plantation whereon I now live with all negroes & stock for her use during her natur- al life or widowhood, at her death all the named property to be divided in the following manner. I give to my son, ALLEN MATHIS, a negro boy named Tom over & above his equal part. At the death of my wife, SUSANNAH, the property to be sold & the money divided among my chn: LEWIS, ALLEN, WILLIAM, JOHN MATHIS, ELIZABETH MCDANIEL, POLLY MOORE, BETSY MOORE, POLLY MCCOMBS, my granddaughter, in place of her mother SUCKY NOWLIN, decd. NANCY MASON, to share equal with the rest of my chn. Her part to be put to the use of her chn. I also leave $1 to THOMAS MASON, I also leave $1 to JAMES NOWLIN. I appoint my sons LEWIS & ALLEN MATHIS my executors. Wit: SHELDRAKE MCCOMBS, WILLIAM COVINGTON.
Signed: JOHN MATHIS.

Page 121. 13 Dec. 1827. Recorded, May Court 1830. I, DANIEL MCGUINN, being of sound mind & perfect memory. First I give unto my mother, SARAH MCGUINN, the rent of my real estate during her life. I give unto my brothers, MICHAEL MCGUINN, & JOHN MCGUINN, my real & per- sonal estate to each an equal share. I do appoint my friend MICHAEL MCGUINN my executor. Wit: EDW. MCGUINN, jurat.
Signed: DANIEL MCGUINN.

Page 122. 8 March 1827. Recorded, June Court 1830. I, JOSHUA TAYLOR,
being weak in body but of perfect sound mind & memory. All
my just debts to be paid. To my dtr., MARY CAMP, I give one negro boy
named Wilkey & one negro girl named Caty during her & her husband CLA-
BORN CAMP'S life time, & not subject to their debts or contracts, at
their death to be the property of their two dtrs. & their heirs, VINEY
& SARAH CAMP. To son, ROBERT TAYLOR, I give one cow worth $8. To my
dtr., FRANCES STEELE, I give one negro girl Isbel and her child Jesee &
her increase, not to be subject to any debts or contracts of ABRAHAM
STEELE during said FRANCIS STEELE'S lifetime. To my son, JESSE TAYLOR,
I give one cow worth $8, & a note of hand of $40 given by him to me
dated 7 Jan. 1808 with interest thereon. To my dtr., OLIVE TAYLOR, I
give one negro boy named Tom, & the tract of land on which I now live,
containing several tracts all adjoining, during her life time or marriage,
in either case one half to go to her son, MILLER ERWIN TAYLOR, also some
household & kitchen furniture, some stock, some tools, and $50 to be
paid unto MILLER ERWIN TAYLOR when he comes of age. To my dtr., HANNAH
DICKEY, I give three negroes named Sam, Matty & Betty. To my dtr.,
RHODA GADD, I give one negro girl named Linda & her increase & a note of
hand given by JAMES GADD payable to JOSHUA TAYLOR, Senr., for $92 with
interest, dated 8 Jan. 1811 & a tract of land lying in Buncombe County,
N.C. I purchased from JAMES GADD if there is such land to be found. To
my dtr., NANCY CHRISTOPHER, I give one negro man named Mark, one boy
named Lewis, one note of hand given by WILLIAM CHRISTOPHER payable to
JOSHUA TAYLOR, the sum of $121.80 with the interest thereon. To my son-
in-law EZEKIEL SCOGGINS I give one cow worth $8 & a note of hand given
him to me for 22 shilling & 6 pence. To my dtr., SARAH GRIZZLE, I give
one negro boy named George, one other named Wilson, which is to be subject to the payment of $50 to the proper use of MILLER ERWIN TAYLOR. To
my son, JOSHUA TAYLOR, I give one negro man named Adam, one woman called
Eve & their increase. One tract of land on Pulloun Creek where WILLIAM
ALLEN now lives. To my g-child, M. E. TAYLOR, negro Jinney, bed & furniture, one small shot gun & $40 for education. To my g-children, M. EUTO
TAYLOR & RHODA SUTTON, I give a tract of land of 100 acres lying on
Mountain & Glighorn Creeks near where JESSE TAYLOR now lives. To my
g-children, MARVILL RABSON, OLIVER, SARAH, STATIA & ALVIRA SCOGGINS, chn.
of EZEKIEL & REBECCA SCOGGINS, each when of age $100. My negro woman
Jenny may choose any of my legatees to live with. I will that negroes
John, Jack & Suckey be sold, to collect all notes not given and money
divided among my seven dtrs. I appoint JOHN BRADLEY, THOMAS EDWARDS, &
ELIAS LYNCH my executors. Wit: BEN H. BRADLEY, Jurat., JAS. O. TERRELL,
jurat., ELIAS LYNCH, jurat. Signed: JOSHUA TAYLOR.

Page 126. 19 Jan. 1820. Recorded, July Court 1830. I, PHILIP DAVIS,
being of sound & perfect mind & memory, being afflicted. I
give unto my beloved son, ROBERT DAVIS, a tract of land, being part of
two tracts, one by entry, one from EVAN WATKINS. Joining lands of
MORELAND, WATKINS, & WAFFORD containing 140 acres, also one horse,
saddle & bridle valued at $80. I give to my beloved dtr., RHODA DAVIS,
a negro girl named Pol, one bed & furniture & a side saddle. I give to
my dtr., FRANCES DAVIS, the negro girl named Rose, one bed & furniture &
a side saddle. I give to my son, JACOB DAVIS, one horse, saddle, bridle
& cloak valued at $80, also a tract of land being part of two tracts,
joining lands of SHARP'S, WATKINS. I give to my son, WILLIAM DAVIS, one
mare, saddle & bridle, a cloak valued at $80, also a tract of land,
joining SHARP'S corner & line. I give to my dtr., SARAH DAVIS, one bed
& furniture & saddle, also the first living child my negro woman Vine
has to her. I give to my dtr., TEMPERANCE DAVIS, one bed & furniture &
side saddle, also the second child my negro woman Vine has to her. I
give to my dtr., POLLY DAVIS, one bed & furniture, one side saddle, also
the third child my negro Vine has to her. Should my said dtrs. not
receive the said negroes they shall have $150 each. I give to my son,
JAMES DAVIS, one tract of land on both sides of the State line, on Hay-
stack Branch & Suck Creek, joining REBECCA WATKINS & E. WATKINS corner,
JACOB DAVIS' line, also a horse, saddle, bridle & cloak when he comes of
age, valued at $80. I give to my son, ABNER B. DAVIS, a tract of land,
on West side of Suck Creek, joining lands of REBECCA WATKINS, PETER &
CHARLES BLACKWELL, also one horse, saddle, bridle & cloak valued at $80
to be given when he comes of age. I give to my son, ALFRED M. DAVIS, a
tract of land on the West side of Suck Creek joining lands of REBECCA

WATKINS line & her corner, also one horse, saddle, bridle & cloak valued at $80 to be his when he comes of age. I give unto my son, PHILIP DAVIS, the several tracts of land where I now live on both sides of the State line and on Suck Creek in N.C. & land in S.C., Spartanburgh District, joining lands of WM. DAVIS & SHARPS line, MORELAND'S corner, R. DAVIS' line, E. WATKINS line, also one horse, saddle, bridle & cloak valued at $80, to be paid when he comes of age. I give unto my beloved wife, NANCY DAVIS, the rest of my estate not before given, Negroes Jim, Eli, & Vine, cattle & live stock, also the tract of land whereon I now live. PHILIP have the benfits from the place where JOHN AMOS lives till A.B. DAVIS & A.M. DAVIS comes of age, also farming tools, household & kitchen furniture until the youngest legatee comes of age, then my smith tools & cross cut saw to fall into the hands of A.B. DAVIS, A.M. DAVIS & PHILIP DAVIS, what money & debts that is due me. I desire that my four youngest sons & two youngest dtrs. to be educated with the benfits of my wife property. I appoint JACOB DAVIS, PHILIP WATKINS, THOMAS LOGAN, WM. DAVIS my executors. Wit: JAMES B. WATKINS, jurat., WM. WATKINS, jurat., JOHN SIMMONS, jurat.   Signed: PHILIP DAVIS.

Page 131. 9 June 1830. Recorded, July Court 1830. I, ABEL HARDIN, being sick in body but of sound memory. After my just debts are paid I give my goods as follows. I give to my beloved wife, MARGARET HARDIN, the negro woman named Sarah and her four chn. Edward, Nelson, Selah & Charlotte and their increase, all my household & kitchen furniture of every discription to be at her disposal. I give my two sons DIAL & DAVIS HARDIN 160 acres of land to be equally divided between them. I appoint my friend ZACHARIAH EARLES my executor. Wit: J. FOUDREN, jurat. WILLIAM ROBERTS.   Signed: ABEL X HARDIN.

Page 132. 3 May 1830. Recorded, Sept. Court 1830. I, CHARLES HILLS, I give unto my son-in-law, HIRAM DUNKIN, all my land of 200 acres on Mountain Creek, because he has agreed to be at all trouble and expense with me & my wife as long as we live which he is to do in a decent & right manner, also I give $50 in trade to my dtr., RACHEL HILLS, and all the remainder of my estate after paying my just debts. I give an equal part to all four of my children, SUSANNAH GREGORY, OLIVE DUNKIN, WILLIAM HILLS, & RACHEL HILLS. I appoint HIRAM DUNKIN & WILLIAM HILLS my executors. Wit: ISAAC ROHM, jurat., WM. HALL, JOHN HALL, jurat.
                    Signed: CHARLES HILLS.

Page 133. 12 July 1828. Recorded, Oct. Court 1830. I, CATHERINE HYDER, being of sound & perfect mind & memory. I give unto my four living children: SUSANNAH LOGAN, BENJAMIN HYDER, NANCY BAGWELL & JOHN HYDER all my real & personal estate to be divided between them, also $90 left in the hands of my son, BENJAMIN HYDER, after my just debts are paid out of it the balance to be divided between the four. I appoint JOHN BRADLEY & BENJAMIN HYDER my executors. Wit: MOSES DICKEY, jurat., WILLIAM G. BAGWELL.   Signed: CATHERINE HYDER.

Page 134. 17 Aug. 1830. Recorded, Jan. Court 1831. I, GEORGE WATSON, being weak in body but of perfect mind & memory. First I will my lawful debts to be paid. I give to my brother, WILLIAM WATSON, $10. I give my brother, HUGH WATSON, $10. I give to my sister, ELIZABETH GETTYS, $10. I give unto my sister, ISABELLA SIMS, $10. All the remainder of my property after the $40 is paid, to my mother, JANE WATSON, & my sister, MARY WATSON, to be equally divided between the two. I give to my brother, JAMES WATSON, all my right & interest in the land. I appoint HUGH WATSON, Junr., my executor. Wit: ELIJAH P. WATSON, jurat. SARAH X WATSON.   Signed: GEORGE WATSON.

Page 135. 16 Dec. 1830. Recorded, Jan. Court 1831. I, WILLIAM K. KERR, being of sound mind & memory, yet weak in body & much afflicted. First I will that my debts be paid. I will unto my beloved wife, KATHERINE KERR, all that mussage of tenements of land of 150 acres on the North side of Main Broad River adjoining ELIAS LYNCH & WILLIAM RUCKER with all household furniture & stock of every kind. The negro woman with her increase & all the outstanding debts. I wish her to have the entire use until her death or marriage. The whole of my estate both real & personal be equally divided among the chn. and the mother in case she should marry. I desire that my wife & executor shall give to all or

each of the chn. as they come of age or marry as much as they think best
to spare not exceeding the amount given to my dtr. that married NORMAN
LYNCH. I appoint my wife, KATHERINE, & HENRY H. KERR my executors.
Wit: TERRELL WILKINS, DAVID GRAY, jurat.
                                Signed: WILLIAM K. KERR.

Page 136. 24 March 1831. Recorded, April Court 1831. FREE ACE, being
           in a low state of body but of perfect mind & memory. I de-
sire my just debts & funeral charges be paid. I give to ROBERT COCKRAM,
Senr., $20 which I have lent to him also the balance of a $40 note on
WILLIAM ERVIN and $20 to JAMES GUFFEY, one cow & calf, 10 yds. flax
cloth, two Scythes & cradles, and one side of soal leather. I give to
JAMES GUFFEY son of JOHN GUFFEY $20 out of a $40 note on WILLIAM ERVIN,
one heifer, one axe, one frow all my leather. I appoint ROBERT COCKRAM,
Senr. & JAMES GUFFEY my executor. Wit: JOHN LONG, jurat. DANIEL WATSON.
                                Signed: FREE X ACE.

Page 137. ? April 1831. Recorded, July Court 1831. I, MARTIN I.
           ELLIOTT, being very infirmed in body but sound in mind & mem-
ory. I desire that my just debts be paid. I give unto my beloved wife,
NANCY ELLIOTT, the tract of land where I now live, my family of negroes,
to wit: Tom, Ellick, Simon, Patty, Rebecca, & her child Erasmus and all
the increase during her natural life or widowhood. After her death or
marriage my will is that my property be sold and the money to be equally
divided between my wife, NANCY, and her eight chn. THOMAS F., ALBERTY T.,
AINSLY S., SIDNEY HARRALSON, PAMELA ANN LEE, EASLY O., NARESSUS N.C.,
PARTHYNA, ELIZABETH ELLIOTT, each to share & share alike. I give to my
wife all the household & kitchen furniture, all stock, all farming tools.
I appoint my wife my executrix. Wit: WILLIAM SLADE, jurat. E. TURNER.
                                Signed: M. I. ELLIOTT.

Page 138. 9 May 1831. Recorded, Sept. Court 1831. I, ROBERT LANKFORD,
           being of sound mind & memory, but of a low state of health.
First I desire my lawful debts be paid. I desire my wife, SEBLA LANKFORD,
shall have all my real & personal estate, during her life time or widowhood. It is my wish that my son, WILLIAM, have a cow, my dtr., CHRIS-
TIANA, to have the gray horse, one breeding sow, one bed & furniture & a
cow. After the death of my wife I wish my estate be divided among my
chn. I appoint my son WILLIAM LANKFORD & EPHRAIM CARROUTH my executor.
Wit: JOHN LANKFORD, ALFRED X FOSTER.
                                Signed: ROBERT X LANKFORD.

Page 139. 17 Dec. 1825. Recorded, Sept. Court 1831. HENRY MONTAGUE,
           LWT. My wife, ELIZABETH MONTAGUE, shall have $700 for her
support out of the money on hand, if not that sum, to be made out of the
money due the est. I give unto my dtr., NANCY SCOTT, one horse, saddle,
one bed & furniture, one cow & calf which she already has, 4 negroes to
wit: Bachus, & Eave, Sucy & Adam to her forever. I give unto my dtr.,
POLLY EARLONE, horse, saddle, one bed & furniture one cow & calf & $300
which she already has and three negroes, Sarah, Bristo & Cook to her
forever. I give unto my dtr., ELIZABETH HAWKINS, one mare & saddle, one
bed & furniture which she has already. I give unto my dtr., CHARLOTTE
MILLER, one horse, saddle, one bed & furniture, one cow & calf and one
negro boy named Peter which she has already and three negroes named Dick,
Andrew & Sam to her forever. I give unto my dtr., JENNY JACKSON, one
mare & saddle, one bed & furniture, one cow & calf, one negro girl named
Doll which she has already, and three negroes named Peter, Charlis &
Fanny to her forever. I give unto my dtr., PROVIDENCE ARTHUR, one horse
& saddle, & $15 which she has already and three negroes named James,
George & Anna and her choice horse & her choice cow & calf, one bed &
furniture. I order it to be so that the land I bought of JOHN ALLEY on
White Oak & Green's Creek be sold and the money divided between my dtr.,
ELIZABETH HAWKINS children when they come of age or marry & that each of
her chn. to have $40 out of my est. in money or property. The balance
of my est. to be sold and the money divided amongst my five dtrs: NANCY
SCOTT, POLLY EARLE, JEANY JACKSON, CHARLOTTE MILLER, PROVIDENCE ARTHUR.
I appoint my sons-in-law, ASPASIA EARLE, & WILLIAM JACKSON my executors.
Wit: JNO. MILLS, Jurat., TYRE G. BLACKWELL, jurat., STEPHEN CAMP.
                                Signed: HENRY MONTAGUE.

Page 141. 23 Aug. 1831. Recorded, Oct. Court 1831. I, LARRANCE COST-
NER, being of sound mind & memory. I give to my wife, NANCY
COSTNER, every thing that I own as long as she lives single viz: My part
in 200 acres of land lying on both sides of First Broad River, joining
lands of ANDERSON ELAM & PETER MOONEY, NATHANIEL THOMPSON, & FREDERICK
GRIGG, with my part of all stock, with household & kitchen furniture,
my gun & crops. My part of brandy that is to be made at JOHN FRONE-
BARGER. After her death the property to be divided among my heirs,
namely THOMAS COSNER, DAVID GIBSON COSNER, & JOSEPH DICKSON COSNER, and
one my wife is pregnant with now, all to have an equal part of my est.
after my just debts are paid. I appoint my friend ANDERSON ELAM, ANDREW
PEALER my executors. Wit: HENRY SCHENCK, Jr., jurat., WILLIAM MARTIN,
SAMUEL X THOMPSON.   Signed: LARRANCE COSTNER.

Page 142. 3 Nov. 1831. Recorded, Jan. Court 1832. I, RICHARD ESKRIDGE,
first I will my lawful debts to be paid. "I direct that my
body be decently intered and that my burial be conducted in a manner
corresponding with my station in life." It is my will that my beloved
wife have all my tract of land where I now live during her lifetime or
widowhood, and after her death or marriage I give my land to my two sons
JESSE & ELIJAH ESKRIDGE to be divided between them, containing 234 acres,
also My negro Hannah. I give to my three sons JOHN G., JESSE, & ELIJAH
ESKRIDGE each of them bed & furniture & a cow & calf. To my wife,
ELIZABETH, I give all the rest of my property, stock, crops, farming
tools, household & kitchen furniture & negroes, Ervin, Phillis, & her
chn. At the death of my wife, my property to be sold & money divided
among all my chn. to wit: WILLIAM S., HAMILTON, RICHARD H., SIMION, JOHN
G., JESSE, ELIJAH, ESKRIDGE, UNICEY MARTIN, SALLY WILKINS. I appoint my
son ELIJAH ESKRIDGE my executor. Wit: W. SLADE, jurat., D. DOBBINS.
Signed: RICHARD ESKRIDGE.

Page 144. 6 Dec. 1831. Recorded, Jan. Court 1832. I, WILLIAM STEWART,
being very sick weak in body but of perfect mind & memory.
I give to my beloved wife, LURNA, 200 acres of land whereon I now live
& one mare, 2 cows & 1 calf, all hogs, Farming tools & household furniture during her natural life at her death all property that is left, I
will to my son, WILLIAM STEWART. I give PEGGY JONES $5, I give LURENA
SIMONS $5. I give my granddaughter, PEGGY STEWART, one mare. I appoint
my wife LURINA & my son WILLIAM STEWART executors. Wit: ROBERT JOHNSTON
(affirms), SARAH X STEWART, jurat.   Signed: WILLIAM X STEWART.

Page 145. 24 May 1831. Recorded, Jan. Court 1832. I, THOMAS WEST,
being very sick & weak in body but of perfect mind & memory.
First I desire my just debts to be paid. I give to my beloved wife,
ELIZABETH WEST, all my estate both real & personal, during her natural
life, and privileged to traffic & dispose of the same amongst my chn. or
as her needs may require. At her death my will is that my youngest sons
ISAAC & WILLIAM WEST to have all my land where I now live, to be divided
between them equally. The rest of my property to be equally divided
among all my chn., except one bed & furniture to ISAAC, by sale or otherwise, viz: DELILAH, JOHN, SARAH, PHEBE, THOMAS, ELIZABETH, MARY, ISAAC
I WILLIAM. I appoint JOSEPH DIVINNEY & my son ? WEST executors. Wit:
JOHN PRUETT, jurat., JAMES X LEWIS. Signed: THOMAS WEST.

Page 147. 16 Jan. 1827. Recorded, March Court 1832. I, WILLIAM MURRAY,
being of sound & perfect mind & memory. First I give unto my
son, JABEZ MURRAY, 5 shillings. I give unto my son, WM. D. MURRAY, 5
shillings. I give unto my dtr., RACHEL STREET, 5 shillings. The balance
of my estate I give unto my son, JOHN MURRAY, for the support of my
loving wife, CESAL MURRAY, & my son, MORDECAI MURRAY. I appoint my
friend, JOHN MURRAY, executor. Wit: AMOS MCCURRAY, JOHN SWIESY.
Signed: WM. MURRAY.

Page 148. 29 Sept. 1831. Recorded, March Court 1832. I, WILLIAM
COLLINS, being sick & weak in body but of perfect mind &
memory. After paying my just debts, I give to my wife, SALLY COLLINS,
all my estate both real & personal for her to possess & enjoy during her
life, and at ther death the remainder or what is left I give unto CARTER
& SALLY BIRCH for them & their heirs forever. I appoint my beloved wife,
SALLY COLLINS, my executor. Wit: JAMES M. WEBB, jurat., EDWARD GOODE,

jurat.   Signed: WILLIAM COLLINS.

Page 149.   12 Feb. 1830.   Recorded, April Court 1832.   I, PHILIP HENSON,
          being of sound mind & memory.   First I will that my wife,
SUSANNAH, have the land where I now live, with two other tract adjoining
one of 50 acres, one of 100 acres during her life time or widowhood.   At
her decease, to descend to BENJAMIN FRANKLIN HENSON forever, in case she
should marry her title to cease to the use of B.F. HENSON in manner
aforesaid.   It is my will that my wife have sole use of all my stock &
furniture, farming tools & at her death or experation of widowhood to be
divided between BENJAMIN F. & PHILIP HENSON, Junr., or the heirs of last
named sons.   To my son PHILIP I will 100 acres of land including the
cross road or Poor's ford old road, former muster ground.   I appoint my
sons PHILIPS & BENJAMIN F. HENSON my executors.   Wit: JAMES S. TERRELL,
ZADOCK D. HARRIS, jurat.   Signed: PHILIP X HENSON.

Page 150.   19 March 1831.   Recorded, April Court 1832.   I, WILLIAM
          MCENTIRE, being of sound mind & memory.   I give to my beloved
wife, REBECCA MCENTIRE, 4 negroes named, Brister, Bob, Bine & Nan, all
cattle, stock, farming tools, household & kitchen furniture during her
natural life or widowhood with the upper part of the plantation where I
live, with waggon & smith tools.   I give unto my dtr., RHODA M. BRAYER,
three negroes named Phebe, Lucinda & Dick.   I give unto my dtr., RACHEL
COVINGTON, three negroes named Eve, Hannah & Rhody.   At the death of my
wife one negro woman named Bine, & 200 acres of land, joining lands of
GEORGE ROYSTER'S land & AARON ROSS land.   I give to my beloved son,
PRICE MCENTIRE, three negroes named, Adam, Sally & Abram, at the death of
my wife one negro named Bob, also the plantation where he lives, and the
home place where I now live.   I give to my dtr., DULCINIA MCENTIRE, three
negroes named Rosannah, Susan, & Peter.   Also a negro man at the decease
of my wife, one horse, saddle, & bridle, two cows & calves & two feather
beds & furniture, & $150 in money.   I give unto my grandson JOSEPH W.
MCENTIRE, 120 acres of land, adjoining land of GEORGE ROYSTER, DAVID
COVINGTON, & PRICE MCENTIRE, including the place where my son, SAMUEL
MCENTIRE, lived to be his when he comes of age, also one bed & furniture.
I appoint PRICE W. MCENTIRE & my wife REBECCA MCENTIRE my executors.
Wit: ALEXANDER BEATY, jurat., JESSE SPURLIN.
                                          Signed: WM. MCENTIRE.

Page 152.   12 May 1832.   Recorded, July Court 1832.   I, DAVID JACKSON,
          being of sound & perfect memory, having arrived at an advanced
age.   I will that my just debts & funeral exepnses be paid.   I give to
my wife, MARGARET JACKSON, & my three dtrs. named FRANCES, POLLY & LINDAY
I give a part of my land (land discribed, joining DAVID JACKSON, Junr.
land).   I give to my sons, HARMAN & REUBEN JACKSON, the balance of my
land to be divided between them.   I give to my wife, MARGARET, one mare,
my stock of hogs & one old steer.   I appoint JAMES BLACKWELL my executor.
Wit: EPHRAIM X JACKSON, jurat., WILLIAM COCKRAM.
                                          Signed: DAVID X JACKSON.

Page 153.   6 Aug. 1832.   Recorded, Sept. Court 1832.   I, JOHN WALL, being
          of sound mind & memory.   After all my debts are paid, I give
unto my wife, LUCY WALL, all the land where I now live during natural
life or widowhood and farming tools & improvements & at her death or
marriage the property to descend to my two youngest sons, JOHN H. WALL
& JEPTHA A. WALL, Also the household & kitchen furniture.   The children
that are not married to receive to same as those that are married.   Chn.
HARTWLL WALL, REBECCA J. WELLS, WILLIS WALL, KINCHIN WALL, ANGELITA
WALKER, LUCINDA WALL, JOHN H. WALL, JEPTHAH WALL, DRUCILLA WALL, & CHASEY
WALL.   The following property to be sold & the money to pay my debts &
the use of the family, one mare, one yoke of steers, one still, one cow
& calf, one tract of land of 120 acres that KINCHEN WALL bought of
WILLIAM GREEN, to make payment on debts to KINTHEN WALL, ALFRED MCKINNEY
& ANNA DEPRIEST for which I am bound.   I appoint my son HARTWELL WALL &
WILLIS WALL my executors.   Wit: JAMES M. WEBB, ABRAHAM PADGETT, jurat.,
JOHN PADGETT, jurat.   Signed: JOHN WALL.

Page 155.   4 Sept. 1832.   Recorded, Oct. Court 1832.   I, JAMES GUFFEY,
          being very sick & weak in body but of perfect mind & memory.
I give unto my well beloved wife, MARTHA GUFFEY, one third part of my

88

real estate with my dwelling house during her natural life, my horse, her saddle, one choice bed & furniture, household items, named. I give unto my two sons, JOHN & JAMES GUFFEY, my plantation to be equally divided between them, JOHN the upper part & JAMES the lower part. My sons to pay my dtr., JENNY R. HOPPISS, the sum of $150 each. The remainder of my property to be sold and the money divided among my three chn. I appoint my son JOHN GUFFEY & SAMUEL HOPPISS my executors. Wit: THOMAS M. BRATTON, jurat., WILLIAM O. WALLIS, jurat.
Signed: JAMES X GUFFEY.

Page 157. 28 Aug. 1832. Recorded, Oct. Court 1832. I, MOSES HENDERSON, being of sound mind & memory. I give to my beloved wife, NANCY HENDERSON, all my goods & chattels, lands & tenements during the time she remains my widow, except the land & property named. I give unto my son, PHILIP, one rifle gun, & $10 now due on JOSEPH BLACK, one horse colt, hogs & 100 acres of land when he comes of age. I give unto my dtr., PROVIDENCE HENDERSON, her choice of cattle, furniture & $4. I appoint my wife, NANCY HENDERSON & JOHN SMITH my executors. Wit: WILLIAM BUTLER, jurat., GEO. MCKINNY, jurat., TALTON X SMITH.
Signed: MOSES HENDERSON.

Page 158. 30 July 1832. Recorded, Oct. Court 1832. I, DAVID JACKSON, being of sound mind & memory. I will that my just debts if any there be to be paid, with my funeral expenses. The remainder of my estate both real & personal I will to my wife, NANCY, to despose of as she may think proper. (No executor named). Wit: REUBEN X JACKSON, jurat., EDWD. MCGUINN.   Signed: DAVID X JACKSON.

Page 159. 20 June 1832. Recorded, Dec. Court 1832. I, WILLIAM GREEN, in common health and memory. I give unto my wife, MARY GREEN, my negro woman named Peggy with the child she is now with, one cow & calf, 1 bed & furniture, with all her clothes, 1 pot & pan, one oven, one horse & saddle to be worth $50. All her cupbard furniture. The remainder of my estate after my debts are paid, I give unto my grandson, WILLIAM M. GREEN, having provided for my children heretofor, with one shilling sterling which I now will to them each. I appoint WM. WALTON & PETER MOONEY my executors. Wit: WILLIAM BAXTER, jurat., CATHER X BAXTER.
Signed: WM. GREEN.

Page 160. 14 June 1831. Recorded, July Court 1833. I, ROBERT HILLS, sick & weakly in body but of perfect mind & memory. I give to my beloved wife, MARY HILLS, all my stock, & tools, household furniture to dispose of at her will. To support the family as long as she remains my widow. In case of marriage the property to be valued and divided between her & her six children. To the chn. of my first wife, MARY, I give one dollar each, ROBERSON HILLS, SARAH HALFORD, & MARGARET EARLY & to MARGARET'S chn. one dollar each. The balance to be equally divided amongst my wife and ARA HILLS, DELILAH & LIZZA HILLS. I give to my son, ARA HILLS, one colt, and the land at the decease of his mother, that is if he stays with her & does a child's part, if not the land to be sold and the money divided amongst the three named. I appoint THOMAS MARLOW my executor. Wit: LONEY F. COOK, jurat., LUCY BATES.
Signed: R. HILLS.

Page 161. 19 Nov. 1832. Recorded, Sept. Court 1833. I, MARY MCMURRY, being of sound mind & memory. My just debts & funeral expenses to be paid. The remainder both real & personal to my dtr. SARAH MCMURRY. I appoint my friend DAVID THOMPSON executor. Wit: JOHN X THOMPSON, EDW. MCGWINN, jurat., MARY X MCMURRY.
Signed: MARY MCMURRY.

Page 162. 4 Dec. 1826. Recorded, Sept. Court 1833. I, THOMAS CAPEL, being aged & infirmed but of sound mind & memory. I allow my just debts & burial expenses to be paid. I give unto my friend and near kinsman DAVID WILSON the whole of my estate both real & personal and every thing that I may die possessed. The said DAVID shall have & hold full right & title to all my land & premises, according to the deeds in my possession. I appoint my friend DAVID WILSON & HENRY M. KERR my executors. Wit: HENRY M. KERR, JOHN LOGAN, jurat.
Signed: THOMAS CAPEL.

Page 163.   18 Dec. 1832.   Recorded, Oct. Court 1833.   I, SUSANNAH RUCKER,
          being sick in body but of sound mind & memory.   I will &
desire that my just debts with a decent burial.   I give to my dtr.,
SARAH, the remains of all my property, including the land where I now
live, one cow, one sow & pigs, all household & kitchen furniture, Also
I desire that my beloved son, WILLIAM RUCKER, to act as guardian to see
that my dtr., SARAH, shall be done justly by. (No executor named). Wit:
M. MILLS, THOMAS EDWARDS, jurat.   Signed: SUSANNAH X RUCKER.

WILL BOOK "E"

Page 1. Sept. 1830. Recorded, Jan. Court 1834. I, JOSEPH FORBIS, being
of sound & perfect mind & memory. I give to my son, JOHN S.
FORBIS, one fifty nine dollar note dated 14 Jan. 1822 against himself &
my crosscut saw. I give unto my son, WILLIAM FORBIS, the plantation
where I now live, including all the land I hold, except 100 acres, also
my negro boy named, Loudon, my blacksmith tools, farming tools. I give
to my dtr., ELIZABETH FORBIS, 50 acres of land, my negro woman, Peg, one
bed & furniture. I give to my dtr., MARY FORBIS, 50 acres of land, my
negro boy, Jacob, my loom, & one bed & furniture, I give unto my two dtrs.
my clock, I allow my dtrs. to have their living & possession of the house
as long as they are single. My still to be sold & the ready money to be
equally divided among my son WILLIAM & my two dtrs. Also I allow my
stock, Balance of household & kitchen furniture to be divided among my
son WILLIAM & my dtrs. MARY & ELIZABETH. I appoint my son WILLIAM FORBIS
& JOHN WILSON my executors. Wit: GEORGE HENDRICKS, jurat. SAMUEL WILSON,
jurat. WILLIAM X HENDRICKS.   Signed: JOSEPH X FORBIS.

Page 2. 12 Dec. 1833. Recorded, Jan. Court 1834. I, DANIEL LATTIMRE,
being of sound memory & understanding. After paying my just
debts & funeral charges. I give to my dear beloved wife, SARAH LATTIMORE,
all my lands where I now live, except 50 acres, excluding the spring &
building of my son, JOHN LATTIMORE, which is his right & proper forever.
Also one negro boy named, Ward, & one negro woman, Nance, also all my
stock of horses, cattle, sheep, hogs. For her to give to JOSEPH, DOBBINS,
SUSANNAH, RACHEL & MARGARET the five youngest chn. a horse, all my household & kitchen furniture, farming tools, grain on hand at my decease. I
give to my son, JOHN, $5. I give to my son, SAMUEL, $5. I give to my
dtr., CATHERINE LATTIMORE, $5. I give to my dtr., JEMIMAH MCENTIRE a
negro woman, Nell, & her child, Nance. I give to my dtr., SUSANNAH one
negro girl named, Jinn. I give to my dtr., RACHEL, a negro girl named,
Poll. I give to my dtr., MARGARET a negro girl worth $350 to be raised
from my personal estate, when she arrives at 18 yrs. I give to my son,
JOSEPH, two negro boys, Alston & Nelson, also one half of the plantation
where I now live, at the marriage or death of his mother. I give to my
son, DANIEL D. LATTIMORE 2 negro boys, Sampson & Cudjo, also one half of
the plantation where I now live. I appoint my 2 sons, JOHN & SAMUEL
LATTIMORE my executors. Wit: ADAM WHISNANT, jurat. THOMPSON EVANS,
jurat.   Signed: DANIEL LATTIMORE.

Page 4. --, -- 1833. Recorded Jan. Court 1834. I, CHARLES LEWIS, give
to my beloved wife, ELIZABETH LEWIS, my mansion house & land
thereon, during her natural life. Also one negro woman, one negro boy &
girl of her choice, also one horse, 2 cows, 2 beds & furniture. After
the death of my wife my will is that her property shall be sold at public
sale and the money be equally divided among my chns. GEORGE, PITMAN, JOHN,
CHARLES, PRESTON, TALIAFERRO, WILLIAM, MARY, SARAH, MILDRE, ELIZABETH, &
NANCY. I give unto my sons all my lands lying in Rutherford County to be
equally divided among them. I give to my dtr. NANCY WHITESIDE one negro
girl. I appoint my sons-in-law MOSES ZIMMIONS & EDWARD PATTERSON my executors. Wit: DANIEL MCCORMICK, jurat. GEORGE GLACK, jurat. JOHN GREER,
jurat.   Signed: CHARLES LEWIS.

Page 6. 19 April 1834. Recorded, July Court 1834. I, JOHN B. IRVINE,
I give unto my wife and child together the one she is now with
all my real & personal property. My watch to be sold and the money used
to pay my debts. I appoint my brother BATTLE ERVINE my executor who has
a note of $250 against SAMUEL COXE, with other papers. I desire that Mr.
JOHN BOWDEN to collect the money due me here. If my wife wish to remove
to S.C. she is to take all or any part of said property with her. (Wife
& children not named.) Wit: M. A. BOSTIC, ADAM BEATY, jurat.
                        Signed: JOHN B. IRWIN.

Page 7. 24 June 1834. Recorded, Sept. Court 1834. I, JOHN POPE, Senr.
being of sound and perfect mind. I give unto my beloved wife
PENELOPE all land in N.C. & all my negroes viz. Rose, James, Jenny and
her four children, & all my estate of all discription in N.C. during her
natural life or widowhood. I appoint my son CARTER to assist his mother
in the management of the est. when called on. I give unto my sons CARTER

POPE & JOHN T. POPE a tract of land containing 700 acres of land in S.C.
on South Pacolet, to be equally divided between them, each to pay the
other legatees the sum of $150. At the death of my wife the property in
N.C. to be divided between my children. I appoint my son CARTER POPE &
PHILIP WATKINS executors. Wit: JOSHUA CAMP, jurat. DAVID POPE, jurat.
JACOB PHILIPS.   Signed: JOHN X POPE, SR.

Page 8. 6 Aug. 1834. Recorded, Oct. Court 1834. I, WILLIAM WILLIAMS,
           being very sick in body, but of perfect mind & memory. I give
unto my beloved wife NANCY WILLIAMS all my property, after my just debts
are paid. I appoint my son WALTER WILLIAMS my executor. Wit: PETER
COWARD, jurat. WM. GIBBS.   Signed: WM. WILLIAMS.

Page 9. 3 Oct. 1834. Recorded, Oct. Court 1834. I, WILLIAM GUFFEY,
           Senr. being in a weak state of health, but of perfect mind &
memory. First I allow my just debts to be paid and burial expenses, from
the personal est. I give unto my beloved wife ISABELLA GUFFEY all my
household & kitchen furniture, all farming tools, 2 cows & a calf, one
horse, with corn & fodder, with three head of hogs during her life time,
at her decease to be divided between my sons ISAAC & SAMUEL GUFFEY. I
give unto my son JAMES GUFFEY 30 3/4 acres of land on the South side of
the land I now live on, line to run from East to West. One cow & calf,
all the corn & fodder he has made this year. I give unto my son ROBERT
W. GUFFEY 30 3/4 acres of land, lying next to my son JAMES' land, one bull
& one heifer. I give unto my son ISAAC & my son SAMUEL R. GUFFEY the
balance of my old tract of land joining ROBERT'S line, both to maintain
their mother during her life. I give unto my son WILLIAM GUFFEY 50 acres
of land, joining BICKERSTAFF'S plantation, one heifer, & fodder. I give
to my son JOHN the balance of that tract of land joining WALKER'S, one cow
& calf, one mare called Peg. I give unto THOMAS'S heirs, each one a dollar
when my horse Guib is sold. I appoint my sons SAMUEL GUFFEY my executors.
Wit: JAMES GUFFEY, jurat. THOMAS GUFFEY, jurat.
                                    Signed: WILLIAM X GUFFEY.

Page 10. 10 Sept. 1833. Recorded, Jan. Court 1835. I, JOHN BALDRIDGE,
           being far advanced in life, but of sound mind & memory. I
allow all lawfull debts & funeral expenses to be paid. I give unto my
wife SARAH BALDRIDGE the land I now live on, my negro Nance, one horse,
two cows & calves, my hogs & sheep, & farming tools, household furniture,
all crops during her natural life or widowhood. "Nance to take care of
my silly daughter during her natural life that is POLLY CLARKE." I also
allow my wife the property & negro girl Harriett that I received from her
when we married. I allow my mill to be rented & my wife to receive the
profits to assist in supporting the family. The balance of my property
not herein mentioned to be sold and divided as following. $50 to Little
Brittain Church. I give to my son-in-law WILLIAM MCGROVE & my dtr. NANCY,
his wife, $10, they having receive their full share. I give to my dtr.
REBECCA & her son, SAMUEL BALDRIDGE, all my mechanical tools, except my
smith tools. I give to my son-in-law, WILLIAM PORTER, & my dtr. PEGGY,
his wife, $500. I give to the chn. of my dtr., BETSY, decd. & former
wife of, THOMAS SMART, $500. At the decease of my wife I allow my plan-
tation to be sold & at the death of my silly dtr. negro Nance & her issue
if any, to be sold, & the money divided as follows. REBECCA & her son
SAMUEL one share, WILLIAM PORTER & his wife PEGGY one share, The chn. of
my dtr. BETSY one share, my son JOHN BALDRIDGE one share. I give to the
heirs of my son, DORANTON BALDRIDGE, one share. To my son WILLIAM BALD-
RIDGE one share. My son JOSEPH BALDRIDGE one share. I appoint JOHN
CARSON and ANDREW LOGAN my executors. Wit: JAMES WATSON, WILLIAM ALLEN,
jurat.   Signed: JOHN BALDRIDGE.

Page 12. 24 Aug. 1832. Recorded, Jan. Court 1835. I, ROBERT TAYLOR, I
           direct all my just debts & funeral expenses to be paid. I give
to my beloved wife a negro girl Sinda & Ben her life time, and a tract
of land joining MCFADDIN her life time, also one bed & kitchen furniture,
two cows & calves. I give to my dtr. MIRA, a negro girl named, Mariah, &
other property she has received, valued at $352. I give to my dtr.,
CYNTHIA, negro girl Arbella, & other property valued at $477. I give to
my son, JOHN B. TAYLOR, a tract of land lying on Green Branch, also a
negro boy named, Alfred, with other property, valued $691. I give to my
son JAMES S. TAYLOR, a negro boy named Dick & other property, valued to

92

$1,024. I give to my dtr., FRANCES & her heirs, except ANN, which is now living on waters of Stone Cutters, & a cow, valued to $233, also a negro boy named Joe. I give to my dtr. DRUCILLA a tract of land lying in the County Buncombe on the waters of Broad River, also a negro girl named Lucy. I give ELIAS LYNCH TAYLOR a negro boy named Watt. I give to ROBERT a negro boy named Harry. I give to HARVEY C. TAYLOR a negro boy named Warren. My plantation to be divided by JOHN MCFADDIN & WM. TABOR for my three youngest son, LYNCH, ROBERT, & HARVEY, also each a horse valued at $60. I appoint my sons-in-law JOHN MCFADDIN & WILLIAN TABOR my executors. Wit: JOSHUA TAYLOR, jurat. MILLER TAYLOR, jurat. JESSE TAYLOR, jurat.
Signed: ROBERT TAYLOR.

Page 14. 18 March 1835. Recorded, April Court 1835. I, WILLIAM ARTHUR, being in sound mind & perfect memory. I desire that all my property be sold at public sale, and the money divided as follows, after payment of my just & lawfull debts, I give unto WILLIAM FORTINBERRY $50. To ADOLPHUS RAY son of SALLY RAY $50 when he comes 21 yrs. of age. The balance to be divided among my brothers & sisters. I appoint WILLIAM BABER & JAMES ARTHUR my executors. Wit: PHILIP GROSS, jurat. CHARLES L.H. SCHIFFILIN.
Signed: WILLIAM X ARTHUR.

Page 15. 12 June 1833. Recorded, April Court 1835. I, GEORGE BLANTON, being in perfect mind & memory. I will my beloved wife, PRIS-CILLA BLANTON, the mansion house & farm and $300, also all household items, except as the children marry off they are to have a bed & furniture worth $30. I give unto MARGARET BLANTON, Mary a negro, about 13 yrs. old. To WILLIAM BEATY SAWYERS BLANTON, Matilda a girl about 17 yrs. old. To JAMES HILL BLANTON, Clarrissa a negro, about 11 months old and money enough to make her worth $350. To GILFORD EAVES BLANTON $350. To a child expected in a few months $350. The above named negroes & money to stay in the hands of my wife PRISCILLA until said chn. come of age. I appoint my brother CHARLES BLANTON & my brother-in-law HOUSEN HARRELL my executors. Wit: SAMUEL HARRELL, jurat. A. D. HARRELL, jurat.
Signed: GEORGE BLANTON.

Page 16. 29 Aug. 1834. Recorded, July Court 1835. I, MARTHA WADE, of sound mind & memory. When property is divided according to terms of decease husband WILLIAM WADE by executors & heirs of EDWARD WASHINGTON WADE which division I wish to be made as soon as possible, all property to be divided into five equal parts and divised as follows. To JOHN BOOKER one fifth part. To SHIELDS BOOKER one fifth part. To JABEZ BOOK-ER one fifth part. To MARTHA OVERTON WADE one fifth part. And to the orphan children of EDMOND BOOKER one fifth part, to be equally divided among them, the said property to stay in the hands of the executors until the chn. come of age. The negro property is not to be sold if possible, and the children not taken from their mother under the age of 6 yrs. I appoint JOHN BOOKER and SHIELDS BOOKER of Spartanburg District, S.C. my executors. I MARTHA WADE amend this my last will as follows, I give SHIELDS BOOKER all the money & notes that I may die possess of, he first paying any debts I may owe, funeral expenses, including a tombstone. The name of MARTHA OVERTON WADE is a mistake, it should be MARTHA OVERTON BOOKER. Wit: JAMES JACKSON, WILLIAM JACKSON, jurat. JOHN MOORE, jurat.
Signed: MARTHA WADE.

Page not numbered. "As information." SANFORD YOUNG aged 79 yrs. old interred this July the 5th, 1899 says he was born Sept. 16, 1820 and that he is the person referred to in the will of ANDREW YOUNG, dec'd. that he was about 13 yrs. old when Mr. YOUNG Killed himself. He says he remembers very well the time Mr. YOUNG killed himself with a pistol on the day before he Mr. YOUNG went out in the chimney corner and was writing most of the day. He went to bed as usual and on next morning sent me to mill before breakfast and went himself and laid "warm" for a fence. After I came back from mill I was sent to help work on the public road in his place. About 10 oclock we heard a gun shot and, RUFFUS MILLS, the youngest of JOHN MILLS, came to us and told us that Mr. YOUNG had killed himself. He lived on the head waters of Back Branch the lands of Capt. J. C. CANUP, Poke County, and that his mother & sister (of said ANDREW YOUNG) heard the shot they were going up the branch to his house having started to see him when they heard the shot, and as they were on their way they found him dead on the path he having a flint lock pistol in his hand empty. A large wound through his head, the ball passing through and striking a small sappling post oak. His mother lived in the forks of Shop Branch & Back Branch. He was very fond of hunting and often taken me with him there being much game, deer, turkey etc. I remember he was very kind to his wife and to me also he often abused and cussed the nullifies." Wit: T. C. SMITH, M. O. DICKERSON, C.S.C.

Signed: SANFORD X YOUNG.

Page 18. 8 Jan. 1833. Recorded, April Court 1835. ANDREW YOUNG. I write these few lines to let all persons know that doing this murder is my own fault and no body else, and I wish my dear wife to take it as easy as possible and I wish her to get SANFORD in her third of the property if she chooses for she has raised him. I hope the rest wont be so ungracious but to agree to it as it is my wish. If I had to marry fifty times I don't want to have better wife than she has been to me. Given under my hand & seal.   Signed: ANDREW YOUNG.
"The foregoing should have entered at April--See the minutes of that term for its probate. Page 232, Book A. of estates."

Page 18. 14 Oct. 1834. Recorded, Oct. Court 1835. I, GEORGE WALTON, I give unto my beloved wife NANCY WALTON, all the property I may die possessed with, viz. All real estate, all slaves, all perishable property, all household & kitchen Furniture with all things belonging to the house, money, notes, book accounts, dues & demands. If think proper to dispose of the negroes, I wish them to go in families, not to separate them. At her death one half of what may remain to be equally divided with the heirs of THOMAS & MARTHA WALTON of Morganton, N.C. CLARISSA FLEMMING of Philadelphia, Pa. and WILLIAM H. WALTON. I appoint my wife NANCY WALTON my sole executrix. Wit: THOS. A. MCENTIRE, jurat. JOHN M. M. CALDWELL.   Signed: GEORGE WALTON.

Page 19. (No date). Recorded, Oct. Court 1835. I, ANDREW MILLER, Senr. being of sound mind & memory. I give to my beloved wife plantation on which I live and adjoining lands. All stock, horses, & household furniture and the following negroes, viz: Jun, Lucy, Phil, Dolly, Granberry, & Maria. I give to my son ANDREW a negro boy Cartiller. Son JOHN, a negro boy Edmund. Son WILLIAM, a negro boy Raleigh. Son HARRY, negro boy Martin. Son CARR, negro boy Henry. My dtr. ELIZABETH a negro girl Fanny. Dtr. NANCY, negro girl Kizzy. Dtr. MARTHA, negro girl Leah. I give to my son JAMES 4 lots in Rutherfordton, N.C. which I purchased at the sale of Bowen's estate. I give to my dtr. POLLY a tract of land on Hoopers Creek in Buncombe County, N. C. patent # 383. I give to my sons JOHN & WILLIAM a tract of wood land ajoining the town of Rutherfordton, known as Sally's Fork, patent #781. The lands not divised in Rutherford-ton & Buncombe Counties to be sold within two yrs. by my executors and money put in trust. Also I divised all my negroes not otherwise given, to my executors in trust, to be sold on the plantation. I desire that each of my children shall receive an equal share of property or cash as possible. I appoint my beloved Wife ANNA guardian of my minor children, ELIZABETH, NANCY, MARTHA, HARRY, & CARR. I desire my boys to have a good English Education. I give to my sons HARRY & CARR the plantation on which I now live at the death of their mother. Each child to receive a horse, bridle & saddle when their mother thinks proper, as the other has receive the same. To following are advancements I have already made to some of my chn. which is to be regarded as whole or part of their share, JOHN & WILLIAM the house & lot I bought from BOWEN. To ANDREW 300 acres of land on Henry's Creek. To POLLY one negro girl Nicey. To DAVID 250 acres in Buncombe Co. on Henry's Creek, and a negro boy Julius. To JAMES one negro boy Waldo. I appoint my wife ANNA, my sons JAMES & JOHN MILLER executors. Wit: THOMAS DEWS, Jr. Test. (Jurat).

Signed: ANDREW MILLER.

Page 21. 18 July 1833. Recorded, Oct. Court 1835. I, RICHARD MCCLURE, of Broad River. Being old & infirmed, but of sound mind & memory. I give all my real estate to LEVI MCCLURE. I give to my son RICHARD MCCLURE $50 in money or a horse. I give to my dtr. SARAH $20 in money, in addition to her bedding & clothing. I give to my dtr. POLLY, widow of JAMES WRAGG (torn) and her children as long as she & my son LEVI may both choose to have it so live together and by their industry upon the said real estate be maintained and the children be schooled. Should

94

they separate, POLLY to have the land from a line on the bank of the river
to a place now known as Frank's Cabbins. The land is for the use of dtr.
POLLY & her chn. so long as she lives. Should POLLY marry or move away,
the land to be the property of my son LEVI. My estate shall be charged
with the maintaince of my wife ANN, she to live with my son LEVI or dtr.
POLLY WRAGG as she does now. Be it understood that her provisions &
clothings is in any event to be at the expense of my dtr. POLLY. Should
my son LEVI sell the estate here in given. He is to supply dtr. POLLY
with a similar house with in 12 months. All my other chn. must be contented with the little they have already had, as I have nothing more to
give them, except as a aged poor father blessing & his prayers for their
welfare. I appoint My son LEVI executor. Wit: JOS. MCD. CARSON, & T. C.
CARSON, jurat.   Signed: RICHARD MCCLURE.

Page 24. 10 Sept. 1835. Recorded, Dec. Court 1835. I, THOMAS LYLES, of
          White Oak Creek, being feeble of body but of sound & perfect
mind & memory. I direct all my debts be paid as soon as possible. I
give to my beloved wife ALEE all the property I got with her by marriage.
(stock & household items named). I give to my wife ALEE & dtr. LILLIA
the tract of land where I now live & the fresh bottom joining EPHRAIM
LYLES part. Also my negro man Dick & his wife Lize and her two chn. for
the support during her natural life. I allow my son EPHRAIM LYLES the land
where he now lives, containing 100 acres, also another tract of 14 acres
joining the above land. I also give him my negro man named Aaron. I
will that my negroes not mentioned before viz. Nell, Hannah, Sawncy,
Reubin, Phillis, Sall, Marion, Lott, Sarah, & Abram, should be put in lots
for the legatees or put up for sale. I will that my chn. share as follow,
my son JOHN, THOMAS, WILLIAM & EPHRAIM and dtrs. SALLY, ELIZABETH, SILLEA
and the chn. of my dtr. ANN BARNETT, decd. and the chn. of my dtr. AGNESS
STEEDMAN, decd. should share alike. I give to my son ROBERT LYLES $10.
I give to my nephew AUBSEAH LYLES one bed & furniture & $50. Likewise at
the death of my wife, the property I left her to be sold and the money
equally divided amongst my legatees, except my son ROBERT as I left him
before all I intended. I appoint my son JOHN LYLES executor. Wit:
ZACHARIAH JOHNS, jurat. THOMAS X MILLER, jurat.
                                        Signed: THOMAS LYLES.

Page 26. 2 March 1835. Recorded, March Court 1836. I, JOHN ELLISON,
          Senr. Being old & infirmed in body but of sound mind & memory.
First I will my just debts to be paid. I give unto my son JOHN 185 acres
of land, by his paying the rest of the legatees $25 within 2 yrs. of my
decease. Land joining MARTIN THOMPSON, & my son WILLIAM where he now
lives I give unto my son WILLIAM, by his paying $50 to the rest of the leg-
atees within two yrs. of my death. I give unto my son JONATHAN my saddle.
To my dtr. JUDAH PACK'S five chn. one $25 note with interest that is
against DANIEL EDWARDS. I give to SAMUEL PACK $1. I give to my dtr.
DELILAH NEWMAN the red cow that I loaned her to cow her $25 to make her
equal with the rest. I give unto my step-son, MOSES HALL, my bay mare.
All the rest of my property, with 25 acres of land on the mountain, with
all the notes that I hold to be equal divided between, SARAH PACK, JONA-
THAN ELLISON, NANCY PACK, LUCY HALBIRD, DELILAH NEWMAN, & JUDAH PACK'S
chn. These chn. to have equal with the other five named above. I appoint
my son JOHN ELLISON, executor. Wit: LUKE WALDROP, jurat. MARTIN THOMP-
SON, jurat.   Signed: JOHN X ELLISON.

Page 27. 28 Dec. 1832. Recorded, March Court 1836. I, BARTHOLOMEW
          BOLTON, being of sound mind & memory. First, after paying my
just debts & funeral expenses. I give unto my wife my personal property,
also my tract of land lying on First Broad River, joining land of AARON
ROSS corner, CHARLES M. ROYSTER line & DAVID CARRINGTON corner. After
the death of my wife JANE BOLTON, I give unto my grandson BARTHOLMEW
GREENLIE all the above named land. I give unto my dtr. MARY NOWLIN 5
shillings. I give to my son WILLIAM BOLTON 5 shillings. I give unto
my son JOHN BOLTON one feather bed & three blankets. My request is that
my grand-son BARTHOLMEW GREENLIE cultivate the land and support his
grand-mother during her life time. I appoint my friends BARTHOLMEW
GREENLIE & AARON ROSS my executors. Wit: JOHN S. GLADDIN, MOSES ROSS,
JESSE SPURLIN, jurat.   Signed: BARTHOLMEW X BOLTON.

Page 29. 25 July 1836. Recorded, Oct. Court 1836. I, MARY WALKER,

95

being of sound mind & memory. I give unto my sister ELIZABETH
BLACKWOOD $1 her full share of my estate. I give unto my sister MARTHA
SERVICE $1, her full share. I give unto my sister MARGARET ADAMS $1 her
full share. I give unto my deceased sister RACHEL WHITESIDE'S children
$1 divided amongst. I give unto my sister JANET WILSON my feather beds
& furniture, my wearing clothes, my chest & contents, and the balance of
my estate, except one $50 note, that I give to my niece MARY WILSON, on
PRIER MCENTIRE. I give to my nephew SAMUEL WILSON one clock. I appoint
my brother-in-law JOHN WILSON executor. Wit: GEO. CABANISS, jurat.
WILLIAM FORBES, jurat.   Signed: MARY X WALKER.

age 30. 17 May 1827. Recorded, Oct. Court 1836. I, JAMES GRAY, being
          of sound mind & memory and in good health. First, I want all my
just debts to be paid. I give unto my son DAVID GRAY all the land whereon
I now live on Green River on the North side, with the mansion house, with
$1200 to be raised from the perishable property to make him equal with
what I have conveyed unto son SAMUEL GRAY. The residue of my whole estate
to be equally divided between my son DAVID GRAY and the heirs of my son
SAMUEL GRAY. I appoint my son DAVID GRAY & friend JAMES MORRIS my executors. Wit: JAMES MORRIS, jurat. ELIZABETH MORRIS, D. DICKEY.
                                        Signed: JAMES GRAY.

Page 31. 11 June 1831. Recorded, Dec. Court 1836. DAVID COLBRATH, being
          in proper health and proper in my senses. I give all my house-
hold furniture, stock, hogs, horses to my loving wife (not named). I
give one half of said property at the decease of my wife unto my dtr.
JAIN COLBRATH and the other half unto dtr. CATHERINE to be divided equally.
I give unto HENRY FAGINS $1. I give unto EDWARD COLBRATH $1. I give unto
JOHN COLBRATH $1. I give unto HENRY COLBRATH $1. I give unto MARY MC-
HANN $1. I appoint HUMPHREY PARISH & ROBERT MCAFEE my executors. Wit:
WILLIAM BUTLER, EDWARD COLBRATH, jurat.   Signed: DAVID X CALBRATH.

Page 32. 7 Jan. 1831. Recorded, Dec. Court 1836. I, ELIZABETH HAYNES,
          being in a low state of health but of perfect mind & memory.
First, all my just debts be paid. I give unto my dtr. CATHERINE LACKEY
during her life and her heirs after her death, namely, HUGH HENRY HAYNES,
SARAH TAMON ? LACKEY the following articles to be divided between them,
(stock & household items, named). I appoint my son-in-law HUGH LACKEY my
executor. Wit: LIVERETT PARSONS, jurat. MICHAEL TANNER, jurat.
                                        Signed: ELIZABETH X HAYNES.

Page 33. 11 June 1836. Recorded, Spring Court 1837. I, DANIEL WATSON,
          being in bad health but in perfect mind & memory. I give unto
my executors as much of my stock, crops & furniture as they may need to
sell to pay my just debts. I give unto my beloved wife JINCEY the balance
of my crop, stock, furniture & tools also all my land during her life or
widowhood for her & the children support. At my wife death what property
that is left to be sold & equally divided among my legatees. (Not named).
"Signed and sealed without witness, knowing my hand writing & signature
are easily proven." I appoint HUGH WATSON my executor & my wife executrix, and after her decease, PATRICK WATSON executor to sell & divide the
estate.   Signed: DAVID WATSON.

Page 33. 22 May 1837. Recorded, July Court 1837. I, GEORGE MORRIS, now
          in a low state of health but in the usual state of mind. First,
my just debts should be paid. I give unto my affectionate wife MARY
MORRIS all my lands & property, including the mansion house in which I
now live during her natural life or widowhood, at her decease to be
divided amongst CATHARINE METCALFE, SALLY MORRIS, THOMAS MORRIS & CHURCH-
WELL MORRIS. Wife to choose one of her sons to manage the plantation for
the support of herself & dtr. SALLY as long as she is single. I appoint
my sons THOMAS MORRIS & CHURCHWELL MORRIS, jurat. JAMES MORRIS.
                                        Signed: GEORGE X MORRIS.

Page 35. 19 Jan. 1830. Recorded, July Court 1837. I, WILLIAM NIX,
          growing old and infirmed and afflicted with pain, yet of per-
fect mind & memory. First I will my just debts & funeral charges be paid.
I leave all lands, stock, and household furniture to my beloved wife JANE
and SAMUEL H. NIX, GEORGE W. NIX, & AARON NIX they are to care for their
mother. I give to son ROBERT A. NIX one cow & calf. To the chn. of my

former wife I give JOHN NIX 5 shilling, BETSY MCCLURE 5 shillings, LEBAN-
ON NIX 5 shilling, CALEB NIX 5 shillings, WILLIAM NIX 5 shillings, NANCY
THOMPSON 5 shillings, SUSANNA GREEN 5 dollars, REBECCA DAVIS 5 shillings.
My smith tools I give unto my wife JANE NIX, SAMUEL NIX, & GEORGE W. NIX,
& AARON NIX. I give unto JOSEPH NIX 5 shillings. I appoint my wife JANE
executrix & friend THOMAS EDWARDS & ALANSON MCHANN executors. Wit: ALAN-
SON MCHANN, jurat. THOMAS EDWARDS, jurat.

Signed: WILLIAM X NIX.

Page 36. 29 March 1837. Recorded, Sept. Court 1837. I, ALEXANDER BALD-
RIDGE, being far advanced in life but of sound mind & memory.
I allow all lawfull debts & funeral expenses be paid from my personal
estate. I give unto my beloved wife JANE BALDRIDGE the plantation that I
now live on, her choice of two horses, all farming tools & two waggons,
three cows & calves, all sheep, twenty head of hogs, my negro man named
Frank, boy named John also Lucy & Esther. The profit from my mill, grain
& fodder at my death, household & kitchen furniture & $100 in cash, during
her natural life or widowhood. Also all property that she brought with
her when we married. I give unto my son-in-law WILLIAM ALLEN $500 in
cash. I give unto my son-in-law & dtr. JAMES C. & JANE GALLICK $10 in
cash as they have received a full share before. At my decease I allow
what property not mentioned in this will to be equally divided amongst
my grand children, that is the chn. of JOHN ALLEN & wife REBECCA, chn. of
WILLIAM ALLEN & wife NANCY. At my wife decease what property left to be
divided among the chn. of JOHN & REBECCA & WILLIAM & NANCY ALLEN. I
appoint my wife JANE BALDRIDGE & friend JOHN CARSON executors. Wit:
FRANCIS LOGAN, jurat. B. LOGAN, jurat. Signed: ALEXANDER BALDRIDGE.

Page 37. 14 Oct. 1835. Recorded, Sept. Court 1837. I, ISAAC LEDBETTER,
being in sound mind & memory. I will all my just debts paid &
burial expenses. I will my wife ZILLA LEDBETTER should hold the tract of
land wheron my house stands on & that part above the lane on the Widows'
Creek bought from JOHN BRADLEY during her natural life, also the negro
Violet & girl Caroline until my youngest child come of age. Then I will
that my wife ZILLA LEDBETTER shall have the choice of all the negroes,
and the rest divided amongst my chn. and one half of my stock all household & kitchen furniture. I desire that the rest of my lands be rented
out until my youngest child come of age, then to be sold or divided. I
will that ISAAC HAMPTON LEDBETTER shall have $500 first, then the rest to
LEDBETTER, my son & DRURY BRADLEY my executors. Wit: H. HARRIS, jurat.
JOHN M. BRADLEY.   Signed: ISAAC LEDBETTER.

Page 38. 15 Feb. 1818. Recorded, Oct. Court 1837. I, WILLIAM CRAIN,
being sick and weak in body yet of perfect mind & memory. I
give unto my wife ELIZABETH CRAIN 150 acres of land, including my plantation & premises during her life, also all my stock of horses, cattle,
sheep & hogs for her use. At her decease my present plantation including
the 150 acres to fall to my son MARTIN CRAIN. I give unto WILLIAM JAMES
COLLINS 50 acres joining my present plantation. I give to my son HIRAM
CRAIN 150 acres from a 300 acres survey in Pendleton District, S.C. he
may have a choice of the tracts, but not to separate the survey. I give
unto JAMES CRAIN'S two dtrs. EUNICE & SUSEY the other 150 acres of the
survey to be divided between them. 100 acres of land lying in Spartan-
burgh Dist., S.C. on Lawson's Fork to be sold & the money divided amongst
JOHN CRAIN, POLLY YOUNGBLOOD, WILLIAM CRAIN, SALLY LEDBETTER, DELILA
CRAIN, and JAMES CRAIN. I appoint my wife ELIZABETH CRAIN & son HIRAM
CRAIN my executors. Wit: JOHN LUSK, JAMES X ROSS, jurat.

Signed: WM. CRAIN.

Page 39. 24 Aug. 1834. Recorded, Fall Court 1837. I, HENRY MCKINNEY,
farmer, being of perfect mind. I give to my beloved wife
NANCY one horse that I got from my son WILLIAM, also 150 acres of land in
Spartanburg Dist., S.C. on waters of Buck Creek. The above item to be
disposed of at her own discretion. I desire that my wife NANCY have full
use & benefit of the 125 acres of land on which I now live, with the
horse I got from SETH RUSSELL, and all other stock & household furniture.
As my dtrs. marry off they are to receive 16 pounds of feathers each.
The reason I leave nothing to my first 6 chn. is that they have more than
I can leave the last eight. I appoint my son WHITLOCK MCKINNEY sole
executor and to act as guardian of my minor chn. if necessary. Wit: JOHN

H. BEDFORD, ALANSOM PADGETT, STEPHEN CAMP, jurat.
                                    Signed: HENRY MCKINNEY.
--HENRY MCKINNEY the testator to the forgoing will acknowledge the same to
me in the present shape (i.e.) with the words "widowhood or marriage"
erased or struck out and that he assigned the same the 21 July 1835.
Attest: M. R. ALEXANDER (jurat)..

Page 41. 22 Sept. 1837. Recorded, Jan. Court 1838. I, JOSEPH GREEN, I
          direct all my just debts, funeral expenses and doctors fees be
paid from the first money. I desire that my wife NANCY have all my land
viz. the tract we now live on containing 173 acres, another tract of 120
acres lying on Abahills Creek. Wife NANCY GREEN to have the use & benfit
of my personal property after my just debts are paid. After the decease
of my wife NANCY that all my real & personal property to be equally
divided amongst my chn. WILLIAM GREEN, ELIZABETH GREEN, JOHN GREEN, JOSEPH
P. GREEN, GEORGE GREEN, ALFRED P. GREEN, JAMES JEFFERSON GREEN, WHITTEN
GREEN & Dr. FRANCIS MARION GREEN. I appoint my wife NANCY GREEN & friend
JESSE CHITWOOD my executors. Wit: JOHN GREEN, jurat. SAMUEL MELTON,
jurat.   Signed: JOSEPH GREEN.

Page 43. 2 Jan. 1838. Recorded, March Court 1838. I, JONATHAN ROBERSON,
          being feeble in body but of perfect mind & memory. First my
just debts to be paid from my personal property. I give unto my beloved
wife JANE ROBERSON the ballance of my estate during her life or widowhood.
At my wife's decease my land to be equally divided between my sons WILLIAM
ROBERSON & JONATHAN H. ROBERSON. What personal property remains I allow
to be equally divided among my six chn. now at home viz. JANE ROBERSON,
CATHARINE, REBECCA, WILLIAM, JONATHAN & MIRA ROBERSON. I allow my wife
to have my little grand daughter Jane long taught to read her Bible. I
appoint my son JAMES ROBERSON my executor. Wit: HUGH WATSON, Jurat.
JACOB YELTON, jurat.   Signed: JONATHAN X ROBERSON.

Page 43. 25 Feb. 1838. Recorded, March Court 1838. I, JOHN WHITAKER,
          being of sound & perfect mind & memory. I give unto my dtr.
SABRAY NANNY wife of EDMUND NANNY my carry all waggon & harness with $25
in cash, also I give unto her son DRURY NANNY my rifle gun. I give unto
my dtr. RACHEL $160 in cash. I give unto my dtr. LUCINDA $140 in cash.
My pewter basin, two dishes, nine plates to be divided among my dtrs.
The other personal property to be sold to pay my debts, if any is left,
it to be divided among my dtrs. I appoint my friend JAMES ALLEN & MADISON
KOONE executors. Wit: JOHN KOONE, jurat. JAMES NANNY, jurat.
                                    Signed: JOHN WHITAKER.

Page 45. 20 Jan. 1838. Recorded, Spring Court 1838. I, JOB WRIGHT,
          being of sound mind & perfect memory. I give unto my wife
POLLY WRIGHT my tract of land where on I now live & all other property of
every kind after my just debts are paid, during her life time, at her
death to be sold & equally divided between my lawful heirs & their heirs
forever. I appoint my son NEWTON WRIGHT & SAMUEL THOMPSON my executors.
Wit: R. T. HORD, jurat. REBECCA THOMPSON.
                                    Signed: JOB X WRIGHT.

Page 45. 19 April 1832. Recorded, Spring Court 1838. I, JOHN N. CRUSE,
          being weakly in body but sound in mind & memory. I desire to
be decently buried and my just debts to be paid. I leave my wife JANE
my plantation, stock & household furniture during her natural life or
widowhood, then to be divided between my two dtrs. ELIZABETH & PATSY,
also I will that my wife JANE to have my negro woman, until my dtrs. come
of age, my negro girl Mima to be used or sold as the case may be. I
appoint JAMES MCHANN & TOLIVER DAVIS my executors. Wit: HARBART HARTON,
WILLIAM WOOD, jurat.   Signed: JOHN N. X CRUSE.

Page 46. 21 Jan. 1835. Recorded, June Court 1838. I, JERRY GILES, Senr.
          being of sound & disposing mind & memory. I will unto my wife
SARAH the tract of land on which I now live, containing 50 acres during
her life or widowhood, at her death or should she marry then the land to
go to the chn. I had by said SARAH. I also give to my wife SARAH all
personal property except one cow & one feather bed & furniture which I
give unto CATHARINE SANFORD dtr. of my wife SARAH. I give unto my son
JEREMIAH the above named 50 acres of land, on the lower end of the plan-

tation. I appoint my son JEREMIAH & wife SARAH GILES my executors. Wit:
JAMES D. HORTON, jurat. DANIEL FEAGINS, jurat.
                              Signed: JEREMIAH X GILES.

Page 47. 15 March 1838. Recorded, June Court 1838. I, WILLIAM JOLLY,
        being of sound mind & memory, but weak in body. First I allow
my just debts to be paid. I give unto my beloved wife RACHEL JOLLY the
tract of land I now live on, containing 150 acres, stock, household &
kitchen items (names) the Bible & hymn book, one note of hand. The balance of the personal property to be sold and divided among my six chn.
REBECCA WOOD, KIZIAH HANEY, MARTHA BLANTON, JOHN JOLLY, RACHEL DAVIS &
PETER JOLLY. I appoint my son PETER JOLLY sole executor. I will that my
son PETER to take his mother to live with him until death or marriage.
Wit: WILLIAM HARDIN, jurat. JOSEPH X BRADLEY, jurat. CLABORN BLANTON.
                              Signed: WILLIAM JOLLY.

Page 49. 21 Dec. 1837. Recorded, Sept. Court 1838. I, AUDLEY HAMILTON,
        feeling the decline of life. Having some property both real &
personal and having no legitimate issue of my body, but having an illiti-
mate son by the name of BENJAMIN HAMILTON, born of the body of a certain
LUVICY BIGGERSTAFF. I give unto said BENJAMIN HAMILTON two negroes named
Toliver & Adam. I give unto LUVICEY BIGGERSTAFF the plantation I now live
on lying on Cane Creek which I bought of JOHN WITHEROW, all my stock,
farming tools, household & kitchen furniture, one negro named Andy during
her natural life at her death all the estate to my reputed son BENJAMIN
forever. I give unto my nephew AUDLEY MARTIN two tracts of land on
Sandy Run one purchased of JACOB CARRELL & DENNIS CARRELL. I appoint my
son BENJAMIN HAMILTON & friend Genl. JOHN CARSON my executors. Wit: HUGH
WATSON, Junr., jurat. JAMES LOGAN, jurat.   Signed: A. HAMILTON.

Page 50. 13 March 1838. Recorded, Fall Court 1838. I, WILLIAM STEWART,
        being of sound mind & memory. I will all my just debts be paid.
The balance of my estate I desire that my wife & unmarried children live
on the plantation as usual and receive their support. I give my gun unto
son JOHN, the other to be sold. My wife ELIZABETH may sell any stock she
thinks proper or necessary to the use of the family. I appoint my friend
AARON D. MCFARLAND & wife ELIZABETH my executors. Wit: JONA. H. JONES,
jurat. SAMUEL MCFARLAND, jurat.   Signed: WILLIAM X STEWART.

Page 51. No date. Recorded, Fall Court 1838. I, THOMAS DEWS, do make
        this my L & T. I give to my father THOMAS DEWS, Senr. and my
mother all my estate real & personal and after the decease of them to fall
to my sister JULIA. I appoint JOSHUA ROBERTS, Esq. my executor. Wit:
NAT. W. ALEXANDER, E. A. MCCLEUINE.   Signed: THOAS. DEWS, JR.

Page 52. 23 Aug. 1838. Recorded, Fall Court 1838. I, HENRY PETTIE,
        being of sound & perfect mind & memory. First my just debts to
be paid. I leave unto my wife ANNA PETTIE my four slaves, also household
& kitchen furniture, also one horse and my waggon & harness, also my
stock of cattle, hogs, sheep during her life time or widowhood, at her
death I give to my son HENRY PETTIE my negro boy Wait called Pompey. To
my son JOHN PETTIE negro boy called Green with all the farming tools.
What property remains that is not given, to be sold and to my dtr. ELIZA-
BETH MOONEY $25. To my dtr. HANNAH MCDANIEL $15. The remainder to be
divided among all my dtrs. I appoint my son JOHN PETTIE my executor, in
case of death or inability, WILLIAM TONEY. Wit: J.S. WARD, jurat. WILLIAM
ELLIOTT, jurat.   Signed: HENRY PETTIE.

Page 53. 17 May 1835. Recorded, Fall Court 1838. I, WILLIAM BAXTER, Jr.
        being of sound mind & memory. First I want my just debts paid,
then the balance of my property to be sold* and the money put on interest,
and money collected yearly and loaned again or the note renewed including
the money of the past year to be equally divided between my dtr. SARAH
CATHARINE & sons WILLIAM GEORGE MARION and JAMES NEWTON BAXTER (no commas)
when they arrive at the age of 21 yrs. or marry then they to receive the
amount due them. I want them educated and made a good English scholar.
I appoint WM. BAXTER, Senr. & JAMES YOUNG, Senr. my executors and for the
raising & clothing of the children. *My land estate I don't wish it sold
but rented out yearly until the chn. come of age, then to be equally
divided among them. Wit: CATHERINE X BAXTER, ELIZABE BAXTER, DAVID

BAXTER, jurat.   Signed: WM. BAXTER, JR.

Page 54. 9 March 1839. Recorded, Spring Court 1839. I, WILLIAM LUCUS,
          being of sound mind & memory. I give unto my wife MARY after
my just debts are paid to have during her life time all my property of
every kind lands, negroes, cattle, household & kitchen furniture & farming tools, except one horse I have reserved for my grand-son HENRY LUCUS.
After the death of my wife MARY, all property except my land and negroes
Sam & Kato shall be sold, and after her debts & funeral expenses are paid
from my personal property. $10 to be given to the Sundy School of Palm
Tree Church to purchase books for said school by the direction of HENRY
SCHENCK, with the advice of said society. The balance to be equally
divided in 3 parts chn. JOHN, JAMES & NANCY PARKER my dtr. I give unto
my son JOHN forever all that tract of land which he lives on, also part
of the tract which I live on, on the East side of old LUCUS FORD, except
one acre to reserve the spring. I give unto my son JAMES forever all
that tract of land called the home tract, that was deeded to me by HARRIS,
and run out by FRANK ALEXANDER, my wearing clothes. I have give unto my
dtr. NANCY & her husband ANDREW PARKER one tract of land called the Roper
tract & I also give him $1. "Should my old servants, Cato & Sam survive
my wife, I will them to my sons JOHN & JAMES and they must support them
or else they must be supported out of the land I have given them." I
appoint my friend HENRY SCHENCK executor. Wit: BARTLETT CROWDER, BERRY
N. GRIGG, jurat.   Signed: WILLIAM LUCUS.

Page 56. 26 Feb. 1839. Recorded, Sept. Court 1839. I, MARGARET WITHROW,
          being of advance years, but of sound & perfect mind & memory.
After my just debts & funeral expenses are paid, the balance to be divided
as follows, I give unto my niece HANNAH WEBB $10. I give to JAMES WITHROW
all my estate both real & personal except one gray mare. I give unto
JAMES WITHROW'S dtr., MARGARET LOTSANNA WITHROW one gray mare. I appoint
JAMES WITHROW & SAMUEL S. GIDNEY executors. Wit: SAMUEL S. GIDNEY,
jurat, ROBERT PRICE, jurat.   Signed: MARGARET X WITHROW.

Page 57. 16 May 1838. Recorded, Fall Court 1839. I, REBECCA WALDROP,
          being weak in body but of perfect mind & memory. To my beloved
sister MARY ANN WALDROP, I give the following property, one cow & calf,
household & kitchen furniture, also my part of the land which my father
JECHONIAS WALDROP, Senr. decd. willed to his heirs sister POLLY WALDROP,
decd. with my claim on her bed & furniture, after my just debts are paid
the balance of the property. I appoint JECHONIAS WALDROP, Jr. my sole
executor. Wit: THOMAS LITTLEJOHN, jurat. JOEL LITTLEJOHN, jurat.
                                          Signed: REBECCA X WALDROP.

Page 58. 4 July 1814. Recorded, Fall Court 1839. I, THOMAS WHAREY, do
          find that old age coming on, at present in reasonable health,
but perfect mind & memory. All my just debts to be paid. To my beloved
wife LETTICE I give during her natural life that part of my plantation
whereon I now live containing 100 acres, at my wife's death, I will the
same to my son JAMES WHAREY. Also I will that my beloved ----ther (torn)
JANE KILLPATRICK shall have --nds (torn) belonging to me on the East side
of said line. As to the Mountain tract of land, my son & dtr. may sell,
keep or divide it. My personal property to be divided into three lots,
one for my wife, one for my son JAMES and one for dtr. JANE. I appoint
my wife LETTICE executrix & brother GEORGE WHAREY, my son JAMES WHREY, &
friend DAVID DICKEY, and JAMES ERWIN my executors. Wit: D. DICKEY,
SUSANNAH X REAVES.   Signed: THOMAS WHREY.

Page 59. 3 May 1839. Recorded, Dec. Court 1839. I, WILLIAM CROWDER,
          being of sound & perfect mind & memory. First I give unto my
wife LUCY my mare, cows, her bed, kitchen furniture, 10 head hogs, also
her spinning wheel during her natural life, she to have her support from
the plantation, the balance of personal property to be sold to pay just
debts & wife support, in the care of JARREL CROWDER & SAMUEL THOMSON,
Senr. At the decease of wife NANCY the remaining property to be sold
and money equally divided among the heirs of JERREL CROWDER & ABSOLAM
WARLICK, I further will to my son JARREL my gun. I will to my dtr. POLLY
GRIGG, my dtr. PATSY MARTIN, my son WILLIAM CROWDER each of them $1. I
appoint my friend SAMUEL THOMSON & son JARREL CROWDER my executors. Wit:
HENRY SCHINCK, W. A. TISDALE, jurat.   Signed: WILLIAM X CROWDER.

Page 61. 9 May 1838. Recorded, Dec. Court 1839. I, ANDREW PEELER, being
of sound mind & memory. I give unto my wife ANNA PEELER all
the lands I now live on during her natural life also my negro woman named
Patience & her dtr. Elizabeth. I give to JOHN & DAVID PEELER my two sons
all the above named land after wife ANNA PEELER'S death to be divided
between them. I give to my dtr. ELIZABETH LONNON half of the above named
negroes after the death of said ANNA. I give unto my dtr. MARY LONNON'S
heirs the other of the value of the named negroes. I give to my dtr.
ELIZABETH & MARY and sons JOHN & DAVID all stock, household & kitchen
furniture after ANNA'S decease. I give unto MARY LONNON $1. I appoint
my sons JOHN & DAVID LONNON executors. Wit: ANDERSON S. ELAM, jurat.
THOMAS POOL.   Signed: ANDREW PEELER.

Page 62. -- -- 1837. Recorded, March 1840. ANN DOGGETT, being of sound
mind & memory. I give to my dtr. ELIZABETH ELLIOTT $5. To my
son CHARLES Y. DOGGETT $5. To my son JAMES P. DOGGETT a negro boy named
Armstead. To my dtr. SARAH GOUDELOCK a negro girl named Maria which she
now has. I give to my sons GEORGE, RICHARD L., COLEMAN DOGGETT the
following negroes Abram, Frederick, Little Jasper, Mahala. After paying
$300 out said negroes by my executors to FANNY MCBRYER. To my son JAMES
one bed & furniture & kitchen furniture. To R. L. DOGGETT one feather
bed & furniture. To my sons R. L. & JAMES DOGGETT my flock of sheep.
To my grand-dtr. SARAH ANN DOGGETT one counterpin and one to my grand dtr.
SARAH ANN GOUDELOCK. I appoint my two sons COLEMAN & JAMES DOGGETT my
executors. Wit: DAVID HAMRICK, jurat. JOSEPH POPE.
                                      Signed: ANN DOGGETT.

Page 63. 4 Dec. 1839. Recorded, March Court 1840. ELIJAH THOMPSON.
This the will of ELIJAH THOMPSON. "We consider him to be in
his right mind." (Nuncupative will). ELIJAH THOMPSON, Senr. to have the
mountain land, and RAMSON THOMPSON $30 extra Dec. 28, 1840 due unto him.
ELVIRA THOMPSON the land, a bed & furniture. AMBROSE THOMPSON $18 which
he owed ELIJAH THOMPSON, Senr. ELIJAH the river place & AMBROSE the
Elson place. MARGARET THOMPSON his wife the remainder of his property
for her life time. At her death sold according to law and divided amongst
my heirs. (Executors not named.) Wit: JOHN ELLISON, jurat. WILLIAM
GARRETT, jurat.   Signed: ELIJAH X THOMPSON.

Page 64. 28 Jany. 1840. Recorded, Spring Court 1840. I, SAMUEL MCCRAW,
being in bad health but perfect mind & memory. I give unto my
loving wife SUSANNA MCCRAW the whole of my household & kitchen furniture
and stock of all kinds enough for her support, also my horse & waggon I
give unto my wife & family for their use, also my smith tools to my wife
& family and at her death I give them to my son ABNER B. MCCRAW. I give
unto my son WILLIS B. MCCRAW one bed & male saddle. I give unto my dtr.
PAGGY DUGAN one bed. I give unto my granddaughter POLLY ANN HUMPHRES,
LUCINDA HUMPHRES, RANEY HUMPHRES four head of cattle, my dtr. BETSY
HUMPHRES to have the use of said cattle for her use & support, until her
chn. come of age. WILLIAM HUMPHRES to have no right or claim to said
cattle. (No executors named.) Wit: G. B. PALMER, jurat. JOSIAH MCCRAW,
jurat.   Signed: SAMUEL MCCRAW.

Page 65. 7 May 1840. Recorded, June Court 1840. I, JAMES MOREHEAD,
being feeble in body but of perfect mind & memory. Being
possessed with 200 acres of land, lying on waters of Robertson Creek where
I now reside. I give unto my dtr. ELIZABETH GUFFIE & her heirs for wait-
ing on me in my sickness and my son ANDREW MOOREHEAD the 200 acres of land
to be divided between them. I appoint my son DAVID MOOREHEAD my executor.
Wit: JOHN HAIMON, jurat. JAMES FINDLEY LONG, jurat.
                                      Signed: JAMES X MOOREHEAD.

Page 66. 31 July 1838. Recorded, July Court 1840. I, MARY WATSON being
advanced in life but of sound mind & memory. First I give unto
my granddaughter MARY M. PATTEN one negro girl named Alvery, one beaureaw
(Bureau) made by MARK MOORE, one bed & furniture with a stand of curtains
with the bed made by JOHN MENTAETH. I give unto my grandson ADOLPHUS L.
PATTEN one negro boy named George, one house clock, one bed & furniture,
one table, half of my cupbord furniture. I give unto my granddaughter
HARRIET N. PATTEN one bed & furniture. I allow my negro woman named
Tilley and all my other estate not mentioned to be sold and the money

101

divided as follows, first I give unto my dtr. NANCY M. JEFFERSON $50. I
allow $50 to RACHEL C. & CHARITY E. PATTEN my grandchildren to purchase
them beds when they come to need them. I allow $25 to Little Britan
Church to be paid in five yrs. to any presbyterean minister that may labor
in the church. I allow my grandson GEORGE W. JEFFERSON $100. The balance
to be divided among MARGARET M., HARRIET A., RACHAEL C. and CHARITY E.
PATTEN my grand-chn. I appoint my kinsman and friend JAMES W. CARSON my
executor. Wit: JON. CARSON, jurat. FRANCES LOGAN, jurat.
                                        Signed: MARY X WATSON.

Page 68. 1 Aug. 1839. Recorded, Sept. Court 1840. I, JOSIAH DURHAM,
        first after my death my executors shall sell at Logan's sale
grounds, on Saturday and on twelve months credit, my negro girl Mary, &
my watch, my debts to be paid & the balance to be loaned out. The balance
of my property I leave to my wife POLLY during her life or widowhood or
until the children come of age. At my wife's death Peter to be hired out
and the land & other property sold & the money loaned out. My wife to
have a child part, when the youngest come of age Peter is to be sold and
the money divided among them all. I allow the children to have a common
education. I appoint my friend EDMUND JONES, & WILLIAM HAMBRICK & my
son ELIJAH my executors. Wit: JEFFERSON R. HAMRICK, jurat. JOHN MCSWAIN,
jurat. GEORGE MCSWAIN.   Signed: J. DURHAM.

Page 69. 6 Oct. 1840. Recorded, Fall Court 1840. I, HUMPREY PARISH,
        give unto my grand-son WATSON P. ABRAHAM all the messuage &
tenements whereon I now live, containing 118 acres, the Farmer tract of
100 acres, the TOM WELCH tract of 185 acres, the JOHN CULBRETH tract of
112, the JOSEPH PETEY tract of 100 acres, the ANDREW MILLER tract of 100
acres in fee simple. Also my waggon & team of 4 horses, 20 head of hogs,
his choice of 15 head of cattle, 11 head of sheep, 4 beds & furniture,
household & kitchen furniture, farming tools, including the wheat fan.
Also 500 busels of corn, 8 stacks of oats, my shot gun, called the crowder
gun. Also negroes, George & his wife Alsea, Lina, Minerva, Mcentire,
Owen, Hammer, Granville, & all black smith tools. I give unto my granddtr. MARY JOHNSON MILLER my negro named Julia, Also I give to my granddtr. MARY MCFARLAND my negro named Jensy. The rest of my negroes not
named (18) in number, my executor shall make an equal division between my
two dtrs. LYDIA W. ABRAHAM and ELIZABETH MILLER. My tract of land lying
on Green River whereon my daughter-in-law HARRIET PARISH now lives, shall
have the use & benfit of all until her youngst child comes of age. I
give unto HUMPHREY and WALKER PARISH & MARY ANN PARISH $250 to be paid
when they come of age. I will that HUMPHREY shall have negro man Sterling
Grand-children THOMAS STEEL, ANN P. STEEL, MARTHA JANE STEEL each in be-
coming of age $250. All notes and money to pay the bequeaths of MARY ANN
PARISH & ROBERT STEEL. I appoint EDMUND BRYAN & WATSON P. ABRAHAM my
executors. Wit: A. MILLER, E. BRYAN, jurat. ELIZABETH MILLER, SARAH X
BLACK, jurat.   Signed: HUMPHREY X PARISH.

Page 72. 13 March 1835. Recorded, Dec. Court 1840. I, ABSOLUM HUNT,
        Being in perfect mind & memory and health. I want all my just
debts paid. I give unto my wife MARTHA HUNT her full support from the
land whereon I now live, during her life or widowhood also a negro woman
named Lucy, one horse, one cow & calf, all the beds, except my dtr.
CINTHEY & LETTIA which they are to keep, until called for, also my son
ELIJAH & ELISHA HUNT all my lands, ELISHA to have the lower plantation on
the Bedford tract. The other to be equal divided between WILLIAM & ELIJAH,
my three sons to pay my dtrs. the sum of $650, that is ELISHA to pay $250,
WILLIAM & ELIJAH to pay $200 each. My dtrs. LEVICY SIMMONS, ELIZABETH
VANZANT & CINTHEY and LETTIA the balance of my property with the afore-
said sum. I give unto CINTHEY & LETTICE one walnut chest each made by
HENRY HAWSER. I appoint my son WILLIAM & ELIJAH HUNT my executors. Wit:
JOSEPH TAYLOR, jurat. HENRY HAWSER, jurat.
                                        Signed: ABSOLUM X HUNT.

Page 74. 15 Sept. 1840. Recorded, Feb. Court 1841. I, WYATT E. HYNES,
        being very sick & weak in body but of perfect mind & memory.
I give unto MARY my wife all the property of every discription that I
possess after all my debts are paid during her natural life. At the
expiration of which I give it unto my beloved granddaughter MARY MARGARET
BAXTER. (No executors named.) Wit: LEWIS CAMP, Junr., jurat. LITTLE B.

HINES, jurat.   Signed: Not signed.

Page 75. 16 Dec. 1840. Recorded, Feb. Court 1841. I, JAMES MCKINNY,
          being of sound mind & memory. After all my just debts & funeral
expenses are paid, "I give unto BETTY YOUNG in consideration of services
rendered in former days a comfortable support and my negro girl Mamdy to
wait on her during her natural life." I appoint THOS. BAXTER as guardian
of said BETSY & property. I give all the property both real & personal
to my son ALFRED MCKINNY and I do appoint THOMAS BAXTER as his guardian.
Lands lying near the High Sholes known as the Old Tract, and the Sharpe
Tract near JOHN MCDANIELS. I appoint THOMAS BAXTER my executor. Wit:
THOMAS VASSE, jurat. MARION AMOS & TEMPY AMOS.
                                    Signed: JAMES MCKINNY.

Page 76. 1 Jan. 1841. Recorded, Feb. Court 1841. ANTHONY STREET, I
          give to my dtr. RACHEL FORBES one sow & 5 pigs, one still &
vessels, fire shovel & tongs. One cow to my granddaughter SALLY FORBES.
One bed & furniture to my sons JOHN & JAMES to be divided between the
two. Then the balance of my property, which is one cow & 2 yearlings to
be sold and divided amongst the rest of my heirs. JAMES & JOHN to have
an equal part with the rest. (No executor named here.) Wit: JAMES PRICE,
jurat. WILLIAM L. PRICE, ROBERT T. PRICE, executor.
                                    Signed: ANTHONY STREET.

Page 77. 16 Feb. 1841. Recorded, March Court 1841. I, WILLIAM GRAYSON,
          being very low & weak in body but of perfect mind & memory.
First I want my just debts paid. I give unto my son BENJAMIN all the
tract of land whereon I now live, joining lands of SPENCER MELTON & J. H.
JONES & others. I give unto my dtr. PATSY QUEEN one lot of land deeded
to me by the heirs of BENJAMIN GRAYSON decd. being a part of the dower
laid off and set apart for RACHEL GRAYSON, decd. widow of JOS. GRAYSON.
I give unto my dtr. ELIZABETH one lot granted to JOS. GRAYSON, Junr. being
part of the above mentioned dower. I give unto my dtr. SALLY DEVINEY,
one lot granted to myself being part of the above mentioned dower and one
lot granted to me from ISAAC GRAYSON a part of above mentioned dower I
want sold, and all other property belonging to me, that is stock, horses,
hogs, household & kitchen furniture, still, farming tools, the money
arising to pay my just debts and the surplus divided among my son BENJAMIN
GRAYSON, dtrs. SALLY DEVINEY, PATSY QUEEN & ELIZABETH GRAYSON. I appoint
my son BENJAMIN GRAYSON my executor. Wit: JOSEPH TAYLOR, jurat. JOHN M.
GRAYSON, JOS. D. G. DEVINEY, W. T. HOWSER, jurat.
                                    Signed: WM. GRAYSON.

Page 78. 18 Dec. 1833. Recorded, March Court 1841. I, THOMAS UPTON,
          being in good health and haveing the use of my perfect senses.
I give unto my beloved wife RUTHA UPTON all property that belongs to me.
After her death to be divided among the chn. DANIEL UPTON, EDWARD UPTON,
THOMAS UPTON, POLLY HILL, REBECCA WEST, ELIZABETH WEST, SARAH WALKER. I
appoint DANIEL UPTON my executor. Wit. THOMAS J. (jurat) sic.
                                    Signed: THOMAS X UPTON.

Page 79. 20 July 1832. Recorded, Spring Court 1841. I, JOHN MOORE, do
          make and ordain this instrument written by myself. ect. To my
dear wife I give all property I received with her, to be desposed of at
her descretion. I also give her $3,000 in money when collected, I give
her a life estate in the house and the land I bought from ROBERT HAMILTON,
also the entries of land adjoining it, also the Dodd & Sherry place and
the land on Machine Creek. I give also two negro men of her choice & two
negro women, all household furniture of every kind, except bedding which
my children are to have a share when they come of age or marry. My wife
to have my carriage and two horses and a child part of my stock. I desire my wife & children to live together until of age or marry. My land
is not to be sold unless to purchase other land more convenient. My
negroes not to be seperated from the family, no child under the age of
eight taken from its mother. No negro that has a wife or husband in the
neighborhood shall be sent out of it without their consent. I will that
when my property is divided my dtrs. to receive their share in money or
personal property. In the case of my death while WILLIAM GRAHAM lives
with me it is my wish that he carry on the store so long as it may be
profitable, he be allowed his board for two years and one third of the net

profit, Should he choose to remain & carry on the buisness he to have one
half of the profit. The business of JAMES NESBITT & myself on the Tyger
and the business now run by FRANCES WARD have considerable debts. I give
unto my wife a child part of all profits that may arise from my farms,
store and mills. My children to have a good English education. I leave
$100 to the laid out for the education of the poor in the neighborhood.
I appoint my wife SARAH executrix. ROBERT G. TWITTY, AMBROSE MILLS, Esq.
& JAMES NESBITT Junr. of Spartanburg, S.C. my executor.
                         Signed: JOHN MOORE.
I, JOHN MOORE, do make this a codicil to my will dated 20 July 1832.
Should my wife SARAH out live me of which there is every probability. I
leave her sole executor of my last will & testament, advising her to con-
sult with her brother ROBERT G. TWITTY believeing he will render considerable service to my wife & children, as he living in the area will be
more use. As WILLIAM T. GRAHAM & JAS. NESBITT has left my employment
and AMBROSE MILLS names has been erased from my will as executor. Dated
28 April 1834.

Page 84. 12 Oct. 1832. Recorded, Fall Court 1841. I, RUSSELL TWITTY, I
          will that my brother, ROBERT G. TWITTY, pay over to JANE EMILY
and WILLIAM (no commas) when they arrive at proper age the balance due me
for my lot of land deeded to him & two negroes boys Ransom & Reubun now
in the possession of him & my mother, making a total of $900 to be paid
as stated. I, will my watch to WILLIAM to be given him at proper age. I
will that all notes due me be collected & put to interest by my brother
ROBERT and expended in educating the children. In case any of the above
named chn. which are the three youngest children of MATILDA COULTER, so
called, should die then such estate shall revert to my brother & sister.
I appoint my brother ROBERT G. TWITTY sole executor. Wit: GUILFORD EAVES.
                         Signed: RUSSELL TWITTY.

Page 85. 9 April 1839. Recorded, Feb. Court 1842. I, JOHN COLLINS,
          being sick & weak in body, but of perfect mind & memory. I
give to my well beloved dtrs. SALLY & LUCINDA all the cattle that belongs
to me, beds & bedding, also my man, also my son-in-law JAMES B. WILKIE
should take & collect all my notes that I have in my possession. It is
my will that my son, RUSSELL should possess that 100 acres of land in the
mountains, it is my will my two sons DANIEL & JOHN should receive $1 each
out of the notes collected. (No executor named.) Wit: WILLIAM WILKIE,
Senr., jurat. T. D. WILKIE, jurat.   Signed: JOHN X COLLINS.

Page 87. 20 Feb. 1842. Recorded, Spring Court 1842. I, Colo. JOHN
          MILLS, of White Oak, Being of sound mind & memory. I will all
my just debts be paid. I give to my son WILLIAM MILLS the tract of land
he now lives on, including the ROBERT LOGAN tract & LEANDER CORRUTH entry
of 100 acres, & so much of the Rock House tract below the new road. I
give unto my son GEORGE MILLS the land where the mansion house & plantation is located, lands on White Oak Mt. above PATRICK MURROW'S land, land
I purchased of SAMUEL YOUNG'S heirs, the tract of land where the grist
mill is purchased of JAMES YOUNG, also the Ross place, & the lands purchased of FRANK ALEXANDER, also all land on Mill Creek & Rock Branch. I
give to my son GOVAN MILLS the land whereon he now lives on the Pacolet
River, including the GEORGE LOGAN lands which I bought of Dr. McEntire,
with the Shields tract & Clouds entry, I will that the Corruth entry above
named to my son WILLIAM be divided so as to give one half only to WILLIAM
& the other to GOVAN. I give to my son COLUMBUS MILLS all my Packolet
lands on both sides of the stream, above son WILLIAM lands, including
the WILLIAM LOGAN tract, the Rock House tract, the place I bought of
Brandon, & the JACK LANKFORD place. I give my son COLUMBUS the above
land upon the condition that he give up all rights, titles, & interest to
my son RUFUS MILLS that he may have on a tract of 640 acres tract of land
lying in Alabama where RUFUS is now living in Russell County. I give to
my grandson JOHN C. CAMP a tract on White Oak joining lands of son GEORGE,
that I bought of PADDY MURROW, also the lands I bought of SAMUEL YOUNG
estate, & the ANDREW YOUNG tract, not already given to son GEORGE. I
give to my grandson JOHN M. DEAN all the tract of land on White Oak called
the East Wood tract containing 200 acres. I give to my granddtr. LOUISA
CAMP all my lands on Green River that I bought of PADDY MURROW & my
Kilpatrick purchase. The remaining lands to be sold and money applied to
my just debts. I give to my son WILLIAM negroes, Mary, Andy, Bons, Isaac,

Dina, Anaka, Armulla, Green, & half my books, rifle, powder horn & shot
bag. I give to my son GEORGE negroes, Stephen, Alsy, Joe Ann, Abram,
Milly, Darcus, Lucy & Bob, & my shot gun, powder horn & sideboard, common
chairs, bed & furniture & my saddle. I give to my son GOVAN the negroes,
Glass, Baz, Burdo, Prince, Hannah, Buster, Adam, Abram, & my shot gun &
powder horn. I give to my son COLUMBUS the negroes, Anthony, Jim, Flint,
Simeon, Satira, Fed & half of my books. I give to my son RUFUS, negroes
Mose, Lida, Jerry, Rose, Horace, Shadnik, Tom, Phillis. I give to my
granddtr. I give to my grandson JOHN C. CAMP, negroes Henry, Martha, &
Hawkins, I give to my granddtr. LOUISA CAMP, negroes Rachel, Jimmy,
Polden, & one bed & furniture complete, her mother's fruit baskets, the
caster candlesticks tray, one lady's saddle in place of my riding saddle.
The balance of my property to be sold applied to the payment of my debts.
I will that my sons WILLIAM & COLUMBUS be guardian of my grandchn. LOUISA
& JOHN CAMP. I also appoint them & GOVEN my executors. I have given
unto JOHN M. DEAN by bill of sale recorded in Rutherfordton County, neg-
roes Delia, Anderson, Orange, Harvey, Ruby & June & her child. Wit: JOS
M. D. CARSON & WALTER DUFFY.   Signed: JHO. MILLS.
CODICIL: Dated 6 March 1842. The items given to son RUFUS to be void.
          The same given to son COLUMBUS in trust for RUFUS and his law-
ful heirs forever. RUFUS may sell or trade any part of the legacy with
said son COLUMBUS. The negro Cato to be given to granddtr. LOUISA CAMP.
CODICIL #2. Dated 12 March 1842. Negro Polden to be taken from LOUISA &
          given to son COLUMBUS, negro boy Fed given to LOUISA in lieu
of Polden. Wit: JOS. M. D. CARSON & WALTER DUFFY.
                                         Signed: JHO. MILLS.

Page 92. 3 Feb. 1841. Recorded, Spring Court 1842. I, JOHN LOGAN, Senr.
          being of sound mind. My just debts to be paid. I give unto
MARTHA LOGAN during her natural life or widowhood my plantation whereon I
now live, known as the Panter tract & the following negroes, Moses, George,
Gilford, Molly, Little Harriet, all personal property not divised in this
will, all debts due me to be collected. At marriage or death of my wife
her property to be divided as follows, the plantation to be divided between my dtrs. MARY ADALINE & MARTHA LOUISA. The furniture belonging to
the house at my wife's death to be divided between my two dtrs. The personal property given to my wife, at her death to be divided among my
three chn. GEORGE, JOHN & SUSAN. The tracts of land known as JOHN S.
HARDIN, WM. BRIDGES & Widow BLANTONS to be sold and money divided among
my three dtrs. ADALINE, LOUISA & SUSAN. I give unto GEORGE my Milikin
tract, the ditches cut to turn Cain Creek to be the line between said
tract & Mr. Panther tract, also my interest in a patent on Connonways
Creek, held by ANDREW LOGAN, also my interest in a lease on THOS. COGGINS
land, known as the Owen mine, also the tract of land I bought of LAWSON
ALEXANDER, also the THOMAS FREEMAN land purchased by ROBERT BURTON, known
as the Bryant tract also the following negroes, Phillis, Willy, Adophus,
Gilley, Charles. I give unto my son JOHN the tract of land Sandy Run,
known as the SAMUEL MOORE place, also the EDMUND HAMNCK tract, also the
Scruggs place & the following negroes Joannah, Bones, Vina, Caesar, &
Joannahs youngest child. I give to my dtr. ADALINE the lower end of the
Moore tract called the Dey tract, the East side of the Powell tract, also
the Alexander land, & the following negroes Clarissa, Washington & Hender-
son. I give to my dtr. LOUISA the upper end of the Moore land, the West
side of the Powell tract, also the following negroes Abner, Harnit & Jane.
I give to my dtr. SUSAN my lots in Rutherfordton, & two tract joining
known as the ANDREW MILLER & RICHARD LEWIS tracts, all land on Cathey
Creek, & the following negroes, Sarah, John & Marshal. I give to the
heirs of my son LAWDON U. LOGAN, decd. $5 each. I appoint my sons GEORGE
W. LOGAN & JOHN W. LOGAN my executor. Wit: B. W. ANDREWS, jurat. JOSEPH
S. WALLIS, jurat.   Signed: JOHN LOGAN.

Page 95. 23 Nov. 1840. Recorded, Spring Court. I, GEORGE HAY, being in
          health and of sound mind. I request all my just debts be paid.
I give unto my beloved wife MARTHA HAY all the residue of my worldly
estate of land whereon I now live with all my stock, Household & kitchen
Furniture, to have during her natural life and at her death or marriage,
the property aforsaid I give unto my son GEORGE HAY (alias WESSON) to his
own proper use forever. (No executor named.) Wit: WILLIAM HUNTLEY,
jurat. JOHN LANCASTER, jurat.   Signed: GEORGE P. HAY.

Page 96.   15 Feb. 1832.   Recorded, Spring Court 1842.   AARON DEVINEY,
being of sound mind & memory.   I give unto my beloved wife
SARAH the plantation I now live on, with her choice of the household &
kitchen furniture, one horse of her choice, two cows & calves, eight head
hogs, all my books & $50 in money & our bed & furniture during natural
life and at her death I want all the above named property sold and equally
divided among my dtrs. except my books.   ELIZABETH STUART & her heirs if
she will take it for $450.   I give to my son ROBERT $1.   I give unto my
dtr. ANN DEVINEY one horse worth $60, or that much money over & above her
part with the rest of my dtrs.   Unto my son ROBERT'S chn. one child part
divided among them JOHN BRACKET, WM. DEVINEY, JOSEPH G. DEVINEY, JENKINS
DEVINEY, BENJ. DEVINEY, AARON J. DEVINEY, SARAH PRUIT, ROBERT DEVINEY, Jr.
I give unto my grandson AARON D. MCFARLAND $25.   Grandson AARON D. WALTERS
$25.   Grandson AARON D. LOVE $25.   Also AARON D. MCFARLAND Jr. & AARON
T. DUNLOP each $25 when they come of age.   Executors to take money for a
head stone for my wife SARAH.   I appoint JAMES MCFARLAND, & AARON D. MC-
FARLAND, Jr. my executors.   Wit: WM. M. MCFARLAND, GEORGE MCFARLAND, A.D.
MCFARLAND, ALFRED MCFARLAND.   Signed: AARON DEVINEY.

Page 98.   13 May 1842.   Recorded, June Court 1842.   I, EPHRAIM CARRUTH,
being of sound mind & disposing memory.   I give unto my son
EDWIN LUSTER CARRUTH my mountain tract of land, joining my home tract &
AMBROS MILLS tract, containing 82½ acres.   I give my home tract where I
reside to my two youngest sons, to be divided equally between them,
WILLIAM PERRY CARRUTH & EPHRAIM ALEXANDER CARRUTH, I will that my wife
SUSANNAH CARRUTH retain possession & control, also all household furniture,
all stock of hogs, cattle, sheep & still, with vessels for her use in
using the fruit from the place at any time, and the proceeds applied to
the support of the chn.   The property named above given during her life
time and at her death to be equally divided between all my lawfull heirs.
The shares I purchased of BENJAMIN LANKFORD in my Mother-in-law's estate
on the waters of Shinca on Tryon Mountain.   My lawful share by my wife,
I leave for my executors to manage for my young chn.   I wish my gun to be
sold and the money applied to making the chimney etc. on my new house.   I
appoint SAMUEL LUCAS, & wife SUSANNAH my executors.   Wit: WILLIAM S.
MILLS, COLUMBUS MILLS.   Signed: EPHRAIM CARRUTH.

 Page 99.   7 Jan. 1842.   Recorded, July Court 1842.   I, NATHAN MCDANIEL,
being weak in body but of sound mind & memory.   First I want
all my just debts paid.   I give unto my beloved wife TEMPY MCDANIEL, my
land & stock of all kinds, household & kitchen furniture, except a filly
& a sow and pigs which my son JETHRO claims.   The land & property left at
my wife's death or marriage to be sold and money divided among my eight
chn.   I appoint MICAJAH MCCALL my executor.   Wit: THOMAS S. MCDANIEL,
MOSES WILKERSON, Jr.   Signed: NATHAN MCDANIELS.

Page 100.   13 Feb. 1842.   Recorded, Sept. Court 1842.   I, HEZEKIAH BLANK-
ENSHIP, being in sound mind & memory but low in body.   First
I will all my just debts be paid.   Then I give unto my beloved wife SUSANN-
AH BLANKENSHIP all my land, and one negro girl named Unis, with all my
stock of horses, Cattle & hog, all household & kitchen furniture, all
working tools during her life time or widowhood.   At her death all property to be sold and the money divided among all my chn. (not named).   I
appoint my wife SUSANNAH BLANKENSHIP my executor.   Wit: JNO. ROOKER, &
WM. BLANKENSHIP.   Signed: HEZEKIAH X BLANKENSHIP.

Page 101.   29 April 1842.   Recorded, Fall Court 1842.   I, JAMES WHOREY, of
Goochland County, Virginia.   First, I desire that a mortgage
of my land to the amount of $1,000 to be paid off & cancelled to the
trustees of the church fund in Providence Congregation & that all my just
debts be paid.   I authorized my executors to dispose of my land in this
county & vest the money in property for the benfit of my children.   Wife
has power to sell any personal property she thinks advisable.   I appoint
my friend & brother-in-law WILLIAM S. MARTIN of Cumberland & my beloved
wife ELIZA F. WHOREY my executor.   Wit: G. W. PAYNE, Jr., G. W. HARRIS.
                              Signed: JAMES WHOREY.

29 April 1842.   The above will was probated in Goochland Co., Va. by wife
ELZA & WM. S. MARTIN as executors.   Bond set at $12,000.   The above will
was proved before the Clerk of Court of Goochland Co., Va. on the 20 June
1842.   On the third day of October 1842 the Clerk of Court certify is a

true copy of the above will.   Signed: W. MILLER, C.G.C.

Page 102. 5 May 1842. Recorded, Fall Court 1842. I, JACOB WALKER,Being
          sick in body but of sound mind & memory. I will unto my dtr.
HARRIETT my two negroes named Eliza & Clerasy & $100 in money. I give
unto my dtr. MARY ELIZABETH LILA & SARAH ANN (no commas) $150 each more
than equal share. I give to my son GEORGE the same amount above his
equal part. I divise that the rest of my estate be divided between my
chn. JOHN, JAMES, JOSEPH, FELIX, STANHOPE, ANDREW & GEORGE, MARY ELIZABETH,
LELIA, & SARAH ANN. I give unto my son FELIX the share of my son JOSEPH
& STANHOPE in trust as my son FELIX may thank they need the sum. I give
unto my dtrs. & son GEORGE support for one year from my crop. My single
chn. to have all beds & furnishings. I appoint my son JOHN W. & JAMES M.
WALKER my executors. Wit: JOMES M. MILLER, JASON MCKENNY, MATILDA X
TIGGINS, JOS. M. BLACK.   Signed: J. WALKER.

Page 104. 9 Oct. 1842. Recorded, Fall Court 1842. I, JOHN ABRAMS,
          being of sound & disosing memory. I give to my beloved wife
the land where I now live and the following negroes, George, Jacob, Nutty,
& Mariah, also one waggon, one horse. The mill tract I leave for the
benfit of my wife & chn. except for my son WATSON P. ABRAMS, I give $100
as he has his share already. The land I live on to my wife, at her death
to be divided among the chn. except WATSON. I wish that WILL S. MILES,
DR. CALLOWAY, & COLUMBUS MILES to lot off the rest of my negroes equally
for my nine children viz. MARY, NATHANIEL, JAMES, ASPUE, NANCY, HUMPHREY,
ROBERT, DENNIS, & ANN. I wish my stock of cattle, hogs, Sheep & horse
to be sold. I appoint my son NATHANIEL G. ABRAMS & ROBERT MCFARLAND my
executors. Wit: WILL S. MILES, JOS. W. CALLOWAY.
                              Signed: JOHN ABRAMS.

Page 105. 2 Nov. 1841. Recorded, June Court 1843. GEORGE JONES, being
          in possession of my usual strength of mind. First I wish all
honest & just demands on me to be discharged. I desire my wife ELIZABETH
to have the following negroes viz. Ben, Phebe & their son Charles & Eliza
and her dtr. Juda, one carriage & 2 horses, 3 mules & the new waggon, 10
cows & calves, 60 head hogs, one third of Real estate and household furniture. The estate to be under controll of my wife during her life time.
I leave Hary & his wife & their boy Guiden in care of my wife for the
support of my son GEORGE and he is not subject to any debts, hereafter
made except the one owed to my son WILLIAM, which debt I desire paid from
the estate, I wish my wife to appoint a guardian for my son GEORGE. I
leave my dtr. MARY the following negroes, Milly & her 3 chn. Jane, Robert
& Uery, Man named Ernie & Sam, Jacob & Joe, woman called Lucinda, one
Forte Piano, one horse, saddle & bridle. I give unto my son JOHN, negroes,
Lewis, Ben, Dodd, Dock, woman named Milly (dtr. of Ben & Phebe) & her
child named George, a girl named Peg, one young horse, I have given him
the sum of $4,000. I have given to my son THOMAS the sum of $4,000,
I now give him a negro boy named Anthony with $700. I have given to my
son EDMOND the sum of $5,964, also I give him a negro boy named Oliver
Perry and at my death to have my silver watch. I have unto my son WILLIAM
cash & property worth $4,080. I have given my dtr. CAROLINE YOUNG cash &
property worth $4,055. I have given my son EDWIN $3,974. I have given
my son GEORGE cash & property worth $3,689. I appoint my son EDWIN
guardian of my son JOHN & dtr. MARY during their infancy. I appoint my
sons WILLIAM & ERWIN my executors. Wit: WILLIS FOSTER, EPHRAIM LITTLEJOHN.
                              Signed: GEORGE JONES.
CODICIL. Dated 15 Oct. 1842. I hereby appoint my son JOHN as an execu-
          tor with WILLIAM & ERWIN to my will dated 2 Nov. 1841. Also
JOHN is to assist his mother in the managment of her property, and of the
property of my son GEORGE and his support. I.wish my wife to give my son
GEORGE a comfortable support as is common in this part of the country,
and after her death I wish his guardian to supply the same. I give unto
my wife ELIZABETH all household & kitchen furniture, also a negro girl
named Het dtr. of Hary & Rachel, also a man named Sutton during her natural life, Said negro Sutton now in possession of my son-in-law Doctor
ROBERT MC. YOUNG of Cass County, Ga. Wit: WILLIS FOSTER & EPHRAIM LITTLE-
JOHN.   Signed: GEORGE JONES.

Page 110. 23 Aug. 1843. Recorded, Sept Court 1843. I, JOHN LONG, being
          weak in body but sound mind & memory. I give unto my beloved

107

wife ISABELLA LONG one negro man named David, also 2 cows & calves, 2
good feather beds & necessary furniture, one bureau, one chest and $50 in
gold and silver, side saddle, flax wheel, wheat & corn, during her natural
life. I give to my son ANDREW B. LONG ½ of the crops gathered and ½ of
the crop to be gathered. The balance of my property not given to be sold
and the money divided among my chn. & the chn. of my son JOHN A. LONG,
decd. I appoint my two sons WILLIAM & ANDREW LONG my executors. Wit:
J. M. CARSON, JNO. CARSON.   Signed: JOHN LONG.

Page 111. 10 Feb. 1843. Recorded, Sept. Court 1843. I, MOURNING HANES,
              being of perfect mind & memory. I make & ordain my friend
D. B. FREEMAN my executor. What property I have left to be sold and
equally divided among my chn. when they come of age. Wit: FRANCIS C.
HANES, PLEASANT H. HANES.   Signed: MOURNING X HANES.
P.S. Others witnesses to this will, JOHN FREEMAN, JOHN NIX & WM. W. NIX.

Page 113. 9 Oct. 1841. Recorded, Fall Court 1843. I, ROBERT WEBB, being
              of sound mind & memory. After all my just debts & funeral
expenses are paid. I give unto my beloved PEGGY the tract of land whereon I now live, containing 200 acres, also a tract joining the old tract &
Miss BLANTON'S possession of 50 acres, and a tract joining JOHN BURGES
possession of 150 acres, two negroes boys named Marion & Prince, 3 negro
girls named Anna, Rose & Julia, a negro man called Howard, & woman Judith,
five cows & calves, three horses, all beds & furnitures, household &
kitchen furniture at her death or marriage the negroes, Marion, Prince,
Anna, Rose & Julia to belong to my youngest son JESSE I. WEBB and my
youngest dtr. MALINDA WEBB, also the tract of land I bought of HARBERT
HORTON lying on old tract joining BOSWELL BOSTICK being part of the JOHN
BUFORD tract containing 100 acres, also negroes Ivey & Moses, one horse,
saddle & bridle. I give to my youngest dtr. MALINDA WEBB a negro boy
named King & girl named Charlotte, with 2 good feather beds & furniture,
one good horse, saddle & bridle. I give unto my son ALFRED WEBB, a negro
man called Daniel. I give unto my son ROBERT $1. I give unto my son
JAMES' heirs if any $1. I give unto my son ELISHA WEBB $1. I give unto
my dtr. DRUCILLA ASLY $1. The balance of my property to be sold and
equally divided among my sons, CLINTON WEBB, IVY WEBB, & dtrs. TEMPY HILL,
HETY GOODE, DELILA MCBRAYER, EDITH MAGNESS, DEDEMS WEIR, SALLY KINCADE.
I appoint JOHN BURGE & WOODY BURGE my executors. Wit: J. M. WEBB, JOHN
HARRELL.   Signed: ROBERT G. WEBB.
N.B. Acknowledge before me.. J. W. GREEN, this Dec. 16, 1842.

Page 116. 10 Oct. 1843. Recorded, Feb. Court 1844. I, WILLIAM THOMPSON,
              direct that the sum of $400 be given to the Rutherfordton
Presbyterian Church for painting & fencing the church. I direct that
$2,000 in trust for the support of a pastor, useing only the interest on
the said sum, trustees are EDMUND BRYAN, JOHN B. MILLER & MATHEW H. DAVIS.
I direct the sum of $500 set apart for the salary of the pastor of the
above named church. I direct that $1,000 for the building of the Male
Accademy in Rutherfordton. I give unto my servant boy Joseph all my
wearing apparel & $10 in cash. I wish my executors to allow Joseph to
select his own master. I allow my executors to pay my physicians a
reasonable sum for their service. I allow the sum of $50 to the pastor
for a funeral service, and $150 to Rev. Mr. NASH pastor of the above named
church as a testimonial of my respect & esteem. I allow $450 to purchase
a negro girl to be given to Miss ELIZA A. CRAYTON, for her own use & her
heirs forever, in case of her death without issue the said negro to fall
to her brother JOHN M. CRAYTON. I also give unto JOHN M. CRAYTON the sum
$400 in cash. I give unto JAMES H. MILLER the son of my friend JOHN B.
MILLER the sum of $400 when he comes of age, in case of his death the sum
to be paid to SARAH L. the dtr. of JOHN B. MILLER, and he is to be trustee of said sum. I also give unto JAMES my "my patent lever silver watch
with the chain & other appendages attached to it." I give unto SARAH the
sum of $400 the dtr. of JOHN B. MILLER, until she is of age. I give MARY
VIRGINIA the dtr. of EDMUND BRYAN my gold watch & $300 when she comes of
age, in case of her death property to go to her brother ANDREW RUFUS, and
the father EDMUND BRYAN to be trustee. I give unto MARY CRAYTON $300 for
my executors to purchase a negro girl for her use, in the same manner as
her sister ELIZA. I appoint my friends EDMUND BRYAN & JOHN B. MILLER my
executors. Wit: W. E. MILLS, MAT. W. DAVIS.
                                        Signed: WILLIAM THOMPSON.

CODICIL. Dated 15 Dec. 1843. First I desire that the bequest of $2,000
be reduced to $1,700 to the support of the pastor of the Pres-
byterian Church of Rutherfordton. I desire that the bequest of $1,000
given to the erection of the Male Academy be reduced to $800. I desire
that the sum of $500 be given unto ANDREW RUFUS BRYAN when he comes of
age and I appoint his father EDMUND BRYAN his trustee. Wit: W. C. MILLS,
L. B. BRYAN.   Signed: WILLIAM THOMPSON.

Page 121. 9 Dec. 1836. Recorded, Feb. Court 1844. (Nuncupative will)
THOMAS HUTCHINS says he wants what he has left to the support
of SARAH his wife and WILLIAM DAWSON his grandchild, he says not to sell
or take anything away, He wants ISAAC his son to take care of them. He
says agreeable to the article when WILLIAM was bound unto him he wants
WILLIAM to have the sorrel mare, he says WILLIAM has 3 head of cattle of
his own. He want ISAAC his son & WILLIAM his grandchild to have the land
at the death of their mother. Wit: WM. PROCTOR, JAMES GETTYS.
                          Signed: THOMAS X HUTCHINS.

Page 122. 28 Nov. 1842. Recorded, Feb. Court 1844. Translation (original written in German). When I die my wife will lose her
anuity of brother LENZ, to make up this loss I have put my son AUGUSTUS
in such position that nobody can attack him as to my property. I wish
AUGUSTUS would take my negroes & tools at a low estimate. The ballance
he shall add it to the capital which is in the coinage business to enlarge
it. This captial, he needs ---- to advance money or else he will have to
coin every day, I believe he can issue as much as my wife & servant need
for a living. I wish that all my property as well as this capital shall
be divided into equal shares among my five children after the death of
my wife. "My son-in-law who should not be of a solid character should
have interest of their share but not have the power to make use of the
capital." If AUGUSTUS has no objections against the above he will sign
it with his own hand. Signed, AUGUSTUS BECHTLER. Wit: CHRISTOPHER
BECHTLER, Junr., H. C. G. SCHAEFFER, HENRY MILLER.
                          Signed: CHRISTOPHER BECHTLER,
                                   Senr.

Page 123. Same will written in German, attested by CHRISTOPHER BETCHLER,
Jr. & HENRY C. G. SCHAEFFER, and HENRY MILLER that the above
translation was correct.

Page 124. 8 March 1844. Recorded, Spring Court 1844. I, RODNY TOMS,
now being in bad health but of perfect mind & memory. I will
that all my just debts & funeral charges be paid. I give unto my beloved
wife MATILDA the plantation on which I now live, with all cattle, hams,
hogs, grain farming tools & my interest both real & personal in the estate
of ROBERT WEBB, decd. as assured in his said WEBB'S will. Also my boys
King & Bob to use until my child JAMES MADISON or any other that may be
born come of age, at which time the plantation & negroes King & Bob to
descend to my child or children. Also I give her negro girl Hannah. I
give unto my mother PAMELIA TOMS my negro girl Eliza until her death then
to my child or chn. when of age. I give unto my sister ELIZABETH my
negro girl Gin during her life, then to descend to my child or chn. at
age. The two named negroes given to my mother & sister is not to be removed from this county. I wish my brother EDWARD TOMS to collect all
debts & dues that may coming to me or my estate. I appoint WILLIAM TOMS
& JAMES GOODE my executors, My brother EDWARD to have power over my son
JAMES M. or any other born chn. to give them a good English education.
Wit: J. M. WEBB & G. W. BABER.   Signed: RODNEY TOMS.
CODICIL. 8 March 1844. I direct that my executors make over to my
brother THOMAS TOMS a tract of land joining my mothers, contain-
ing 164 acres, after the balance of the sum has been paid, being $64.
Wit: G. W. BABER & J. M. WEBB.   Signed: RODNEY TOMS.

Page 129. To the Justice & Clerk of Court of Pleas & Superior Court of
Rutherford County. Whereas lately in our Superior Court a
paper writing purposing to be the last will & testament of GEORGE PAINTER,
decd. the finding of the jury and judgement of the court declared it to
be true and ordered it to be recorded. This 9 Feb. 1844.
                          Signed: I. W. WEBB, Clk.

Page 130. 30 Aug. 1828. Recorded, Fall Court 1844. I, GEORGE PAINTER,
          being very weak in body but of perfect mind & memory. First
I give to my dtr. CATY TRUELOVE 10 shillings. I give unto my daughter
BARBARY FREEMAN 10 shillings. I give unto my son LEONARD PAINTER 10
shillings. I give unto my son GEORGE PAINTER 10 shillings. I give unto
my son MICHAEL PAINTER 10 shillings. I give unto my dtr. EVE DECK 10
shillings. I give unto my dtr. ELIZABETH PAINTER 10 shillings. I give
unto BENJAMIN FREEMAN PAINTER 10 shillings. I give unto my son JOEL
PAINTER 10 shillings. I give unto my beloved wife 170 acres of land
whereon I now live. Also my mill & machine. I give unto my wife REBECCA
HARRIS PAINTER 2 negroes, Major & Cherry, my horse, household furniture,
working tools. I give unto CATY BURNETT one bed & furniture and one cow
& calf. I appoint BENJAMIN FREEMAN my executor & my wife REBECCA PAINTER
executrix. At her death property to be divided among the children. Wit:
ROBERT JOHNSON, DAVID JOHNSON.   Signed: GEORGE PAINTER.

Page 133. 22 July 1844. Recorded, Summer Court 5 Aug. 1844. I, ELIAS
          UPCHURCH, being weak in body but of perfect mind & memory.
First I desire all my just debts to be paid. I wish my wife to hold &
possess my land and all property I may have at my death, until her death
and then to be sold according to law and money divided among my children.
I appoint my wife ANNA UPCHURCH & JOHN TOMBLIN my executors. Wit: I. W.
WEBB, MORRIS LOGAN.   Signed: ELIAS X UPCHURCH.

Page 134. 29 May 1844. Recorded, Summer Court 1844. I, ANN E. BIRCHETT,
          after payment of my just debts & demands the balance disposed
as follows. To my brother KERR B. MILLER the negro boy James & child
Hamett. I give to my brother HARVY A. MILLER the negro boy named Henderson, also my household furniture, lot in the town of Rutherfordton, adjoining the property of F. L. COXE, also my tract of land containing 40
acres, also $4,000 and my gold watch with it appendages. I give unto
sisters NANCY & MARTHA, each the sum of $1,000 also a bed with furniture,
the balance to go to my brother HARVY. I give to my nephew WILLIAM the
son of DAVID B. MILLER the sum of $1,000, this sum to remain in the hands
of my brother H. W. MILLER until he comes of age. I give to my brother
JAHU MILLER the sum of $400 and my brother W. H. MILLER $500. The balance
of my estate to be divided among my three nieces the dtrs. of Brother
DAVID B. MILLER. I request the note that I hold on my brother ANDREW T.
MILLER shall be given up to him. I desire that my executors to sell my
lands to fullfill my bequests. I appoint my brother HARVY A. MILLER &
friend ROBERT G. TWITTY my executors. Wit: JOSEPH W. CALLOWAY, LEMUEL
MURRAY, MAT W. DAVIS.   Signed: A. E. BURCHETT.
CODICIL.   Dated 25 July 1844. I give unto the two children of my brother
          JAMES A. MILLER $400, to be equally divided between them, this
sum to be taken from the sum I gave unto HARVY MILLER. I give unto my
mother ANNA MILLER $100. Wit: MAT W. DAVID, WM. TWITTY.
                                          Signed: A. E. BURCHETT.

Page 137. 15 Sept. 1843. Recorded, Summer Court 1844. I, TERRELL WIL-
          KINS, being in perfect mind. First I desire my just debts
paid. I give to my beloved wife all home plantation during her natural
life, also the choice of two negro men Arthur & Cepted? also Lucy, Truci.
Fran and Tild, Caty & Louisa which she may choose, two horses, tools,
household & kitchen furniture, cattle, hogs & sheep. At her death to be
divided as follows, ELIZABETH TWITTY, JOHN H., WILLIAM, JAMES T., THOMAS,
MELISA, EVELINE & SAMUEL WILKINS and their heirs. ELIZABETH, JOHN,
WILLIAM, JAMES & THOMAS they have received a part equal, all but JOHN he
is $40 behind in his home. MILISA & EVELINE to have Agness & her child-
ren & Hampton. Also horse, saddle, bridle to be worth $70, each a bed &
furniture to make them equal. SAMUEL to have Arthur & bed & furniture to
make him equal. MILISSA & EVELINA to have the home plantation at their
mother's death. My Watson land containing 380 acres to JAMES & SAMUEL.
Negroes to be taken at valuation and to be kept with my children, none
less than 8 yrs. old taken from their mother. The old negroes to be
taken care of at the expense of the estate. I appoint my son THOMAS &
my wife SARAH WILKINS my executors. NOTE: "The land that old free Bob
died on be paid for and you are requested and authorized to make a title
to said Bob heirs according to law."   Signed: TERRELL WILKINS.

Page 139. 22 May 1844. Recorded, Summer Court 1844. I, MARY MCSHEEA, being in feeble health but of sound mind & memory. I will my just debts and funeral charges be paid. I give unto SAMUEL S. GIDNEY & his issue my lot of land in the town of Cheraw, S. C. on the corner of Market & Green street # 135. after my decease in trust for the sole & separate use of ELIZABETH JOHNSON my dtr. the wife of DANIEL JOHNSON during her natural life and to her heirs forever. I give unto SAMUEL S. GIDNEY & his heirs three negroes named, Sam, Peggy & Aleck in trust for the sole use & benfit of ELIZABETH JOHNSON my dtr. wife of DANIEL JOHNSON during her natural life & her heirs forever. I give unto SAMUEL S. GIDNEY a tract of land lying on the road from Rutherfordton to Lincolnton joining lands of JESSE CHITWOOD & others containing 64 acres in trust for the sole & separate use & benfit of ELIZABETH JOHNSON my dtr. wife of DANIEL JOHNSON to her & her heirs forever. I give unto SAMUEL S. GIDNEY & his heirs all my household & kitchen furniture, clothing, money and all the est. both real & personal that I may die with, in trust for ELIZABETH JOHNSON my dtr. & wife of DANIEL JOHNSON, during her natural life & her heirs forever. I appoint DANIEL JOHNSON my executor. Wit: REUBEN MARTIN, RHODES GLOVER.   Signed: MARY MCSHEEA.

Page 143. 8 July 1844. Recorded, Fall Court 1844. I, JOHN MOORE, being in perfect mind & memory. First I desire my just debts to be paid. The rest of my property to my wife ELIZABETH during her life or widowhood, for the purpose of raising our children and support for herself. At her death the property to be equally divided among the chn. My son JACKSON MOORE equal with the rest of my chn. I appoint JACKSON MOORE & my wife ELIZABETH MOORE executors. Wit: JAMES T. WILKINS, jurat, DAVIC GRAY.   Signed: JOHN MOORE.

Page 143. 23 Aug. 1844. Recorded, Dec. Court 1844. I, ROBERT HUMPHREY, being weak in body but in perfect mind & memory. I give to my grandson WILLIAM A. MCFADDIN 50 acres of land, adjoining JOHN KEETER. I give unto my grandson ROBERT GRANT 25 acres joining the first tract. I give unto DINAH HUMPHREY 25 acres joining the second tract. I give unto MAY SARGENT 25 acres joining the third tract. I give unto PRISCILLA HARRISS 20 acres joining the fourth tract. I appoint JOHN GILKEY my executor. Wit: JOHN R. MORRIS & ICHABOD KEETER.
                          Signed: ROBERT X HUMPHREY.

Page 145. 18 Jan. 1844. Recorded, Feb. Court 1845. I, LITTLETON SIMS, being very low in health but sound in mind & memory. I want all my just debts paid first. I give my wife all the property she brought here when we married also one cow. I give to my granddaughter HANNAH SIMS all my beds and household & kitchen furniture. I give unto RACHEL and JAMES SIMS the tract of land lying on First Broad River which I bought from JOHN A. LONG. JAMES to have the lower part with the house and RACHEL the upper part containing 200 acres. I give unto ANDREW H. SIMS the tract of land where I live containing 150 acres, he is to pay JOHN A. LONG the sum of $300 for which LONG holds my note, to be paid in three years, and a tract of land lying on Mountain Creek containing 232 acres to be sold and money divided between RACHEL OSBORN & HANNAH dtr. of A. H. SIMS, also one note that I hold against GEORGE CLENINGER, which I gave to WASHINGTON OSBORN in the sum of $100. I give to my son A. H. SIMS my farming tools, stones, flax wheel. I give unto JAMES SIMS his note which I hold in the amount of $300. One colt unto Doctor LITTLETON SIMS and negro boy called Nat. I also give unto A. H. SIMS 2 negroes Willis & Mannuel. I give unto LEANDER wife of BYNUM W. BARBER one mare. I give unto MARY ELEANOR dtr. of WM. GETTY one horse. The executors to take the cattle and pay unto JANE PRICE, JAMES SIMS, SUSANNAH COWAN, NANCY MELTON, RACHEL OSBORN, ELIZABETH CLENINGER and WILLIAM SIMS chn. of A. H. SIMS. I give JANE PRICE the poultry. I appoint A. H. SIMS my executor. Wit: JAMES L. TAYLOR, ELISHA HUNT.   Signed: LITTLETON X SIMS.

Page 147. 6 Oct. 1844. Recorded, Spring Court 1845. I, EDWARD HAMILTON, being of sound mind & memory. I give unto my mother JANE HAMILTON, Senr. in consideration of her love and kind treatment of me in my last illness all my estate both real & personal as follows, my share of a certain tract of land known by the name of Wells tract, lying on second Broad River, now in possession of my brother ARCHIBALD HAMILTON. My negro boy named Tom, my horse, saddle & bridle, with all notes due me, the persons and amount I do not remember. The note I hold on my brother

111

ARCHIBALD HAMILTON I will to him. I appoint WILLIAM G. MITCHELL my executor. Wit: M. C. DICKERSON, WALTER DUFFY. Signed: EDWARD HAMILTON.

Page 148. 17 Oct. 1844. Recorded, Spring Court 1845. I, LEWIS WEBB,
being in bad health but of sound mind & memory. All my just debts to be paid from the money due me. I give unto my beloved wife ELIZABETH all my remaining property, including the household & Kitchen furniture, all to be applied to her support and raising of my children. I give unto my wife 50 acres of land joining lands of JOHN GOOD, the Widow GOOD & JOHN GOOD, Senr. with my dwelling house during her natural life then to my three sons BRYAN, DANIEL & JAMES, I also give unto my three sons above named all the remaining of my lands after my chn. come of age. My part of my father's DANIEL WEBBS estate to be divided among my dtrs. & wife. I appoint my brother JAMES M. WEBB my executor. Wit: DAVID TATE.   Signed: LEWIS WEBB.

Page 151. 22 March 1844. Recorded, June Court 1845. I, JAMES QUEEN,
being in the use of my perfect senses. I give unto my beloved wife SARAH QUEEN the home plantation down to the cross fence, her choice of my horse, one cow & calf, one half of hogs, all household & kitchen furniture, negro woman named Mill. JAMASON QUEEN to have the lower part of my plantation below the cross fence. At my wife's death all the remaining property to go to my son HAMPTON, he to pay my debts. I appoint JAMASON QUEEN & JAMES HAUL my executor. Wit: ALFRED JONES, EDWARD X UPTON.   Signed: JAMES X QUEEN.

Page 153. 14 Dec. 1845. Recorded, Feb. Court 1846. I, STEPHEN CAMP,
being of sound mind & memory. Having given unto DAVID K. FISHER & my dtr. his wife EULIA and my son GEORGE C. CAMP their part of my estate. I now give the rest of my estate unto ELIZA GREEN, ELIAS A. CAMP, ADAM P. CAMP & WILLIAM C. CAMP my chn. after paying my just debts, to be equally divided among them. I appoint ADAM P. CAMP my executor. Wit: M. R. ALEXANDER, jurat. M. D. BUTLER, JO. C. DANIEL.
Signed: S. X CAMP.

Page 155. 15 Jan. 1846. Recorded, March Court 1846. I, WALTER SORRELS,
being far advanced in age & weak in body but of sound mind & memory. I allow all my just debts to be paid. I give unto my wife MARY all the property I got with her at our marriage also one cow & calf, all meat on hand. I give unto my dtr. NANCY GREEN $5 & what THOS. GREEN owes me. The balance of my property to be sold and the proceeds divided equally between my dtrs. CATY MOORE & REBECKAH BARTLETT. I appoint my son CHARLES & ESRAE P. SORRELS my executors. Wit: J. GILKEY, jurat. ANDREW FLACK, Jr., jurat.   Signed: WALTER X SORRELS.

Page 157. 29 July 1845. Recorded, Spring Court 1846. I, ELIZABETH
BRIDGES, being sound memory. First I desire my just debts & funeral charges be paid. I give unto my son ANDREW BRIDGES, DICEY LEWIS and SUIDA, one beauro, one mare, a clock, pot vessels and kitchen furniture, and ANDERSON and my beloved son JAMES BRIDGES to have my stock of cattle, hogs, sheep divided equally between them, JAMES to have the cupboard & chest, my son WILEY to have the trunk. I give unto my dtrs. my bedsteads & furniture to be equally divided between them. In consideration of the love & special affection I have for my son ANDERSON, I appoint him my executor. Wit: A. EDWARDS, jurat. JOHN TEAL, jurat.
Signed: ELIZABETH X BRIDGES.

Page 158. 4 April 1846. Recorded, Spring Court 1846. I, THOMAS L. MC-
ENTIRE, being sound in mind & memory. First after paying my just debts & funeral expenses. I give unto my nephew WILLIAM THOMAS MCENTIRE my negro man Bonaparte & wife Delphia & their chn. Alice, Alfred, Felix, Tilmon & my negro man Bill son of Delphia & my old woman Darkey for the purpose of his supporting her during her life. I give unto my nephew JOHN YOUNG MCENTIRE my negro man Westley & Eveline & her chn. Lafayetta, Buck & Dice. I give unto my nephew WILLIAM T. MCENTIRE his choice of the bed & furniture, the next of the bed & furniture to my man Bill, the balance of beds & clothing to the negroes according to their families size. My wearing apparel to be divided among my negro men. The balance of my estate I leave unto my nieces & nephews to wit: MARTHA

ANN MCENTIRE, WILLIAM THOMAS MCENTIRE, JOHN YOUNG MCENTIRE, JANE ELIZA
MCENTIRE, LAURA EUGENE MCENTIRE, chn. of JOHN & MARY JANE MCENTIRE, MARTHA
MELINDA ERWIN, THOMAS GEORGE WALTON, WILLIAM MCENTIRE WALTON, & ELIZABETH
TILMAN, AVERY, chn. of THOMAS & MARTHA WALTON. I appoint JOHN MCENTIRE
my executor. Wit: W. H. WALTON, jurat. & C. L. HARRIS, jurat.
Signed: THOMAS L. MCENTIRE.
CODICIL. Dated 4 April 1846. Negroes left to nephews WM. THOMAS & JOHN
        Y. MCENTIRE to be keep in possession of executor until the ne-
phews are of age, not having to pay the rent to said nephews. Property
left unto others nices & nephews to be sold and proceeds divided equally
among them. Wit: C. L. HARRIS, Jurat. W. H. WALTON, jurat.
Signed: THOS. L. MCENTIRE.

Page 162. 10 July 1846. Recorded, Aug. Court 1846. I, EDWARD WALDROPE,
        Senr., being in possession of my mental faculties. My present
wife MARY ANN shall remain in the mansion house where I now live under
the care & charge of my son ASBERRY as long as she remains single or
death, also a note I hold on ZACHARIAH WALDROPE in the sum of $170 and
interest, two cows & calves, two feather beds & furniture, I also leave
unto my son ASBERRY WALDROPE my mansion house and plantation of 129 acres,
that I bought from RICHARD LEWIS, joining lands of AARON FOWLER & lying
on Green River, also all my horses, hogs, tools, and outstanding debts
of every kind. To my several chn. CATHERINE THOMPSON, ALFRED WALDROPE,
DAVIDSON WALDROPE, JONATHAN WALDROPE, SARAH SPLAWN, CASWELL WALDROPE,
PRESCILLA OWENS, LEVINA WOOD, EDWARD P. WALDROPE, & JANE WALDROPE $1 each.
I appoint my wife ANN WALDROPE & my son ASBERRY WALDROPE my executors.
Wit: JAMES MORRIS, jurat. AARON FOWLER, jurat.
Signed: EDWARD WALDROPE.

Page 165. 19 Feb. 1839. Recorded, Sept. Court 1846. I, JOHN CARSON,
        being advanced in life but of sound mind & memory. First I
give unto my wife MARY all my estate both real & personal after paying
my lawfull debts, during her natural life, I allow her to dispose of the
household & kitchen furniture when we are both dead, and the land as
follows, begining at THOMAS LOGAN'S line at Earley's ditch to the road,
up the creek to Cochans line all on the east of these bounds I give unto
my son WILLIAM P. CARSON. From the creek bridge up the lane about 100
yrds. East of my dwelling house, due West to Baldridge's line all land
North of these bounds, I give unto my son GEORGE W. CARSON, the remaining
land I give unto my son OLIVER P. CARSON, I allow my sons GEORGE W., &
OLIVER P. CARSON each to give to my dtr. ISABELLA C. CARSON $125 each.
I have made a deed of gift to my dtr. ISABELLA C. CARSON for a negro girl
named Julia Ann. I give to my grandson HENRY K. SMART one horse & saddle
& a cow & calf. At our death I allow all my personal property to be sold
and equally divided among POLLY S. CARSON, wife of FELIX W. CARSON, JAMES
W. CARSON, JANE CARSON, wife of WILLIAM CARSON, SIDNEY B. SMART, wife of
HIRAM SMART, MARY ANN GETTYS, wife of WILLIAM GETTYS, and A. M. CARSON.
I give to my son OLIVER P. CARSON my gold watch, it being a relect that I
do not wish to go out of the family. I allow my books to be divided among
GEORGE W., WM. P., A. M., & O. P. CARSON. I appoint my sons JAMES W. &
OLIVER P. CARSON my executors. Wit: JAMES LOGAN, jurat. WILLIAM ERWIN,
jurat.   Signed: JNO. CARSON.

Page 166. 7 April 1837. Recorded, Sept. Court 1846. I, WILLIAM STATON,
        being weak in body but of sound mind & memory. I desire all
my just debts to be paid and my wish is that my wife NANCY STATTON have
the balance during her life if she out live me. My will is that there
shall be an equal divide with all my children. JAMES STATTON & ANDERSON
STATTON to be equal in the divide with my children. I appoint JAMES &
ANDERSON STATTON my executors. Wit: JOHN FLEUI, jurat & JOHN TWITTY,
jurat.   Signed: WILLIAM X STATTON.

Page 169. 14 July 1846. Recorded, Fall Court 1846. I, PLEASANT FORTUNE,
        being of sound mind & memory. Executors to pay just debts &
funeral expenses. I give unto my wife ELIZABETH one third of the land
and premises that I now own, joining DAVID MOREHEAD land, during her natural life, then to my son PLEASANT FORTUNE, also the other two thirds of
my lands in fee simple, and one horse, one cow & calf, bed & furniture,
tools. I also give to my wife two beds & furniture, one cow & calf, my
cupboard, clock, kitchen furniture. I desire the remainder of my property

to be sold and the proceeds divided among the remaining part of my child-
ren, except PLEASANT. I appoint my son PLEASANT FORTUNE & my son-in-law
MILTON GOLD my executors. Wit: A. G. LOGAN, jurat., J. M. WEBB, jurat.
Signed: PLEASANT FORTUNE.

Page 171. 15 March 1847. Recorded, Spring Court 1847. I, JOSEPH GREEN,
being of sound mind & memory. I desire that my just debts &
funeral expenses to be paid. I give unto my beloved wife MARY GREEN,
about 100 acres of land, joining lands of Weeks corner or called Goldney
corner, including Akins house, during her natural life, then to my son
JOSEPH W. GREEN, also a boy named Bob, George, Hannah, Artimenta, Adolphus, Minerva, & Margaret and at her death, Bob to belong to my son JOSEPH.
The remainder to be disposed of if necessary to pay her debts and the
overpluss to be divided equally between the mother & six children of JOHN
BURGESS & the eight chn. of DRUCILLA MCBRIERS. All my stock, cattle,
grain, household & kitchen furniture, tools, interest in the blacksmith
shop to be the property of my wife MARY during her life time, then to be
sold by the executors and the proceeds divided among the chn. of JOHN
BURGES & DRUSCILLA MCBRIERS. I have before portioned off LEAR BURGE of
two negroes & other property. Also I have given to DRUCILLS MCBRIERS the
same. I give to my son JOSEPH W. one girl named Claricy & one boy Toliver,
& furniture. I appoint my son JOSEPH my executor. Wit: JOHN TEAL, SAMUEL
MELTON, ABNER GREEN.   Signed: JOSEPH GREEN.

Page 173. 16 March 1847. Recorded, Spring Court 1847. I, GUION BOLYN,
being of sound mind & memory. My executor to pay all funeral
expenses & other just debts. First I give to my oldest sister JANE BOLYN
$200 in cash, also to my sister ELIZABETH $200 in cash, also to my aunt
MARY PARKER in consequence of her misfortune $100 in cash, and the residue
of my estate be equally divided between my father RUTTAIN BOLYN & my
mother MARGARET BOLYN and my three brothers, G. R. BOLYN, JOSEPH & JOHN
BOLYN. I appoint my friend N. M. FLOYD & G. R. BOLYN of York Dist., S.C.
as my executors. No witnesses.   Signed: GION X BOLYN.

Page 175. 24 July 1847. Recorded, Aug. Court 1847. I, WILLIAM SMART,
being of sound mind & memory. First I wish my executor to pay
my just debts & funeral expenses. I give to my beloved wife MARGARET 100
acres of land to be taken from the lower end of the home place, also
about 6 acres from the JAMES & ROBERT GUFFY tract and the REID GUFFY tract,
also an equal share of the personal property, after her years allowance
being first taken out, also one bed & furniture. The residue of my real
property to be rented by my executor until my youngest child comes of age,
then to be equally divided between my four chn. by each one of the girls
paying over to CORNELIUS my youngest child $12 in cash. I appoint my
friend SAMUEL ANDERSON my executor. Wit: GEORGE W. GUFFY, WM. MONTEITH,
Jr.   Signed: WILLIAM X SMART.

Page 176. 25 Nov. 1847. Recorded, Feb. Court 1848. I, HANAH DOBBINS,
being of sound mind & memory. First I will that my just debts
& funeral expenses be paid. I give unto my dtr. ARTAMINCY HARRILL, 2
mares, 1 three horse waggon, 3 cows & calves, hogs, six feather beds &
furniture, bureau, one clock, loom & wheel, one negro girl named Sarah
about three yrs. old. I give unto my son JOHN CALLAHAN $6 in cash. I
appoint A. S. HARRILL my sole executor. Wit: D. BEAN, ROBERT H. WILSON.
Signed: HANNAH X DOBBINS.

Page 177. 31 May 1848. Recorded, Sept. Court 1848. I, WILLIAM WEST,
being in a state of bad health, but of sound mind & memory.
I will that my just debts & funeral expenses be paid. I leave to WILLIAM
M. ERWIN my saddle, bridle and blanket. I leave unto JAMES S. ERWIN my
rifle gun. I do not desire my clothing to be sold, I leave them all to
WILLIAM M., & JAMES S. ERWIN. I appoint my friend WILLIAM ERWIN my ex-
ecutor. Wit: JOHN A. WATSON, A. B. LONG.
Signed: WM. WEST.

Page 178. 11 Nov. 1843. Recorded, Fall Court 1848. I, HENRY KEETER,
being weak in body but of sound mind & memory. I give unto my
son ADEN KEETER all my land on Cathey's Creek being the place I now live,
also where my son ICHABOD now lives and to him all my land on Mountain
Creek and my bed and furniture. I also give unto my son ADEN one bed &

furniture. I give unto my dtr. AMY CALLAHAN one bed & furniture. I give unto my sons all my loose property to be divided between them, that is ADEN & ICHABOD. Also I appoint my sons ADEN & ICHABOD my lawfull executors. Wit: ZACHARIAH SMITH, RAIL X HILL.

Signed: HENRY KEETER.

Page 180. 17 Dec. 1848. Recorded, Feb. Court 1849. I, JOSHUA CAMP, being weak in body but of perfect mind & memory. First I desire my just debts and funeral expenses be paid. I give unto my wife NANCY CAMP all my estate both real & personal that I may die possessed of until my son GEORGE J. CAMP becomes the age of twenty one. Should either of my dtrs. marry, I wish them to have a negro girl worth $500, also a horse worth $50, saddle worth $10 and household & kitchen furniture that my wife thinks she can spare. I wish my wife to save what money she can to educate my son GEORGE, he also to have a negro boy worth $500. I wish my wife to have four negroes, two men & two women, one third of the land during her natural life. I appoint my son J. T. CAMP executor & my wife NANCY Executris. Wit: D. SCRUGGS, THOMAS WILKINS, LEWIS CAMP.

Signed: JOSHUA CAMP.

Page 182. 17 Oct. 1845. Recorded, Feb. Court 1849. I, AMBROSE MILLS, of Green River, being of sound disposing mind & memory. First I desire all my just debts be paid, for this purpose I set aside nine negroes to be hired out to wit, Patrick, Perry, Harvy, Jeff, Aramster, Benson, Ben, Guy & Lucus. Then the said negroes to be divided between my three chn. to wit. JANE ANN the wife of JONAS KING, WILLIAM E. MILLS, & MARY AMANDA the wife of ADOLPHUS MILLS. I give unto my beloved wife NANCY MILLS the right & privilege of residing in my mansion house, with land to support her during her life. I wish the whole of my land be under the management of my son WILLIAM, as it is to be his after her death. I also give unto my wife negroes, Mariah, old Guy & Milley his wife & Mariah chn. Butler, Larkin, Frank & George. Stock (named) during life time, then to his chn. Except the four chn. of MARIAH they are for his grand chn. to wit. AMBROSE MILLS the son of WILLIAM E., AMBROSE WALTER the son of my dtr. AMANDA & WILLIAM AMBROSE WASHINGTON KING the son of my dtr. JAN. I give unto my dtr. JANE the wife of JONAS KING four lots in the town of Rome, Ga. they being formerly belonging to my son THOMAS & since bought by my son WILLIAM, lots to be purchased from WILLIAM by my estate, also the following negroes, Nancy & her children, Anay, Harriet, Minty, Mitchell & Rachel & her child, July Ann. I give unto my son WILLIAM all land on Green River, with the home place, with negroes to wit. Little Sam, Ester & her chn. Ellis & Tom and her youngest child, Milley, Gusta & Mary. I give unto my dtr. MARY AMANDA the wife of ADOLPHUS MILLS all land on North Pacolet River in the County of Henderson, also negroes, Big Sam & his wife Judy, Aggy & her chn. Eliza & James & Young Judy & her child Luciesa. I appoint my son WILLIAM E. MILLS my sole executor. No witnesses. Signed: AMBROSE MILLS or A. MILLS. CIDICIL. Whereas I, AMBROSE MILLS, of Polk County, present this as a codicil to my will of 17 Oct. 1845. This 28 Oct. 1848. I hereby despose of two negroes bought since my will was made, named Nelson & Andrew. I give to my son WILLIAM the negro named Nelson and to my dtr. MARY ANN the negro Andrew. Wit: JAMES MORRIS, SADON POG.

Signed: A. MILLS.

Page 187. 15 Jan. 1849. Recorded, Spring Court 1849. I, REBECCA DALTON, first I desire all my just debts & funeral expenses to be paid from the proceeds of my cattle. My loom with all fixtures belonging I give to my sister LUSINDA & all the rest of my property both real & personal and a negro girl named Catharine and my interest in the plantation that I now live on, being where my father lived & died and the remainder of my property to my mother ELIZABETH DALTON at her death. I direct that the property be divided between my two sisters & my brother, viz. CALEB JACKSON DALTON, LUSINDA DALTON, & NANCY DALTON and to my sister POLLY NEALON shall have $1. I appoint my neighbor JOHN GILKEY my executor. Wit: WILLIAM COSTON, CELA X BLACK.

Signed: REBECCA X DALTON.

Page 188. 8 May 1848. Recorded, Spring Court 1849. I, MICHAEL HESTER, of the County of Polk, N. C. Being low in health, but sound in mind & memory. I will that my wife MARY HESTER & grandson JAMES M.

115

HESTER after paying my debts to have all I possess both real & personal,
to be divided between them, at my wife's death grandson is to have all.
I desire that my wife & grandson to care for my dtr. SALLY HESTER during
her life time. No executor named. Wit: S. W. WALKER, B. E. BLANTON,
J. G. LANCASTER.   Signed: MICHAEL X HESTER.

Page 188.   21 March 1849. Recorded, Spring Court 1849. I, MARY ALLEN
            WATSON, first I direct that my funeral expenses & just debts
be paid. I give to my sister ELIZABETH GETTIS $10. To my sister IBBY
SIMMS $10. Also to the above named sister I leave furniture to be divided
between them. I leave to my nephew JOHN CALDWELL, son of my brother
JAMES one bed & furniture & side table. I leave to MARY ELIZABETH my
niece & dtr. of JAMES WATSON one chest. I leave to GEORGE PATTEN my
nephew, son of brother JAMES WATSON one writing table. To my niece
ISABELLA dtr. of JAMES GETTY my side saddle. To my niece MARY ELIZABETH
dtr. of JAMES WATSON five white counterpin. Notes on WM. CANSTIN for the
sum of $75 & one on ALFRED CALLAHAN for $34 with interest and a pension
check claim to be set apart for JOHN CALDWELL, GEORGE PATTEN, MARY ELIZA-
BETH & ISABELLA JANE sons & dtr. of JAMES WATSON my brother, until they
are of age. I appoint my brother JAMES WATSON my executor. Wit: WILLIAM
FLACK, WILLIAM ALLEN, J. H. FORNEY.   Signed: MARY ALLEN X WATSON.

Page 191.   24 May 1849. Recorded, Aug. Court 1849. I, ISAAC WILLIAMS,
            being of sound mind & memory. First my executor to pay my
funeral expenses & just debts. I direct my executor to sell all my working tools, books, wearing clothes with all personal property. I direct
my executor to purchase a good tomb stone in Columbia, S. C. or Augusta,
Ga. & lettered with my birth day which is 29 Jan. 1800 & the date of my
death. After paying my debts the executor to use the remainder for his
own use. I appoint PRESTON N. LONG my executor. Wit: SAMUEL ANDREWS,
N. P. WALLIS.   Signed: ISAAC X WILLIAMS.

Page 193.   15 April 1848. Recorded, Sept. Court 1849. I, DANIEL MELTON,
            being of sound and perfect mind & memory. First I want all my
just debts paid. I want my executor to pay unto my son DANIEL MELTON, Jr.
$100 extra and before a division is made. The remaining part of my est.
to be divided among all my lawful heirs. I divide my land into three
tracts, my home place of 200 acres, joining lands of WM. J. LONG, & A. H.
SIMS. Another tract of 70 acres is to be sold with my other property. I
Appoint my son DANIEL MELTON, JR. & JOHN M. GRAYSON my executors. Wit:
L. D. DAVIS, THOS. X DAVIS.   Signed: DANIEL X MELTON.

Page 195.   27 Dec. 1849. Recorded, Spring Court 1850. I, SAMUEL BIGGER-
            STAFF, being of sound mind & memory. Executor to pay funeral
expenses & just debts. I give unto my beloved wife SARAH BIGGERSTAFF 80
acres of land on the upper end of my old tract, for a dower & to include
the mansion house during her natural life. I give unto my son SAMUEL
BIGGERSTAFF 134 acres on both sides of Robertson Creek. Son JOSEPH 58
acres on both sides of Roberson Creek, joining SAMUEL'S. I give unto my
son AARON 58 acres on both sides of Robertson Creek. I appoint my sons
BENJAMIN & SAMUEL BIGGERSTAFF my executors. Wit: JAMES BABER, SENR.,
JAMES BABER, JR.   Signed: SAMUEL BIGGERSTAFF.

Page 197.   15 March 1837. Recorded, Spring Court 1850. I, THOMAS GREEN-
            WAY, being of sound mind & memory. I wish five disinterested
men to divide the tract of land that belongs to GIAEON my brother and myself, all my land to stand and benfit the family until the youngest comes
of age. My will is the stock of goods, surplus money to be used for the
family's benfit. When the youngest child comes of age, all property to
be sold and divided among my chn. ELIZA ANN IRVINE ELIZABETH MARY & JAMES
(no commas). I appoint ROBERT MCFARLAND & my son IRVINE GREENWAY after
he come of age my executors. Wit: R. L. ABRAMS, D. M. ABRAMS.
                                       Signed: THOM. GREENWAY.

Page 198.   10 Sept. 1849. Recorded, Spring Court 1850. "We the under-
            signed were called on by WM. WHITE at JOHNSON KEETERS where he
had previously resided for more than ten days, while in his last sickness
to hear witness to his will or devise of the manner in wich he desired
his property disposed of after his death and he died then on the 29 Aug.
1849. Declare that it was his desire and will that after his death, all

116

his personal property should be sold and after paying all his just debts the proceeds thereof to be equally divided between all his children in this country and his grandson WM. WHITE after paying LUCY WHITE something or some small amount. In witness of this request we caused this his will as expressed to us to be put in writing and signed by each of us this 10 Sept. 1849." (Will of WM. WHITE.)   Signed: JOSEPH HEAD, JAMES ERLEY.

Page 199. 30 Jan. 1838. Recorded June Court 1850. I, JOHN DENTON, being
          of sound mind & disposing memory & being advanced in years.
I desire my just debts if any to be paid. To my wife SARAH I leave all
my property both real & personal during her life time. My dtrs. AGGY &
SALLY to live with wife and have support also JOHN my grandson the son of
SALLY to have same support as his mother. At my wife's death I give
unto AGGY & SALLY and her son JOHN 100 acres of land each and also to
JOHN I give one bed & furniture & one horse. To my dtr. MARY HUDSON one
bed & furniture. To AGGY & SALLY the remainder of my property of every
kind. Haveing heretofore given to my dtr. NANCY CLOUD the same amount of
property. Wit: JOHN MOORE, ELI F. LITTLEJOHN.
                                        Signed: JOHN X DENTON.
CODICIL. Dated 14 Feb. 1838. Having not named an executor to my will,
          do by this codicil appoint JOHN W. HAMPTON my executor. Wit:
JOHN MOORE, ELI F. LITTLEJOHN.   Signed: JOHN X DENTON.

Page 202. 4 June 1850. Recorded Aug. Court 1850. I, WILLIAM E. MILLS,
           of Green River. It is my will & desire that all my just debts
shall be paid, to sell negroes Ellis, Sam & Luke for that purpose, any
overplus to be put into the estate. I give unto my wife ANN ELIZA one
third of all my land. I give unto my three chn. AMBROSE, SARAH LOUISE and
ANN ELIZA all my land lying on Green River to be held jointly subject to
a dower of their mother. My lot & premises in Rutherfordton should be
sold & proceeds applied to my debts or the estate. I give unto my wife &
chn. all personal property to be given to them as they come of age. My
wife to pay strict attention to the raising, training & education of my
chn. or have a suitable guardian appointed. I give unto my son AMBROSE
my gold watch to be given to him when proper, in the meantime to be worn
by his mother. I appoint my friends L. A. MILLS, & LARKIN B. BRYEN as
executors. Wit: E. BRYEN, JONATHAN KING.
                                        Signed: W. E. MILLS.

Page 205. 4 Sept. 1848. Recorded, Spring Court 1851. I, DANIEL SISK,
           being weak in body but of sound mind & memory. I give unto
my beloved wife LEANNER all my land & farming tools during her natural
life, then I give to my son ROBERT SISK. I also give unto my wife my mare
& saddle all household & kitchen furniture and one cow. ROBERT I give
my hogs & 3 head sheep. I give to my dtr. ELLENOR one cow & 3 head of
sheep. I give to my dtr. POLLY $1. I appoint AARON MCFARLAND my executor.
Wit: JOS. TAYLOR, MOSES BLACK.   Signed: DANIEL X SISK.

Page 206. 4 Aug. 1849. Recorded, Aug. Court 1851. I, ROBERT COCHRAN,
           being of sound mind & perfect memory. First I wish my funeral
expenses & just debts to be paid. I give unto my wife LETITIA COCHRAN
the plantation on which I now live with the mansion house, all household
& kitchen furniture not hereafter disposed of, all farming tools, my
negro man Andrew & woman Mary & her child Lucinda, horses & cattle for her
support. Son REID COCHRAN as trustee, manager to care for the above.
The negroes to be divided between my sons WM. K. & REID COCHRAN. The
land I gave my wife, at her death, I give the same unto my son REID. The
other property I gave to my wife to be sold and the proceeds applied to
the legacy hereafter named. I give to my grandsons BENJAMIN, JOSEPH,
JOHN, & GEORGE sons of SARAH the widow of JOHN COCHRAN, decd. 50 acres of
land where she now lives, during her widowhood and then to the above
named chn. I give to my dtr. FRANCIS NORVILL my negro girl named Priscilla now in her possession. I give unto my dtr. MARY GUFFY my negro
girl Adline. I give unto my granddaughter MARTHA L. GUFFY my negro girl
Elizabeth, 2 beds & furniture & a horse, saddle & bridle worth $60. I
give to my sons WM. K. & REID all my negroes not already given, to be
divided between them. I give unto my dtr. NANCY S. MOORE $1. I give unto
my grandchn. GEORGE W., CYNTHIA R., ROBERT N., & ELIZABETH E. GUFFY $25
each. I give unto my grandchn. the chn. of REBECCA LONG $25 each. (Not
named). I appoint my son REID COCHRAN & GEORGE W. LOGAN my executors.

                                117

Wit: A. B. LONG, WILLIAM LONG.   Signed: ROBT. COCHRAN.

Page 209. 21 Aug. 1851. Recorded, Sept. Court 1851. I, JAMES TONEY,
          now in my proper mind, viewing the situation of my family. I
want all my funeral charges & just debts paid. I give unto my wife
MARGARET the plantation whereon we now live, with all crops, one mare,
cattle, hogs, farming tools & household & kitchen furniture for her support. I desire that she & my executor sell my land on Robertson Creek
and put the proceeds on interest for my two sons WILLIAM S. & MICAJAH
MC. TONEY. Executor to sell my negro boy if unruly or to be the property
of wife. I appoint SIMEON MCCURRY my executor. Wit: HENRY A. TONEY,
SMITH MCCURRY, jurat.   Signed: JAMES X TONEY.

Page 210. 23 May 1851. Recorded, Sept. Court 1851. I, ALBERT G. FORNEY,
          I give unto my wife ELIZABETH one third of my plantation with
my dwelling house, during her natural life, then to my two chn. I give to
her my two negroes Alphonso & Eliza to dispose of as she may wish. Also
one third of my other negroes during her natural life, then to my two chn.
also my household & kitchen furniture, with as much stock of cattle,
horses, hogs & sheep as she may need. The balance of my property to belong to my chn. MARY MARGARET & JAMES MILLER. All negroes to be valued
and the wife & each child to have a third, excepting my negro named Lawson who is not to be taken in account. As my chn. are both infants, I
appoint my brother-in-law ALBERT G. LOGAN sole guardian of said chn.
Executor & guardian to keep family together, and educate the chn. and
manage their property to their benfit or marriage or the age of twenty
one. I appoint my wife ELIZABETH & brother JAMES H. FORNEY my executrix
& executor. Wit: W. M. HEAD, jurat. N. P. WALLIS, jurat.
                                      Signed: A. G. FORNEY.

Page 213. 18 Feb. 1851. Recorded, Fall Court 1851. I, WILLIAM WATKINS,
          being this day in ill health but in sense and memory sound.
I desire my funeral charges & just debts to be paid. I give to my beloved wife SARAH the use & benfit of the tract of land on which I now
live, with three others tracts containing 355 acres during her natural
life or widowhood, with the following negroes, Ann, Jane, Dark, Susinna,
Major, John, Mary, Adaline, Joseph, Nelson, Thomas, Hannah, Julia Ann,
Harriett, Elick & Spencer with all horses, cattle, hogs, tools, household
& kitchen furniture during her natural life or widowhood. After which I
wish my negroes to be divided into eight lots as equal as can, and drawn for
by my distributers. I desire all my land & personal property to be sold,
except my negroes, and divided among, NANCY, AMOS, MARY BYERS, PHILIP
WATKINS, MARTHA HARRIS, ALFRED M. WATKINS, SUSEN WOOD, LOUISA ROBBS &
TEMPERANCE BYARS. I appoint my son PHILIP WATKINS and son-in-law THOMP-
SON ROBBS my executors. Wit: D. SCRUGGS, M. W. SIMMONS, jurat. GREEN
HICKS, jurat.   Signed: WM. WATKINS.

Page 214. 22 May 1851. Recorded, Fall Court 1851. I, JAMES N. EGERTON,
          being old & infirm but of a sound mind & memory. All just
debts to be paid. I give unto my beloved wife TERSULA my negroes Craton
& Mary Ann during her life or widowhood, with all my household & kitchen
furniture & the use of the house to live in. I leave my land 321 acres
where I now live to my son BENJAMIN F. EDGERTON at $2,000. I leave my
dtr. MALISSA, little Het, Joshua & Elyah at $1,000. I have also given
unto my son JAMES $1800, and my son THOMAS $1,000. My dtr. SARAH WHITE-
SIDE $1,000. I have given to my dtr. LOUISA KING $1,000. To my dtr.
MANERVA WHITESIDE $1,000. To MARTHA MILLS one thousand dollars in land,
one negro girl Evaline. My negroes to be divided into lots and taken or
drawn. I allow three beds & furniture & sideboard, one walnut table to
be sold. Each to have a cow & calf. Old Het to be taken by my wife and
cared for or son B. F. during her life time. Land, stock, & tools etc.
on Kelly's Creek to be sold and divided among my sons. I appoint my sons
JAMES, THOMAS & BENJAMIN EGERTON my executors. Wit: LUKE WALDROP, jurat.
JOHN PEARSON, jurat.   Signed: JAMES N. EGERTON.

Page 216. 5 Sept. 1851. Recorded, Fall Court 1851. I, JOHN LYLES, being
          in a state of declining health but of sound mind. I direct
all my debts & funeral expenses to be paid. I give to my dtr. ANN FEAGAN
the wife of JACKSON FEAGAN, The land whereon they now live & the Liles
& Steadman tracts lying on Hinton Creek of Main Broad River, also negro

girl named Jane now in their possession, also $500 in cash. I give to my
dtr. ELIZABETH, wife of GEORGE FEAGAN all the land on Pacolet River lying
in Rutherford Co., N.C. & Spartanburg Co., S.C. known as the THOMAS
BLACKWELL tract, joining the "grave yard" and WILLIAM LILES, JOHN MCFAR-
LAND & Blackwell line. I also give her negro girl Jane & her two chn.
already born. I give to my dtr. SARAH wife of DANIEL FEAGAN all the land
lying on the Pacolet River, lying in Rutherford Co., N.C. & Spartanburg
Co., S.C. joining lands of Bullinton or Jackson line, Millicans corner,
Moore corner, near the halter shop, Moore line, Johnston line, & ELIZA-
BETH FEAGAN land. I give unto my dtr. HARRIETT wife of ANDREW MCDOWELL
land lying on the Pacolet River, in Rutherford Co., N.C. & Spartanburg
Co., S.C. known by the name of the Millican tract & Walker tracts. Also
a negro girl named Charlotte. I give to my dtr. ALTHA ADALINE wife of
JOSEPH BLACKWELL, the land where they now live, lying on the South side of
the Pacolet River, lying in Spartanburg Co., S.C. known as the Bullington
tract, also negro girl Harriett. I give unto my dtr. LILLY wife of
GEORGE BLACKWELL all the land known as the Price tract, at the mouth of
White Oak on the South side of Green River, joining the tract left my
stepmother for her maintainance at fathers death and (other description)
also a negro girl named Mary now in her possession. I give to my son
HENRY, all the land on White Oak, with the mansion house, where my father
THOMAS LYLES onced lived, joining land of Dtr. LILLY, Mcfarland line,
McFarland & JASON CARSON corner, Millers corner, also negro boy named
Grover. I give unto my son THOMAS, all the land whereon he now lives,
on the Broad River known as the Walker lands, also a negro girl named
Angeline now in his possession. I give unto my son JOHN, all the land
known as the Stephen Camp tract & part of my joining lands (described)
also negro girl named Harriett. I give to my son ROBERT a tract of land
lying on Green Creek of Green River the lower part of the lands which I
now live, including the mansion house, (described) also a negro boy named
Lewis. I give unto my dtr. MARY LOUISA all the balance of the lands
where I now live, being the upper part, joining the grave yard, and lands
I bought of the estate of MATAGE & JAMES BLACKWELL., also I give her two
negroes named Caroline & Selena. Household & kitchen items named, her
property to be held for her until marriage or of age, brother HENRY as
her guardian. Sons HENRY & ROBERT to have household & kitchen furniture
named. My mansion house being given to son ROBERT, I direct that my son
HENRY & dtr. MARY LOUISA be permitted to live in the same for one year
after my death. I appoint my son HENRY my executor. Wit: J. M. WEBB,
jurat. OLIVER ARMS, jurat.   Signed: JOHN LILES.

Page 226. 4 March 1852. Recorded, Spring Court 1852. Being of sound
               disposing mind & memory. I give unto my wife JANI M. COXE,
all household & kitchen furniture, farm tools, also in lieu of her dower
one third of my land, on Stone Cutter & Floyd Creeks, including the dwelling house. I give to my chn. TENCH C. COXE, JOSEPH COXE, & FRANKLIN COXE
my books and the remaining two thirds of my land, and after my wife's
death, her third to be divided between them. I give unto TENCH CHARLES
COXE my son hereinafter named executor my lots & tracts of land in Browns-
ville, Tenn. to sell the same and apply the proceeds as directed. His
father TENCH COXE, Esq. now deceased, left will, place not named, mentioned mines belonging to the estate. I appoint my son TENCH C. COXE executor. Wit: MAT W. DAVIS, O. BARTLETT, JOHN GRAY BYNUM.
                                 Signed: FRANCIS S. COXE.

Page 229. 23 Dec. 27. Recorded, Fall Court 1852. I, FREDERIC JOHNSON,
               being aged & feeble but of perfect sense & memory. First I
give unto my wife during her natural life all my estate of land & property
I am possessed of at my death, after the decease of my wife EDA, then to
become the property of my youngest dtr. MARY M. JOHNSON, except $5 to be
divided among my other chn. (Not named) No executor named. Wit: HOWEL
WESTBROOK, LEWIS X JOHNSON.   Signed: FREDERIC X JOHNSON.

Page 229. 31 Dec. 1850. Recorded, Fall Court 1852. LEONARD DANIEL, I
               give unto my son WILLIAM G. DANIEL my negro boy Jeff, also a
tract of land whereon I now live including my dwelling house, joining
lands of ARCHIBALD LOLLER & JAMES MCCLURE, McEntire line, Hay's line, all
land North of this line. I give unto the heirs of my dtr. NANCY BABER,
the other part of the above land lying South said line, for her support,
no part of thereof or money from my estate shall be applied to the pay-

119

ments of JOHN BABER debts, and he shall have no power or access whatever
to the same. I give unto the heirs of MARY BABER my negro girl Milly, no
part there of or money that might arise from my est. shall be applied to
the payment of ROBERT BABER debts, he is to have no power or access to
the same. I give unto my dtr. ELIZABETH BLACK my negro girl Rilla. I
give unto my dtr. MARTHA MCKINNY my negro girl Mariah. I give unto my
granddaughter WHITSON BABER & her heirs my negro boy Anderson & a child
of Rilla, age about 18 months, also my filly, saddle & bridle. I give
unto my brother CHISHOLM DANIEL my old deer gun. I give unto my son
CHISHOLM DANIEL one fourth part after the distribution aforsaid, being
negroes, Dick, Martin, and Sam, with all stock of horses, cattle, hogs,
blacksmith & farming tools, household & kitchen furniture. The remaining
property to be divided among ELIZABETH BLACK, MARTHA MCKINNY, W. G.
DANIEL, & the heirs of NANCY & MARY BABER. I appoint JOHN MCKINNY &
CHISHOLM DANIEL my executor. Wit: ISAAC MCCLURE, JAMES A. MCCLURE.
                                   Signed: LEONARD DANIEL.

Page 232. 17 Nov. 1845. Recorded, Feb. Court 1853. I, WILLIAM BAXTER,
           being of sound mind & memory. First I will my just debts &
funeral expenses be paid. I give unto my dtr. MARGARET COSTEN all notes
I hold on her husband JOHN CASTAN. I Give unto my son JAMES P. BAXTER
all the notes I hold on him. I give unto my dtr. MARY TODD all the notes
I hold on her husband JOHN TODD. I give unto my dtr. CAROLINE HILL $250.
I give unto my dtr. SARAH SUTTLE my Flin tract, except 50 yds. off the
North side, she is to discount $600 from the residue of my est. I give
unto my chn. JOSEPH, THOMAS, JANE EAVES, ELIZABETH HARRILL, ESTHER MC-
DOWELL, DURHAM & JOHN BAXTER $1 each, all have received negroes & land.
I give unto my son DAVID BAXTER my land lying on the island road known
as the old Stone place. I give unto my son GEORGE W. my negro boy Richard, & my mill tract of land & 25 acres lying between the Widow TOMS &
ABEL HILL & $600. I give unto my son ELISHA my negro boy Dick & the
land I bought from JOHN JOHNSTON, except what was given unto son GEORGE
from this tract & two 50 tracts I bought from WILLIAM WEBB, also the 50
yrd. strip on the North side of the Flin tract. Also $50 to buy him a
horse and the same property to ELISHA & $250 to my son TAYLOR BAXTER when
he comes of the age of twenty one yrs. I give to my son TAYLOR my negro
boy Francis, my Hopper tract of land & 100 acre I entered on the waters
of Blacks Branch & my Holland tract of 50 acres & $500. I also give unto
sons ELISHA & TAYLOR my negro boy Jim to be hired out until ELISHA is
twenty one yrs. old. I give unto my nephew JOHN BAXTER $85. I give unto
my sons, JOHN & GEORGE W. BAXTER five negroes, Bet, the wife of Hillis,
Milly, Harriett, & her child & Miriah, in trust for support of my dtr.
ESTHER MCDOWELL DURHAM, during her natural life & her heirs. The remainder of my estate to be sold and the proceeds be equally divided among my
chn. JOSEPH, THOMAS, SARAH SUTTLES, JANE EAVES, ELIZABETH HARRILL, ESTHER
MCDOWELL DURHAM, JOHN, DAVID, GEORGE W., ELISHA & TAYLOR BAXTER. Chn.
that has received a full share & due no more, JAMES P. BAXTER, MARGARET
COSTEN, MARY TODD, CAROLINE HILL furthur becouse she has no heirs, my
decd. sons ANDREW & WILLIAM BAXTER & the dtr. of said WILLIAM SARAH CAT-
HERINE COSTEN. I appoint my sons JOSEPH, THOMAS, & JOHN BAXTER & my
son-in-law SPENCER EAVES my executors and guardians of my minor children.
Wit: J. MCENTIRE, jurat. E. BRYAN.   Signed: WILLIAM BAXTER.
CODICIL. Dated 7 Feb. 1851. This codicil left in possession of JOHN
          MCENTIRE for safe keeping. Son-in-law AMOS HARRILL has a habit
of intoxication and his conduct can not be calculated safely, he may
leave a large family with no support, all property left to ELIZABETH to
be taken by sons JOHN & GEORGE BAXTER in trust for ELIZABETH HARRILL and
her children, if she should die the said property to belong to the chn.
negroes to be hired out and the rent applied for their support. By the
last will, negroes was given in trust unto JOHN & GEORGE BAXTER for the
use of ESTHER DURHAM, the wife of MICAJAH DURHAM, since the said negroes
was given unto said DURHAM, who returned them to me, saying they could
not remain with him without absolute title, I am not perpared to keep
them. I desire my sons JOHN & GEORGE BAXTER to sell them and the proceeds to be vested in good stock and the interest going to my dtr. ESTHER
during her life time, then to her chn. The note I hold on AMOS HARRILL
is to be taken as so much cash advanced. Wit: C. H. HAYNES, Jurat. GEORGE
MCDANIEL, Jurat.   Signed: WM. BAXTER.
COCICIL #2. Dated 20 July 1852. In hands of JOHN MCENTIRE for safe
             keeping. I hereby declair that the power given to sons

JOHN & GEORGE BAXTER over the estate or property of my dtr. ESTHER DURHAM to extend over the property of my dtr. ELIZABETH HARRILL and her heirs. Wit: SABUN SMITH, jurat., THOMAS MORRIS, jurat.

Signed: WM. BAXTER.

Page 242. 8 Jan. 1853. Recorded, Feb. Court 1853. I, JOHN MCFADDEN, first I direct my just debts & funeral expenses be paid. I give unto my wife, MARTHA MCFADDEN, all my land & houses belonging to me during her life time, also household & kitchen furniture, also negro boy Ben, two mares, all cattle, hogs, & waggon. I give to my dtr., MARY M. MCFADDEN, one bed & furniture, I give unto my dtr., MARTHA C. MCFADDEN, one bed & furniture. I give to my son, JAMES T. MCFADDEN, one saddle. I direct that Doe to be sold on 12 months credit, to educate my youngest chn. SARAH, ELIZABETH & JOHN. At wife's death the property to be divided among all my chn. I appoint E. L. TAYLOR my executor. Wit: JAS. L. TAYLOR, jurat. J. W. VANDIVER, jurat.   Signed: JOHN MCFADDEN.

Page 243. 6 Dec. 1852. Recorded, March Court 1853. I, RICHARD ROBERTSON, being of sound and disposing mind & memory. I give all my beds & bed clothing to the 3 girls that are single, ARTY LOUISA, HETTY CATHARINE, & JULIAN. I will that the chn. have a home & land to live on until the youngest come of age, with all stock of cattle, hogs, one horse, & tools. I appoint my son ALFRED ROBERTSON & JOHN H. WALL executors. The balance of my property to be sold, when the youngest child come of age and the proceed to pay my just debts. If any is left to be divided among all my chn. Wit: LEWIS PADGETT, jurat. JOHN H. WALL.

Signed: RICHARD X ROBERTSON.
CODICIL. Dated 5 Jan. 1853. I RICHARD ROBERTSON do desire that all my property both real & personal shall be sold at my decease. Except the beds & clothing, which I gave to my three dtrs. Wit: LEWIS PADGETT, jurat. JOHN H. WALL.   Signed: RICHARD X ROBERTSON.

Page 145. 17 June 1851. Recorded, Spring Court 1853. I, WILLIAM HENDERSON, desire my funeral charges & just debts if any shall be paid. I give unto my son, MICHAEL, the negro Hannah & her two chn. Henry & George. I give unto WESTLEY EDWARDS & his wife, SARAH, my land on the mountain where he now lives. I give unto my two sons DAVID & WILLIAM HENDERSON, & my granddaughter, SARAH, & her husband, FENALE FOSTER, all my land adjoining the land which I deeded to my son MICHAEL to be divided between them. The balance to be divided among seven of my children, to wit. The heirs of JAMES HENDERSON, the heirs of REBECCA PACK, the heirs of JOEL HENDERSON, WILLIAM THOMPSON & his wife NANCY, WILLIAM HENDERSON, DAVID HENDERSON, & TOLIVER SMITH & his wife ELIZABETH. I appoint my son MICHAEL HENDERSON & J. W. HAMPTON my executors. Wit: JESSE RHODES, jurat. N. B. HAMPTON.   Signed: WILLIAM X HENDERSON.

Page 247. 10 May 1853. Recorded, Aug. Court 1853. I, GEORGE MCKINNY, being in sound & disposing mind & memory. I give unto my wife MIRA my negro girl Charlotte which I agreed in a marriage contract to do. I give unto my son JAMES MCKINNY, my negro Andrew. I give unto my dtr., MARY SUTTLE, my negro Sarah & the debt which her husband, JOSEPH SUTTLE, is due to me for the land & the balance of the price of the mill. I give unto my dtr., MARY WALKER, my negro Malinda. I give unto my dtr., ELIZABETH CAMP, my negro Primus Nicy & her child Lofa during her natural life & at her death to be divided among my other chn. I give unto my son, THOMAS MCKINNY, $200 in trust for the use & maintainance of my dtr., JANE MORRIS. I give unto my sons, JOHN M. & THOMAS MCKINNY, my home tract of land to be equally divided between them. I give unto my son, THOMAS MCKINNEY, my negro Henry. I direct my executor to sell the rest & remainder of my property and apply the proceeds as follows, to pay JAMES MCKINNY $750. MARY SUTTLE $750. NANCY WALKER $750. ELIZABETH CAMP $750. To THOMAS MCKINNY in trust for the use & maintainance of my dtr. JANE MORRIS. Any amount over to be divided among my chn. I appoint my son THOMAS MCKINNY my executor. Wit: JOHN L. MCDOWELL, jurat. MILLER MCKINNY.

Signed: GEORGE MCKINNY.

Page 251. 15 Aug. 1853. Recorded, Fall Court 1853. I, R. L. PRICE, First I direct that all my lands to my wife during her life time or widowhood, at the expiration of either to become the property of my three chn. (no names of wife or chn. given). I appoint ROBERT PRICE and TILFORD?

121

my executors. Wit: P. P. PRICE, jurat.   Signed: R. L. PRICE.

Page 251.   31 Aug. 1853. Recorded, Fall Court 1853. I, JAMES BLACKWELL,
          being of sound mind & memory. I wish all my just debts to be
paid. I will unto my wife, MARY, during her life time all my land lying
on both sides of Green River, containing 900 acres also seven negroes,
Albert, Walton, Lonuon, Jason, Vina, Esther & Sarah, all stock of horses,
cattle, hogs, farming tools. At her death to become the property of my
dtr., LITITIA VERNON, and her children. I will unto my dtr., LITITIA, &
her children the rest of my negroes being 34 in number. It is my wish
that my friend WILLIAM L. MILLS to act as my executor, to act as he may
think proper with the above named property for the benfit of my dtr. &
grandchildren. Wit: O. P. EARLE, jurat. TYRA G. RIDINGS, THOMAS A.
SNOWDEN.   Signed: JAMES BLACKWELL.

Page 253.   11 Feb. 1829. Recorded, Fall Court 1853. I, JOSEPH CARPENTER,
          I give unto my son, HIRAM, $10. I give unto my son, WILLIAM
J., $10. I give unto my son, EMMANUEL M., $10. I give unto my son,
DANIEL J., $10. I give unto my son, JOHN H., $10. I give unto my dtr.,
MARIAH, $10. I give unto my son, SAMUEL, $10. I give unto my son, JAMES,
$10. I give unto my dtr., NANCY WALTON, $10. I give unto my dtr., MIRA
ISENA, $10. All the rest of my estate both real & personal I give unto
my wife, ELIZABETH, to be her absolute property. I appoint my wife,
ELIZABETH, & sons, HIRAM, WILLIAM my executors. Wit: JAMES CARPENTER,
ORVILLE KEE WILSON, R. K. WILSON, jurat.
                                 Signed: JOS. CARPENTER.

Page 255.   19 Jan. 1854. Recorded, Feb. Court 1854. I, WILLIAM WATSON,
          being feeble in body but of perfect mind & memory. First all
my just debts to be paid. I leave to my son, HUGH WATSON, $15. I give to
my son, JAMES R. WATSON, $10. I give to my son, DANIEL WATSON, three
lots of land, one of 50 acres, one of 40 acres & one of 25 acres, which
lot PRESTON GOFORTH is to have 12½ acres if he pays the sum of $7. I
give to my son, JOHN WATSON, all the land that lies above the before
mention land, containing 150 acres, being my home tract, also one bed &
furniture, he is to pay out of his legacy $50. I give unto my 3 dtrs.
ELIZABETH, MARGARET & CATHERINE all my unnamed beds & furniture. I ordered my books sold & divided among my chn. JOHN excepted. I give unto
MARGARET one chest. I give unto SARAH WATSON who now lives with me one
cow & calf, forty weight of bacon, five head of geese & $6. The balance
to be sold & proceeds divided among dtrs., ELIZABETH, MARGARET & CATHERINE.
I appoint my son, JOHN WATSON, & son-in-law, HUGH WATSON, my executors.
Wit: PRESTON GOFORTH, THOMAS MCDANIEL, jurat.
                                 Signed: WILLIAM WATSON.

Page 258.   20 April 1842. Recorded, July Court 1854. I, WILLIAM LONG,
          being feeble in body but of perfect mind & memory. First my
just debts to be paid. I allow the deeds made by me to my sons to stand.
I allow the bill of sale made by me to my chn. for negro to stand. I allow my son, THOMAS LONG, to pay my granddaughter, JANE BALDRIDGE, $50 at
any time she comes for it. I allow my son, WILLIAM J. LONG, to pay grand
son, JOHN BALDRIDGE, $25, also said WILLIAM to pay two $50 notes I hold
on him, one to my dtr., MARY M. LONG, & the other to dtr., LUSINDA STAF-
FORD. I leave my broad axe & cross cut saw to my sons, JAMES T. LONG, &
PRESTON N. LONG. I give to my beloved JANE one bay mare, saddle, bridle,
with all household & kitchen furniture to be at her own disposal. I
appoint my son, WILLIAM J. & PRESTON N. LONG, my executors. Wit: HUGH
WATSON, jurat. JOHN FARLAND.   Signed: WILLIAM X LONG.

Page 260.   12 Jan. 1854. Recorded, March Court, 1854. I, LUKE WALDROPE,
          being old & infirme but of sound mind & memory. All my just
debts to be paid. I have already given to sons SAMUEL & MERCER a pony &
bedding worth $50 each. I have given to my son JOSEPH C. a pony worth
$40 & I give him feather bed & furniture to make him equal. My dtrs.
PATSY & JANE I have given a bed & furniture, JANE has received a bee hive,
PATSY ALMURA. I have already given to my dtrs. HARRIET A. & REBECCA each
a feather bed & furniture & a bee hive. All the balance of my lands,
horses, cattle, sheep, fowls & household & kitchen furniture, I give to
my beloved wife SARAH during her life time or widowhood with the privi-
ledge of AMANDA, REBECCA & JOSEPH living with her. If JOHN CUD stays

until he is 21, he is to have 2 suits of clothes worth $10. The balance of my property to be divided among TERRILL F., MERCER R., SAMUEL MC., JOSEPH C. & PATSY A., HARRIET A., JANE, REBECCA. JOSEPH to have the land by paying son TERRILL the sum of $55, he having stayed & kept his father & mother in their old age. I appoint JAMES JACKSON my son-in-law & JOSEPH C. WALDROPE my executors. Wit: I. M. HAMILTON, jurat. JOHN LITTLE-JOHN, jurat. JACKSON WALDROPE, jurat.   Signed: LUKE WALDROPE.

Page 263. 8 March 1844. Recorded, Spring Court 1854. I, WILLIAM PARKER, being of sound mind & memory. All funeral expenses and just debts to be paid. I give unto my beloved wife, POLLY PARKER, all my property both real & personal during her natural life. I give to my son, THOMAS, all that tract of land whereon he now lives and negro girl Nancy. I give unto my son, ELIJAH, all that tract of land whereon he now lives, with negro Alfred. I give to my grandson, JOHN, son of ELIJAH one negro girl named Jane. I give to my son, JAMES, 3 negroes, Jack, James & Lil & Lil increase. I give to my dtr., SALLY, negro named Abby and at my wife's death to get all household & kitchen furniture. I give to my son, JOHN, $10. I give to my son WILLIAM $10. I give to my dtr. NANCY $10. I give to my grandson JOHN MCKEY $10. I hereby appoint my sons, THOMAS & ELYJAH, guardian of my son JAMES if they out live him, they are to divide his estate between themselves. I Appoint my sons, THOMAS & ELYJAH, my executors. Wit: M. WILKERSON, SR., JETHRO WILKERSON.
                                       Signed: WILLIAM X PARKER.

Page 265. 9 Sept. 1853. Recorded, Spring Court 1854. I, ARCHIBALD LOLLAR, being of sound mind & memory. First my funeral charges & just debts to be paid. I give to my wife all the land that I now own, all stock of horses, cattle, sheep, & hogs, my ox cart, her choice of carriage, all household & kitchen furniture, farming tools, all blacksmith tools, my threshing machine, fan mill also $250 in money, my negroes Felix & Milly as long as she is a widow, also negro girl Sarah to hold & assign as she may choose to do. I give to my dtr., MARTHA, negro girl Alvira & her children. I give to my dtr., JANE, a negro girl Jane. I give to my son LEWIS a negro named Sam at $400 provided he returns home from California before my son THOMAS shall arrive to the age of 21 years if not then Sam to belong to son THOMAS at $400. I give unto my son, LEONARD, negro John. I give to my dtr., ELIZABETH, negro girl Elvira. The balance of my property to be sold & divided among my chn. to wit. MARY, ISAAC, DAVID, LEWIS, LEONARD, ELIZABETH, & THOMAS. Each to account for what they have been advanced. As THOMAS is a minor, I hereby appoint my wife as his guardian of his person & his estate until he arrives of full age, and my executors to retain from the estate $80 for a horse, saddle over his share. I Appoint my wife & my son, LEONARD, my lawfull executors. Wit: EDWARD TOMS, jurat. J. R. TWITTY, jurat.
                                       Signed: ARCHIBALD LOLLAR.

Page 268. 27 Oct. 1849. Recorded, Spring Court 1854. I, WILLIAM HAMMEN, being of sound & disposing mind & memory. I will that my just debts be paid. I give unto my beloved wife PHEBE the tract of land whereon I now reside, containing 116 acres, also a tract of land of 49 acres lying on North Packolet River, that I bought from Mrs. ELENOR WHITTON, also the land I purchased from WILLIAM W. DEVENPORT, & SAMUEL C. HANNEN, all household & kitchen furniture, horses, cattle, hogs etc. during her natural life or widowhood. Should she remarry then I appoint WILL S. MILLS, my executor, to sell the land and make an equal division among the heirs of my said wife. I deem that the heirs of my first wife will have an equal or better share than the chn. by the present wife. Wit: JESSE EVANS, BENJAMIN PAGE, jurat.   Signed: WILLIAM X HAMMEN.

Page 270. 18 March 1854. Recorded, Aug. Court 1854. I, J. M. WEBB, Being in sound mind & memory. I desire that my body be interr- ed in the garden between my two wives, and a stone put up for myself & my last wife with engraving. To JAMES PINCKNEY WEBB & GEORGE MILTON WEBB. I have already given $430, he to receive $128.94 to make him equal with PINCKNEY & MELTON. The rest of the chn. to be educated, & given a horse & saddle, and when of age to receive $558.04 each. C. J. WEBB has agreed to come home & live upon the place and care for the children as a father, also run the plantation. The goods in the store to be sold at action. I appoint my sons, C. J. WEBB, & G. M. WEBB, my executors, in case either

one can't act, then son SHROD L. WEBB to act when of age. TOLIVER DAVIS
& GEORGE MELTON WEBB to be advisors to C. J. WEBB if needed. Executors
to sell land on High Sholes to pay my debts. Wit: JOSEPH W. CALLOWAY,
EDWARD GOODE, jurat.   Signed: J. M. WEBB.

Page 277.   8 April 1854. Recorded, Aug. Court 1854. State of Alabama,
            Autauga County. OSBERN R. HOLLYFIELD a citizen of Rutherford
County, N. C. now in the county aforsaid. Being in low health, but of
sound mind. Property in Rutherford County to be kept in possession of my
parents, ELIJAH & ERNSY? HOLLYFIELD. The sum of $1200 to be placed in
the hands of the trustees as herein named to purchase what is called the
Logan Place on which my parents reside. I give unto my sister PRISSY my
gold watch & chain as an extra legacy. It is my will that my just debts
be paid, and after the death of my parents, all the property found in
their possession as given to them by me during their life time shall
revert to my estate and be divided equally as follows, RANSOM, EAY, PRISSY,
CYNTHIA HOLLYFIELD (alias) LOVELACE, NORCISSA, ABRAM, NOAH, and my nephew
HARVEY HOLLYFIELD and their heirs forever. I appoint my friend, WILLIAM
JAMES SMITH, my executor, he is a citizen of Spartanburg Co., S.C. He is
to collect all debts due to me & to pay all my debts, and matters of
business in the States of Ala., Ga. & S. C. I leave my friend LEONARD
DECK of Rutherford County, N. C. to be my legal trustee and represent my
parents. Wit: GEORGE W. STINE, W. NUNN, T. M. WALKER, jurat.
                                       Signed: O. R. HOLLYFIELD.

Page 280.   22 Nov. 1853. Recorded, Fall Court 1854. I, JETHRO WILKERSON,
            being of sound mind & memory. First I desire my just debts to
be paid. I give unto my wife, POLLY WILKERSON, one half of the bottom
land, and the mansion house, farm tools, 10 head of cattle, all hogs,
household & kitchen furniture, two horses, two negroes, Ned & Able,
during her natural life or widowhood. I give unto my son PERMINTER WILKER-
SON the other half of the bottom land where he now lives. At her death
the land she has to fall to son MOSES. My son MOSES to have the blacksmith tools, son PERMINTER my rifle gun. Balance of my property to be
sold & proceeds divided equally among my dtrs. REBECCA PARKER, NANCY
PARKER, POLLY FRADY, TEMPY NANNY, ALTHEY MORGAN, LINDY WILKERSON, Dtr.
LINDY to have $100 over and above the rest of my dtrs. I appoint my
sons, MOSES & PERMINTER WILKERSON, my executors. Wit: M. WILKERSON, Senr.,
jurat. M. HALL, jurat.   Signed: JETHRO WILKERSON.

Page 282.   25 Sept. 1854. Recorded, Fall Court 1854. WILLIAM DAVIS,
            being sound in mind but not in body. I give unto my son, WM.
DAVIS, all the tract of land I now live on, with the mill and all the
improvements of 192 acres, and he must take care of his mother during her
life time, also the balance of a note given to me for $64.32. I give to
my wife, CELY DAVIS, one cow & calf, all the household & kitchen furniture.
I give unto my granddaughter, SALLY L. TEAL, $10. I give unto my grand-
daughter, CELY C. TEAL, $10. I give unto my granddaughter, NANCY B. TEAL,
$10. I give unto my granddaughter, MARY H. TEAL, $10. I give unto my
dtr., LUCINDA DAVIS, the tract of land she now lives on and the heirs of
her body. The balance of my property sold and the money due me collected
and equally divided among my chn. NOAH, JOHN, JAMES, LUCINDA DAVIS & SALLY
ROGERS. I appoint my sons, JOHN & WILLIAM DAVIS, my executors. Wit: A.
HARRILL, jurat., N. M. FLOYD, jurat.   Signed: WILLIAM X DAVIS.

Page 284.   26 Aug. 1846. Recorded, Fall Court 1854. I, WILLIAM PADGETT,
            being this day of sound mind & memory. I give unto my dtr.,
POLLY, one horse, bridle and saddle, with all the living property that I
have, both hogs, cattle, sheep, with farming tools, with all household &
kitchen furniture. I give unto my wife, MANERVA, $1. I give unto ABRAM
PADGETT $1. I give unto MANSFIELD PADGETT $1. I give unto my dtr.,
ENSY HOLLISFIELD, $1. I give unto EPHRAIM PADGETT $1. I give unto my
dtr., LYAIR WALL, $1. I give unto my dtr., LELAH WETHERS, $1. I give
unto my son, JOHN, $1. No executor. Wit: D. PANNELL, jurat. ALASON
PADGETT.   Signed: WILLIAM X PADGETT.

Page 285.   2 Feb. 1837. Recorded, Feb. Court 1855. I, WILLIAM CAMP,
            Being far advanced in life but of sound mind & memory. I give
unto my wife, ELIZABETH, one tract of land formerly owned by GEORGE
JOHNSTON where I now live & one other tract in Burke County, N. C., ex-

cept I may sell it in my life time. One negro woman Tene & negro boy
Wade, all stock of horses, cattle, sheep, & hogs, farming tools & household & kitchen furniture to remain in her possession & at her disposal,
at her death negro to fall to son JOHN CAMP. I give unto my grandchn.
WILLIAM, HENRY, & JOHN NANNY the heirs of Mary, three tract of land, one
the Hunter tract of 63 acres, & one the Hamrick tract on Squaw branch of
50 acres, joining land of ELIZABETH KEETER to be equally divided among
said chn. I appoint my son, JOHN CAMP & JOHN GUILKY, my executors. Wit:
JOHN CROSS, JOSEPH U. WHITESIDES.   Signed: WILLIAM X CAMP.

Page 286. 25 April 1855. Recorded, Spring Court 1855. I, JAMES PRICE,
          having advanced in life but of sound mind & memory. I give
unto my wife, MARY PRICE, all my land during her natural life, also her
resident in the house we now live in with all furniture, all stock of
horses, cattle, sheep, hogs, waggon, blacksmith tools, after the death
of my wife, I give unto my chn., FREEMAN, FRANKLIN & ELIZABETH, the tract
of land where FRANKLIN now lives, to be divided among them, FRANKLIN the
lower part, F. A. the middle part, & ELIZABETH the upper part. To son
JAMES H. & DELARQUIS the tract of land known as the Julius tract, with
DELARQUIS taking the North part. Son, BENNET PRICE, has received his
share. I give to my three dtrs., ELLEN, ELIZABETH & ANNIE, the plantation I now live on to be divided among them. Son, HAMPTON PRICE, to have
his share of land heretofore named. I allow my son, WADE, $5 in cash. I
have four grandchildren who are bound to me, they are to live with my
wife & dtrs. and to receive as I am bound by the Court to give. I appoint
my wife executrix. Wit: W. M. C. GETTYS, W. H. ATKIN.
                                        Signed: JAMES PRICE.

Page 288. 27 Jan. 1852. Recorded, Spring Court 1855. I, Mrs. CELEY
          WEBB, being of sound mind & memory, but in bad health. I give
unto my dtr., SELEY, my household & kitchen furniture of every kind &
moveable property. My dtr., SELEY, to pay my funeral expenses & just
debts. I also give SELEY my negro boy Simon. I appoint my dtr. Executrix. Wit: THOMAS BAXTER, LEWIS PADGETT.
                                     Signed: MRS. CELEY X WEBB.

Page 289. 1 Feb. 1853. Recorded, Spring Court 1855. I, GEORGE GROVE,
          being of sound mind & memory. I desire my just debts & funeral
charges to be paid. I give unto my dtr., MALINDA, my home tract of land
where I now live, also 40 acres lying West of my home tract, joining
lands of L. A. MILLS, NICHERS, & HALE. The remainder to be divided among
WM. M. GROVES, SAMUEL ANDREWS, WILLIAM IRWIN. I give unto my dtr. MALINDA
all the money on hand at death, also all household & kitchen furniture.
Stock of cattle, hogs & sheep. I give unto my dtr. CYNTHA ERWIN one
feather bed. I appoint my son-in-law, SAMUEL ANDREW, my executor. Wit:
A. B. LONG, A. R. WALLACE.   Signed: GEORGE GROVES.
(The above will was proved 4 Monday in March 1855.)

Page 291. 26 June 1855. Recorded, Aug. Court 1855. I, WILLIAM TONEY,
          doth will to my wife, SARAH TONEY, all the property that we
now have on hand, the old cow to be sold to pay debts, and for her to
settle with JOSHUA about the mare, and take his note for the balance to
pay debts. My wife, SARAH TONEY, & JEFFERSON TONEY to divide the land,
she to keep her part for maintenance during her life time, then to be
divided between DORCHUS TAYLOR & NANCY BIGGERSTAFF. No executor. Wit:
SAMUEL L. WHITESIDES.   Signed: WILLIAM TONEY.

Page 292. 27 Feb. 1855. Recorded, Aug. Court 1855. I, JAMES MORRIS,
          Senr., I give to my wife, ELIZABETH MORRIS, all my household
& kitchen furniture, except the piano & secretary. Also negroes Wiley,
Benton, Jerry, Sally, Mira, Emily, Pattsy, Elizabeth with one horse & the
coach. I give to my son, JAMES B. MORRIS, the home place with the joining
lands made by the county processor lying on Broad River, joining land of
R. G. TWITTY, THOMAS MOORE, containing 136 acres, also 100 acres now
called the Carver land, also negroes Ben, Dick, Teriser, also 4 horses,
smith tools, wagons, buggy & secretary. I give to my grandson DAVID M.
GREENLEE, the son of my dtr. ELIZA, two negroes between the ages of seven
& ten yrs. I give unto my dtr., MARY M., wife of JAMES D. BININGS the
following negroes, Nelly, & her child Becky, Ritta & Harriet & Billy, I
give to my son-in-law, J. D. BININGS, $50. I give to my dtr. MARTHA L.,

the wife of ERASTUS ROWLEY the following negroes, Tomsin, & her child
Hannah, Letty & Angeline also Milly, Also to ERASTUS ROWLEY $40. I give
unto my dtr., JANE E., wife of SAMUEL WILKINS the following negroes, Ann
& her child Sarah, Fanny, & Rachel & Harvey. I give to my dtr., MATILDA
C. MORRIS, negroes, Little Vina & her child Merva, Mahalor, Little Abe,
with the piano bought for her. I will that the lands of the Dickey,
Rucker, & Garrett places be sold and proceeds divided among my wife &
four dtrs. named above. The remaining property not given or sold to be
equally divided among my wife & five chn. I appoint JAMES D. BININGS,
ERASTUS ROWLEY, & SAMUEL WILKING my executors. Wit: EDMOND FOSTER, jurat.
JAMES M. GARRETT, jurat.   Signed: JAMES MORRIS.

Page 295. 11 July 1855. Recorded, Aug. Court 1855. I, A. W. WHITESIDE,
          give unto my wife, ELIZA, during her life all my land on the
South side of Broad River, including the dwelling house, and that part
lying on the North side above the cross fence on the said river with the
mill, & the Scott's place, and negroes, Mary & her Chn. Cindia, Jack, &
Harriett and Andy, also one half of my horses, cattle, hogs, sheep, the
household & kitchen furniture. I desire that my son, JONATHAN, to manage
the property for his mother & my afflicted son, JOHN. I give unto my
son-in-law, MADISON LYNCH, & his wife, I give the negroes Hannah & Oliver
& their chn. and the property I have put in their possession and the sum
of $1500. I give unto my son-in-law, B. L. BLANTON, & his wife all the
property I have put in their possession with negroes, Mira & Manda &
their chn. with the sum of $1500. To my son, JONATHAN, all my lands on
Broad River & Buffalo Creek with several other tracts. I give to my
afflicted son, JOHN, negroes Harris & Sal, and I appoint my son, JONATH-
AN, his guardian of his property & him. I give unto my granddaughter,
ELIZA E. HETTRICK, the sum of $1500 to be loaned out on interest until
she is 21 yrs. old, should she die the money to be divided between my
dtrs., MADISON LYNCH'S wife & BLANTON'S wife & son JONATHAN. After my
death I desire my executor to sell negroes, David & Ethel and their chn.
Dick & Bill. Duch & her child Peter. I also give unto LOUISA E. HETTICK
the sum of $1500. All property not named to be sold & proceeds given
as legacys in this will. I appoint W. M. SHIPP & M. E. LYNCH, my executors. Wit: T. R. EDGERTON, T. H. W. WHITESIDE, jurat.
                                        Signed: A. W. WHITESIDE.

Page 298. 28 April 1855. Recorded, Aug. Court 1855. I, PRESTON GOFORTH,
          being of sound mind & memory. First I desire my just debts
& funeral charges to be paid. I give unto my beloved wife, PARTHENA B.
GOFORTH, all the plantation on which we live, also farming tools, mare,
cow & calf, household & kitchen furniture, books as the big Bible, Baptist
hymn book, Cherekee Physician. I give to my second dtr. $20 extra account
of her being lame. Land on the Fork to be sold with other items not named
and the proceeds divided among all my chn. I appoint my sons W. C.
GOFORTH & JOHN E. GOFORTH my executors. Wit: W. B. ANDREWS, jurat. JOHN
R. GOFORTH, jurat.   Signed: PRESTON GOFORTH.

Page 301. 2 Oct. 1854. Sept. Court 1855. I, DAVID BROWN, being of
          sound mind & memory. I direct that all my just debts & funeral
charges to be paid. I direct that the whole of my property, both real &
personal shall be and remain the property of my wife, ISABELLA BROWN, &
her heirs, if she should die before me I desire that the estate be equally
divided among my chn. as they come of age. Wife to keep or dispose of
my negroes, Malinda & her chn. Jiles & John as she think best. If wife
should marry again, the property to be sold and divided among her & chn.
share & share alike. I appoint SAMUEL YOUNG & JOHN GILLESPIE, my executors. Wit: ANDREW J. SCOGGIN, JOHN MATHERNY, jurat.
                                        Signed: DAVID BROWN.

Page 303. 19 March 1855. Recorded, Fall Court 1855. I, JOSHUA TAYLOR,
          give unto my beloved wife, STACY, the plantation whereon I
now reside with negroes, Soloman, Hett, Mary & child Jerry, Elizabeth &
Jane during her natural life, also all household & kitchen furniture, two
horses, 4 cows & calves, all hogs & hams, & one years provision. I give
unto my dtr., MANERVA TOMS, the negro girl she now has Elvira and Tom &
Harriett, during her life, then to her chn. I give unto my son, WILLIAM
W. TAYLOR, the mountain tract of land of 100 acres. I give unto my son
OLIVER P. TAYLOR, a tract of mountain land called the Steel place of 100

126

acres. I will unto my five sons, JOHN A., ELYAH A., OLIVER P., FRANKLIN
L. JOSHUA L. TAYLOR the balance of my property, and at wife's death, ex-
cept the land, to be part of the property that is to be valued and put
into lots, with the oldest son having first choice. The land given to my
wife at her death to belong to sons OLIVER P. & JOSHUA L. TAYLOR. Son
WILLIAM has not been given as much as the rest, I desire that the others
to "do him justice." I appoint my sons WILLIAM W., JOHN A., & ELIJAH A.
TAYLOR my executors. Wit: ROBERT G. TWITTY, ELIAS L. TAYLOR.
Signed: JOSHUA TAYLOR.
CODICIL. Dated 6 Aug. 1855. I will to my wife, STACY, negroes Mary &
her child to dispose of as she thinks best at her death. Also
the plantation given to my wife to belong to son OLIVER P. at his mother's
death & four negroes, Lynch, Jerry, Lewis & Rachel.
CODICIL #2. Dated 6 Aug. 1855. I give unto OLIVER P. negroes, Henry,
George, Juda & Martha. Wit: ROBERT G. TWITTY, E. L. TAYLOR.
Signed: JOSHUA TAYLOR.

Page 305. 4 Sept. 1855. Recorded, Fall Court 1855. I, JACOB MAGNESS,
being of sound mind & memory, but weak in body. I order my
executor to pay my just debts & funeral charges. At my death I desire
all my property both real & personal to be sold on 12 months credit, and
proceeds divided among my five chn. ROBERT, BENJAMIN, ELIZA, WILLIAM &
SARAH. I have loaned sons BENJAMIN & WILLIAM $50 each. I not having
their notes, if they do not pay me in my life time, I desire that the
amount to be taken from each share. (No executor named). Wit: HOUSEN
HARRILL.
Signed: JACOB X MAGNESS.

Page 307. 28 Jan. 1856. Recorded, Feb. Court 1856. I, JAMES CHERRY,
being far advanced in age but of sound mind & memory. I allow
my just debts to be paid with my funeral expenses. I give to my wife
ELIZABETH CHERRY negroes, Squire, Tener, Craton, Alfred, George Tener, &
Queen with all stock of cattle, hogs, & sheep, tools, household & kitchen
furniture, one half of my land including the mansion house. I give unto
my dtr. SINTHY ANN CHERRY, negroes, Fanny, Van, Squire, Henry, July,
Austin, & Clarison, also one young mare, also the other half of my land.
Executor to help in the education of my dtr. he may sell part or all of
her property for her use & benfit, to sell my new wagon to school dtr.
I appoint my friend JOHN GILKEY my executor. Should dtr. SINTHY ANN die
before full age, negroes to the property of JOHN GILKEY, and the land to
be sold & proceeds divided among the heirs of my sister MARY WALLIS. Wit:
JOHN KEETER, jurat. JOHN A. JUSTICE, jurat.
Signed: JAS. CHERRY.

Page 309. 8 Jan. 1856. Recorded, Feb. Court 1856. I, JESSE CHITWOOD,
being of sound mind & memory. Executor to pay all debts &
funeral expenses. I give unto my wife the tract of land whereon I now
reside, joining lands of JAMES OWENS, ASSA SWEEZY, JONAS BEDFORD & I. M.
CHITWOOD during her natural life. I allow my youngest dtr. SARAH 40 acres
lying on Coburns Branch, joining lands of JAMES OWENS & RAYMOND OWENS,
the upper part to be her part at the death of her mother SARAH CHITWOOD.
At the death of my wife her land to be divided among WILLIAM, J. M.
CHITWOOD & SARAH CHETWOOD. The balance of my property to be divided
among my five chn. WILLIAM CHETWOOD, ELIZABETH the wife of ALEXANDER
GETTY, J. M. CHITWOOD, NANCY the wife of BENJ. A. JENKINS & SARAH CHIT-
WOOD. Except the chn. of my oldest dtr. MARGARET (wife of CHARLES BIRD)
to have $10 paid at the death of my wife SARAH as their share. My son
JOHN CHITWOOD to have $150 as his share. I appoint AMOS HARRILL, DANIEL
P. GOLD & JAS GREEN men to divide the property among the 5 chn. As my
dtr. SARAH is under age & will not be of full age until 7 March 1860 I
hereby appoint my son WILLIAM as her guardian. I also appoint my sons
W. C. CHITWOOD & J. M. CHITWOOD my executors. Wit: J. W. PRICE, jurat.
LEWIS JUSTICE, jurat.
Signed: JESSE CHITWOOD.

Page 313. 29 March 1848. Recorded, Spring Court 1856. I, JOHN GUFFY,
Sr. being declining in body but of sound mind & memory. First
of all my just debts & funeral charges be paid. I give unto my son
ARCHIBALD W. GUFFY a tract of land on Big Camp Creek containing 166 acres,
being where he now lives, also one set of blacksmith tools which he said
ARCHY has in his possession. I give unto my son JOHN L. GUFFY the tract
of land lying on Little Camp Creek, where I now live and said JOHN now

lives, containing 158 acres, JOHN L. binds himself to support his mother & me during our natural lives. JOHN to have all my interest in our new waggon. I give unto my son JAMES GUFFY the sum of 10 shillings if called for. I give unto my son THOMAS GUFFY the sum of 10 shillings if called for. I give unto my dtr. FANNY GUFFY one cupboard, one table & one big pot. I give unto the heirs of my dtr. ELIZABETH LITTLE $10 if called for. I give unto granddaughter ELENDER SPRATT, one feather bed & furniture, one cow, our stand of curtains, one cotton wheel which property she now has. I give to grandson JOHN A. GUFFY, one bed & furniture. I give unto my beloved wife ELIZABETH GUFFY the remaining property, that is cattle, hogs, & sheep, household & kitchen furniture if she out lives me, and at her death to my dtr. FANNY, except one spotted heifer, I allow my grand-daughter MATILDA GUFFY "for washing." I appoint my son ARCHY V. & JOHN L. GUFFY my executors. Wit: A. B. LONG, Jurat. M. P. LONG.
Signed: JOHN GUFFY.

Page 316. 24 July 1856. Recorded, Aug. Court 1856. I, ELIZABETH CARPENTER, being of sound mind & memory. First I desire my executor to pay my funeral expenses & just debts. I give unto my dtr. MERCY SARAH BRADLEY one negro boy, Lafayett & one half of my land, with the dwelling house & half of the household & kitchen furniture forever. I give unto my dtr. NANCY W. EDWARDS one negro girl, Clarisa & one half of all my land, with half of the household & kitchen furniture forever. I give unto JAMES J. JONES one horse colt for the natural love & affection I have for him. All remaining property of negroes, stock, tools & notes to be sold and proceeds divided among my sons, HIRAM, WM. I., E. MORTON, DANIEL T., JOHN, SAMUEL A., & JAMES CARPENTER. I appoint my two sons E. M. & JAMES CARPENTER to divide the land for my dtrs. Also I appoint them my executors. Wit: LAWSEN EVES, jurat. P. A. CARPENTER, jurat.
Signed: ELIZABETH X CARPENTER.
CODICIL. I desire that $100 more to each of my dtrs. be paid from the notes when collected, as they are in bad health. Dated 2 Aug. 1856. Wit: J. BRISON WALKER, Junr., Jurat.
Signed: ELIZABETH X CARPENTER.

Page 320. 14 June 1856. Recorded, Fall Court 1856. I, THOMAS NANNY, Senr. being advanced in age but of sound mind & memory. First from my personal property my funeral expenses be paid. I give unto my wife MARY all my land to support her and the children who are minors during life or widowhood. I also give to my wife all stock of cattle, horses, hogs, sheep & household & kitchen furniture. Wife to pay son MARTIN for working in the crop, wife to give the single sons an equal share as sons AMOS & CEBERN have had. Also to give to my two dtrs. MARY SELENA & GRISSILLER enough to make them equal to what the married dtrs. has received. I appoint my sons AMOS & CEBERN NANNY my executors. Wit: T. B. JUSTICE, jurat. JOHN FLACK, jurat.
Signed: THOMAS X NANNY.

Page 322. 16 March 1852. Recorded, Fall Court 1856. I, ANDREW HUDLOW, Senr. being of sound mind & Memory. First I direct that all my just debts to be paid. I direct that all my estate both real & per-sonal be sold by my executors, and after paying my debts, the money divided as follows, son MICHAEL HUDLOW & grandchildren if alive ANDREW HUDLOW, JR., JOSEPH HUDLOW, WILLIAM HUDLOW, THOMAS HUDLOW, & MARTHA HILL the wife of ASSPH HILL, BARBARA GOODE wife of ABRAHAM GOODE, ELIZABETH TANNER wife of JAMES TANNER, SARAH BABER wife of JAMES BABER, NATHAN HUDLOW, MARY HUDLOW. I appoint my grandson ANDREW HUDLOW & A. H. LOGAN my executors. Wit: PHILIP H. GROSE, jurat. THOMAS I. HARLEN, jurat.
Signed: ANDREW X HUDLOW.

Page 323. 1 Sept. 1856. Recorded, Fall Court 1856. I, WILLIAM SHAMWELL, being of sound mind & memory. Executor to pay just debts & funeral expenses. I give unto my beloved wife ELIZABETH SHAMWELL, the plantation & all loose property that I may die possessed of, during her natural life or widowhood, then to go to my son ELISHA M. SHAMWELL to be his part of my estate. The remainder part of my estate to go to my dtr. EMALINE SHAMWELL. I appoint my friend DUGGER FREMAN my executor. Wit: JOHN FREEMAN, Senr., jurat. JOHN M. FREEMAN.
Signed: WILLIAM SHAMWELL.

Page 325. 27 Nov. 1826. Recorded, Spring Court 1857. I, ZACHARIAH JOHNS,
being of sound mind & memory. All debts to be paid. I give
unto my beloved wife MARTHA all my personal property of every kind during
her natural life, also to enjoy the benfits of the plantation during her
life time, then divided among my chn. The plantation in the fork of
Broad River & Green River unto sons JAMES JOHNS & JOHN JOHNS where I now
reside. Joinings land of Burges & Shearer. Land surveyed by FRANCES
ALEXANDER 23 April 1821. JAMES JOHNS to have the land he now lives on &
JOHN to have the land where I now reside. I appoint my wife MARTHA JOHNS
my executrix & JOHN JOHNS my executor. Wit: ANDREW YOUNG, FRANCES ALEX-
ANDER, JAMES MILLER, A. E. MILLER,   Signed: ZACHARIAH JOHNS.

Page 326. 5 March 1857. Recorded, Spring Court 1857. I, HUGH WATSON,
being of sound mind & memory but in feeble health. I direct
all my debts to be paid. My tract of land where on I now reside, giving
dtr. ANN C. WATSON my lower or large house & my son HUGH C. WATSON the
upper or small house, also one chest, one bed & furniture, one third of
my books. I give unto ANN C. WATSON one third of the books, which to
include the large Bible, also all hogs, one mare, tools, & household &
kitchen furniture. I give unto my dtr. REBECCA A. GOFORTH one third of
my books. All money & notes collected and after paying my debts to be
equally divided among my three chn. I appoint JOHN A. WATSON my executor.
Wit: SAMUEL ANDREW, jurat. DANIEL WATSON, jurat.
                                    Signed: HUGH X WATSON.

Page 327. 20 Oct. 1850. Recorded, Spring Court 1857. I, JOHN MCENTIRE,
being of sound mind & memory. I will my just debts & funeral
expenses shall be paid. I give unto my wife, MARY JANE MCENTIRE, my
dwelling house & lot in the town of Rutherfordton, all household & kitchen
furniture & at her death to go to my youngest dtr. LAURA E. MCENTIRE, also negroes, Minerva, & her five chn. Sarah, James, Edmond, Tolliver, &
Madison & her husband Levi, and at her death said negroes to belong to my
dtr. LAURA. I give unto my wife negroes, Hannah, & her dtr. Allie, & all
of Hannah's increase, Carolie & her child Nell & her increase & Drew &
Ellie during her natural life then to my second dtr. JANE E. MCENTIRE. I
also give unto my wife 3 tracts of land known as the McFaddin, Bradley &
Taylor lying on Mountain Creek during her life then divided between my
youngest dtrs. JANE E. & LAURA E. I give unto my dtr. MARTHA A. MCENTIRE
the following negroes, Charlotte, Griffin her son, William, Mary, Jane,
Noah & all of Charlotte's increase, also Mary & her dtr. Lizzy, Primmis
also the sum of $3,000. I give unto my sons WM. THOMAS & JOHN YOUNG
MCENTIRE my store house & lot in Rutherfordton, also 3 tracts that I
bought from ISAAC CRATONS sale, containing 60 acres, also the land I
bought of NANCY WALTON containing 23 acres. To WILLIAM I give the Parish
tract containing 200 acres, with the mill tract, joining McDowell land.
To JOHN Y. 57 acres I bought of WESLEY MCGUIN, joining the land of Bryan,
Miller, & Harris also on tract on Floyd Creek known as the McKinny tract
containing 1,000 acres. I give to my wife 30 acres of land joining Bryan
& Millers that I bought of Doctor JOHN MILLER, at wife death to belong
to dtr. LAURA E. I give unto my dtr. JANE E. the tract of land that I
bought of heirs of JOHN & ANDREW MILLER, joining lands of Twitty, Logan,
etc. also the sum of $4,000 in cash. I give my dtr. MARTHA ANN the tract
of land I bought of Hampton, joining the land of J. G. BYNUM, TWITTY &
others, containing 100 acres. I give unto my son, WILLIAM, negroes, Bill,
Clarisa, & her son Ransom, & Unity and the sum of $3,000. I give unto my
son, JOHN Y., negroes, David, & his wife Clarsia & her son Arthur & George
& Joe also the sum of $3,000. The balance of negroes to my wife, MARY
JANE, with the sum of $3,000. I appoint her my executrix. (No witnesses)
                                    Signed: J. MCENTIRE.

Page 332. 6 April 1857. Recorded, Aug. Court 1857. I, JAMES GARRET,
After paying my just debts I give unto my beloved wife CILIA
my land, containing 100 acres, that I bought of my father, I have nearly
paid for but have no deed, one mare & colt, one small waggon, one yoke of
oxen & my crop after my rents are paid, wife may sell land or other property to pay my debts, as they have increased in my trying to pay for my
land, this will is made in place of one I made a few days ago. I appoint
my wife CILIA my sole executor, but not having been doing busness, I wish
her to act under the advice of ROBT. G. TWITTY & FENDAL FOSTER. Wit:
JAMES L. FOSTER, Jurat. S.P. FOSTER.   Signed: JAMES M. GARRETT.

Page 332. 12 Aug. 1857. Recorded, Aug. Court 1857. I, CELIA GARRETT, want all my just debts to be paid. I give to my mother one bed stead & furniture. I will unto my mother-in-law SARAH GARRET one bed & furniture. I will my wearing clothes to my sister. I will one counter-pin and one quilt to ADITINE TURNER. I will that the balance of my pro-perty to be sold and pay off the debts, if any overplus to be divided between my mother and mother-in-law. I appoint ROBT. G. TWITTY my ex-ecutor. Wit: JAS. B. MORRIS, J. L. GRAY, jurat.
Signed: CILIA X GARRETT.

Page 333. 15 May 1847. Recorded, Fall Court 1857. I, WILLIAM MCKINNEY, of Cleveland County, being under the decay of nature but of sound mind & memory. After my just debts are paid, I give unto my two sons WILLIS MCKINNEY & WILLIAM H. MCKINNEY all my lands to be divided be-tween them. I give unto my dtr., SALLY, one good bed & furniture & $150 in money. To the rest of my dtrs. SUSANNAH JONES, POLLY JONES, BEDY MCDANIEL, LATHY GREEN $50 to each. The balance of my property to be sold and divided among my chn. to wit. SUSANNA JONES, POLLY JONES, BEDY MC-DANIEL, SALLY MCKINNEY, BURNICE MCKINNEY, WILLIS MCKINNEY, WILLIAM H. MC-KINNEY, & LETHY GREEN. I appoint my two sons-in-law EDMOND JONES, ZACHA-RIAH MCDANIELS my executors. Wit: EDWARD P. JONES, jurat. WILLIAM A. JONES.
Signed: WILLIAM MCKINNEY.

Page 334. 28 Sept. 1857. Recorded, Fall Court 1857. I, DAVID MILLER, being of sound mind & disposing memory but of feeble health. I direct that my just debts be paid. I give unto my beloved wife, MARY MILLER, during her natural life or widowhood one third of my land & four negroes (two men & two women, her choice) the land to include the home whereon we now reside, all household & kitchen furniture, stock of all kinds, tools, note of hand on J. B. & W. H. MILLER & $150 in U. S. coins, and book apts. that may be due me. I give unto my six chn. MARY ANN, CAROLINE, ANDREW, WILLIAM, WELDON & MARTHA all my personal estate of cash, notes, negroes, the cash, notes & negroes falling to the chn. that are under age to be put on interest & negroes hired out until each is 21 yrs. old. Land not given to my wife, be taken by my sons ANDREW, WILLIAM & WELDEN. I desire that my son ANDREW refund to the other chn. what money I have paid to him, he retaining one share. I desire my chn. under age to stay with their mother and their schooling & clothing be paid from their estate. I appoint my wife MARY MILLER & my brother-in-law JOHN B. MILLER my executors. Wit: JNO. M. CRATON, jurat. W. J. T. MILLER.
Signed: DAVID MILLER.
CODICIL. Dated 4 Oct. 1857. I, DAVID MILLER, do make this a codicil to my last will & testament of 28 Sept. 1857. In addition to what I have given to my wife MARY MILLER, also give her two negroes chn. Julia & Wesly they being Harriet's children. Wit: J. L. GRAY, jurat. JOHN CRATON, jurat.
Signed: DAVID X MILLER.

Page 336. 28 Nov. 1857. Recorded, Fall Court 1857. I, JOSEPH STEADMAN, desire that all my just debts to be paid. I will that my eldest dtr., SUSANNAH, & my son, JAMES A., shall have a tract of land lying on Dills Creek, to be equally divided between them. Also one other tract of 150 acres lying on Jarrols Creek. It is my will that my son JOHN & dtrs. MARY, MARGARET & SARAH to share equal with the others. I appoint my neighbors STEPHEN F. BLANTON & JOHN OWENS my executors. Wit: JOSEPH OWENS, DRURY MCDANIELS, jurat.
Signed: JOSEPH X STEADMAN.

Page 338. 13 April 1856. Recorded, March Court 1858. I, DAVID BEAM, being of sound mind & good memory. My executor to pay my just debts. I give unto my beloved wife RACHEL all the land where I now live, except what I have given unto my 4 sons, MARTIN, DAVID, JOHN, & J. W. BEAM. At the death of my wife the land & other property to be sold & pay to each of my dtrs. $100 & the balance of my effects to be divided among my lawfull heirs. I wish HENSON HARRILL & family to have the use of the place where he now lives until the death of my wife, free from rent. I appoint DAVID BEAM my executor. Wit: ZACH. MCDANIEL, O. P. GARDNER, jurat.
Signed: DAVID BEAM.

Page 339. 15 Dec. 1857. Recorded, March Court 1858. I, COLEMAN MCDONALD, being weak in body but of sound mind & memory. I will that my wife SARAH MCDANIEL have all my household & kitchen furniture, stock of

130

cattle, hogs, tools & 158½ acres of land during her life time or widowhood. Except I will that my wife furnish my son WILLIAM a horse, saddle,
my rifle gun when he comes of age. I give unto my son LEWIS MCDONALD
61½ acres of land, said tract is the one I bought from TENCH COX, for
which I have a bond for a right, the land willed to my wife is where I
now live. At the death of my wife the land to be divided between my dtr.
JANE HARDEN & son WILLIAM MCDONALD, and the personal property to be divided among my 3 chn. (No executor named.) Wit: EDWARD TOMS, REUBEN MCDANIEL,
jurat. Signed: COLEMAN MCDONALD.
(Having omitted in the above will to say that the land willed to my son
LEWIS is to immediately descend to him. Wit: EDWARD TOMS, REUBEN MCDANIEL,
jurat.) Signed: COLEMAN MCDONALD.

Page 341. 20 June 1857. Recorded, Spring Court 1858. I, PIMAN LEWIS,
being weak in body but of sound mind & memory. I allow my
debts to be paid. I give to my beloved wife INTHY LEWIS my Head plantation during her life time, also negroes Luke, Senr. & his wife Tabby, all
cattle, hogs, sheep, horses, tools, for the support of family. At wife's
death, property except land to be sold and divided among my heirs. I
give unto my dtr., ELIZABETH LEWIS, negroes, Annis, Tom, Mark, Ann,
Rebecca, Lovett, & John. I give unto my son, C. RUFUS LEWIS, negroes,
Mary, Luke Junr, Noah, George, also the land where I formerly lived
containing 116 acres. I give unto my dtr., M. LOUISA LEWIS, negroes Jane,
Penelopey, Lisey, Adam, Sally, Milly. I give unto my son, PITMAN P.
LEWIS, negroes, Elily, Joseph, Ned, Henry also the land where I now live
called the Head Place, when he arrives of age. I wish all my negroes to
stay on the plantation until each child comes of age. I appoint my wife
INTHY LEWIS & JESSE T. LEWIS my executors. Wit: I. WOOD, jurat.
Signed: PITMAN LEWIS.

Page 342. 18 May 1857. Recorded, Spring Court 1858. I, B. S. BLANTON,
of sound mind & good memory. All just debts & funeral expenses to be paid by my executor. I give unto my beloved wife ALMINA all
household & kitchen furniture, 2 horses, 3 cows & calves, 10 hogs, 200
acres of land with the dwelling house whereon I now live, during her
natural life or widowhood. One negro girl named Mary her own right &
property from her father's estate. I give unto my 3 sons GEORGE W.,
WILLIAM H., & JONATHAN B. BLANTON all the other land I own to be divided
between them, & the 200 acres willed to my wife at her death. All other
property to be sold and after paying my debts, the balance to be divided
among my sons. As the children come of age 21 they are to have as much
household items as wife can spare. I appoint G. E. BLANTON & O. P.
GARDNER my executors. Wit: O. P. BLANTON & O. P. GARDNER , both jurats.
Signed: B. S. BLANTON.

Page 344. 11 March 1858. Recorded, Spring Court 1858. I, JOHN L. WELLS,
being of good mind & sound memory. I give unto my eldest son
RICHARD $70 which he has. I give unto my dtr. ANGELINE WILSON $60 which
she has. I give unto my son JOHN $60 which he has. I give unto my dtr.
HULDAH PHILBECK $55 she has & my executors to pay her $5 more. I give
unto my son MOSES $60 which he has. I give unto my dtr. MARGARET H.,
MILLEY WELLS, WOODY B. WELLS $60 to be paid by my executors. I give unto
my son MARCUS M. C. $60 to be appropriated in sending him to school. I
give unto my son ROBERT R. $100 to be appropriated to send him to school.
I give unto my wife MALINDA all property now on hand during her natural
life or widowhood with all money, on conditions, "that she is not to spend
neither the property or money in riotous living or keeping persons about
her who do not belong to the family." I give unto my sons MARCUS M. C.
& ROBERT R. the tract of land whereon I now live at the death or marriage
of their mother. I appoint my son-in-law WILLIAM G. WILSON & son ROBERT
R. WELLS (when he comes of age) my executors. Wit: WILLIAM DAVIS, jurat,
O. P. GARDNER, jurat. Signed: JOHN L. WELLS.

Page 346. 20 Oct. 1856. Recorded, Spring Court 1858. I, MISS SELAH
WEBB, being of sound mind & memory and in bad health. I give
unto my brother DANIEL WEBB & sister ELIZABETH SCRUGGS all my household
& kitchen furniture, except one bed & furniture, which I give unto MILLY
LUCINDA BOHELO. also one heifer. I also allow my brother & sister above
named all my stock except the one heifer, my brother & sister to pay all
my debts, I allow them my negro boy Simon. I also will to M. L. BOHELO

$10. I appoint my brother DANIEL & ROBERT SCRUGGS my executors. Wit: W. A. HAWKINS, jurat. WILLIAM BLAND, jurat.

Signed: MISS SELAH X WEBB.

Page 347. 23 March 1858. Recorded, Spring Court 1858. I, JAMES LARGENT, "Being in limited circumstances" with eleven children to wit. LINDA, SINTHA, ELIZABETH, AMY or her son WILLIAM, NANCY, ADALINE, SARAH, HUGH, JOHN, NOAH, & JAMES. If my property is divided amongst my heirs, a very small share would fall to each, having been afflicted for several years & been waited upon by my dtr. NANCY & being unable to pay her wages, I do give unto my dtr. NANCY my land, household & kitchen Furniture, stock & my blind mare to her forever. I do give unto my grandson WM. LARGENT my horse colt. All my debts to be paid from the property. (No executor named.) Wit: JOS. REID, W. K. REID, jurat.

Signed: JAS. X LARGENT.

Page 348. 8 May 1858. Recorded, Spring Court 1858. STEPHENS MORGAN. Noncuputive will. Whereas STEPHEN MORGAN being desires of making a will and not having an opportunity of commiting it writing. I, DAVID MORGAN, & JAMES M. RABURN being present the 8 day May 1858. Said MORGAN died on the 14 day this inst. His will was that his wife GRACY MORGAN have controll of all his property, after paying all his just debts, until the youngest child is of age & at that time she to have one third of the land & personal est. and the balance to be divided amongst his children. JAMES, JETHRO, POLLY, JOHN P., GRAYSON, & CRATEN MORGAN. Executors is wife GRACY & J. W. MORGAN. This, 25 day 1858. Signed: DAVID MORGAN & JAMES H. RABURN, both jurat.

Signed: E. TOMS, Clk.

Page 349. 29 July 1858. Recorded, Aug. Court 1858. I, WILLIAM HUTCHENS, being of sound mind & memory. I give unto my wife MARY my fresh lot of land on which I hold a lease during her natural life. The old land to be rented out & the proceeds put on interest, wife to have her support from the crops & the stock. After paying just debts, & the wife needs the balance to be sold and money divided among his heirs. I appoint son JOHN HUTCHENS my executor. Wit: G. E. JOHNSON, Y. R. GUFFY.

Signed: WILLIAM HUTCHINS.

CODICIL. No date. Do add to the the forgoing will, My wife MARY HUTCHINS to have a good comfortable cabbin built on my lot of land for my wife. Wit: G. E. JOHNSON, Y. N. GUFFY, jurat.

Signed: WILLIAM HUTCHINS.

Page 350. 13 July 1858. Recorded, Aug. Court 1858. I, JOHN GREEN, being of sound mind & memory. I give unto my wife ALETHA GREEN all my land & personal estate during her natural life or widowhood for her support, except as herein directed. I give to my son JOHN P. GREEN a colt. I give unto my son DRURY A. GREEN my youngest colt. "I require my wife to sell horse Jim & pay the debts contracted by my son ALNSON GREEN in his life time instead of having a horse." The balance of my estate to be divided (at the death or marriage of my wife) among all my children according to what they have each received. I appoint my wife ALETHA My executor. Wit: ROBERT X GREEN, J. B. MCDANIEL, both jurat.

Signed: JOHN X GREEN.

Page 351. 14 July 1858. Recorded, Sept. Court 1858. I, WILLIAM O. BAGWELL, being of sound mind & memory. After all my just debts & funeral charges are paid, I give unto my wife MARY BAGWELL all my land whereon I now live during her natural life also two negroes, July & Simon, if July has a child in twenty years, I will it to MARY JANE BALLARD the heir of BERNY & ANGELINE BALLARD, MARY JANE to have said child if any at three yrs. of age. I also give unto my wife MARY all the other property durring her natural life, unless STANDHOPE marries & is not willing to live in the house with POLLY, then two good men to say what STANDHOPE shall have to begin house keeping with. "I want my mother NANCY BAGWELL buried decently & paid for out of my property." and I want my wife POLLY to see that it is done. I also want my wife POLLY buried decently & STANDHOPE to see to it. I give unto STANDHOPE all my mountain land, to take possession now & my wife to have the fruit that is grown there, also my negro boy Andrew. I give to STANDHOPE BAGWELL all the property that my wife has at her death. I appoint my friend B. E. ROLLINS my

132

executor. Wit: R. O. LEDBETTER, jurat. WM. H. LOGAN, jurat.
                                        Signed: WM. O. BAGWELL.
CODICIL. Dated 15 July 1858. This is to be a codicil to my last will
          dated the 14 July 1858, my executor to purchase a good & decent
set of tombs for myself & my two deceased babies. My wife to pay for the
same from my estate. Wit: W. H. LOGAN, jurat. T. N. EGERTON.
                                        Signed: WM. O. BAGWELL.

Page 352. 16 Aug. 1858. Recorded, Sept. Court 1858. I, WM. SMITH, Senr.
          being of sound mind & memory. My executor to settle all de-
mands. I give unto my son JAMES T. SMITH 100 acres of land where he now
lives. I give unto my two grandsons MATHEW & RICHARD SMITH 100 acres of
land where I now live, joining the land given to my son J. T. SMITH. My
dtr. POLLY live where JEREMIAH W. SMITH now lives for the space of 10 yrs.
and after that time the land to belong to my two grandsons or the heirs
of J. W. SMITH. In consequence of what my son GESROSE W. SMITH has had
I duct $100 out of his part of the estate. By reason of bad treatment
given me by my son-in-law LEWIS SCOGGIN & my dtr. SALLY SCOGGIN I give
them $5. I give my two granddaughters one bed each (no names given). My
dtr. NANCY WAGGONER is dead and her chn. lives so far away, therefor I
give them $5. My dtr. MENEME is dead, I will that her chn. to have her
part of my estate. Also my dtr. JANE being dead, that her chn. to have
her part of my estate. I give unto dtr. POLLY her equal part of my
estate & $25 extra. That RITTOR have her equal part & $25 extra. I give
unto my dtr. MALINDA HANEY her equal part & $25 extra. I appoint my
friend WM. SMITH, Junr. & DAVE PANNEL my exectors. The balance of my
property to be sold and divided among all my chn. JOHN SMITH, JACOB SMITH,
heirs of JOEL SMITH, & WILLIAM SMITH, Junr. Wit: ABRAHAM PADGETT, jurat.
D. M. PANNEL, jurat. C. B. PANNEL.   Signed: WM. X SMITH SR.

Page 355. 12 Nov. 1856. Recorded, Fall Court 1858. I, PETER FREEMAN,
          being of sound mind & memory. Executor to pay all my just
debts & funeral charges. I give unto my beloved wife, ELIZABETH FREEMAN,
50 acres of land & fire wood during her natural life, then to VINY TRUE-
LOVE. I give unto oldest dtr. RIDLEY GUFFY $10. I give unto my second
dtr. CLARISA MOREHEAD $10. I give unto my third dtr. MARGARET HACKLER?
$10. I give unto my fourth dtr. POLLY LUQUIRE $10. I give unto my fifth
dtr. FAITHY MARIRE MOREHEAD $10. I give unto VINY TRUELOVE $10. I give
to my oldest son PETER $1. I give unto my second son ANDREW $5. I give
unto my third son GEORGE $10. I give unto my wife ELIZABETH the kitchen
furniture, & at her death to belong to dtr. VINY TRUELOVE, also she to
have one bed & furniture. The balance of my property & debts owning to
me, when collected, to pay my debts & legacies, if any surplus shall be
divided among my eight chn. & VINY TRUELOVE. I appoint my friend JOHN
FREEMAN my executor. Wit: W. B. FREEMAN, jurat. JOHN UPCHURCH, jurat.
                                        Signed: PETER X FREEMAN.

Page 357. 11 Oct. 1853. Recorded, Feb. Court 1859. I, S. D. ALEXANDER,
          being of sound mind & memory. I give unto my brother M. R.
ALEXANDER all my real & personal estate, that is the land whereon I now
live, my stock, tools and any other property I may own at death. In lieu
of which he is to support my father & mother. It is my will that the land
shall never be sold for debt. In case he should die before father or
mother, the land shall be theirs. I appoint my brother M. R. ALEXANDER
my executor. Wit: J. L. LORANCE, jurat. CAMEL SMITH.
                                        Signed: S. D. ALEXANDER.

Page 358. 28 Feb. 1859. Recorded, March Court 1859. I, JOHN WASHINGTON
          HARRIS, SR. I give all my property both real & personal to be
sold by my executors as may thik best. The proceeds divised as follows,
all my just debts to be paid. I desire that my wife, SARAH, have the
following negroes, Joseph & Mariah during her natural life. I give unto
my wife 2 beds & furniture of her choice. I desire that $2500 be set
apart for my wife from the sale of my property. The said sum to be
placed in the hands of BEDFORD SHERRILL, he is to pay unto my wife the
interest yearly, and at her death to be equally divided among my children. ELIZABETH SHERRILL, NANCY WILKINS, JOSIAH, LOUISA, & WILLIAM REIGON
chn. of my dtr. LOUISA who is dead, the chn. representing their mother
are getting a child's part. SARAH U. BRITTAIN, C. L. HARRIS, JOHN W.
HARRIS, J. A. HARRIS, W. N. HARRIS. I appoint my son C. L. HARRIS &

133

BEDFORD SHERRILL my executors. Wit: L. P. ERWIN, jurat. G. W. LOGAN, jurat.   Signed: J. W. HARRIS.
CODICIL. Dated 4 March 1859. Instead of negro Maria which I gave unto
          my wife, I now give her negro girl Ginny, also my carriage. My
dtr. SARAH U. BRITTAIN has now in her possession a negro named Catherine,
I desire she to keep her at the value of $325 to be accounted for in her
share of my estate. Wit: L. P. ERWIN, jurat. G. W. LOGAN, jurat.
                                        Signed: J. W. HARRIS.

Page 361. 5 Jan. 1859. Recorded, Spring Court 1859. I, ELIJAH HOLLI-
          FIELD, being of sound mind & memory. The funeral expenses &
just debts to be paid. I give unto my wife EMSEY HOLLIFIELD all property
in lieu of her dower of one third of my real estate during her natural
life. I give unto my two dtrs. NARCISSY & ELIZA HOLLIFIELD all their
bedding & clothing, one trunk that they made & bought for themselves.
The residue of my estate to be sold and divided among my chn. & HARRY C.
HOLLIFIELD to have an equal share. I appoint my friend ABRAHAM P. HOLLI-
FIELD my executor. Wit: JOHN FREEMAN, jurat. PLEASENT FORTURN, jurat.
GEORGE X EARLEY.   Signed: ELIJAH HOLLIFIELD.

Page 362. No date. Recorded, Spring Court 1859. I, ELI GUFFY, do give
          unto my wife LOUCINDA my tract of land known as the Johnson
Place, to use or give as she may see fit. If there is any left after
paying my debts, it to be divided among my wife & my dtr. MARY ALMIRAH
MATILDA BAXTER,. I also give to my dtr. a bed & bureau and the balance of
the furniture to my wife. My wife & JONATHAN ELLIOTT her father my
executor. Wit: J. W. HARRIS, jurat. C. CLEMENTS, jurat.
                                        Signed: ELI GUFFY.

Page 363. 27 April 1859. Recorded, Spring Court 1859. I, B. F. SUTTLE,
          after my just debts are paid, the remainder to be divided as
follows. I put in my three sons as trustees for my daughters to wit.
JOSEPH DRURY D. and WILLIAM SUTTLE, ESTHER HARRILL shall not have her
part unless her husband will bring her back to this country to enjoy it,
to be held for her & her chn. & URSILLER to belong to her & her chn. &
CAROLINE BLAND share to belong to her & her chn. she owes me $200 which
is to be discounted, and the land to be her's & her chn. CATHARINE MAHALY
share to be her's & her chn. and JAMES SUTTLE is to be her trustee, and
to take care of her until she marry if she does. Son GEORGE to have $200
extra. Son BENJAMIN F. is to have $100 extra. Son WILLIAM is to have
$50 extra. I appoint my sons JOSEPH, JAMES & WILLIAM SUTTLE as executors.
Wit: J. G. CAMP, jurat. GEORGE MCDANIEL. Signed: B. F. SUTTLE.

Page 364. 3 May 1859. Recorded, Spring Court 1859. I, GARLAND DICKERSON,
          will that my just debts be paid. I give unto my son, M. O.
DICKERSON, one negro boy named Frank and he is to pay unto MARY M. HORTON
the sum of $200 within 2 yrs. after said negro is in his possession. I
will the balance of my property to my wife ELIZABETH DICKERSON during her
life time and at her death to be divided between SARAH M. BROWN, ROBERT
B. DICKERSON, JULIA A. CARRIER, REBECCA G. THOMPSON, M. O. DICKERSON, MARY
H. HORTON, NANCY W. CARSON, CAROLINE C. BOMAN and my granddaughter, JULIA
H. DICKERSON. I appoint M. O. DICKERSON & O. P. CARSON my executors.
Wit: B. WASHBOURN, jurat. L. P. ERWIN, jurat.
                                        Signed: G. X DICKERSON.

Page 365. 6 Aug. 1858. Recorded, June Court 1859. I, JOHN HUCKABA,
          being of sound mind. I give unto my beloved wife, JANE, 162
acres of land where I now live, also the cattle, hogs, sheep, tools and
crops she may think she may need. She may keep what household & kitchen
furniture as she may think proper, also her side saddle & what money I
have on hand & what is due me, during her life or widowhood. I have
given to my dtrs., RHODY, SARAH and MINLA HACKABA, all my land & property
before named, they may sell and divide the proceeds or divide the property
as it is among themselves. My dtr. LEVINA BRIDGES, wife of WILEY BRIDGES,
to have what she has & no more. Son WILLIAM to have what he has & no
more. Son BENJAMIN what he has and no more. Son BENJAMIN what he has
and no more. My dtr. MARTHA MELTON, wife of LENORE MELTON, to have what
she has and no more, the cause why they received no more is known by good
reason of me. Dtr. RHODY to have one new feather bed, 2 sheets, 3 quilts,
one cover lid & 2 pillows. Dtrs. SARAH & MINLA to have the same as given

134

to RHODY. I appoint my dtrs. RODY & SARAH agents for MINLA MERCILLA
HUCKABA, to manage her share for her. I Appoint my wife, JANE HACKABA,
Executrix & WM. G. WILSON executor. Wit: WM. DAVIS, jurat. NATHAN M.
FLOYD, jurat.   Signed: JOHN X HUCKABA.

Page 368. 16 Feb. 1859. Recorded, Aug. Court 1859. I, JAMES NANNEY,
          I give unto my wife SARY NANNEY all the land that I own & all
horses, cattle, hogs during her life or widowhood, at her marriage or
death the property to be divided among my chn. I leave my son, THOMAS
NANNEY, executor. Wit: JOHN FLACK, jurat. GEORGE W. HILL, jurat.
                                      Signed: JAMES X NANNEY.

Page 368. 27 Aug. 1858. Recorded, Aug. Court 1859. I, JOHN HARRISON,
          being in the decline of life & weak in body, but of perfect
mind & memory. First I direct my just debts to be paid, then I give to
my beloved wife REBECCA HARRISON all my estate both real & personal,
during her natural life and at her death, I give to my dtr. MARTHA NOR-
VILLE and at her decease the estate both real & personal to my sons,
SIMEON & JAMES R. HARRISON, on condition that they pay to my sons EDMOND
& HARDING C. HARRISON & to dtrs., ELIZABETH SMILEY & SALLY BUSOUT? the
sum of $5. I appoint my son, S. HARRISON, my executor. Wit: JOSEPH
BIGGERSTAFF, jurat. ROBERT R. GETTY, jurat.
                                      Signed: JOHN X HARRISON.

Page 370. 13 Aug. 1859. Recorded, Fall Court 1859. I, MARTHA HAY, am
          in my proper mind as much as I was in my life. I give unto
MARGARET J. ROACH $100 after my just debts are paid, also my best bed &
furniture with a set of plates, with cups & saucers & bureau. I give
unto my granddtrs. SOPHRONIA & LOUISA SUTTLE $500 each. I give unto my
two grandsons GEORGE & VINSON SUTTLES all my land on Leghorn Creek, which
land my dtr. POLLY SUTTLES to live on during her life time, the land
rented out & the money put on interest until they come of age. All my
perishable property with household & kitchen furniture to be sold & the
money to pay legacy to my granddaughters. I appoint my brother WILLIAM
WESTON, GEORGE THOMPSON & HAMBLETON HORNE my executors & guardian of said
chn. I leave my notes in FIELDING TURNER'S hands & what he does or say
is my will when delivered to my executors. Wit: J. TURNER, jurat. C.
BLANTON, jurat.   Signed: MARTHA X HAY.

Page 371. 23 June 1858. Recorded, Fall Court 1859. Being of sound &
          good memory. I desire my executors to pay all funeral charges
& just debts. I give unto my beloved wife 350 acres of land known as the
GEORGE BLANTON & ALFRED WEBB tracts and all rent that may be due from
said land. I also give unto my wife PRISCILLA one negro man named
Emanuel & one woman named Nancy, at death or marriage to another person
the said negro Nancy to return to my estate. Also I give her $400 in
money, household items (named) all property she brought with her, two
cows & two hogs. I give unto my sons JOHN, WILLIAM P. & JULIUS C. BURGE
two tracts of land containing 550 acres to be equally divided among them,
so that WILLIAM P. shall have the place whereon I now live. I give unto
my son JOHN, negro man Harry. I give unto my son WILLIAM P. negro man
Eli. I give unto my son JULIUS C. negro named Sidney, also each to have
their bed & furniture, and the horses they are now useing. All other
property to be sold and money divided among my heirs. I appoint my sons
WILLIAM P. & JULIUS C. BURGE my executors. Wit: O. P. GARDNER, N. M.
FLOYD, jurat.   Signed: JOHN BURGE.

Page 373. 27 Dec. 1859. Recorded, Spring Court 1860. I, NANCY WALTON,
          being of sound & disposing mind & memory. I give unto my
grandniece HENRIETTA, dtr. of WM. C. ERWIN, of Morganton, N.C., my negro
boy named William about 12 yrs. old. I give unto my grandniece LAURA,
dtr. of WM. C. ERWIN, a negro boy named Nocovus or Dock about 10 yrs. old.
I give unto my grandniece, ELLA, dtr. of WM. C. ERWIN, a negro boy named
Franklin about 7 yrs. old. I give unto WM. M. WALTON as trustee the
following negroes, Rachel, Minta & her two chn. Martha about 16 yrs. and
Walter about 12 yrs., Jane age about 18 yrs. The said trustee to hold
the negroes & their increase for the sole & separate use & benfit of my
grandnieces CLARA wife of JOHN H. MURPHY & LOUISA wife of J. CHEESEBROUGH
during their natural life & at the death of them to their heirs, in case
of either not having issue then to the children of the other. I give

135

unto my nephew W. H. WALTON $100 in addition to the other property given
to him. I give unto my grandnieces MARTHA, ELISA & CLARA dtrs. of Gen.
C. M. AVERY to be divided between them, the stock which I hold in the
bank of N. C. in the amount of $1600. I give unto my great grandniece
MATILDA & IDA dtrs. of WM. T. MCENTIRE $500. I desire that after my
death my negroes Minta, Jane & Martha each to have a common bed and
clothing. Any property not willed to be sold and money due me collected,
to pay my debts & funeral expenses, then to pay the legatees named. I
give to my nephew THOS. GEO. WALTON my negro man Frank. I appoint my
nephew THOS. GEO. WALTON executor. Wit: G. W. LOGAN, jurat. C. L. HARRIS,
jurat.   Signed: NANCY WALTON.

Page 375. 21 April 1860. Recorded, Spring Court 1860. I, REBECCA
          MATHIS, after my just debts are paid, for the kind treatment
and attention of J. R. NELON & family I leave to said NELON my bed &
furniture & wearing clothes, all pots & shelf wear and if I leave any
money at my death, I leave it to them & any other property that I may
have, I leave it to them. (No executor named.) Wit: MARTIN WALKER,
jurat. JN. SHITLE.   Signed: REBECCA X MATHIS.

Page 376. 20 April 1857. Recorded, Aug. Court 1860. I, ABRAHAM GOODE,
          first I will all my just debts to be paid of my stock property.
At my death I want my negroes all sold in the usual way and the proceeds
divided as follows, except my grandson RODNEY DOGWOOD I leave him $5 only.
My dtr. MARY MOORE to have her equal share, but at her death the amount
to be refunded to my other children of their heirs the same to be keep
secure by my executor. My dtr. RACHEL BABER to have her share but not
subject to her husband's control, at her death the same to go to her chn.
I appoint my sons JAMES & WILLIAM my executor. Wit: ROBT. G. TWITTY,
jurat. C. E. GREEN.   Signed: ABRAHAM X GOODE.

Page 376. 8 July 1860. Recorded, Aug. Court 1860. I, PLEASANT EARLES,
          being of sound & perfect mind & memory. I give unto my be-
loved wife all the land and all the property that I have after settling
my just debts. After selling the horse and wheat & oats then sell enough
land to settle my debts, then at her death it is to go to my two little
brothers JOSHUA & PINKNEY. I appoint my father my executor. Wit: JOHN
B. SWEEZY, jurat. J. S. HUTCHINS.   Signed: PLESANT X EARLES.

Page 377. 30 Oct. 1859. Recorded, Aug. Court 1860. I, GEORGE KOON,
being of sound mind & memory. I give unto my dtr. RUTH BLANKINSHIP my
negro girl named Nancy now in her possession. I give unto my dtr.
MIRIAM NANNEY one negro girl named Mandah and her mother Judah. I give
unto my dtr. ARMINTHA ADAIR one negro girl named Eliza. I give unto my
dtr. POLLY RAY one negro girl named Matildah. I direct my executors to
sell negro Leander or Spencer and $200 to be paid to my grandson HUMPHREY
P. MORGAN also to my granddaughter NANCY MORGAN the sum of $200, also to
my grandson ALBERT F. MORGAN the balance of the proceeds of the sale. I
give to my beloved wife AREHESTER KOON 3 cows & calves, hogs, sheep, &
one horse, her choice of household & kitchen furniture. I give my wife
one negro man named Terry, Spence, Sina & her boys John, Frank, Lynch, &
Marcus, at my wife's death or marriage said negroes to be sold, and the
proceeds divided as follows, I give unto my son JOHN KOON the sum of $1.
I give unto his sons G. W., JOHN W., THALES E. C., JAMES H. KOON and his
dtr. CATHARINE ALATHA AN KOON one eighth part of the proceeds from the
sale of negroes. I give unto my son MADISON KOON, DUVALT KOON, RUTH
BLANKINSHIP, MIRIAM NANNEY, ARAMINTHA ADAIR, POLLY RAY & my grandsons
H. P. MORGAN, A. D. MORGAN, & my granddaughter NANCY MORGAN, the last
named chn. to have their mother's part. The balance of my property to be
sold and divided among my heirs, giving my decd. dtr. DAMARIS MORGAN'S
children her part. I appoint MADISON KOON & DUVALT KOON my executors.
Wit: NOAH KOON, jurat. AMOS NANNEY, jurat.

                                                Signed: GEORGE KOON.

Page 380. 28 Nov. 1859. Recorded, Fall Court 1860. I, GEORGE FLACK,
          being sound in mind but frail in body. I give unto my son
JOHN FLACK $20. I give unto my dtr. JANE LEWIS $2000. I give unto my
son ANDREW FLACK all my land where I now live containing 140 acres, also
75 acres known as the Sercy Place, also 170 acres joining said lands,
also one negro man named Charlie, one named Delphe and her son named

JOSEPH. I give unto my grandson GEORGE FLACK 2 negroes Zeremagah & Anna.
I give unto my grandson MILLS H. FLACK all my land on Cove & Cedar Creeks
& joining lands of 30 acres & one tract of 80 acres, with 250 acres known
as the Ledbetter place. I give unto ANDREW FLACK all stock, tools,
household & kitchen furniture. I appoint my son ANDREW FLACK my executor.
Wit: A. M. LEDBATTER, jurat. J. P. SORRELS, Jr., jurat.
                              Signed: GEORGE FLACK.

Page 381. 2 Jan. 1856. Recorded, Fall Court 1860. I, JAMES WILSON,
          being of sound mind & memory. My executor shall pay my just
debts. I give unto my son WILLIAM G. WILSON 100 acres of land whereon I
now live, including the dwelling house where said WM. G. WILSON hath
lived, also my waggon & blacksmith tools. I give to my dtr. POLLY WILSON
the remaining land that I have, with the dwelling house I now live in,
with all out buildings, all horses, cattle, sheep. In case my dtr. POLLY
should marry, the land to be in trust to my son WM. G. as trustee for my
dtr. use & benfit only or to her heirs forever. I appoint my son WM. G.
WILSON my executor. Wit: O. P. GARDNER, WM. A. BRIDGES, jurat.
                              Signed: JAMES WILSON.

Page 382. 15 Dec. 1859. Recorded, Fall Court 1860. I, FRANEY MELTON,
          now of Rutherford Co., N. C. I give all my personal property
about the house to my sister MARGARET MELTON. I also will all my interest
in the tract where we now live it being the land of SILAS MELTON, decd.
unto MARGARET MELTON, which joins land with WM. FORTUNE. Sister LETTIA
VICKERS to give her right to the said land as I have given her $25 for
her interest in the SILAS MELTON decd. property. I give to my brother
A. G. MELTON should have me buried for the note of $31 I hold on him. I
appoint my brother A. G. MELTON my executor. Wit: WILLIAMSON FORTURN,
jurat. B. C. FORTUNE.   Signed: FRANEY X MELTON.

Page 382. 19 Dec. 1859. Recorded, Fall court 1860. I, MARY ROSE, being
          of sound mind & memory. First my just debts to be paid, I
give all my estate both real & personal as follows. I give unto my dtr.,
ELIZABETH LOGAN $1. I give unto my dtr. MARGARET LOUERY $1. I give unto
my dtr. CATHARINE WEAST $1. I also give unto my son, ADA M. WEAST $1.
The remaining part of my estate I give unto my dtr. NANCY E. WEAST, of
household & kitchen furniture also my money & notes I may have. I appoint
my grandson JOSEPH H. WEAST my executor. Wit: W. B. CARSON, J. H.
DUPRIEST, jurat.   Signed: MARY X ROSE.

Page 383. 12 Sept. 1848. Recorded Fall Court 1860. I, CORNELIUS CLE-
          MENTS, Sr. being weak in body but of perfect mind & memory. I
give unto my son ANDREW 64 acres of land whereon he now lives (the meet-
ing house and grave yard excepted) also my smith tools. I give unto my
son, JOSEPH CLEMENTS, my rifle gun, JOSEPH having conveyed his part of
the land to ROBERT W. GUFFY, the rest of the land whereon I live containing 125 acres being conveyed unto my two dtrs. SARAH & ELIZABETH C.
CLEMENTS that still lives with me, I give my mare, all cattle, hogs,
sheep, with household & kitchen furniture & one loom. I allow my three
married dtrs. $10 each, when it can be spared, JANE GUFFY, my dtr. re-
ceived a horse. I appoint my son ANDREW CLEMENTS & PRESTON GOFORTH my
executors. Wit: JOHN WATSON, JAMES C. GOFORTH.
                              Signed: CORNELIUS CLEMENTS.

Page 385. 15 April 1861. Recorded, Aug. Court 1861. I, ANDREW EAVES,
          being of sound & disposing mind. I will that all my just debts
& funeral expenses be paid. I will that my present property, money,
notes which are not named in the following items of this will, to be
equally divided among my dtrs. ELIZABETH HILL, GILFORD & SPENCER EAVES.
I give unto my dtr. ELIZABETH HILL the tract on which I now live and at
her death to my sons GUILFORD & SPENCER EAVES. I give unto my son GUIL-
FORD the tract of land he now lives on containing 400 acres. Provided no
suit ever is brought against me by LAWSON P. EAVES (son of LAWSON EAVES,
decd.) or others, concerning his father's estate on which I was Admnr.
and because of my ingorance of the law may not have been discharged in
strict accordance of the law. I give unto my son GUILFORD a negro named
Moses and $900. I give dtr. ELIZABETH negroes Dan & Mariah. My son
SPENCER a house & lot in Rutherfordton, I give unto my son negroes,
Wilson, Mira. I give unto my grandchildren, the chn. of my deceased dtr.

137

CATHERINE SULLINS who may be alive at my death $100 each. I appoint my son SPENCER EAVES my executor. Wit: E. TUMS, M. D. BUTLER, jurat.
                                         Signed: ANDREW X EAVES.

Page 11. 16 April 1855. Recorded, Aug. Court 1861. I, JOHN C. GETTYS, having advanced in life but of sound & memory. I give to my beloved wife ELIZA E. GETTYS my dwelling house, two beds & furniture, one chest, loom, cow & calf and a note on ABSALOM WHISNANT of $100, which is to be loaned out yearly and the interest paid to her. I leave my wife in the care of my sons JAMES & JOHN GETTYS. I give unto my sons JAMES & JOHN GETTYS the plantation where I now live, they are to pay my youngest son ROBERT GETTYS in cash to make him equal in value to their land. I give unto my three sons all cash, & notes due me after paying my doctor bills and to pay to each of my married chn. $5, that is, NANCY PRICE, BETSY GETTYS, SMYTH GETTYS, & PATSY MOREHEAD also POLLY TONEY. I also allow all stock of every kind to be divided among my three sons. My wife to have a gentle beast to ride to meetings & also when conveneint to go with her. I appoint my sons JAMES & JOHN GETTYS my executors. Wit: W. M. GETTYS, JAS. MCFARLAND, jurat. GEO. P. MCFARLAND.
                                         Signed: JNO. C. GETTYS.

Page 389. 8 May 1824. Recorded, Dec. Court 1861. I, WILLIAM TOMS, being in a sickly state but of sound mind & memory. I give unto my wife PAMELA all that tract of land I bought of MILES CASTILLO to do as she please with it, but subject to the same conditions I am bound to by bond that is if CAMP comes forward and pays up the two notes of $50 each with interest she to make title for same. I give my wife the said 2 notes. I give my wife all the tract of land where I now live that I bought of ROBERT WEBB, to use as she sees fit, or to be divided at her death among our chn. JAMES WILLIAM EDWARD RODNEY (no commas) I appoint my wife PAMELA my executrix. Wit: WILLIAM BAXTER, ALFRED WEBB.
                                         Signed: WILLIAMS TOMS.
CODICIL. Dated 10 April 1828. This to be a codicil to my last will dated 8 May 1824. I give unto my dtr. POLLY the 6 silver spoons all the same set with the sugar nippers that is kept in the chest and at her mothers decease I do give her my 2 silver tables & large spoon.
                                         Signed: WILLIAM TOMS.

Page 391. 14 Nov. 1857. Recorded, Feb. Court 1862. JAMES HILL. I being of sound mind. I will all my real & personal estate to DELPHA my wife during her widowhood and that she not to sell the land or any part of it. Should my wife marry again, I will my estate both real & personal be sold and the proceeds divided her & the childre, she taking a child part. I appoint my son GEORGE HILL my executor. Wit: MADISON, jurat. RANDLE NANNEY.   Signed: JAMES HILLS.

Page 391. 27 Dec. 1861. Recorded, Feb. Court 1862. I, JESSE LOOKADOO, being of sound & disposing mind & memory. I will all my just debts & funeral expenses be paid. I give unto my beloved wife MARTHA LOOKADOO all that tract of land called the old place including my dwelling house during her natural life and at her death it is to belong to my son G. W. LOOKADOO, also my wife to have 4 negroes (not named), her choice horse, mule, 6 head cattle, 20 head hogs, 12 head sheep, plenty of feed, tools, waggon, household & kitchen furniture and $300 in money. At her death the personal property to be divided as, the negroes to my son G. W. LOOKADOO & all the rest to belong to my 2 granddaughters MARTHA & MARGA-RET SPURLIN. I also give unto my said granddaughters all that tract of land known as the JAMES SPURLIN tract, joining lands of M. SPURLIN, also one negro girl named Mary, I also give unto them a tract of land of 200 acres to be laid off the West side of the Wright place and a negro named Rosaline, if either should die, the property to belong to the other, if both should die and leave no heirs the property to belong to G. W. LOOKA-DOO. I give unto my son G. W. LOOKADOO the balance of my property of all kinds. I appoint my son G. W. LOOKADOO & A. S. HARRILL my executors. Wit: D. BEAM, J. B. MCDANIEL, jurat.   Signed: JESSE LOOKADOO.

Page 393. 2 June 1861. Recorded, Feb. Court 1862. I, SAMUEL HARRILL, give unto my illegitimate daughter MARTHA SUSANNA JOHNSON, of Cleveland County, all my property real & personal that I possess now or hereafter at any time or any way, for her to enjoy the same absolute &

& forever. I appoint A. S. HERRILL my elder brother my executor and he is directed as soon as the said MARTHA S. JOHNSON shall arrive at the age of 21 yrs. to deliver over to her the said property & he is directed to support her wants until the coming of age. Wit: L. F. CHURCHILL, C. BURNETT, jurat.   Signed: S. C. HARRILL.

Page 394. 14 Feb. 1862. Recorded, Feb. Court 1862. I, GEORGE EDWARDS, will that all my just debts & funeral expenses be paid. I give unto my beloved wife TEMPERANCE all my lands with all personal property, one negro boy named Spad, all horses, cattle, hogs, household & kitchen furniture for her use during her natural life or widowhood, at her marriage or death, I give unto my dtr. MALINDA SPURLIN 65 acres of land where she now lives, by her paying my executor $2.50 per acre for 15 acres. I give unto my dtr. MARTHA JAMES 50 acres of land including the house that her husband ROBERT JAMES built. I give unto my dtr. MARY ANN MCDANIEL, JANE DAVIS, BIDDY C. COOPER and AMELIA B. COLLINS each 50 acres of land. At death or marriage of wife executor to sell all personal property and divide equally the proceeds among all my chn. I appoint JOHN B. MCDANIEL my executor. Wit: L. W. GREEN, jurat. RANSOM BLANTON, jurat.   Signed: GEORGE EDWARDS.

Page 395. 21 Sept. 1861. Recorded, Spring Court 1862. I, JOHN EDWARDS, being of sound mind & memory. First my executor to pay all my just debts. I give unto my beloved wife MARGARET EDWARDS all my personal property of which I possess during her natural life and at her death, I desire my executor sell the same and divide the proceeds equally between my chn. SALLY N., JAMES M., CAROLINE & JOHN EDWARDS. I will unto my three chn. SALLY, CAROLINE & JOHN the tract of land whereon I now reside, to be divided among them, but let the girls have the mansion house. I will my executor to sell a tract of land in Rutherford County of about 100 acres, joining lands of ABRAM WHITAKER & J. M. EDWARDS or the wife may wish the land, if so she to take it during her life time. I appoint my son JAMES M. EDWARDS my executor and he is to have $50 from the estate for executing this my will. Wit: D. BEAM, R. H. WILSON, jurat.
                                        Signed; JOHN EDWARDS.

Page 396. 25 July 1854. Recorded, Spring Court 1862. I, THOMAS MORRIS, I desire that my just debts & funeral expenses be paid first. I give unto my beloved wife MARY all my property both real & personal during her life time or widowhood, for the purpose of raising and educating my children. In case my wife should marry again, I desire my property sold according to law & proceeds divided equally. Should a child marry, my wife & executor shall give them what they can spare. I hereby appoint my father-in-law to act as guardian for my children until they are of age. I appoint my wife executrix & my father-in-law JOSEPH BAXTER exect. Wit: R. L. GILKEY, jurat. CHURCHILL MORRIS.
                                        Signed: THOMAS MORRIS.

Page 398. 26 March 1862. Recorded, Aug. Court 1862. I, HESEKIAH BLANKENSHIP, being of sound mind & memory. First my funeral expenses & just debts to be paid. All my effects of money, horses, hogs, cattle, sheep, household & kitchen furniture both now in possession of WM. FORTUNE. I give to my beloved wife SUSANNAH. My will is that my beloved friend and father-in-law P. N. LONG executor, having power to receive & receipt at present for all monies in the hands of WM. FORTUNE, admnr. of my father's estate. Wit: K. G. MCCROW, jurat. J. C. LONG.
                                    Signed: HESEKIAH BLANKENSHIP.

Page 398. 30 April 1862. Recorded, Aug. Court 1869. I, REUBEN MCDANIEL, Jr. being in perfect mind. All my just debts to be paid. To my beloved father & mother SAMPSON and LEAH MCDANIEL to have & hold my estate both real & personal during their natural life, to live upon & enjoy as long as they may live. If any is left at their death, it to return to my estate and be divided as follow, LOUCINCY MCCOMBS to receive $5, and GUILFORD & SARAH MCDANIELS to divided the balance. The three named legatees was brother & sisters. I appoint THOMAS WILKINS my executor. Wit: THOMAS WILKINS, W. T. WILKINS, jurat.
                                    Signed: REUBEN MCDANIELS, JR.

Page 399. 22 July 1862. Recorded, Aug. Court 1862. I, ALFRED WL WILLI-

AMS, being of sound mind. I will unto my children JAMES
A. WILLIAMS & ALFRED B. WILLIAMS all my estate, right, title and interest
accruing unto me in any manner whatsoever. I appoint my father JAMES
WILLIAMS my executor. Wit: MARY SWEEZY, jurat. JOHN M. M. PRICE, jurat.
Signed: ALFRED W. X WILLIAMS.

Page 400. 2 April 1857. Recorded, Aug. Court. I, THOMAS ROBBINS, being
in proper mind and memory, but somewhat paralized in body. I
give unto my beloved wife NANCY ROBBINS all my property to hold during
her life time. At her death the land to be divided as, begining at
father's old corner SW to speculation line all below to belong to P.
BRISCOS line to be for JOSEPH ROBBINS, PHILIP ROBBINS, CHESTERFIELD
ROBBINS and their heirs. The remaining part to on both sides of river to
MARGARET NODINE, TLEBY FLYN & SARRAH SPLAN and JANE HESTER and their
heirs. I appoint JOSEPH ROBBINS & JOHN NODINE my executors. Wit: A.
PADGETT, A. LANCASTER, jurat.   Signed: THOMAS RONNINS.

Page 401. 6 July 1856. Recorded, Aug. Court 1862. WILLIAM GOODE, at
my death, my wife SALLY to hold & keep all my property after
paying my just debts, during her life or widowhood. I want her to give
the three youngest MARTHA, PETER DUFFY & WM. THOMAS a horse, saddle, cow
& calf each. If she should marry the chn. to have the property. I
appoint my brother JAMES GOODE executor. Wit: W. H. GREEN, jurat.
Signed: WILLIAM GOODE.

Page 402. 18 July 1860. Recorded, Aug. Court 1862. I, STACY TAYLOR,
being of sound mind & memory. My executor to pay my funeral
expenses & just debts. I give unto my son OLIVER P. TAYLOR my whole
estate. one negro girl Mary, 22 yrs. old & one negro girl named Minerva
about 7 yrs. old. all my stock, of horses, hogs, sheep and cattle, household & kitchen furniture, all grain in storage & growing crops. I appoint
my friend MADISON LYNCH & ELIAS L. TAYLOR my executor. Wit: J. B. CORN-
WELL, J. L. GRAY.   Signed: STACY X TAYLOR.

Page 403. 2 Feb. 1860. Recorded, Sept. Court 1862. I, ELIZABETH
WHITESIDES, being of sound mind & memory. I wish my executor
to pay my funeral expenses & just debts. I give unto my dtr. A. C.
BLANTON, wife of B. S. BLANTON, decd. my negro girl Easter, now in their
possession. I will the remainder of my property that I may have at my
death to be divided between my two dtrs. S. E. LYNCH, the wife of E. M.
LYNCH & A. C. BLANTON not taking the property willed by my husband A. M.
BLANTON, decd. I appoint my son-in-law E. M. LYNCH my executor. Wit:
R. O. LEDBETTER, jurat. T. R. EGERTON. Signed: ELIZABETH WHITESIDES.

Page 404. No date. Recorded, Fall Court 1862. I, JOSEPH G. PRICE, being
of sound mind & memory and having enlisted as a soldier for
the term of three years in the service of the Confederate States of
America. My real estate, I desire and will that my beloved wife DRUCILLY
to have sole use if I not return. If she remarry my land to be rented
out and the proceeds applied to the education of my dtr. LYDDIA, ELIZA-
BETH (states dtr. but has a comma) I appoint Bother-in-law A. C. WHIS-
NANT my executor. Wit: JOHN WHISNANT, jurat.
Signed: JOSEPH G. PRICE.

Page 405. 29 May 1861. Recorded, Dec. Court 1862. I, G. W. KOONE, being
of sound mind. It is my desire that my just debts be paid. I
give unto MARGARET and SALINA A. LYNCH two beds & furniture. The rest of
my estate with my interest in my grand father KOON'S estate which he
willed to me at my grand mother KOON'S death, I give unto my sister CAT-
HARINE A. A. KOONE. I appoint NORMAN LYNCH my executor. Wit: WM. DAVEN-
PORT, T. H. W. WHITESIDE, jurat.   Signed: G. W. KOONE.

Page 405. 30 June 1862. Recorded, Dec. Court 1862. I, JEREMIAH WEBB,
being of sound mind & memory but feeble in Body. I give unto
my beloved wife CINDRILLA all the property I possess both real & personal
during her natural life and at her death, I will what property that remain belong to JAMES MCALLEN. I appoint my friend W. G. WILSON my executor. I desire that my just debts to be paid. Wit: D. BEAM, W. G. WILSON,
jurat.   Signed: J. WEBB.

Page 407. 25 Sept. 1861. Recorded, March Court 1863. I, ALEXANDER
HAMILTON SHOTWELL being of sound mind & body. In view of the
uncertainties of life and dangers incident to a Military Campaign in which
I am about to engage. All my estate both real & personal in the State of
N. C. I give unto my wife JANE ELIZA one third of the property, and the
other two thirds divided equally among my heirs at law. I appoint my
friend JAMES B. MORRIS my executor. Wit: J. W. HARRIS, L. F. CHURCHILL.
Signed: A. H. SHOTWELL.

Page 408. 21 May 1862. Recorded, March Court 1863. WILLIAM ELLIOTT, SR.
being in good mind & memory. My will is for J. W. H. ELLIOTT,
ANDREW ELLIOTT, J. L. ELLIOTT my 3 oldest boys to have my upper plantation. My will is for MILLY DELINDA ELLIOTT, W. H. ELLIOTT, ZILLA MANDA
ELLIOTT to have my home plantation. My will that ARSILLAR CALDING ELLIOTT
to get $100 out of her mother's part, she has $100 out of my part, one
bed & furniture, one heifer. MILLY & MANDY to have a cow & calf.
WILLIAM to have a bed & furniture. HARRIS & JAMES has had a bed & furniture. JAMES to have my little gun & $10. No witnesses. No executor
named. Very, very faint writing. Signed: WILLIAM ELLIOTT.

Page 409. 21 May 1862. Recorded, March Court 1863. I, ANDREW HARMON, I
do make my father ANDREW HARMON, Sr. my sole executor. I give
unto my father ANDREW HARMAN Sr. & my mother DOLLY HARMON and MARGARET
HARMON all my property, except my brother ALFRED HARMON 50¢ & VINEY
SULLINS my niece 50¢ & JOSEPH HARMON 50¢. Wit: JAMES YOUNG, SARAH J.
YOUNG. Signed: ANDREW HARMON.

Page 410. 15 July 1862. Recorded, April Court 1863. I, DAVIDSON WALKER,
being of sound mind. I give unto my wife MARTHA all the tract
of land where I now live, joining the lands of J. W. GREEN & G. W. ROLLINS
during her natural life, at her death or marriage to go to my child or
children if any and if not any unto my brothers & sisters. I give unto
my wife MARTHA all personal property after paying my just debts. I
appoint J. W. GREEN my executor. Wit: G. W. ROLLINS, jurat. J. W. GREEN,
jurat. Signed: DAVIDSON WALKER.

Page 411. 7 March 1857. Recorded, April Court 1863. I, MARY GREEN,
being of sound mind. I give unto my son JOSEPH W. GREEN the
following negroes, Artaminta, Minerva, Margaret & Abram. I give unto my
son JOSEPH the balance of my estate forever. I appoint my son J. W.
GREEN to be my executor, to pay my just debts & funeral expenses. Wit:
G. W. ROLLINS, jurat. WILLIAM DAVIS, jurat.
Signed: MARY GREEN.

Page 412. 13 May 1863. Recorded, June Court 1863. I, J. M. CHITWOOD,
being of sound mind & memory. First my executor to pay my
just debts. I give unto my beloved wife ROSALINE CHITWOOD all my estate
both real & personal, during her natural life & at her death the land to
be divided among the chn. LOUISA ELLER WM EVANS SALLIE AGATHA (no commas)
or any that may be born. I appoint my brother-in-law R. H. MCBRAYER of
Cleveland Co., N. C. my lawful executor. Wit: SAMUEL DAVES, JAMES A. X
DAVES, jurat. Signed: J. M. CHITWOOD.

Page 413. 4 March 1861. Recorded, June Court 1863. I, J. L. TAYLOR,
first I direct my just debts to be paid and funeral expenses.
I give unto my wife the Maple Creek place for her life time & all household & kitchen furniture, 2 cows, 15 hogs, one cart, steer, two negroes,
Obe & Paty to be sold at her death and proceeds divided among my children.
I give unto my son, JAMES M. TAYLOR, the Mountain Creek farm, and all my
interest in MARTHA TAYLORS dowery of land & one negro boy Harry & one
gold watch worth $75 & one horse at $100, which he is to account for. I
give unto my dtr. MARY and JOHN JONES one note of $1200 and two others of
$154 without interest & I have given them 2 mules worth $175, & cows &
furniture worth $50, total of $1579 which is their share of my estate
unless named. I give unto R. L. TAYLOR my Bennick Farm and mill & one
negro named Hamp, one good horse worth $100 & a good saddle & bridle. I
give unto my son H. C. TAYLOR the place I now live on, known as the old
Hider place & one negro Sam, one horse & saddle & bridle worth $120. I
give unto my dtr. MARTHA W. TAYLOR 2 negroes, Souse & July should they
die, she to have $550 worth of other property, and one horse, saddle, and

141

bridle worth $120 & one little place known as the Suttle place. I appoint
J. M. TAYLOR my executor. No witnesses. Signed: JAS. L. TAYLOR.

Page 414. 20 Oct. 1861. Recorded, June Court 1863. I, JONATHAN ELLIOTT,
being of sound mind & memory, and consideration the uncertainty of my life in the war. I give all my estate both real & personal to
brother A. L. ELLIOTT, including all my notes which I have at interest
if I never live to get out of this war, I hope this writing will be
found and established. No witness, no executor.
Signed: JONATHAN ELLIOTT.

Page 414. 6 Feb. 1863. Recorded, June Court 1863. I, ANDREW CLEMENTS,
being weak & frail in body but of perfect mind & memory. I
give unto my son CORNELIUS all my land except 10 acres joining JOHN A.
LONG after my wife MARGARET CLEMENTS death and my three dtrs. that are
single, they are to have their support from the said land while single.
I leave to my three married dtrs. $5 each. I also give to my son CORNEL-
IUS my smith tools. I give to my wife MARGARET & the three single dtrs.
all stock of cattle, hogs, & sheep and all household & kitchen furniture,
one loom. I give unto my son-in-law JOHN A. LONG 10 acres of land join-
ing his own land. I appoint my son CORNELIUS CLEMENTS, Jr. and CORNELIUS
CLEMENTS, Sr. my executors. Wit: ARINGTON HILLS, jurat. GEORGE W. GUFFY.
Signed: ANDREW CLEMENTS.

Page 416. 15 April 1863. Recorded, June Court 1863. I, GUILFORD E.
BLANTON, of Murry Co., Ga. being of sound mind & memory. My
executor to pay my funeral expenses & just debts. I give unto my beloved
wife MARY JANE BLANTON during her life time or widowhood all my effects,
of personal property and money, to be used for herself and raising &
educating my children, should she marry the estate to be equally divided
among my wife & our three chn. CARAH LUTICIA, CHARLES EDGAR, & GEORGE
MARION (all under age). I appoint my wife MARY JANE BLANTON the guardian
of my minor chn. I appoint my wife MARY JANE BLANTON my executor. Wit:
H. HARRILL, jurat. G. M. WEBB, jurat. Z. W. GREEN.
Signed: G. E. BLANTON.

Page 418. 22 July 1853. Recorded, Sept. Court 1863. I, ELIJAH WALKER,
being this day of sound mind & memory. I give unto my beloved
wife AMY WALKER all my estate both real & personal, during her natural
life or widowhood, except that JOHN J. WALKER have one good horse, saddle
& bridle. At the death or marriage of my wife my son J. J. WALKER to
have all the land that I have not deeded to my other sons, the proceeds
kept until her death or marriage then to sell all remaining items and
divided among my chn. SYNTHA PANNEL, A. P. WALKER, T. M. WALKER, S. HAYNES,
WM. WALKER, J. J. WALKER, my granddaughter SARAH B. $1. I appoint A. P.
WALKER, T. M. WALKER & WM. WALKER my executor. What is given to my
children is given as a gift without any account being taken. Wit: D.
PANNEL, jurat. D. M. PANNEL, jurat. Signed: ELIJAH WALKER.

Page 419. 23 June 1863. Recorded, Sept. Court 1863. I, PRISCILLA, being
of sound mind & memory. My executor to pay my funeral charges
& just debts. I give unto my son-in-law G. M. WEBB all my tract of land
whereon he now lives containing 350 acres, lying on the East side of
Second Broad River, joining the land of MARY WEBB or her heirs SAMUEL
HARRILL, Sr. and G. W. LOGAN where A. C. BLANTON now lives, provided G.M.
WEBB is to pay my children $1,000 for said land. All my money and the
said $1,000 & my interest in my father's estate is to be equally divided
among my chn., SUSANNAH YOUNG, MARGARET WRAY, PRISCILLA J. WEBB, & B. S.
BLANTON chn. WILLIAM H. & JOHN BLANTON and my son J. H. BLANTON chn.
JULIA, DOCTOR, DOVA, JANE & HILL BLANTON, my son G. E. BLANTON chn.
CORAH, EDGAR, & GEORGE. I give unto my dtr. SUSANNAH YOUNG my sideboard.
I give unto my dtr. MARAGRET WRAY $14 in lieu of sideboard & Cupboard.
Many household items named. I appoint my son-in-law G. M. WEBB my lawful
executor. Wit: O. P. GARDNER, H. HARRILL, jurat.
Signed: PRISCILLA BURGE.

Page 422. 17 Sept. 1863. Recorded, Oct. Court 1863. I, JOSEPH BRENDLE,
being in sound mind but afflicted. I wish my just debts paid
with my burial expenses. I appoint SMITH MCCARRY my mule & 12 months
support for one man & mule if it is left when I die. I appoint SMITH

142

MCCARRY my agent or guardian for my black boy Isom. I leave my land to
be sold & household property, except I wish my daughter ELIZABETH SAIN to
divide my wearing clothes among the boys. After paying the debts the
balance to be divided as follows, I give my dtr. NANCY'S heirs $5, also
REBECCA TOWERY $5. MARY UPTON $5. SARAH HALL heirs $5. JOSEPH BRINDLE
$5. JOHN BRINDLE $5. HENRY BRINDLE $5. and ELIZABETH SAINES to have
the balance and divide as follows ELIZABETH SAINES to have $3 for one of
HENRY BRINDLE. I appoint SMITH MCCURRY my executor & J. H. JONES to cry
my sale. Wit: JAMES SIMS, jurat. SUSANNAH C. LONG, jurat.
Signed: JOSEPH X BRINDLE.

Page 423. 2 July 1858. Recorded, Dec. Court 1863. I, ELIAS LINCH, I
give unto my beloved wife FRANCES 6 negroes, 2 men, 2 women,
& a boy & girl her choice, household & kitchen furniture, 3 horses or
mules, farming tools, 40 head hogs, 6 cows & calves with 2 more for beef,
15 head sheep, one set of blacksmith tools, $500 in money, a year supply
of feed for stock, at her death the negroes to be sold and the proceeds
divided among my heirs. My property not willed to be sold at my death,
and all my children made equal, what I have advanced to each will appear
in a book. My dtr. REBECCA MINERVIA KING being dead, the balance due her
to be given to her or her husband NOAH KING. My son TOLIVER D. LINCH
being dead & left 4 chn. 2 sons & 2 dtrs. what may be coming to my two
granddaughters, I leave in trust with my son E. M. LYNCH, he to vest in
real estate for their benfit. I appoint my son ELIAS M. LYNCH my executor. Wit: ROBERT G. TWITTY, jurat. WILLIAM L. TWITTY.
Signed: ELIAS LINCH.
CODICIL. Dated 19 Oct. 1860. This to be a codicil to my will of 2 July
1858. What property that would be due my dtr. MALINDA WHITE-
SIDE at my death shall be paid to her six chn., MARTHA ELLIOTT WM JOSEPH
POSEY RICHARD & NOAH WHITESIDE (no commas) their mothers share. Wit:
ROBT. G. TWITTY, jurat.   Signed: ELIAS LINCH.

Page 424. 1 June 1861. Recorded, Dec. Court 1863. I, BRIANT WEBB, being
of sound mind & memory. First my executor shall pay my funeral
expenses & just debts. I give unto my mother ELIZABETH WEBB 55 acres of
land, all my interest in the estate of my brother JAMES, decd. also all
my personal estate. The above to be valid & in full force if I never
should return back home again otherwise to be void and no effect and
lastly I appoint my mother ELIZABETH WEBB my executor. Wit: M. W. SIM-
MONS, jurat. HENRY JENKINS.   Signed: BRIANT X WEBB.

Page 426. 21 April 1858. Recorded, March Court 1864. I, RICHARD H.
HICKS, being of sound mind & memory. My executor to pay all
funeral expenses & my just debts. It is my will that my beloved wife
shall have the use of my estate both real & personal, so long as she
remains a widow and to raise & educate our children. I give to each of
my children when they arrive at 21 yrs. $100. I give all my lans unto
my wife & chn. to be divided equally then the youngest child come of age.
Negroes to be hired out & the money kept on interest. I desire my executors will attend to my store & sell all the goods now on hand until 1 Jan.
next, then close the store by selling to the highest bidder. I appoint
my wife Executrix & MOSE N. SIMMONS executor. Wit: P. A. CARPENTER,
jurat. JAMES HARTON.   Signed: R. H. HICKS.

CODICIL. Dated 3 May 1858, Each child to have a good horse, saddle &
bridle in addition to what was willed to them. Also a bed &
furniture when they come of age. J. A. WEBSTER is appointed executor
with N. W. SIMMONS & MRRE L. HICKS. Wit: PANTHA DURHAM, JOSHUA GEORGE
CAMP, jurat.   Signed: R. H. HICKS.

CODICIL #2. Dated 4 April 1858. If wife remains a widow until youngest
child is 21 and her share not sufficient for her maintainance she is to have Ann & one of her girl children & Jo if alive and
necessary house furniture. Wit: ABRAM LOVELACE ,jurat. PANTHA DURHAM.
Signed: R. H. HICKS.

Page 428. 27 Dec. 1861. Recorded, March Court 1864. I, JOHN WATERS,
being in bad health but sound mind and memory. I allow all
my just debts be paid & the remainder to be disposed of as follows, I
have 500 acres land that I want my son AARON D. WATERS & my dtr. (not

143

named) to share equally, two uninterested men to value the land and put
in shares for, AARON D. WATERS one share, SARAH B. MCENTIRE one share,
JANE DERBERRY one share, heirs of ELIZABETH DERBERRY one share, MARY
PROCTOR one share, RACHEL MOONEY one share. The rest of my chn. I have
given them deeds to their land, JAMES, JOHN, ELISHA, ELIJAH, & A. O.
WATERS and shall not have any share in the other property. All horses
& cattle to be sold & proceeds to go to son A. D. WATERS, heirs & my dtrs.
above named. I appoint ABSOLOM O. WATERS my executor. Wit: JAMES MC-
FARLAND, WILLIAM G. MODE, jurat.   Signed: JOHN X WATERS.

Page 429. 21 March 1817. Recorded, March Court 1864. being in perfect
        mind & memory. First I desire my debts & funeral charges to
be paid.   All my estate to be divided between my step-daughter JANE
SEWARD & JANE WISE my grand step-daughter. I appoint JANE SEWARD & JANE
WISE my executrixs. Wit: D. DICKEY, WILLIAM K. KERR.
                                    Signed: ROBERT NEWTON.

Page 432. LETTER. Richmond, Va. 22 May 1863. Recorded, June Court
        1864. L. A. ROBERTSON to W. WALL. "Dear Uncle: I am again
permitted to drop you a few lines to let you know how I am getting along.
I am as well as could be expected and not very well at that for you know
that my health is not very good at best, tho I must do the best I can
while I stay in the service the health Regiment is as good as could be
expected. I will leave out the war news as you have heard it before we
had to give back from Yorktown to Richmond as you have been informed of
the fact. I will hasten on for my time is limited. I would like to see
you all as I have heretofore but it seems like to me that I never shall
get to see any more pleasure with you all again but if I don't I hope
that we all may meet in that upper and better world than this. Tell
ERVANA WALL that it is very uncertain whether I ever shall live to see
the time rolled round that I can come home and get my shirt that you
made for me. I hope you will live to see me come home and wear it to see
my sweet hart. Tell J. A. WALL that I have not forgot him and I would
like to receive a few lines from him. . . .Uncle I want you and A. M.
ROBERTSON to wind up my business as good as you can if I should happen to
fall in the battle field or die with sickness for life is very uncertain
here. I want ARTY ROBERTSON & JULIAN ROBERTSON to have $25 more than
the rest becouse they have no home. Give JULIAN ROBERTSON my watch &
$25 besides as she is the youngest child. I gave her my watch in with
the $25. All the rest of my property to be divided between all. I want
you to understand it I gave them $25 in money a piece as a gift and they
are to have as the rest in the balance of my property beside what I give
them. You need not say any thing about this unless I should happen to
die. If you see any of them that owes me they can pay the money over to
you and you can take care of it for me. Signed: L. A. ROBERTSON & W. M.
                                                                  WALL.
Direct your letter to Richmond, Va. in care of Capt. H. D. LEE 16 Regiment   N. C. Troops Write as soon as you can.

Page 432. 27 Nov. 1863. Recorded, June Court 1864. I, E. P. MORGAN,
        being in perfect mind & memory. I want all my just debts paid
and the remainder of all my property, I give unto my beloved wife POLLY
MORGAN to use as she sees proper and if she remains my widow until the
youngest child come of age she to have one half of estate, should she
marry before, she to get a child part. I appoint my wife POLLY & my son
PERMINTER H. MORGAN my executors. Wit: M. W. MORGAN, jurat. ELIJAH
MORGAN, jurat.   Signed: E. P. MORGAN.

Page 433. 19 Nov. 1863. Recorded, July Court 1864. I, PHILIP GROSS,
        being of sound mind & memory. My executor to pay all my just
debts. I give unto my beloved wife PRISCILLA GROSS all my tract of land
I now live on, during her life time, with four negroes, all household
& kitchen furniture, one yoke of oxen, one wagon & farming tools stock of
all kinds & $100 in cash. The balance of my negroes to be put in lots &
drawn by my chn. LEANDER GROSS, HENRY D. GROSS, PHILIP H. GROSS, HOIL U.
GROSS & JOHN GROSS. The balance of my property to be sold and proceeds
divided among the above named chn. At the death of my wife the land to
be sold and the money with the notes and money on hand to be divided
among my chn. except I give to my son ELI GROSS $20. Negro Jane that is
afflicated & cannot walk is to live with some of my children and be well

treated and each of my children to bear their part of her support. I
appoint my son HOIL U. & PHILIP H. GROSS my executors. Wit: W. L. GRIFFIN,
jurat. N. H. MORROW, jurat.   Signed: PHILIP GROSS.

Page 436. 3 Jan. 1848. Recorded, Sept. Court 1864. I, MARTHA TAYLOR,
        I wish my just debts paid. I will my negro, Lucy, & one bed
& furniture to my son ELIAS TAYLOR. To my grandson, HARVEY C. T. DAVIS,
one bed & furniture to be kept for him by ELIAS L. TAYLOR until of age.
I give my wearing clothes of every description to be divided between my
dtrs. MARY TABER, SINTHA MCFADDEN & DRUCILLA DAVIS. To my dtr., MIRA
TABER, I give one negro girl, Caroline, now about 6 yrs. old, one bed &
furniture, all horses, cattle & hogs with grain that is on hand. No
executors. Wit: ROBT. G. TWITTY, ALLEN TABER.
                                Signed: MARTHA X TAYLOR.

Page 436. 27 March 1862. Recorded, Sept. Court 1864. I, ELIZABETH
        PARHAM, being of sound mind & memory. I give unto MARTHA HILL
wife of ALEXANDER HILL & her heirs all the property that I may have at
my death, both real & personal. The real property being the tract of
land whereon I now live. This is made in consideration that the said
HILL & wife is to take care of & see that I have plenty to live on during
my life time. If they or their heirs fail or refuse to supply me, then
this will is void. No executor. Wit: M. WILKERSON, SR., jurat. A. O.
LYNCH, jurat.   Signed: ELIZABETH X PARHAM.

Page 437. 24 Oct. 1863. Recorded, Sept. Court 1864. I, DANIEL WEBB,
        being of sound mind & memory. First my executor to pay my
funeral charges & just debts. I give unto my beloved mother, ELIZABETH
WEBB, 56 acres of land, also all my interest in the estate of my brother,
JAMES WEBB, decd. also one mare & mule colt, all personal property during
her natural life and after my mothers death, all my property to belong
to my niece, MARY WEBB. I appoint my mother ELIZABETH WEBB my executrix.
Wit: M. W. SIMMONS, jurat, JOHN W. GOODE, NAT D. SMITH.
                                Signed: DANIEL WEBB.

Page 438. 8 Aug. 1864. Recorded, Sept. Court 1864. I. L. M. SPARKS,
        being of sound mind & memory. My executor to pay my funeral
charges & just debts. I give unto my beloved wife, SARAH SPARKS, all my
property both real & personal during her natural life or widowhood, at
her death or marriage my property to be sold & equally divided among my
lawful heirs, my grand son JAMES L. SPARK, C. L. SPARK, WM. A. SPARK, &
A. E. SPARK or their heirs. In case my said grandson should die leaving
no heirs, his share shall return to my estate. I appoint my sons C. L.
SPARKS & W. A. SPARK my executors. Wit: O. P. GARDNER, E. A. JONES,
jurat.   Signed: L. M. SPARKS.

Page 439. 23 Feb. 1863. Recorded, Sept. Court 1864. I, JOHN LEDBETTER,
        being of sound mind & memory. First my executor to pay my
just debts & funeral expenses. I give unto my wife MARTHA URSULA all my
property both real & personal, and all money due me. I appoint Dr. T. R.
EGERTON my executor. Wit: WM. DEVENPORT, jurat. A. W. WHITESIDE.
                                Signed: JOHN W. LEDBETTER.

Page 440. 20 May 1856. Sept. Court 1864. I, ROBERT G. TWITTY, I give
        unto my beloved wife, MARY WATSON TWITTY, the tract of land on
which I now live, including the dwelling house, except the land in the
bend of the river, during her natural life. I also give her five negroes,
Wade, Clarissa, Puss, Sam & Julia. 4 mules, horse Hickory Dick, as many
cows as she thinks necessary, Carriage, buggy, 4 horses wagon, & farm
tools. I give unto my son, WILLIAM L. TWITTY, my tract of land on
Cathey's Creek known as the Bynum or Hampton land, also my Jamestown land
valued together at & 7,400. Also negroes, Alfred, Frank, Dinah & Little
Boy Bill, one mule, one note on W. A. TANNER for $125 and $700 for com-
pleting his education. I give unto dtr. MARGARET ANNIE a tract of land
on Broad River, known as the Lynch & Erwin tracts valued at $8,000, also
negroes, Jack, Jane & Jim and the Piano I bought her & a horse. I give
to my son FRANCIS LOGAN my Littlejohn land on Broad River, this tract
also divised to my wife as the home place, at her death this land & the
land in the river bend, also negroes, Calvins, Reuben & Emily & his horse,
also my Mountain land known as Washington Harrises, all land given him

valued at $8,000. I give unto my son THEODRICK BURCHET land on Cane
Creek, known as the Patton tract & the 2 Morrison tracts valued at $9,500
& negroes, Kerr, Landrum, & Frances. I give unto my dtr. MARY JANE my
Miller tract on the mountain and my PRESTON LONG & MCCURRY land of Cane
Creek, valued at $8,500, also negroes, Moses, Manan, John & Mary. Child-
ren not to mortgage or sell any of their property before the age of 35
yrs. old. Wife is appointed guardian of the minor children. Having
omitted a clause or any land to my son LOGAN, I divise unto him LOGAN an
interest I hold a contract upon Speculation Company I hereby give said
LOGAN the contract. I Appoint A. G. LOGAN & son WILLIAM my executors.
Wit: W. H. MILLER, jurat. JNO. M. CRATON, jurat.
Signed: ROBERT G. TWITTY.

Page 444. 7 Jan. 1853. Recorded, Dec. Court 1864. I, JOHN DAVENPORT,
being of sound mind & memory. I will that my just debts &
funeral expenses be paid. I will unto son MATHEW all the notes which I
hold on him in the sum of $800. I give unto the children of my dtr.
ELIZABETH DALTON all the notes I hold on their mother, with money added
to make a total of $800. I give unto my dtr. SARAH SEARCY all the notes
I hold on her, and money added to amount to $800. I give unto the child
of my son MARTIN $800. I give unto my son DAVID all notes I hold on him
& $800. I give unto my grandson WILLIAM DAVENPORT son of DAVID DAVENPORT
my home tract of land, and all adjoining lands, also negroes, Jane,
Burton and all Janes chn. born after this will. The remaining property
to be sold and money put into 6 equal parts and given as follows, one
part to son MATHEW DAVENPORT, one part to DAVID DAVENPORT, one part to
dtr. FANNY LYNCH, one part to SARAH SERCY, and one part to chn. of dtr.
ELIZABETH DALTON, one part to the child of my son MARTIN, if not claimed
within seven years from the date of my death, it shall be divided among
the other five. I appoint my son DAVID DAVENPORT & friend T. H. W.
WHITESIDE my executors. Wit: WILLIAM H. LOGAN, jurat. H. W. HARRIS,
J. A. HARRIS.   Signed: JOHN X DAVENPORT.
CODICIL. Dated 4 Nov. 1857, add this codicil to my LS&T. I revoke the
third clause to this extent. I desire to give the children of
ELIZABETH DALTON nothing more than the notes which I hold on their mother,
except JACKSON DALTON whom I give $500. I revoke all clauses in my will
giving to FANNY LYNCH any interest in my property real or personal. I
give unto the child of MARTIN DAVENPORT provided she be living $1,000 in
place of all interest in my will. I give unto my grandson JOHN DAVENPORT
son of WILLIAM DAVENPORT $1,000 to be put on interest until he is 21 yrs.
old. The remainder of my property to be sold and the proceeds divided
among, after paying the money legacies, to chn. of MATHEW DAVENPORT,
DAVID DAVENPORT, & SARAH SEARCY. Wit: C. L. HARRIS, W. H. HARRIS, jurat.
J. W. HARRIS.   Signed: JOHN X DAVENPORT.

Page 447. 5 Oct. 1863. Recorded, Dec. Court 1864. I, WILLIAM RANDAL,
being of sound mind & memory. After my just debts are paid,
I give unto my beloved wife MARY RANDAL all my personal estate and real
estate during her life or widowhood & provided she marries, I give unto
my wife MARY RANDAL the home tract of land & I give unto my dtr. MARTHA
J. NORTON half of my land forever and at the death of my wife, I give
unto my dtr. MARY E. RANDAL the other half of my land, I also give unto
MARY E. RANDAL one horse, saddle & bridle, one cupboard & furniture, I
give unto my dtr. MARTHA J. HORTON the burow, & little table at her
mother's death. I appoint my friend WILLIAM GUFFY my executor. Wit:
WILLIAM MCSWAIN, jurat. MARTIN PANNEL.   Signed: WM. X RANDAL.

Page 449. 20 Aug. 1862. Recorded, Jan. Court 1865. I, NATHANIEL W.
MILLER, being of sound mind & memory. I will that all my just
debts & funeral expenses be paid. I give unto my beloved wife ELIZABETH
J. MILLER all my estate let it consist of whatever it may, unless I should
have heir or heirs born of her body, in that case my wife is to have one
half, should she marry again all my estate is to go to my heirs. All the
property I received by my wife is to be absolutely hers. I appoint WAT-
SON P. ABRAM my executor. Wit: M. O. DICKERSON, jurat. T. B. TWITTY.
Signed: NATHANIEL W. MILLER.

Page 450. 20 Sept. 1862. Recorded, March Court 1865. I, ISAIAH W.
MELTON, being of sound mind & memory. I give unto my beloved
wife LOURANEY & my heirs all my estate both real & personal. I appoint

146

my wife LOURANEY and my father-in-law JOSHUA MELTON my executors to collect my debts and pay my just claims against me. Wit: JOSEPH BIGGERSTAFF,
jurat. SAMUEL BIGGERSTAFF, jurat.   Signed: ISAIAH W. MELTON.

Page 451. 19 July 1862. Recorded, March Court 1865. I, JOHN BURGE,
          being of sound mind and perfect memory. I leave unto my wife
HESTER BURGE the plantation where I now live, also negroes Harry & Rose,
all household & kitchen furniture, farming tools, horses, hogs, cattle
& wagon. I will that my wife to live on the land and half of the proceeds be applied to the maintainance & education of my dtr. EVA. Should
my wife remove from my land, the said land & negroes to be rented out and
half of the proceeds to go to my dtr. EVA. At the death or marriage of
my wife the land & negroes to be divided between my wife HESTER & my dtr.
EVA. If my dtr. EVA die without lawfull issue then my property to be
equally divided between my two brothers J. C. BURGE & WILLIAM P. BURGE &
my sisters MARY WEBB & DRUCILLA REINHARDT, my other brother & sisters I
will $1. each. (No executor). Wit: H. HARRILL, jurat, JAMES HARRILL.
                              Signed: JOHN BURGE.

Page 453. 30 Dec. 1855. Recorded, Aug. Court 1865. I, K. J. MCCURRY,
          being very weak & low body but of perfect sound mind & memory.
I give unto my oldest son LEWIS MCCURRY all that tract of land whereon he
now lives. To PHILY DOWNS one negro boy Jerry. To MARTHA CROW a negro
boy Cisero. To NANCY WHESNANT negro girl ------. To SMITH MCCURRY one
negro Dice. To dtr. MARGARET TONEY two negroes Meg & Nancy. To dtr.
CHRISTENY GRAYSON two negroes, Ann & Frank. To son JOSEPH MCCURRY one
negro boy Sam. Let the land be divided equal & sell the balance of the
property & pay my just debts. Give the heirs of ELIZABETH PROCTOR,
JOSEPH, WILEY, MARGARET, and WILLIAM PROCTOR $1,000 a piece. SIMMON
MCCURRY has had his share & has give me his receipt for same. When property is sold, pay the debts & give MARTHA CROW $600. PHILBY --- $500.
SMITH MCCURRY $200. MARGARET TONEY $300. CHRISTINY GRAYSON $300.
JOSEPH $100. NANCY WHISNANT $3.. I appoint JOSEPH GRAYSON & W. FORTION
my executors. Wit: ELI WHISNANT, ELI EARLEY.
                              Signed: I. K. MCCURRY.
I, WILLIAM FORTION being appointed by K. J. MCCURRY an executor, on ac-
count of ill health relinquish any & all claims as such. This 31 July
1865. . . .
I K. J. GRAYSON, being appointed an executor by K. J. MCCURRY do relin-
quish any right or claim to the above will & enter my dissent. J. C.
GRAYSON. 2 Aug. 1865.

Page 456. 8 Sept. 1859. Recorded, Court of 1865. I, JOHN PERTER MOONEY,
          being in declining years but of sound & disposing mind & memory.
I will that my just debts and funeral expenses be paid. I give unto my
beloved wife CHARLOTTE MOONEY $1200 in money & my negroes, Allen, Sallie,
Ellen, Jerry, Bob, Jasin, Martha, Einley & her choice of three more, one
carriage, one wagon, 6 cows & calves, 15 head of hogs, all household &
kitchen furniture, all farming tools, the use of the plantation & mill
during her natural life & at her death to be sold, & the proceeds equally
divided among my children liveing & the heirs of DRUSILLER HILL, decd. is
to have one sixth part. I also give unto my wife a year's allowance of
400 bushels of corn, 50 bushels of wheat, 1,000 pounds of pork, 50 pounds
of coffee, 100 pounds sugar, one sack of salt. I give unto the chn. of
DRUSILLA HILL decd. my negroes, Hannah, Adaline now in possession of ABLE
HILL & $1500 in cash. I give unto my dtr. NANCY VINA EAVES wife of GIL-
FORD EAVES my negroes, Westly, Manervy now in possession of GILFORD
EAVES. I give unto my dtr. ELIZA HAMILTON wife of L. S. HAMILTON & her
heirs, my negroes, Milley & Cintha, I give unto my grandson LAWSON EAVES
$600 in money, to be taken out of the legacy given to my dtr. ELIZA
HAMILTON. I give unto my son JACOB S. MOONEY my negroes, Ben & Dick
which he now has, & $400 in money. I give unto my son WILLIAM MOONEY my
negroes Henry, Margaret both of which he now has, & $500 in money, which
he has received. I give unto my dtr. CHARLOTTE BRYAN the wife of JAMES
BRYAN my negroes, Philis & Nance now in their possession & negro Becky.
I will that the balance of my negroes, Alford, Lawson, Sam, Isac, Lizzy
& her child Julia to be sold & the proceeds to pay the legacys herein
named, & the balance divided among my chn. living & the chn. of DRUSCILLS
HILL decd. I hereby appoint W. S. HILL trustee of the money for DRUS-
CILLA heirs. I appoint my son WILLIAM A. MOONEY my executor. Wit: J. W.

147

HARRIS, M. O. DICKERSON.   Signed: J. PETER MOONEY.

Page 460.   2 Nov. 1864. Recorded, Will Docket 1865. I, OLIVER WATERS,
            being in sound mind & memory. I desire all my just debts to be
paid, and the remainder of my property be equally divided between my wife
P. B. WATERS & all her heirs. I appoint WILLIAM G. MODE my executor.
Wit: I. T. MODE, ALFORD JONES.   Signed: OLIVER WATERS.

Page 461.   23 Jan. 1864. Recorded, Will Docket. I, MOSES LOGAN, I give
            unto my dtr. NANCY all that tract of land where I now live,
lying on the West side of Second Broad River, all belonging or attached,
machinery, bark mill to her in fee simple. Also negroes, Vine & her
children, Emaline, John, Sarah, Nancy Peggy, Henry, Chany, Mary, &
Guinney, also Emeline chn. Frances, George, & Caroline also Dovey & her
two chn. Amander & Jeff Davis also Milly, Dick & Vince. All stock of
every kind & household & kitchen furniture, farming tools. I give unto
my son negroes, Sal, Dice, Phillis, Peter, Jim, Becan, & her children
Harril, Ester, Levi, Ann & Molenda. ALBERT is to collect all my debts
& to pay all my just debts. I have not memtioned all my children or
grand children as they have received all of my estate which I have for
them. I appoint my son ALBERT LOGAN my executor. Wit: G. W. LOGAN,
jurat. W. A. WILSON, jurat.   Signed: MOSES LOGAN.

Page 463.   18 May 1863. Recorded, Will Docket. I, JOHN DALEY, being of
            sound mind & memory. First all my lawfull debts to be paid.
I give unto my beloved wife the land & all thereon, during her natural
life or widowhood, with all land in Cleveland County. Executors to sell
what land needed to settle my just debts. I appoint my sons J. J. DALEY,
BENJAMIN N. DALEY & JOHN JACKSON DALEY my executors. Wit: O. P. GARDNER,
D. PANNELL, jurat.   Signed: JOHN DALEY.

Page 464.   25 Oct. 1864. Recorded, March Term 1866. I, THOMAS HARRIS,
            being of sound mind & memory. First, after my just debts &
lawfull debts are paid, the remainder of my estate both real & personal
I give unto my wife, land on Dill's Creek & Cove Creek, with each & every
article of property I may own during her natural life, and after her
death to be divided among my heirs. I appoint FELIX LOGAN my executor.
Wit: W. H. LOGAN, jurat. WILLIAM FLINN.   Signed: THOMAS HARRIS.
CODICIL. Dated 24 March 1865. This writing to be a codicil to my last
            Will dated 25 Oct. 1864. As things has changed, I do hereby
devise unto my wife MYRA the interest which may accrue from the selling
of my land to H. LOMAS. Also the farm purchased by HENRY LOMAS & HENRY
POSTSUM to have & hold during her life time, then to be divided among my
heirs. Wit: T. R. EDGERTON, W. H. LOGAN, jurat.
                                          Signed: THOMAS HARRIS.

Page 466.   21 July 1866. Recorded, Sept. Court 1866. I, PHILIP WATKINS,
            Sr. being this day in feeble health, but of sound mind & memory.
My will is that my just debts & funeral expenses be paid. I give unto my
beloved wife PENELOPE WATKINS the use & benfit of all my land, horses, 4
cows, 10 sheep, all hogs, one wagon, farming tools, buggy & blacksmith
tools, the household & kitchen furniture, except what I give unto my dtr.
MARTHA WATKINS $50, one feather bed & furniture, one young cow. I give
unto my dtr. EMELINE WATKINS $50 one feather bed & furniture, one side
saddle & a young cow to be bought from my estate. I appoint my son
KINDRED C. WATKINS & EDMOND C. HARRIS my executors. Wit: J. T. BLACKWOOD,
L. P. HARRIS, J. L. WOOD.   Signed: PHILIP WATKINS.
CODICIL. Dated 21 July 1866. After the death of my wife PENELOPE WAT-
            KINS I desire all my land & other property to be sold & divided
among, MARY DAVIS, TEMPERANCE ARNOLD, ELIZABETH MCMAHAN, MARTHA WATKINS,
EMELINE WATKINS to be made equal with KENDRED C. WATKINS & PHILIP WATKINS.
Wit: J. T. BLACKWOOD, T. P. HARRIS, J. T. WOOD.
                                          Signed: PHILIP WATKINS.

Page 468.   20 June 1866. Recorded, Will Docket Sept. Court 1866. I,
            JAMES MCMAHAN, being of sound mind & memory. I desire my ex-
ecutor to pay my funeral expenses & just debts. I give unto my son
ALFORD M. MCMAHAN one bed & furniture, I give unto my dtr. MARY wife of
J. C. HENSON, one bed & $10 in money. I give unto my dtrs. SARAH &
ISABEL (single girls²) one bay mare & wagon, All cattle, & hogs and all

                                148

Household & kitchen furniture. I appoint my son ALFORD MCMAHAN my executor. Wit: W. S. HILL, jurat. THOS. TOMS.
Signed: JAMES MCMAHAN.

Page 469. 21 Aug. 1865. Recorded, Will Docket 1866. I WALLIS B. MURRAY,
being of sound mind & memory. My executor to pay my funeral
expenses & just debts. I give unto my son JOHN ANTHONY MURRAY all that
tract of land lying in Rutherford Co. on Duncons Creek, adjoining lands
of JOHN ALEXANDER & WILLIAM MARTIN & others. I give unto my son JOHN
MURRY my interest in the land of WILLIAM D. MURRAY, that has not been
divided, supposed to be 55 acres in Cleveland, County on the waters of
Big Hickory, joining lands of DAVIS PUTMAN & STEAVEN HOGUE. I give unto
my son JOHN MURRAY my blacksmith tools, Household items (named) The
family Bible, Prayer Book & Zion Songster. I give unto my nephew one
bed. The remainder of my tools to my brother JOHN ALEXANDER MURRAY to
use as his own until my son come of age. My son is at the age of 11 yrs.
old and I appoint my brother JOHN ALEXANDER MURRAY as his guardian. I
appoint my brother JOHN ALEXANDER MURRAY my executor. Wit: JAMES MURRAY,
JOHN HUNSINGER.
Signed: WILLIS X MURRAY.

Page 474. 16 Aug. 1858. Recorded, Dec. Court 1866. I, WILLIAM SMITH,
Sr. I give unto my son JAMES L. SMITH 100 acres of land including the tract whereon he now lives and taking a piece of land over
the road from the East Line. I give unto my grandsons MATHEW & RICHARD
SMITH 100 acres of land including where I now live joining the land of
JAMES L. SMITH. My Daughter POLLY to live where JEREMIAH W. SMITH now
lives for 10 years and at the end of that time the land to belong to
grandson or the heirs of J. W. SMITH. In view of what son GEORGE W.
SMITH has received $100 is deducted from his share. By reason of bad
treatment given me by my son-in-law LEWIS SCOGGIN and my daughter SALLIE
to have $5. I give unto my two granddaughters one bed each, the bed they
claim. Daughter NANCY WAGGONER, is dead, & her chn. lives vast distance
away I give them $5. MINEME, being dead, her chn. to have her part. My
dtr. JANE being dead, her children to have her part. I also give unto my
dtr. POLLY her equal part of my estate & $25 extra. My dtr. RETTER to
have her equal part & $25 extra. I give unto my dtr. MALINDA HANEY her
equal part & $25 extra. I appoint my friend WM. SMITH, Jr. & DAVE PANNEL
my executors. It is my will that the rest of my property to be sold &
equally divided among my chn. to wit. JOHN, JACOB, the heirs of JOAL, &
WM. SMITH, Jr. Wit. D. M. PANNEL, jurat. C. B. PANNELL.
Signed: WM. X SMITH, SR.

Page 475. Court of Probate. Sept. Term 1858. The within instrument of
writing perposing to be the last will & testament of WM. SMITH
was presented in open Court for probate-ABRAHAM PADGETT & D. M. PANNEL
the subscribing witnesses. It was ordered to be recorded & filed away.
DAVE PANNEL qualified as an executor, WM. SMITH, Jr. did not qualify.
Present, J. L. TAYLOR, JET COVINGTON, & R. H. CARPENTER, Esqs.
Signed: E. JONES, Clk.

Page 476. 16 Oct. 1863. Recorded, Dec. Court 1866. I, RICHARD WELLS,
being of sound mind. I give unto my beloved wife, ELENDER P.
WELLS, all my lands, money, stock during her natural life or widowhood
and then all the above named property to belong unto my dtr. NANCY M.
WELLS & her heirs forever. Should My dtr., NANCY, not have heirs of her
body, then after all my funeral expenses & debts are paid the property
except the land to be divided among my heirs & my wife heirs, the land to
be rented out & the proceeds divided between the church at Brittain &
Pisgah, until my dtr. NANCY comes of the age of twenty one then this to
be void. I appoint my wife, ELENDER P. WELLS, my executrix. Wit: J. P.
ALLEN, jurat. JAS. M. SPRULL, jurat. JANE SPRULL.
Signed: RICHARD WELLS.

Page 478. 2 Nov. 1863. Recorded, March Court 1867. I, ROBERT GATTYS,
I give unto my beloved wife, SARAH P. GATTYS, all my property
both real & personal after paying my just debts, during her natural life.
Should my wife marry again, I will my children to have two thirds of
all my lands & personal estate. I appoint my friend W. MC. GATTYS my
executor. Wit: A. B. MARTEN, EMILY S. GATTYS.
Signed: ROBERT GATTYS.

Page 479. 18 March 1866. Recorded, March Court 1867. I, JOHN J. ALLEN,
being of sound & desposing mind & memory. Executor to pay all
lawful debts & funeral expenses. I give unto beloved sister, JUDETH B.
HAMRICK, in consideration of her services & nursing and tending on me as
I am helpless. All my land, of 50 acres lying on Piney Mountain, adj.
land of R. A. DURHAM & others, with all my personal property I appoint
AMOS HAMRICK my executor.   Signed: JOHN J. ALLEN.
"We the undersigned do certify that we heard JOHN J. ALLEN acknowledge
the above as his last will and testament that witnessed it in his presence
and at his request."   Signed: J. B. MCDANIELS & J. H.
                                              WHITAKER.

Page 479½. 13 Sept. 1860. Recorded, June Court 1867. I, ABRAM WHITAKER,
being of sound & desposing mind & memory. I give unto my
beloved wife, NANCY WHITAKER, after paying my just debts & funeral charges, all my real & personal property during her natural life. After my
wife's death I give all my property unto my dtr., SOPHRONIA LUCRETIA
WHITAKER, for her comfort and support. I appoint my son JOHN WHITAKER my
executor. Wit: J. B. MCDANIEL, P. G. M. WALKER, jurat.
                                Signed: ABRAM X WHITAKER.

Page 480. 31 March 1866. Recorded, June Court 1867. I, HARBERT HARTON,
being of sound mind in both sense & memory. I appoint my two
sons JOHN & ROBERT HARTON my executors, first I will my funeral expenses
& just debts must be paid. I give unto my beloved wife ELIZABETH HARTON
one half of my land, including the mountain house where I now live, with
all cattle, hogs, wagon, farming tools, household & kitchen furniture
during her natural life, then to belong to my son JAMES HARTON, by taking
care of my beloved wife as long as she lives. I give unto my son JAMES
the other half of my land. I hold a note of my son ANSLOM HARTON dated
20 July 1851, I now give him the principle & interest. Remainder of
debts due me to be equally divided among, JOHN M., A. M., ROBERT H.,
T. J., MARY ANN WEBBER, SARAH JANE OATS, & JAMES H. HARTON. I give unto
my son JOHN M. the cupboard & bureau, son JAMES to have no claim of the
household & kitchen furniture. Wit: A. HUDLOW, J. U. WHITESIDES, jurat.
                                Signed: HARBERT HARTON.

Page 482. 26 May 1867. Recorded, Sept. Court 1867. I, DAVID MOSLEY, I
give unto SPENCER MOSLEY (free man of color) 65 acres of land
joining OTHNILE BUTTLER, one ox cart, one yoke of oxen, one bed & furniture, one mare named Fan, one rifle gun, one beareau, one clock, one cupboard, one large looking glass, one spinning wheel, six chairs, 2 hogs,
3 bee gums, & $50 in money & an equal share with JOHN & HARRETT MOSLEY
(free persons of color) of all the money that may be collected after my
death. I give unto JOHN & HARRIETT MOSLEY, the rest of my land divided
between them, one bed & furniture, one shot gun, one large table, one
cupboard, 2 hogs, 2 bee gums, 4 chairs, HARRIETT to have one black heifer,
one bed & furniture, one reel, one spinning wheel, 2 hogs, 2 bee gums,
one foulding table. I appoint G. W. LOGAN my executor. Wit: E. TOMS,
jurat, P. D. GOOD, jurat. W. T. GOOD, jurat.
                                Signed: DAVID X MOSLEY.

Page 484. 22 March 1864. Recorded, Sept. Court 1867. DAVIS MORGAN.
I will my whole estate to my wife BETSEY ELIZABETH, except my
boy Mark. I choose JOSEPH BAXTER my executor, if he don't live, JOHN
FLACK to execute my will. After my death I want the blacks removed from
my children. Mark to be sold and money divided among my wife & heirs.
When my chn. come of age or my wife marry, I desire my executor to sell
off & lot the lands to my wife & heirs. $18.40 EMRY MCFALLS give my wife
to go equal to BETSEY'S heirs. NANCY FLACK my dtr. has received $80.
I want my children schooled. (No witnesses).
                                Signed: DAVIS MORGAN.
"My request is for my oldest children to live on my land all work together
and assist in raising the little children and all agreeable."
                                Signed: DAVIS MORGAN.

Page 485. No date. Recorded, March Court 1868. (Nuncupative will)
JOHN HANEY. "JOHN HANEY verbal will is as follows, his will
& desire is that MARTHA W. HANEY, ANN SELIA D. HANEY should have all his
property both real & personal to use at their pleasure absolutely and

forever. Further it was his will that MARTHA W. HANEY & SELIA D. HANEY
should take care of their mother during her natural life, it was his will
& desire that SELIA D. HANEY & MARTHA W. HANEY should be his sold executrixs. Wit: DAVID MATHENY, HANNAH MATHNEY, JOHN J. DAILY.
Signed: JOHN HANEY.

Page 486. 7 Oct. 1861. Recorded, March Court 1868. I, WM. DYCUS, being
of sound mind & memory. After all my just debts are paid, I
will that wife ELIZABETH have 100 acres of land including the house, one
bed & furniture, working tools, household & kitchen furniture (named)
during her life time or widowhood. The balance of my property both real
& personal to be sold and equally divided between my dtrs., MILLA, SALLY
& SELA. At my wife's death or marriage her property to be sold & divided
the same way. I appoint executor (no name). Wit: F. C. DOBBINS, jurat.
LEWIS DOLLANY?.   Signed: WM. X DYCUS.

Page 487. 15 Jan. 1867. Recorded, March Court 1868. I, DAVID AMOS,
Being in my right mind. I give unto my wife NANCY AMOS all
my land & personal estate during her life time or widowhood. Should my
wife marry again, I want my property divided equally among six children.
My dtr. TEMPY HARDIN has received benfit of my land to the amount of $100,
over the other five chn. After the other five receive that amount, she
is to have an equal share of the balance. At my wife's NANCY death or
marriage the property to be divided as the other. I appoint E. C. HANES
my executor. Wit: JAMES PHILIPS, K. C. WATKINS, R. L. WATKINS.
Signed: DAVID AMOS.

Page 488. 24 March 1868. Recorded, June Court 1868. I, JAMES A. GETTEYS,
being advanced in age but of sound mind & memory. First I
desire my just debts to be paid. I Give unto my beloved wife MARTHA A.
GETTEYS all my estate both real & personal during her life, unless she
marries again, then the whole estate to be divided equally between my
wife & son JOHN ALVIN GETTEYS & my dtr. AMAND GREEN GETTEYS, & my dtr.
MARTHA MOREHEAD GETTEYS. I appoint my wife MARTH A. GETTEYS my executrix.
Wit: WM. G. MOODE, WM. A. MARTIN.   Signed: JAMES A. GETTEYS.

Index
Compiled by
Nanetta Key Burkholder
Lake Jackson, Texas 77566

BEATY (cont.)
  Francis 20
  James 53, 59
  James G. 56
  John 6
BEAVER, Benj. 17
BECHTLER, Augustus 109
  Christopher Junr. 109
  Christopher Senr. 109
  Lenz 109
BEDFORD, H. 98
  J. 18, 24
  James 69
  James Junr. 19
  Jonas 6, 31, 69, 127
  Jonas Junr. 14, 19,
    24, 69
  Jonas Senr. 19
  Raymond 69
  Stephen 69
BELL, James 65
  John 64
  Nancy 80
BENSON, Christopher 4
BERRY, Richard 15
  William 61
BICKERSTAFF, -- 92
BIEDRY, Samuel 49
BIERS, Samuel 61
  William 61
BIGGERSON, Aaron 116
BIGGERSTAFF, Aaron 8
  Benjamin 116
  Joseph 116, 135, 147
  Luvicy 99
  Mary 1
  Nancy 125
  Sally 73, 74
  Samuel 74, 116, 147
  Sarah 116
BILBOW, Mathew 6
BININGS, James D. 125,
  126
  Mary M. 125
BIRCH, Carter 87
  Sally 87
BIRCHETT, Ann E. 110
  Theo 72
  Theo F. 72
  Theodorick 73
  Thro. 67
BIRD, Charles 127
  Margaret 127
BLACK, Cela 115
  Elizabeth 120
  Hugh 79
  Joseph 89
  Margaret 79
  Moses 117
  Sarah 102
BLACKWELL, Altha Adaline
  119
  Charles 65, 84
  Daniel 65
  George 119
  Harriet 65
  Isaah 40
  James 65, 78, 88, 119,
    122
  Joel 40, 65
  John 40
  Joseph 119
  Lilly 119
  Mary 40, 122
  Matage 119
  Molly 40, 54
  Peter 65, 84
  Sally 65
  Sarah 40, 65
  Thomas 119
  Tyre G. 86
  William 40
BLACKWOOD, Elizabeth 96

BLACKWOOD (cont.)
  J. R. 148
BLALOCK, David 78
  John 78
BLANCHARD, Andrew 1
BLAND, Caroline 134
  William 132
BLANKENSHIP, Elijah 64
  Elisha 64
  Hesekiah 139
  Hezekiah 106
  John W. 60
  Susannah 106, 139
  Wm. 106
BLANKINSHIP, Ruth 136
BLANTON, A. C. 140, 142
  A. M. 140
  Almina 131
  B. E. 116
  B. L. 126
  B. S. 131, 140, 142
  Bunel 27
  Burrell 28
  C. 135
  Carah Luticia 142
  Charles 55, 93
  Charles Edgar 142
  Claborn 99
  Corah 142
  Doctor 142
  Dolly 78
  Dova 142
  Edgar 142
  Frances 28, 54
  G. 24
  G. D. 131
  G. E. 142
  George 27, 28, 93, 135,
    142
  George Marion 142
  George W. 131
  Gilford Eaves 93
  Guilford E. 142
  Hill 142
  J. H. 142
  James H. 93
  Jane 142
  Jeremiah 78
  Jerry 76
  John 28, 142
  Jonathan B. 131
  Julia 142
  Margaret 93
  Martha 99
  Mary 28
  Mary Jane 142
  Miss 108
  Peggy 28
  Priscilla 93
  Ransom 139
  Richard 28
  Sarah 54
  Stephen F. 120
  Susanah 27
  Widow 105
  William 27, 28
  William Beaty Sawyers
    93
  William H. 131, 142
  Wm. 33
  Wryley 78
BODDAN, Andw. 13
BOHELO, Milly Lucinda 131
BOIOD, Thomas 21
BOLTON, Bartholomew 95
  Jane 95
  John 95
  William 95
BOLYN, Elizabeth 114
  G. R. 114
  Gion 114
  Guion 114
  Jane 114

BOLYN (cont.)
  John 114
  Joseph 114
  Margaret 114
  Ruttain 114
BOMAN, Caroline C. 134
  William Senr. 24
BOOKER, Edmond 93
  Jabez 93
  John 93
  Martha Overton 93
  Shields 93
BORDIN, Mary 80
BOSTIC, M. A. 91
BOSTICK, Boswell 108
  Charles 47
  Charley 47
  Margaret 47
  Reuben 47
  Richard 47, 55, 65
  Ruth 47
BOULDERIDGE, Sarah 29
BOWDEN, John 91
BOWEN, -- 94
  Joseph 66, 73
  Mary Ann 73
  Milley 73
  Thomas 73
BOWMAN, Elizabeth 24
  William 25, 58
BOYD, Agness 48
  Thomas 18, 21
BRACKET, John 106
BRACKETT, Benj. 1
BRADEN, Rhodda 74
BRADLEY, Ben H. 84
  Drury 97
  Edward 34
  James 30
  John 30, 50, 76, 84,
    85, 97
  John M. 97
  Joseph 99
  Mary 76, 79
  Mercy Sarah 128
  Richard 12, 13, 44, 48
  Robert 34
  Thomas 48
  Willis 30
BRADLY, Nancy 31
BRADON, Robert 55
  Robert M. 55
BRANDON, -- 104
BRATTON, Thomas M. 89
BRAYER, David W. 50
  Rhoda M. 88
BRENDLE, Joseph 142
BRICHETT, T. 73
BRIDGES, Anderson 112
  Andrew 112
  Ann 28
  Aron 42
  Betsey 28
  Catherine 28
  Dicy 38
  Elizbabeth 63, 67, 112
  Frances 65
  James 38, 57, 64, 112
  Jesse 35
  John 14, 22
  Levina 134
  Samuel 57
  Sally 35
  Wiley 112, 134
  William 15
  Wm. 105
  Wm. A. 137
BRIGGS, David 30
  Esther 30
  Jesse 30
  Molley 17
  Molly 18
BRINDLE, Henry 143

HAMBRICK, Feby 32
   George 32
   James 57
   John 57
   Mary 57
   Moses 57
   Nancy 57
   Price 57
   Richard 57
   Samuel 57
   Sarah 57
   William 102
HAMILL, John 62
HAMILTON, Abby 71
   Andrew 62
   Archibald 11, 112
   Audley 65, 71, 99
   Benjamin 99
   Edward 111, 112
   Eliza 147
   Elonor 62
   I. M. 123
   James 62
   Jane Senr. 111
   Jas. 43
   Jesse 62
   John 62
   Joseph 36, 55, 66, 71
   L. S. 147
   Lawson Eaves 147
   Nancy 62, 71
   Noble 56
   Nobles 37
   Robert 62, 103
   Sarah 20, 66, 71
   Silviy 71
   William 62
HAMMEN, Phebe 123
   William 123
HAMMER, Jane 49
HAMMRICK, Nathaniel 19
HAMNCK, Edmund 105
HAMPTON, Adam 32
   Alice 32
   Andrew 10, 31, 32
   Benjamin 32
   Betsey 22
   Catherine 32
   Elizabeth 32
   J. 20
   J. W. 121
   James 22
   John 32
   Johnathan 4
   Jonathan 1, 4, 7, 10,
      12, 13, 22, 30, 31,
      32, 34, 35, 36, 46,
      53, 54, 76
   Jonathen 9
   Jonathon 81
   Mary 22, 32
   Michel 32
   N. 46
   N. B. 121
   Nancy 32
   Noah 22
   Rachel 32
   Susannah 32
   Washington 31, 32
HAMRICK, Amos 150
   Ann 35
   David 72, 101
   Delilah 72
   Eliza 35
   George 35
   James 35
   Jefferson R. 102
   Jenny 35
   Jeremiah 72
   Judeth B. 150
   Lorenzo D. 72
   Nancy 72
   Narcissa 72

HAMRICK (cont.)
   Nathan 72
   Precella 35
   Rebecca 35
   William 35, 72
HAMRIGHT, Frederick 1
HANE, Nicholas 13, 14
HANES, E. C. 151
   Francis C. 108
   Mourning 108
   Pleasant H. 108
HANEY, Ann Selia D. 150
   John 62, 150, 151
   Kiziah 99
   Malinda 133, 149
   Martha W. 150, 151
   Robert 26, 47
   Selia D. 151
HANNEN, Samuel C. 123
HANNON, Edwin 59
HANNONS, Edward 7
HARDEN, Jane 131
   John 47
   Joseph 58
   Robert 28
HARDIN, Able 85
   David 42, 85
   Dial 85
   Elijah 5
   John S. 105
   Hamner 42
   Jno. 42
   Johnathan 20
   John 10, 42
   Jonathan 5, 20
   Joseph 5, 42
   Margaret 85
   Molly 35
   Rebecca 42
   Robt 42
   Sally 42
   Susanna 42
   Tempy 151
   William 99
HARLEN, Thomas I. 128
HARMAN, Andrew Sr. 141
HARMON, Alfred 141
   Andrew 141
   Dolly 141
   Edwin 46
   Elizabeth 8
   Margaret 35, 141
HAROLD, Samual 35
HARRALSON, Sidney 86
HARRELL, A. D. 93
   Betsey 47
   Housen 79, 93
   James 47
   John 47, 108
   Martha 74
   Polly 47
   Samuel 93
   Sarah 67
   Susannah 74
HARRETL, Joseph 17
HARRILL, A. 124
   A. S. 114, 138, 139
   Amos 120, 127
   Artamincy 114
   Elizabeth 120, 121
   Esther 134
   H. 142, 147
   Henson 130
   Housen 127
   James 147
   S. C. 139
   Samuel 138
   Samuel Sr. 142
HARRIS, -- 100
   Amny 22
   Betsy 22
   C. L. 113, 133, 136,
     146

HARRIS (cont.)
   Charles 66
   Daniel 66
   Deletha 66
   Edmond C. 148
   Elizabeth 50
   Francis 22
   G. W. 106
   H. 76, 83, 97
   H. W. 146
   Isaac 50
   J. A. 133, 146
   J. W. 134, 141, 146,
     147, 18
   James 49, 66, 82
   John 22, 66
   John W. 83, 133
   John Washington 83
   John Washington Sr.
     133
   Judah 22
   L. P. 148
   Leaven 66
   Lewis 83
   Louisa 133
   Martha 1118
   Mathew 66
   Myra 148
   Patience 82
   Peter 22
   Priscilla 111
   Reubin 22
   Robert 66
   Sally 22, 42
   Sarah 66, 80, 133
   Thomas 148
   W. H. 146
   W. N. 133
   William 83
   Zadoc 34, 60
   Zadock 66, 82, 83
   Zadock D. 88
   Zador 49
HARRISON, Edmond 135
   Harding C. 135
   Martha Norville 135
   Rebecca 135
   Simeon 135
   James R. 135
   John 135
HARRISS, James 34
HARROLD, Frances 38
   Gilbert 38
   Housan 38
   John 38
   Richard 38
   Samuel 38
   Street 38
   Susannah 35
HARTON, A. M. 150
   Ansolm 150
   Elizabeth 150
   Harbart 98, 150
   James 143, 150
   James H. 150
   John 150
   John M. 150
   Robert 150
   Robert H. 150
   T. J. 150
HAUL, James 112
HAWKINS, Benj. 47
   Benjamin 31, 46
   Elizabeth 63, 86
   Fanny 2
   Henry 63
   Jane 63
   John 2, 3
   Joseph 63
   Michael 38
   Patty 2
   Philip 2
   Thomas 13

HAWKINS (cont.)
  W. A. 132
  William 2, 14, 15,
    17, 38
  Wm. 14
  Wm. Junr. 14
HAWSER, Henry 102
HAY, George 46, 105
  George P. 105
  Martha 105, 135
  Sally 47
HAYNE, S. S. 142
HAYNES, C. H. 120
  Elizabeth 96
  Hugh Henry 96
HAYS, Martha 2
  Samuel 2
  Will 4
HEAD, Joseph 117
  Mary 35
  W. M. 118
HEADEN, John 30
HEART, Ephraim 65
HEATHERLY, Neomy 5
HEFLIN, Betsy 78
  Polly 78
HENDERSON, Allen 49
  Benjamin 51
  Betsey 24
  David 121
  Elizabeth 51
  Gabrile 49
  James 121
  Joel 121
  Michael 121
  Moses 89
  Nancy 89
  Phebe 81
  Phiba 51
  Philip 89
  Providence 89
  William 4, 24, 121
HENDRICKS, George 91
  William 91
HENRY, John 43
  Robert 64
  Turner 48
HENSON, Benjamin Franklin
    88
  Elizabeth 63
  J. C. 148
  Mary 148
  Philip 2, 35, 49, 63,
    88
  Sarah 63
  Susannah 88
  Thomas 70
HESLEP, Mary 13
  Thomas 13
HESTER, Alfred 75
  James M. 115, 116
  Jane 140
  Mary 115
  Michael 115, 116
  Sarah 33
  Sally 116
HETHERLY, Amey 5
  Samuel 5
HETTICK, Louisa E. 126
HETTRICK, Eliza E. 126
HEYER, Metta 113
HICKS, Benj. 31
  Berry 35
  Berryman 42
  Caty 75
  Green 118
  Jas. 58
  John 66
  M. L. 143
  Mary 42
  Richard 42
  Richard H. 143
  Thomas 58

HICKS (cont.)
  William 42
HIENS, Fanny 39
HILL, Abel 120, 147
  Alexander 145
  Asaph 46
  Assph 128
  Caroline 120
  Charles 50
  Charley 45
  Delpha 138
  Drusiller 147
  Elizabeth 1, 137
  George 138
  George W. 135
  James 46, 138
  Martha 128, 145
  Polly 50, 103
  Rail 115
  Reubin 46
  Robert 50
  Tempy 108
  W. S. 147, 149
  William 46
HILLS, Ara 89
  Arington 142
  Charles 85
  Delilah 89
  Lizza 89
  Mary 89
  Rachel 85
  Roberson 89
  Robert 89
  William 85
HILTERBRAND, John 17
HINES, Little B. 102, 103
HOBBS, Martha 74
  Mary 74
HOGAN, Edward 15
  Michael 5, 14, 19
  Richard 27
  Shadrack 4
HOGEN, Tilpha 59
HOGUE, Jesse 61
  Louis 61
  Stephen 19, 21, 149
HOLLAND, J. P. 37
  James 6, 9, 15, 16, 18
  John 24
  William 50
HOLLIFIELD, Abraham P. 134
  Elijah 134
  Eliza 134
  Emsey 134
  Harry C. 134
  Narcissy 134
HOLLIN, John 24
HOLLISFIELD, Ensy 124
HOLLYFIELD, Abram 124
  Cynthia 124
  Eay 124
  Elijah 145
  Ernsy 124
  Harvey 124
  Lovelace 124
  Noah 124
  Norcissa 124
  Osbern R. 124
  Prissy 124
  Ransom 124
HONCRIEFFE, John 11
HONEYCUT, Hartwell 34
  Mary 34
HOOD, Fanny 73
HOOKER, John 40
HOOKS, Edy 53
HOOTEL, Martha 25
HOPE, Deborah 59
HOPKINS, La--- 15
HOPPISS, Jenny R. 89
  Samuel 89
HOPSON, Edward 8
  Nevill 26

HOPSON (cont.)
  William 17
HORD, John 65, 71
  R. T. 98
HORN, Hamblin 50
  Henry 50
  James 50
  Jesse 50
  John 50
  Mary 50
HORNE, Hambleton 135
HORTON, Harbert 78, 108
  James D. 99
  Martha J. 146
  Mary H. 134
  Mary M. 134
  Touson 26
  Townsend 56
  Townson 13
  William 20, 63
HOUGE, Stephen 25
HOUGEN, William 25
HOUSE, Jacob 52
  William 48
HOW---, Elizabeth 50
HOWEL, Jno. 61
  John 61
HOWELL, James 43
  John 43
  Malachi 40
HOWSER, W. T. 103
HOYLE, David 43
  Henry 33
  John 52, 83
  Nancy 43
  Rebecca 83
HUCKABA, Benjamin 134
  Jane 134
  John 134, 135
  Minla 134
  Rhoda 134
  Rhody 134, 135
  Sarah 134, 135
  William 134
HUDDLESTON, David Junr.
    7, 8
  James 79
HUDDLESTONS, David 2
  Davis 2
  Hannah 2
  James 2
  John 2
  Mary 2
  William 2
HUDLONG, Barbra 35
HUDLOW, A. 150
  Andrew 128
  Andrew Jr. 128
  Andrew Senr. 128
  Joseph 128
  Mary 128
  Michael 78, 128
  Nathan 128
  Thomas 128
  William 128
HUDSON, Mary 117
HUEY, Dorcus 17
HUGGINS, John 60
  Margaret 60
  Robert 60
HUGHES, John 1, 18, 29
  Martha 29
HUGHS, John 29
  Lewis 29
HULL, William 83
HUMPHERY, James 31
HUMPHRES, Betsy 101
  Lucinda 101
  Polly Ann 101
  Raney 101
  William 101
HUMPHREY, Deidomus 52
  Dinah 111

MC MURRY (cont.)
  Andrew 29
  Cathern 43
  Elenor 29
  James 29, 43
  Jane 29
  Jean 29
  John 29, 43
  Margaret 29
  Margarett 43
  Margret 29
  Mary 29, 43
  Patsey 43
  Samuel 29, 43
  Sarah 43, 89
  Thomas 29
  William 3, 42, 43
MC MURTRY, Caty 76
MC NEALY, James 83
MC NEELY, James 68
MC RAN, Mary 33
  Susannah 33
MC REYNOLDS, Hugh 52
MC SHEEA, Mary 110, 111
MC SWAIN, George 102
  John 102
  Lurany 74
  William 146
MEANS, Robert 27
MECHAEL, Jacob 76
MECRUM, Jacob 42
MELTON, A. G. 137
  Abner 64, 65
  Alfred 80
  Betsey 45
  Cornilus 29, 41, 64,
    65
  Cyrus 44
  Daniel 116
  Daniel Jr. 116
  Elijah 61
  Francey 137
  Green 65
  Hiram 65
  Isaiah W. 146, 147
  John 44, 60
  Joshua 80, 147
  Lenore 134
  Louraney 146, 147
  Margaret 137
  Martha 134
  Marvill 65
  Nancy 111
  Peggy 81
  Samuel 76, 98, 114
  Sarah 45, 59, 80
  Shadrack Green 65
  Silas 137
  Sindrey 65
  Spencer 103
  Telitha Cuma 65
  William 60
MENTAETH, John 101
METCALF, Anthony 15
  Warner 15
METCALFE, Catharine 96
METTON, Jno. 21
MICHAEL, Jacob 69, 73
MILES, Columbus 107
  Daniel 15
  Will S. 107
MILLER, A. 102
  A. E. 129
  Agness 81
  Agnis 1
  Andrew 4, 17, 18, 30,
    31, 94, 102, 105,
    129, 130
  Andrew T. 110
  Andw. 17
  Anna 94, 110
  Betsy 34
  Caroline 130

MILLER (cont.)
  Carr 94
  Charlotte 86
  David 1, 30, 31, 34,
    72, 94, 130
  David B. 110
  Elizabeth 94, 102
  Elizabeth J. 146
  H. W. 110
  Harry 94
  Harvy 110
  Harvy A. 110
  Henry 109
  I. 11, 23
  J. B. 130
  Jahu 110
  James 1, 6, 7, 8, 10,
    11, 12, 15, 16, 24,
    27, 81, 94, 129
  James A. 110
  James H. 108
  James Junr. 24
  Jno. 24
  John 1, 11, 12, 17,
    30, 31, 34, 72, 94,
    129
  John B. 108, 130
  John Twitty 72
  Jomes M. 107
  Joseph 23
  Kerr B. 110
  Martha 94, 110, 130
  Martha Ann 130
  Mary 130
  Mary Johnson 102
  Nancy 94, 110
  Nathaniel W. 146
  Polly 30, 94
  Sarah L. 108
  Sucky 34
  Susanna 72, 73
  Susannah 11, 12, 34,
    59
  Thomas 95
  W. 107
  W. H. 110, 130, 146
  Weldon 130
  William 34, 94, 110,
    130
MILLERS, James 35
MILLES, Henry 26
MILLICAN, William 31
MILLIGAN, James 46
  Joseph 46
MILLIGANY, R. 40
MILLS, Adolphus 115
  Amanda 115
  Ambrose 19, 20, 72,
    104, 106, 115, 117
  Ann Eliza 117
  Anna 1, 19, 20
  Columbus 104, 105, 106
  George 104, 105
  Govan 104, 105
  Jho. 105
  Jno. 86
  John 19, 93, 104
  L. A. 117, 125
  M. 90
  Martha 118
  Mary Amanda 115
  Milly 19, 20
  Nancy 115
  Pamilea 19
  Ruffus 93
  Rufus 104, 105
  Sarah Louis 117
  Thomas 19, 115
  Twitty 19
  W. C. 109
  W. E. 108
  Widow 1
  Will S. 123

MILLS (cont.)
  William 1, 11, 19, 20,
    34, 40, 104, 105,
    115
  William E. 115, 117
  William L. 122
  William S. 106
MIRIA, Susannah 72
MITCHELL, Andrew 31
  George 79
  Jane 31
  John 31
  Martha 31
  Nancy 31
  Peggy 31
  Polly 31
  William 31
  William G. 112
MODE, I. T. 148
  Isaac 39
  Mary 39
  Samuel 39
  William 39
  William G. 144, 148
MOFFITT, David 22
MONFORD, Joseph 3
MONROE, Henry 54
  William 12
MONTAGUE, Elizabeth 86
  Henry 86
MONTEITH, Wm. 114
MOODE, William 39
  Wm. G. 151
MOONEY, Adam 58, 59
  Beckey 78
  Betsey 78
  Caty 59
  Charlotte 147
  Christyne 59
  David 75
  Elizabeth 99
  Fanny 59
  Henry 59
  J. Peter 148
  Jacob 78
  Jacob S. 147
  John Perter 147
  Jonathan 75
  Mary 78
  Olif 59
  Peggy 78
  Peter 59, 78, 87, 89
  Rachel 59, 144
  Sally 78
  Susannah 59
  Susy 78
  Suza 78
  William 147
  William A. 147
MOORE, Aaron 8
  Ann 8
  Betsy 83
  Caty 112
  Elisha 8
  Elizabeth 55, 63, 111
  Farmer 74
  George 3, 55
  Jackson 111
  James 48, 55, 76
  John 8, 36, 38, 40, 51,
    52, 57, 70, 72, 74,
    81, 93, 103, 104,
    111, 117
  Joseph 2, 55, 76
  Joseph Jr. 2
  Joseph Sr. 2
  Lemuel 19, 49, 55, 60,
    66
  Margaret 8
  Mark 101
  Mary 8, 136
  Michael 40, 46
  Mose 5

QUEEN (cont.)
William Lewis 12
QUIN, Edward M. 66
QUINN, Hugh 55
RA-----, Phebe 38
RABB, Robert 40
RABURN, James H. 132
James M. 132
RAGAN, Widow 27
RAGEN, Catharine 27
RAKESTRAW, Jesse 1
RAMSOUR, David 30
RAN--, Mary 32
RANDAL, Mary 146
Mary E. 146
William 146
RANDLE, Rachel 82
Susanna W. 54
RANNEGES, Jeremiah 28
RAWLINS, Charles 12
RAY, Adolphus 93
Polly 136
Sally 93
RAYNOLDS, Phebe 38
Thomas 38
READER, James 61
Lucy 61
Thomas 61
William 61
REAGAN, Caty 27
John 26
REAVES, Susannah 100
REAVIS, Betsey 30
David 56
James 16, 29
Joseph 56
Lucynda 30
Martha 30
Morgan 30
Polly 30
Rebecca 56
Samuel 56
Samuel A. 56
Washington 30
Wilson 30
REDEY, Margaret 66
REED, Archibald 73
Elizabeth 79
James 28
Jane 73, 82
John 28, 73, 79
John Junr. 73
Rachel 28
Samuel 28
Sarah 28, 79
William 28
REID, Jos. 132
W. K. 132
REIGON, William 133
REINHARD, Emmaline E. 60
REINHARDT, David 60
Drucilla 147
Margaret 60
RENFRO, Peter 9
RENFROE, Peter 9
REOU, Marcuril 18
REPPY, Edward 51
REYNOLDS, Catherine 79
Elijah 49
Elizabeth 49
George 49
Hamilton 38, 49
Henry 52
Hugh W. 22
Jesse 49
John 49
Lucy 47
Sarah 49
Thomas 49, 57
Unice 49
RHODES, Jesse 121
RICHARDSON, Charles 20,
25, 35, 69

RICHARDSON (cont.)
Charles Jr. 35
Charles Senr. 69
Elizabeth 69
Hiram 69
Hymen 69
Isabella 69
James 69
Jesse 15, 68
John L. 68
Mary 69
William 69
RIDINGS, Tyra G. 122
RIGGS, Israel 23, 40
Timothy 8, 14, 22
RIGHT, Richard 32
RILLEN, William 21
RIPPEY, Edward 71
ROACH, Margaret J. 135
Susannah 78
ROBBINS, Chesterfield 140
Elijah 18
Joseph 140
Nancy 35, 140
Philip 35, 140
Thomas 140
William 2, 31
Wm. 35
ROBBS, Louisa 118
Thompson 118
ROBERSON, Catharine 98
James 98
Jane 98
Jonathan 98
Jonathan H. 98
Mira 98
Polly 32
Rebecca 98
William 98
ROBERTS, J. 53
James 49
Jno. 29
John 31
Joshua 5, 99
M. 42
Martin 29, 59
Robert Jno. 28
W. 43, 58
William 85
ROBERTSON, A. M. 144
Alfred 121
Arty 144
Arty Louisa 121
Catherine 60, 121
George 50, 60
Hetty 121
Israel 50
Julian 121, 144
L. A. 144
Martha 50
Richard 121
Sarah 50
Thomas 50
William 2, 8, 30
ROBINS, James 52
John 52
Philip 52
Sarah 52
Thomas 52
William 52
ROBINSON, Benjamin 30
Elizabeth 30
Jonathan 30
Mary 13
Rebecca 30
Thomas 13, 19, 30
Thomas Junr. 13
Thomas Senr. 13
William 13, 30
ROBISON, T. 24
RODES, Thomas 66
ROGERS, Sally 124
ROHM, Isaac 85

ROLLANS, William 17
ROLLINS, B. E. 132
G. W. 141
ROOKER, Edmond 81
Jno. 106
John 73
Martha 81
Wm. 61
ROPER, -- 100
Joseph 18, 21
ROSE, Mary 137
ROSS, Aaron 88, 95
Charles 21
John 61
L. A. 40
Moses 61, 95
S. A. 80
Samuel 53
Sarah 80
Solomon 47
Solomon A. 51, 80
ROWLAND, Michael 19
Mildred 1
Thomas 1, 4, 9, 32
ROWLEY, Erastus 126
Martha L. 125
ROYSTER, Charles M. 95
George 88
RUCKER, Sarah 90
Susannah 90
William 85, 90
RUE, Benjamin 3
RUFF, Henry 40
RUGGY, Reid 114
RUPH, Samuel 5
RUSSELL, -- 44
Felby 7
George 7, 57
Jeremiah 9
Mary 7, 23, 24, 49
May 7
Seth 97
RUTHERFORD, James 13, 26,
56
SAIN, Elizabeth 143
SAINES, Elizabeth 143
SANDON, Henry 62
SANFORD, Catharine 98
SARGENT, May 111
SCHAFFER, H. C. G. 109
Henry C. G. 109
SCHENCK, Henry 100
Henry Jr. 87
SCHIFFILIN, Charles L. H.
93
SCHINCK, Henry 100
SCHROEBEL, John 76
Sally 76
Thomas 76
SCHUFFELIN, Charles 71
SCOGGEN, Polly 47
Sally 47
SCOGGIN, Andrew J. 126
Elizabeth 40
Frances 40
Jasse 40
Jeremiah 40
Jesse 40
Lemuel 40
Lewis 133, 149
Richard 40
Sally 133
SCOGGINS, Alvira 84
Ezekiel 84
Oliver 84
Rebecca 84
Sarah 32, 84
Statia 84
SCOTT, Betsy 70
Dunlap 47, 70
James 23, 28, 57
Jas. 36
John 28, 57, 70